Veterinary Forensics

Investigation, Evidence Collection, and Expert Testimony

Veterinary Forensics

Investigation, Evidence Collection, and Expert Testimony

Edited by
Ernest R. Rogers
Adam W. Stern

CRC Press
Taylor & Francis Group
Boca Raton London New York

CRC Press is an imprint of the
Taylor & Francis Group, an **informa** business

CRC Press
Taylor & Francis Group
6000 Broken Sound Parkway NW, Suite 300
Boca Raton, FL 33487-2742

First issued in paperback 2020

ISBN-13: 978-1-4987-6317-2 (hbk)
ISBN-13: 978-0-367-77824-8 (pbk)

Library of Congress Cataloging-in-Publication Data

Names: Rogers, Ernest R. editor. | Stern, Adam W., editor.
Title: Veterinary forensics : investigation, evidence collection, and expert testimony / edited by Ernest R. Rogers and Adam W. Stern.
Description: Boca Raton, FL : CRC Press, 2018. | Includes bibliographical references and index.
Identifiers: LCCN 2017035472| ISBN 9781498763172 (hardback : alk. paper) | ISBN 9781315153421 (ebook)
Subjects: LCSH: Veterinary forensic medicine.
Classification: LCC SF769.47 .V486 2018 | DDC 636.089/415--dc23
LC record available at https://lccn.loc.gov/2017035472

Visit the Taylor & Francis Web site at
http://www.taylorandfrancis.com

and the CRC Press Web site at
http://www.crcpress.com

Contents

Preface

Since the time of the first book on forensics, Hsi Duan Yu (1248 AD), forensic sciences have been moving forward with increases in science and technology. Propelling these advances are societal needs to assign responsibility for animal crimes and other violent acts. Furthermore, forensic medicine and science has been an essential element for law enforcement.

Forensic science is not concerned with justice and injustice or innocence versus guilt, it is concerned with the science and medicine that can incriminate or exculpate the individual based on the evidence. As scientists, we will use the best and acceptable scientific techniques supported by the most current responsible journal articles that will lead to reproducible results.

The art and science of forensics is not without its failures. The concept of *ipse dixit* ("he himself said it") is no longer an acceptable defense for the opinion of an expert witness in a court of law. To this end, scientific testimony has been guided by several entities including the Frye test (1923, *Frye v. United States*), the guidelines of the Federal Rules of Evidence 702 (1975), and the Daubert test (1993, *Daubert v. Merrell Dow Pharmaceuticals*). These have been the standard, in many courts, for admitting expert witness opinion. These guidelines establish the rules for scientific/medical expert witness testimony.

The goal of this text is to provide those in veterinary medicine, law enforcement, lawyers, the judiciary, animal control officers, and others with guidance in the collection of evidence, development of criminal and civil case documentation, and then the presentation of scientific and medical opinions and conclusions in a court of law. The chapters in this book are written by experts in their fields. This was done to give the reader information that directly reflects the thoughts of the best forensic scientists in the business. These experts have many years of experience and for the most accurate and current information it would be best for you to hear directly from them.

Preface

This book is written as both a guide and to ensure that all forensic and expert witnesses meet the current expectations and standards for veterinary forensic medicine and science. We hope you enjoy this book.

> The greatness of a nation and its moral progress can be judged by the way its animals are treated.
>
> **Mohandas Gandhi (1869–1948)**

> The time will come when men such as I will look upon murder of animals as they now look upon the murder of men.
>
> **Leonardo da Vinci (1452–1519)**

Acknowledgments

I have been fortunate in my life, both for my life experiences that have brought me to the opportunity to become involved with this project and for the support of friends and family. Thank you.

First, I must thank my parents, my father, my first hero, Roy (1920–1983) and my mother, my second hero, D. Lorraine (1929–1985), for their wisdom, guidance, and love. They both gave me the fortitude and fighting spirit to move forward through adversity and good fortune. Thank you.

My mentors and veterinary heroes have been a guiding force in my life, Doctor Daniel Urtnowski (1927–2001) and his wife, Judith. They both encouraged me to seek my goals and excel to the best of my ability. Thank you.

This book would not be possible without the many authors' contributions and sacrifices to make the individual chapters come to life. I owe a great debt of gratitude to my co-editor, Dr. Adam Wayne Stern, who kept me honest and organized. His insight in the chapters and subject matter has been enlightening. Thank you.

Thanks to all those unnamed persons who have influenced my decisions to both work in forensic veterinary medicine and develop the skills for this burgeoning area.

Thanks to everyone.

Ernest R. Rogers

I would like to thank all the contributors of this textbook. If it were not for them, this book would not have been possible. All the authors had numerous other commitments while simultaneously writing this book and I am indebted to the time they took out of their busy schedules to write this book and I truly appreciate their commitment to see this book to completion.

I would like to thank the CRC Press/Taylor & Francis publication team for supporting us during the writing of this textbook. A special thanks to Mark Listewnik who helped us throughout this process.

My mentors at Oklahoma State University and the Oklahoma Animal Disease Diagnostic Laboratory taught me so much throughout my anatomic pathology residency and played a huge role in getting me where I am today. Specifically, I would like to thank Drs. Jerry Richey, Timothy Snider, Melanie Breshears, Bradley Njaa, Anthony Confer, Gregory Campbell, Catherine

Lamm, and Roger Panciera. It was all of you who pushed me to keep on describing those lesions and explained to me the pathogenesis to so many different disease processes. I am forever thankful for your guidance.

I want to thank my wife Trish and my daughters Hailey and Alexa for supporting me (and missing me) during all those extra hours I put into working on this book and for encouraging me to get it done. Last, I want to thank my parents Randi and Jack and sister Marissa for their support throughout the years.

Adam W. Stern

Editors

Ernest R. Rogers, DVM, PhD, CCI, CMI-Level V, has been working in veterinary medicine since the age of 9 as a kennel person, technician, or veterinarian. This has always been his dream profession.

His first encounter with veterinary forensic medicine was on a police ride-along with Roanoke County Police in Virginia (1996) when they came across a crime scene involving animal abuse. He was asked to give expert testimony for a prosecution that was successful.

Since that time he has been involved with multiple cases both for law enforcement and defense as an expert witness, crime scene investigator, medical examiner and pathologist, and a consultant. Now, in 2017, he feels that some of his acquired knowledge should be placed in a book and so, the resulting text.

He holds a BSc (Hons) Biology (Biomedical Sciences, Guelph, 1985), BA Psychology (Learning and Neuro-Psychology, Guelph, 1985), DVM (Veterinary Medicine, Tuskegee, 1991), and PhD (Toxicology and Pharmacology, Virginia Tech, 2004) obtained from universities in Canada and the United States. He has had the opportunity to complete college-level courses in Criminal Investigation, Criminal Procedure, Criminal Law, and Arson Investigation (Raritan Valley Community College). He has completed certifications in Medical Investigation (CMI-Level V, American College of Forensic Examiner Institute, 2013) and Crime Scene Investigator (CCI, ACFEI, 2015), and was granted the Diplomate Status for the American Board of Forensic Medicine (ACFEI, 2014–2017), and must maintain this status with continuing education. These certifications have been granted after a review of his professional education, forensic casework, and forensic experience. This includes a review of his years in forensics, over 6 years with the New Jersey Society for the Prevention of Cruelty to Animals (Humane Police), and most recently as an expert consultant. In 2012, he started a forensic investigation company, Animal Forensic Investigations LLC. As a consultant, he has testified for law enforcement, prosecutors, and defense attorneys in both municipal and state judicial (superior court) venues as an expert witness. He has given lectures to both law enforcement and veterinary audiences in America through forensic and veterinary continuing education organizations. He is a member in good standing for the International Association for Identification and New Jersey Association of Forensic Scientists based on his professional activities.

Dr. Rogers feels fortunate to be working in this field and hopes this book becomes a positive addition to the science and investigation of animal-related crimes and forensic medicine.

Adam W. Stern, DVM, CMI-IV, CFC, Diplomate ACVP, is a Clinical Associate Professor at the Veterinary Diagnostic Laboratory, University of Illinois. Dr. Stern received his Bachelor of Science in Biology from George Washington University (2003) and Doctor of Veterinary Medicine from the University of Prince Edward Island, Atlantic Veterinary College (2007). He is a Board Certified Veterinary Pathologist and is a Certified Forensic Consultant and Certified Medical Investigator through the American College of Forensic Examiners Institute. Additionally, Dr. Stern has expertise in veterinary forensic pathology and dermatopathology. Dr. Stern is the section head of both the Forensics Section (Midwest Center for Veterinary Forensics) and the Pathology Section in the Veterinary Diagnostic Laboratory. He currently teaches the course Veterinary Forensic Medicine to second and third veterinary students, which is one of a few forensic courses taught to veterinary students in North America. He has given lectures about veterinary forensics both nationally and internationally. Dr. Stern is a member of the International Veterinary Forensic Sciences Association, is the current treasurer, and is a member of the pathology-working group within this organization. Dr. Stern has been involved in numerous forensic investigations of cases of animal cruelty and has served as an expert witness on numerous occasions. He started a forensic consulting company, Stern Veterinary Forensics Consulting, LLC in 2014.

Contributors

Melissa Bain
Clinical Animal Behavior Service
William R. Pritchard Veterinary Medical Teaching Hospital
University of California, Davis
Davis, California

Jon-Henry Barr
J.H. Barr & Associates, LLC
Clark, New Jersey

Julie Brinker
Humane Society of Missouri
St. Louis, Missouri

Jason W. Brooks
Animal Diagnostic Laboratory
Department of Veterinary and Biomedical Sciences
The Pennsylvania State University
University Park, Pennsylvania

Katherine E. Kling
Veterinary Teaching Hospital
University of Illinois Urbana–Champaign
Urbana, Illinois

Janice Kritchevsky
College of Veterinary Medicine
Department of Veterinary Clinical Sciences
Purdue University
West Lafayette, Indiana

Kevin Parmalee
North East Crime Scene Institute
Hillsborough, New Jersey

Ernest R. Rogers
Animal Forensic Investigations, LLC
Bedminster, New Jersey

Martha Smith-Blackmore
Forensic Veterinary Investigations, LLC
Boston, Massachusetts

Elizabeth Stelow
William R. Pritchard Veterinary Medical Teaching Hospital
University of California, Davis
Davis, California

Adam W. Stern
Veterinary Diagnostic Laboratory
University of Illinois Urbana–Champaign
Urbana, Illinois

Mee-Ja Sula
Biomedical and Diagnostic Sciences
College of Veterinary Medicine
University of Tennessee
Knoxville, Tennessee

Debra Teachout
Pulaski Animal Hospital
Chicago, Illinois

Elizabeth Watson
University of Florida Veterinary Forensic Medicine and Veterinary Imaging
Summerland Key, Florida

Kristen M. Webb
Allegheny College
Department of Biology
Meadville, Pennsylvania

Jennifer Woolf
Woolf Veterinary Forensics Consulting, Inc.
Dublin, California

Anita Zannin
AZ Forensic Associates
Amherst, New York

1

An Introduction to Animal Abuse and Associated Human Behaviors

Ernest R. Rogers

Contents

Introduction

Humans have, for thousands of years, interacted with animals for food, companionship, assistance with human disabilities or frailties, for facilitation of jobs requiring great strength or speed, to assist with herding livestock, hunting, and to facilitate or enhance the speed of travel. Further, the role of the canine and equine partners in law enforcement and military operations is commonly recognized (Turner 1980). The relationship between humans and beast has resulted in the domestication of a multitude of animal species. As the human–animal bond has strengthened and animals have been invited to become more intimate with human life, an increase in animal abuse incidents has been documented (Rollins 2007, 2011).

According to the American Veterinary Medical Association, the "human-animal bond is a mutually beneficial and dynamic relationship between people and animals that is influenced by behaviours that are essential to the health and well-being of both" (American Veterinary Medical Association 2017a). The human–animal bond has been recognized as a beneficial quality interaction, revered and practiced in many societies around the world. Unfortunately, not all human–animal interactions are positive for the animal involved. There are two broad categories of animal abuse: active aggression and passive abuse (Holsing 2009). Active aggression includes those crimes against animals that involve a depraved mind (*mens rea* of malicious intent). These acts include but are not limited to burning, slapping, kicking, shooting, stabbing, or any form of physical assault. The second category of animal abuse is passive abuse, where negligence and/or ignorance of husbandry or animal nutrition and failure to obtain veterinary care are the inciting acts that can result in the abuse (Animal Legal Defense Fund 2009). It is not unusual for the forensic veterinarian to be required to develop an opinion about the perpetrator's mind-set (*mens rea*) but only with the evidence surrounding the act itself (*actus reus*). We have seen specific crimes against animals that have been due to human greed and criminality as well as those crimes that have been due to psychiatric illness or willful ignorance of the needs of our animal companions, for whom they were responsible.

There are laws in all 50 states relating to animal abuse. These statutes vary by state and vary with respect both to the species protected and to the penalties imposed. In most states, penalties range from a simple summons to a misdemeanor, up to and including a felony. Individual state laws can be reviewed and are available on the Internet through state and federal government websites. The Federal Bureau of Investigation has included the crimes related to animal abuse in the National Incident-Based Reporting System to assist in the development of statistics as an aid to pursue these crimes (Federal Bureau of Investigation 2016, 2017).

Though laws vary among states and provinces, the animal laws of New Jersey are representative of these laws in general. Under NJ Statute 4:22-17 (Cruelty; disorderly persons offence), it states: "it shall be unlawful to overdrive, overload, drive when overloaded, overwork, deprive of necessary sustenance, abuse, or needlessly kill a living animal or creature" (Animal Legal and Historical Center 2017). It is important to be aware of updates to existing legislation as there may be changes to the definitions and penalties of existing law as the animal cruelty statutes develop (Friedman 2013).

There are some beliefs, among laypersons, that animal abuse is a precursor to serial murder. This theory is referred to as "The MacDonald Triad." The MacDonald triad refers to the three childhood behaviors (bedwetting [beyond the age of 5 years], fire starting/arson, and animal abuse) that serve as predictors of serial killer patterns and behavior (MacDonald 1963; Wright and

Hensley 2003). Though there are some examples of childhood animal abuse behavior being a common factor for some serial murderers, most individuals charged with childhood acts of animal abuse and cruelty do not become murderers as adults (Overton et al. 2012). Much of social science research suggests that most childhood offenders of crimes against animals are much more likely to have adult issues with sexual abuse, domestic violence, child abuse, and other socially inappropriate crimes (Hensley et al. 2010; Monsalve et al. 2017; Patterson-Kane and Piper 2009; Upadhya 2017).

In this chapter, there will be a review of some of the issues that are precipitated by the close relationship between animals and humans that may result in animal abuse. The interactions discussed in this chapter represent some of the more common negative engagements that humans can have with animals that may result in animal abuse. The understanding of these specific crimes against animals will help the reader to better characterize their approach and mind-set to each suspected crime and crime scene. The appropriate collection of evidence is essential to the successful prosecution of the individual responsible for the crime. It is important to note that not all abuses are with a malicious mind. This chapter is not meant to be a comprehensive review of all crimes against animals, but merely an overview of those activities that are common and that the reader may encounter as a forensic veterinarian. In general, by disregarding animal cruelty in the social science literature, we have "dismissed an opportunity to identify behaviors that may be an indicator or precursor of violence against humans" (Merz-Perez et al. 2001). There is an ethical responsibility for all veterinarians from the general practitioner to the forensic veterinarian to recognize and report animal abuse in their practice (Monsalve et al. 2017).

Domestic Violence and Animal Abuse

Domestic violence is a term relating to physical or psychological abuse of a spouse or partner. Domestic violence is not limited to married or cohabitating intimate individuals but may also include siblings, children, and the elderly who may simply share common living spaces. The acts involved in domestic violence span a gradient from psychological abuse to physical abuse to rape and murder (Golding 2002). The goal of the intimidation or abuse is to humiliate, coerce, or otherwise force the domestic partner to engage in an act that he or she may not otherwise complete (Faver and Cavazos 2007). Although there is a large amount of literature compiled for violence against women, women may also be the initiator and perpetrator of violent acts against others (Febres et al. 2012).

Animal abuse is just one of the four predictors of domestic violence. These four predictors of perpetrator initiated abuse include: (1) poor academic performance or failure to graduate from high school, (2) fair or poor mental health, (3) problems with drugs or alcohol, and (4) a history of pet or animal abuse (Walton-Moss et al. 2005). Numerous studies have linked animal abuse and violence against humans (Degenhardt 2005; Gullone 2011).

Domestic violence statistics suggest that nearly 20 people per minute are physically abused and 1 in 3 women and 1 in 4 men have been a victim of physical abuse by their intimate partner within their lifetime. Further, victims of intimate partner abuse have an economic impact of 8 million days of lost or paid work productivity per year (National Coalition Against Domestic Violence 2017). Another study showed that of the 307 men arrested for domestic violence, 41% had committed at least one act of animal abuse since the age of 18 (Febres et al. 2014). The cycle of abuse can start in childhood. The more often a child has perpetrated animal abuse or is exposed to animal or family abuse, the more likely he or she will become an abuser (Ascione 2007; Gullone 2011; McEwen et al. 2014).

It has also been reported that 19% of victims of domestic violence involves a weapon (National Coalition Against Domestic Violence 2017). Due to the high prevalence of domestic violence, it is imperative to review and report animal abuse to the appropriate authorities. Up to 70% of female victims of interpersonal violence who own pets report that their pets were threatened or harmed by their intimate partner (Doctors Foster and Smith Educational Staff 2017).

Based on the national statistics and information to date, the collection of evidence in animal abuse cases where human abuse is also suspected is critical and may aid in the indictment and prosecution of the abuser. The collection of evidence from a deceased pet often surrounds the accurate description and documentation of the physical force or use of a weapon that was used to abuse or kill the animal. Weapons can include knives or other form of cutting implements, guns and projectiles, blunt objects, and strangulation. In committing the crime of animal abuse, the perpetrator may be bitten or scratched; therefore, preservation and collection of any potential sources of DNA should be a priority. If the animal is alive at the scene and until DNA samples are collected, the animal should not have access to either food or water, so as to maintain the integrity of the potential evidence. The immediate collection of any possible sources of DNA such as blood or hair must be a priority. At the crime scene, if the animal is deceased the extremities and head should be isolated until appropriate samples can be obtained and it is essential to place protective paper covers over all 4 feet and the head/mouth. These areas are often a source of perpetrator DNA including blood or hair. DNA analysis may be essential to demonstrate the perpetrator's presence at the scene of the crime. As the animal is attacked, there is often struggle on the animal's part to fight to survive which may result in the transfer of DNA between the perpetrator and the animal. To avoid contamination of the animal's body, personal protective equipment is required. For more information regarding examination of bite wounds or an animal that is suspected to be a biter, the reader is referred to Chapter 10 (Bitemarks: Examination and Analysis).

Early examination of the animal's remains for petechial hemorrhage of the sclera or bruising of the neck may be significant in the determination of cause of death. It should be noted that deaths by strangulation do not always result in fracture of the bones of the neck. Drowning or blunt force trauma may be present but should not be assumed as the cause of death without a complete forensic necropsy. Once the body is examined on scene, it should be placed in a clean transport container and immediately transported to the necropsy laboratory for further examination.

Coordination with law enforcement both at the crime scene and with respect to any documentation or follow-up investigation is imperative and, in most cases, completed in a very short timeframe. The investigator should be aware that in some states there exists access to an Animal Abuse Directory and this represents a list of convicted animal abusers (O'Connor 2013). This directory serves as a "do not adopt" list but may also be helpful in the search for evidence of prior acts of animal abuse. This is one element that may be used to identify potential perpetrators who may have been involved in inflicting injuries in domestic abuse cases. This information is confidential and is usually available only to law enforcement. Domestic violence can be a consequence of childhood history of animal abuse or may be coincident with animal abuse. In all cases the speed, accuracy, and comprehensive collection and documentation of all available evidence is essential to a successful investigation.

Hoarding

Hoarding represents a behavior where an individual accumulates multiple items of small to no value and maintains them within their sphere of control, their living accommodations. This is considered a psychiatric illness and as such has been given designation in the Diagnostic and Statistical Manual of Mental Disease (DSM-5) (American Psychiatric Association 2013). Hoarding is classified under the broad class of obsessive compulsive disorders (OCD) (American Psychiatric Association 2013; Frost et al. 2015). Hoarding has been traditionally discussed in the realm of inanimate objects that accumulate in a person's environment and for which the individual accumulating these items has a reticence to give up, throw out, or otherwise part with them (American Psychiatric Association 2013). Since animals are legally, in most states and provinces, considered property, the definition for hoarding remains in place. More recently, hoarding—including animal hoarding—has been diagnostically redefined as a psychological syndrome that has been separated from OCD (American Psychiatric Association 2016; Frost et al. 2015). This redefinition is currently controversial among psychiatric and clinical psychological professionals (Frost et al. 2015).

For this illness, there are multiple diagnostic criteria to define the syndrome (Table 1.1). As with all medical diagnosis, not all symptoms need to be present to make the diagnosis. Often the hoarder feels that there is no one else capable of caring for the animals (feral, companion animals, and/or livestock) as well as they can. Often, without specific training or education in animal care and husbandry, the hoarder will adopt multiple feral intact male and female animals. These animals are rarely separated and will become sexually mature resulting in numerous pregnant animals. The newborns within months become mature and the cycle continues. The hoarder is very quickly overwhelmed by the need to care, feed, and clean up after the

Table 1.1 Summary of the Diagnostic Criteria for Hoarding Including Animal Hoarding

Perceived need to save items and distress at discarding items
Accumulation of possessions that compromises living areas
Clinical distress or impairment in other areas of life
Hoarding not attributable to other medical condition, mental disorder, or condition
Excessive acquisition and difficulty discarding
With good insight or fair insight recognizing hoarding is problematic
With poor insight hoarding beliefs are not problematic despite evidence
With absent insight delusional beliefs that there is no problem

Sources: 1. American Psychiatric Association. 2013. *Diagnostic and Statistical Manual of Mental Disorders*, 5th ed. American Psychiatric Association, Arlington, VA. 2. American Psychiatric Association. 2016. *Supplement to Diagnostic and Statistical Manual of Mental Disorders.* American Psychiatric Association, Arlington, VA.

animals to maintain a sanitary environment with an overload of animals. The environment very rapidly deteriorates and eventually becomes uninhabitable due to massive accumulations of feces and dead, dying, and/or sick animals. Hoarders are not limited to animals and it is often the case that the navigation of the living environment is extremely difficult and dangerous due to hoarding of inanimate objects.

Often the first responders to a hoarding situation are the local health department and/or animal control officers. Discovery of this situation occurs by neighbor complaints of foul odors or seeing multiple animals (beyond the statutory limit for the locality) in and around the hoarder's location. The general practitioner is often suspicious of a hoarding situation where clients, over time, return with multiple animals. These animals are usually in poor health, suffering from parasitic infections (both external and internal), are thin to emaciated, have open wounds and healing scars, overgrown claws, and unkempt fur. There may be multiple intact males, females, and pregnant females owned by the suspected hoarder. The veterinarian's level of suspicion should rise if there are multiple deaths among a client's animals that may be explained by poor husbandry and nutrition.

The general practitioner or forensic veterinarian may be asked to respond to the hoarding location to aid in the triage of animals. Triage is the process of establishing those animals that need little help immediately, those animals that require medical support to survive, and those animals that are found dead or, for humane reasons, need to be euthanized.

The collection of evidence is the same for hoarders and the investigation of industrial breeding sites (puppy and kitten mills). The approach and local environs of the hoarder location must be documented like any other crime scene. The grounds surrounding the home should be inspected for newly disturbed soil and burial sites. When found, these sites should be fully marked and excavated carefully to identify all deceased animals to determine the cause of death of these animals.

Due to the nature of a hoarding situation, there are increased dangers of zoonotic disease and the potential for human infection. Feral cat/dog bites, overwhelming odors (such as ammonia and putrefaction), potential exposure to external or internal parasites, and fecal contamination require the use of appropriate personal protective equipment (PPE). In general, PPE should include: Tyvek® coveralls with hood, protective boots, occlusive vinyl/rubber gloves, safety eyewear, mask or respirator, and heavy leather gloves to prevent scratches and bites if handling animals. To ensure the proper handling of the free-range animals the use of fishing retrieval nets, blankets, rabies poles, and multiple hard plastic transportation cages are often the most useful tools. To limit the spread of contamination, the establishment of a cleansing station should be set up at each access point. All responders who have entered the premises should decontaminate upon exiting the scene.

The collection of crime scene evidence is essential to assist in a successful prosecution. The initial approach to the crime scene should include a video and photographic review of the surroundings and the houses and/or out buildings (curtilage, may require search and seizure warrants) to which the animals have access. For more information regarding crime scene investigation, the reader is referred to Chapter 2 (Crime Scene Investigation).

There are occasions when the veterinarian is called in to make an examination after the animals have been contained by law enforcement personnel and animal control officers. These examinations may take place at a veterinary hospital/clinic, animal shelter, or mobile veterinary unit. It is important that the veterinarian must ensure the safety of lay and technical people who are assisting at the hoarding scene during the capture and triage of animals, as well as those assisting at the crime scene. Each animal should be identified by a unique case identification number and when possible be tagged with a temporary identification collar. For more information regarding the forensic physical examination of an animal, the reader is referred to Chapter 5 (Forensic Physical Examination of the Cat and Dog) and Chapter 6 (Forensic Physical Examination of Large Animals).

Examination of an animal must include the photo documentation of each animal, determination of sex of the animal and reproductive status (as is possible), overall health status by documented physical examination, notation of visible scars and identifiable markings, dental health, weight, and an evaluation of body condition score for all live animals (e.g., Purina Body Condition Score). Each examination must be fully documented in individual clinical notes. It is the responsibility of the lead agency to coordinate with the animal control officer, local health officer, and/or the forensic veterinarian to arrange for housing and care of all animals removed from the scene.

The forensic veterinarian is responsible for the triage of animals rescued. There are several levels of medical triage that are observed.

- Triage level 1: Live animals without physical defect or sickness should be housed and cared for at another location or kennel.
- Triage level 2: Animals with signs of disease, trauma, or debilitation that require treatment to survive should be treated by the attending veterinarian who should take charge or direct the medical care and clinical support for these animals.
- Triage level 3: Includes those animals that are so debilitated, injured, or sick that humane euthanasia is appropriate. This should be accomplished as needed and completely documented in the medical records. Any animals euthanized or found dead should have a forensic necropsy performed to best determine the cause of death.

Once on-site, after the crime scene examination is completed, all documentation should be compiled including all photographs, videos, medical notes including treatment plans, forensic necropsy reports, police/crime scene reports, and witness statements. The investigating veterinarian should be aware of the statutes regarding evidence retention that may exist in their local jurisdiction. For example, in New Jersey, all documentation must be preserved for reciprocal discovery until released by the prosecutor or judge overseeing the criminal case (Dow 2011).

Blood Sports

Blood sport defines a classification of animal fighting for entertainment, wagering and profit among individuals of all strata of society (Johnson 2014). The most common form of blood sports includes dog fighting, cockfighting (gamecocks), and hog-dog fighting. In all 50 states and most industrialized countries use of animals for fighting as entertainment is considered animal abuse and is illegal (Animal Legal Defense Fund 2009). Some groups and individuals also consider bull fighting, dog racing, horse racing, and other events cruel and abusive. This section is not meant to be a comprehensive review of animal fighting but merely an introduction to the forensic investigation strategies to approach animal blood sports. Although there are many different types of animal fighting for the purposes of this section, we will limit the discussion to dog fighting and cockfighting.

Dog Fighting

In North America, there is a wealth of legal, law enforcement, and media attention directed toward dog fighting (Adler 2017; Associated Press 2013; Johnson 2014). In some countries dog fighting is considered acceptable. In North America and throughout most of the industrialized world these activities are not only discouraged but are in violation of animal cruelty laws (Animal Legal Defense Fund 2016). Dog fighting is a felony in all 50 states and the District of Colombia (National Humane Education Society 2017).

The veterinarian may suspect that a patient is involved in blood sports based on clinical signs. Fighting dogs often have multiple bite wounds about the head, neck, and fore and hind limbs and often die from blood loss, dehydration, and/or infections (Humane Society of the United States 2017). An owner who makes repeated visits for veterinary care that involves multiple lacerations, fractures, avulsed teeth, fractured crowns, or other injuries that are consistent with dog fighting may be suspected of being involved with dog fighting. The veterinarian may be approached for medical materials by the layperson; these may also be obtained illegally and can be found at the fighting scene (Figure 1.1).

Other items such as fighting and breed specific literature (e.g., *Sporting Dog Journal*, *DMX Year of the Dog*) are commonly found on the premise of dog fighting participants (Hollandsworth 2009). Circumstantial evidence of a dog fighting enterprise would include fight training equipment such as flirt poles (Figure 1.2), spring poles (Figure 1.3), breaking or parting sticks (Figure 1.4), and treadmills or turntables (Figure 1.5) (National Humane Education Society 2017).

Fighting dogs are forced into prolonged running as this exercise increases their endurance (National Humane Education Society 2017). Additional training equipment can include heavy weights attached to thick collars on each animal to increase neck strength. The presence of walled dog fighting rings is a common feature at many dog fights; however, it is important to note

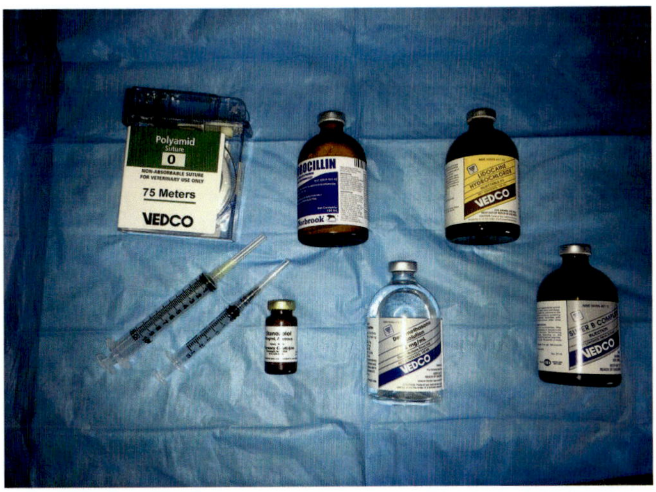

Figure 1.1 Drugs and medications may be found at a dogfight or in the kennel. These can include antibiotics, syringes, steroids, local injectable anesthesia, suture materials, and vitamins.

Figure 1.2 Example of a flirt pole. This is held by the trainer as the dog is teased with the toy. This exercise is used to challenge the dog to chase the target toy. It is thought to decrease reaction times and increase the dog's predatory aggression.

that events, where there are dogs involved in fighting, may occur anywhere including an alley way or parking lot. There may be open areas for fighting and crowd entertainment. Fighting pits are 14–20 square feet and can be carpeted to ensure good footing. These areas are often poorly cleaned and may have remnants of previous fighting events (Mott 2004). Blood evidence (bloodstains) may be the only source of evidence remaining at a site of a previous dog fight. For more information about bloodstains, the reader is referred to Chapter 4 (Bloodstain Pattern Analysis).

Losing or dying dogs may be euthanized by shooting, drowning, or electrocution. Each of these methods of euthanasia is in violation of the American Veterinary Medical Association standards for euthanasia and therefore can be considered animal abuse (American Veterinary Medical Association 2013; Animal Legal Defense Fund 2009). It is essential to determine the cause of death for each deceased animal and all critical evidence should be collected to determine total culpability of the suspected animal fighter. For more

Figure 1.3 Example of a spring pole. A spring pole is usually suspended from a tree limb above the reach of the dog. The goal is to have the dog jump and hold on to the target with its feet off the ground. The expectation is that this will increase bite and neck strength.

Figure 1.4 Example of a break stick. This is used to break the hold of a dog latched onto an opponent. Photo courtesy of Mike Bizelli.

Figure 1.5 Example of a treadmill used to improve a dog's endurance. Although the design of treadmills will vary, the basic structure is a rotating floor with an attachment to the machine restricting the animal to the running surface. Photo courtesy of Mike Bizelli.

information regarding examination of a deceased dog, the reader is referred to Chapter 7 (The Forensic Necropsy).

Individuals who fight dogs may resort to stealing, adopting, or otherwise acquiring small nonfighting animals including dogs, rabbits, and cats that may be housed at the same location as the fighting dogs (Mott 2004). These smaller animals are used as bait to increase blood drive in the fighting dog, often found with tape restraints to avoid any possible injury to the fighting dog (Mott 2004).

When scheduled, these events are advertised by word of mouth and other types of closed communication (e.g., electronic and written scheduled fights). The location of the fight, in urban areas, often involves abandoned or foreclosed housing. Neighbors and innocent bystanders may be aware of a sudden increase in automobile and foot traffic locally. There may be sounds of dogs barking and fighting suggesting a fighting event. In the rural areas often barns and out buildings are set up for dog fighting. When identified, these dog fighting arenas are often filled with individuals who bet on the outcome of any fight. There are thousands of dollars in gambling that pass hands and is the impetus for the observer who attends these fights. Dog fighting events can also attract a criminal element that may carry firearms both for self-protection and to dispatch the losing animals (Davis 1997; Lockwood 2012). In any case, where dog fighting events are suspected to be occurring, the local and state police should be informed. Due to the laws relating to search and seizure, the dangers of armed individuals, and other considerations, law enforcement will take the lead in arrests and investigation. For more information regarding the investigation of a crime scene, the reader is referred to Chapter 2 (Crime Scene Investigation). The forensic veterinarian may be invited to the crime scene for the collection, treatment, and triage of animals and/or to collect physical and biological evidence from the animal. For more information regarding collection of biological evidence from an animal, the reader is referred to Chapter 11 (DNA Evidence Collection and Analysis).

In any investigation of any blood sport, there is equipment and devices that are commonly used in the training of the participants such as a treadmill, break stick, or flirt pole. The investigator should be aware that the presence of training equipment alone may be insufficient to support a criminal charge or indictment of dog fighting. The case must be based on the condition and wounds of the dogs, the presence of equipment, the presence of literature related to dog fighting, and evidence of fighting bouts.

Trunking

Recently, a new aspect of dog fighting has arisen specifically to avoid police detection. Trunking is a surreptitious method of disguise where two fighting dogs are placed in the trunk of a medium to large motor vehicle. Fighting occurs while the vehicle is in motion. Often the perpetrator has distraction of loud music and activity to mask the sounds of the fighting dogs. After an appropriate amount of time, the trunk of the vehicle is opened and the winner declared (Hoffer-Ortiz 2011). In the case of trunking, finding a deceased or mortally wounded dog's body in a location other than a fighting venue may represent a secondary crime scene; therefore, the car then becomes the primary crime scene. Appropriate investigation techniques should be employed in this case (Johnson 2014).

Cockfighting

Cockfighting is when two roosters are encouraged to fight. Cockfighting is illegal in all 50 states. These fights occur in urban, suburban, and rural locations. Gamecocks are the more common fighting species but other birds, finches or canaries, may be used (Brunswick 2009). Gamecocks fight in a small circular fight ring known as a cockpit. These roosters can be outfitted with fighting spurs or gaffs. These weapons are dangerous and have severely injured humans (Daily Mail 2011; New York Post 2011). Fighting continues until one combatant is either killed or too injured to continue. As with dog fighting, the primary goal is gambling.

The collection of evidence should include the examination of the premises and grounds suspected of hosting a cockfight. Further, the triage, documentation, and examination of all animals are a priority. Photographic documentation of fighting equipment and cockpits are essential to the development of a case against the suspects of animal abuse. In addition, there may be other circumstantial evidence including the presence and burial of dead combatants, literature, spurs, and weighing scales. Though illegal in the United States and Canada, this blood sport is practiced in many areas of Asia, the Caribbean, Mexico, Europe, and the Middle East.

Collection of evidence for cockfighting or other blood sport crime scenes is similar to dog fighting and is often circumstantial. Direct physical evidence may be obtained by law enforcement on entering the premises and detaining the observers, trainers, and animal owners.

Failure to Obtain Veterinary Care and Insufficient Care

Previously we reviewed two types of animal abuse, passive and active abuse. Passive abuse is due to an owner failing to meet the husbandry, medical, or nutritional needs of their pets or livestock. Passive abuse includes starvation (Figure 1.6), dehydration, parasite infestation, failure to provide adequate shelter, and/or failure to obtain veterinary care. The need to provide an animal medical care has been recognized as a human responsibility to our companion and working animals (Coleman 2006). The individual accused of this type of crime may claim ignorance or lack of reasonable attention or care. The signs and symptoms of passive abuse must be separated diagnostically from other causes of emaciation, parasitism, dehydration, and so on, that are due to medical conditions separate from that of poor care. The failure to obtain veterinary care can be seen by the practicing veterinarian. Often cases of open infected wounds, emaciation, improperly healed fractures, severe dental disease, and protracted illness related to untreated kidney disease, cancer, infections, and metabolic disease can be recognized. The decision to report these cases is often left to the attending veterinarian. In some jurisdictions, there are professional obligations regarding reporting of animal neglect and cruelty (American Veterinary Medical Association 2017b; Animal Legal Defense Fund 2014; University

Figure 1.6 Example of a dog from an organized dog fighting kennel. Multiple dogs may be housed outdoors, chained and left with minimum housing. It is important to investigate and document the presence of potable water/food and quality of the housing. Examination of the animal should include assessment of the animal's body condition and notation of the presence or absence of wounds (including scars). Photo courtesy of Mike Bizelli.

of Vermont 2017). As of 2014, there are 15 states with mandatory reporting laws and 12 with permissive reporting laws (Animal Legal Defense Fund 2014). Many states have immunity from civil and criminal prosecution for reporting animal abuse (University of Vermont 2017), when in good faith. It is important to recognize that not all jurisdictions offer immunity even if the state requires mandatory reporting for the reporting veterinarian. It should be noted that of the 15 states with mandatory reporting, Kansas, Minnesota, Missouri, and Wisconsin do not offer immunity from prosecution for the veterinarian reporting animal abuse (Animal Legal Defense Fund 2014). The practicing veterinarian is in a good position to make the decision as to whether the patient has suffered from negligence, passive abuse, or active abuse. In some instances, the cause of the animal's condition was not the intended result of the owner's actions and may be resolved by simple client education and care instructions.

Evidence collection for passive or active abuse is best assessed through a complete forensic physical examination including blood, urine, and fecal analysis in order to eliminate metabolic or medical causes for signs and symptoms. The review of husbandry and nutritional conditions either in person or by interview with the responsible owner or guardian is critical to establish abuse. Before committing to any diagnosis of abuse, all other pertinent diagnosis that may account for the signs and symptoms should be eliminated and a comprehensive "rule-out list" created to support a diagnosis of animal abuse. Each diagnosis is eliminated or considered reasonable based on the evidence and referral to the medical and scientific literature. For more information regarding the forensic physical examination of an animal, the reader is referred to Chapter 5 (Forensic Physical Examination of the Cat and Dog) and Chapter 6 (Forensic Physical Examination of Large Animals).

Munchausen's Syndrome by Proxy

Munchausen's Syndrome by Proxy (MSBP) is a term used by medical and psychology professionals to describe an illness where the caregiver projects or creates physiological symptoms or illness on an individual under their care, often children or the elderly (Lasher and Sheridan 2004). Munchausen's Syndrome by Proxy is given a formal mental or psychiatric diagnosis. Munchausen's Syndrome by Proxy was included in the *Diagnostic and Statistical Manual of Mental Disorders* in 2013 (American Psychiatric Association 2013). The disease recognized as MSBP was then reclassified as a factitious disorder imposed on another (FDIA) in 2016 (American Psychiatric Association 2016). It is considered a component of a group of mental illnesses and specifically is a factitious disorder imposed on oneself or a factitious behavior imposed on another (Bursch 2014). A factitious disorder is classified in the *Diagnostic and Statistical Manual of Mental Disorders* as those individuals who falsify or fabricate symptoms or signs of an illness (American Psychiatric Association 2016). In some cases, the falsified disease or illness is embraced by the person presenting themselves as ill. When the fabricated illness or description of signs or symptoms is referred to an individual or animal under the guardianship, control, or care of another person, this is considered MSBP/FDIA (Lasher and Sheridan 2004). The reward for the instigator of these issues is by receiving attention either for recognizing serious disease symptoms that others may have missed or by being part of the cure in resolving the illness. MSBP is difficult to diagnose and is considered a form of child abuse and may extend to pets or other animals (Vannemann et al. 2005). This syndrome has been recognized in children and may be an issue for the clinical veterinarian (Munro and Thursfield 2001; Tucker et al. 2002).

The clinical veterinarian should have an increased level of suspicion when clients have multiple or often sequential hospitalizations of one or more pets. These pets on presentation may have either an unremarkable or confusing medical history. Repeating interview questions, while obtaining the history, may lead to varying answers or outright lying. Once admitted, the results obtained during the examination of the patient (including blood or urine analysis) may not fit the history and clinical signs. Often, while separated from the owner, pets improve with only supportive care (Table 1.2). It is very difficult to confirm a diagnosis of MSBP by the examination of the pet. This is a psychiatric diagnosis, to be made by our medical and psychiatric colleagues. Monitoring of the patient may suggest animal cruelty, which is the purview of the clinical or forensic veterinarian.

The investigation of MSBP surrounds the signs of the medical illness presented. The layperson may have access to a poison or toxin as well as illicit or prescription pharmaceuticals. The key to assessment of the antemortem patient is to collect multiple serial biological samples (blood, urine, and saliva)

Table 1.2 Signs and Symptoms Suggestive of Munchausen's Syndrome by Proxy with Animals
Multiple veterinary visits for apparently minor issues
Increasing severity of signs and symptoms with sequential visits
Caregiver wants to inject themselves in care and treatment programs in hospital
After separation from caregiver, the animal recovers with supportive care
Mild signs of toxicity or poisoning
Post-treatment injury or fractures
Lack of healing for no apparent reason, despite appropriate treatment
Signs, symptoms, and laboratory findings are confusing and inconsistent
History interview doesn't provide a rational reason for illness and there are obvious indications of falsehoods
The suspected illness doesn't follow the usual course or there are unexpected relapses

over time (days to weeks) for laboratory assessment. Since any criminal or legal follow-up will revolve around the potential of intoxication as a method of animal abuse, antemortem and/or postmortem documentation including analytical toxicology, photographic documentation, and histopathology are essential. The identification of appropriate toxicology testing is based on the clinical signs of the patient. In general, the patients' signs will yield insight into the class or chemical nature of the pharmacological, toxicological, or poisonous agent. Further, the development of a timeline of medically significant events can be an aid to the prosecution of serial animal abuse. Postmortem patients should also have appropriate organ specimens collected in duplicate or triplicate and stored in a freezer, 0.9% sodium chloride and 10% neutral buffered formalin. Collection of duplicate or triplicate samples ensure sufficient quantities for security, testing, and reciprocal discovery. For more information regarding toxicology, the reader is referred to Chapter 13 (Veterinary Forensic Toxicology).

Ritual Associated Abuse

The practice of religion is protected by the First Amendment (U.S. Constitution Online 2011) in the United States with comparable laws in other countries. The practice of many religions can involve domestic animals in many positive ways. The investigation of crimes against animals specifically should focus on the procedure and ritual that led to the report of animal abuse. Investigation of religious practices will ultimately lead to a challenge on the regulations as an infringement of religious freedoms (Masoudi 1993).

Some ritual practices have been investigated and don't violate the animal abuse statutes of the United States. There are many religions that require the need for animal sacrifice for completion of their sacred rituals. Humane slaughter has been challenged and is practiced for many religions as exempted from animal welfare acts as compared to the traditionally acceptable mainstream slaughter practices. Mainstream slaughter practices involve the initial stunning of the animals and then the rapid exsanguination (United States Department of Agriculture 2013). Alternative religious animal slaughter practices also fall under the rule of the Humane Methods of Slaughter Act. These alternative practices don't meet the mainstream guidelines but are considered alternative acceptable methods of humane slaughter (United States Department of Agriculture 2017).

Animal abuse investigations must surround rituals where there is the unapproved slaughter of animals. The slaughter of food animals is under the constraints of the Humane Methods of Slaughter Act and, as such, any violation of this act is grounds for animal abuse, based on the abuse act, not the religion or religious ceremonial act that surrounds the abuse. Similarly, the euthanasia of animals is grounded by the guidelines set forth by the American Veterinary Medical Association (2013). Religious practices must remain unchallenged during any animal ceremony investigations. The investigation should focus specifically on the animal abuse act relating to:

1. The method of slaughter or euthanasia.
2. The failure to provide veterinary care or insufficient nutrition or appropriate husbandry protection.
3. The use of inappropriate shelters for size or function.

Inappropriate ritual slaughter may be identified by elements of a practice including challises for collection of blood, sacrificial tables or tablets, candles, remnants of previous animal sacrifices, and/or areas with excessive bloodstaining of ritual surroundings and furnishings. The presence of caldrons, animal bones, blood and other animal remains, or ceremonial knives are suggestive of ritual ceremonies. In some religious events, the presence of specific areas with ceremonial vestiges, furnishings, and clothing may be present (Winburn et al. 2017).

A history of multiple animal adoptions or purchases specifying a specific color or breed is a possible indicator of ritual killings. All elements of the scene must be documented and never touched. Touching religious symbols, artifacts, or objects during an investigation may result in civil litigation against the investigator. Investigations of areas where ritual ceremonies are suspected to have occurred are challenging and personal protection equipment is mandatory. Some of the ritual areas, buildings, or rooms may be protected under the First Amendment as a sanctuary of religious practice. Working with law enforcement forensic specialists is essential to ensure a legal and thorough evidence collection (e.g., search and seizure laws).

The investigations of ritual crimes against animals associated with religious practices are fraught with pitfalls and roadblocks. Some cases may lead to the investigator becoming embroiled in additional legal and civil litigation beyond the initial investigation, if the religious First Amendment protections are violated. The forensic veterinarian should limit their involvement to their specific area of expertise within the scope of medicine and science and the evaluation of the events surrounding the animal abuse.

Conclusion

The investigations of crimes against animals that are intimately tied to human acts will often involve multiple professionals in the investigation for a single case. The forensic veterinarian should expect significant interactions with law enforcement, physicians, psychiatrists, psychologists, and other legal professionals. To this end, the forensic veterinarian should be prepared both in discussions and written communication to ensure the scientific and medical understanding of the terms of abuse. The results of the forensic physical examination, forensic necropsy, and other diagnostic modalities such as analytical toxicology should be reviewed and it is important to avoid colloquialisms and medical shorthand jargon when discussing the findings to law enforcement professionals.

Working with and understanding our clients and patients is one great strength of a veterinarian. We may, on taking a medical history, an interview, or during discussions with clients, recognize subtle signs of questionable mental health, abnormal behavior, or questionable animal practices. The animal patient may confirm the suspicions of abnormal or questionable abusive activity. Further, based on discussions, the medical history, clinical signs, and/or examination findings often give insight into human behaviors and motivations related to animal abuse. In any case that requires follow-up, the veterinarian should defer the investigation to local law enforcement which may include animal control and investigation officers.

The collection of the appropriate evidence and comprehensive documentation is critical to the legal process. The forensic veterinarian must recognize that involvement in these human behavior cases may result in requirements (both legal and ethically) to report and follow-up on animal abuse (Animal Legal Defense Fund 2014). The report of the available evidence and its presentation must be objective without prejudice or biases related to the attending human behavior.

References

Adler, J. 2017. Animal cruelty laws. http://www.jimadler.com/animal-cruelty-laws/ (Accessed May 2, 2017).

Animal Legal and Historical Center. 2017. https://www.animallaw.info/statute/nj-cruelty-consolidated-cruelty-statutes (Accessed May 6, 2017).

Animal Legal Defense Fund. 2009. Animal fighting facts. http://aldf.org/resources/laws-cases/animal-fighting-facts/ (Accessed February 15, 2017).

Animal Legal Defense Fund. 2014. Rankings stat sheet 2014: Category 10 - Veterinarian reporting/immunity. http://aldf.org/wp-content/uploads/2013/04/Vet-reporting-chart-2014.pdf (Accessed March 23, 2017).

Animal Legal Defense Fund. 2016. Animal protection laws of the United States and Canada. http://aldf.org/resources/advocating-for-animals/animal-protection-laws-of-the-united-states-of-america-and-canada/ (Accessed February 15, 2017).

American Psychiatric Association. 2013. *Diagnostic and Statistical Manual of Mental Disorders*, 5th ed. American Psychiatric Association, Arlington, VA.

American Psychiatric Association. 2016. *Supplement to Diagnostic and Statistical Manual of Mental Disorders*. American Psychiatric Association, Arlington, VA.

American Veterinary Medical Association. 2013. Euthanasia guidelines: The gas chamber debate. http://atwork.avma.org/2013/02/26/euthanasia-guidelines-the-gas-chamber-debate/ (Accessed May 2, 2017).

American Veterinary Medical Association. 2017a. The human animal bond. https://www.avma.org/KB/Resources/Reference/human-animal-bond/Pages/Human-Animal-Bond-assistance-animals.aspx (Accessed February 28, 2017).

American Veterinary Medical Association. 2017b. Animal abuse and animal neglect. www.avma.org/KB/Policies/Pages/Animal-Abuse-and-Animal-Neglect.aspx?PF=1 (Accessed May 2, 2017).

Ascione, F.R. 2007. Emerging research on animal abuse as a risk factor for intimate partner violence In: *Intimate Partner Violence*. Kendell-Tackett, K., S. Giacomoni, eds. Civic Research Institute, Kingston, NJ.

Associated Press. 2013. 12 are charged over dogfights. http://www.nytimes.com/2013/08/27/us/12-are-charged-over-dogfights.html (Accessed May 2, 2017).

Brunswick, D. 2009. About 150 birds seized in fighting investigation. http://www.cnn.com/2009/CRIME/07/27/connecticut.finch.fighting/ (Accessed May 2, 2017).

Bursch, B. 2014. Munchausen by proxy and factitious disorder imposed on another. http://www.psychiatrictimes.com/special-reports (Accessed February 27, 2017).

Coleman, P. 2006. Man['s best friend] does not live by bread alone: Imposing a duty to provide veterinary care, *Anim L.* 12:7–37.

Daily Mail. 2011. Champion rooster slashes its owner's throat for being asked to fight once too often. http://www.dailymail.co.uk/news/article-1348653/Indian-police-hunt-killer-rooster-slashes-owners-throat.html (Accessed May 2, 2017).

Davis, S.E. 1997. Blood sport: Dog fighting is big business in California, and just about impossible to stop. *Calif Lawyer.* 17:44.

Degenhardt, B. 2005. Statistical summary of offenders charged with crimes against companion animals July 2001–July 2004. Chicago Police Department.

Doctors Foster and Smith Educational Staff. 2017. Animal cruelty/domestic violence: The link. http://www.peteducation.com/article.cfm?c=2+2100&aid=3120 (Accessed April 1, 2017).

Dow, P. 2011. Attorney general directive regarding retention and transmittal of contemporaneous notes of witness interviews and crime scenes, Directive #2011-2. http://www.nj.gov/lps/dcj/agguide/directives/dir-2011-2-RetentionTransmittal.pdf (Accessed April 11, 2017).

Faver, C.A., A.M. Cavazos. 2007. Animal abuse and domestic violence: A view from the border. *J. Emot Abuse.* 7:59–81.

Febres, J., Shorey, R.C., Brasfield, H., Zucosky, H.C., Ninnemann, A., Elmquist, J., Buccossi, M.M. et al. 2012. Adulthood animal abuse among women court-referred to batterer intervention programs. *J Interpers Violence.* 27:3115–3126.

Febres, J., Brasfield, H., Shorey, R.C., Elmquist, J., Ninnemann, A., Schonbrun, Y.C., Temple, J.R. et al. 2014. Adulthood animal abuse among men arrested for domestic violence. *Violence Against Women.* 20:1059–1077.

Federal Bureau of Investigation. 2016. Tracking animal cruelty. https://www.fbi.gov/news/stories/-tracking-animal-cruelty (Accessed February 28, 2017).

Federal Bureau of Investigation. 2017. SRS to NIBRS. https://www.fbi.gov/services/cjis/cjis-link/srs-to-nibrs-the-path-to-better-ucr-data (Accessed February 28, 2017).

Friedman, M. 2013. Christie signs "Patrick's Law" to increase animal cruelty penalties. http://www.nj.com/politics/index.ssf/2013/08/christie_signs_patricks_law_to_increase_animal_cruelty_penalties.html (Accessed February 28, 2017).

Frost, R.O., Patronek, G., Arluke, A., G. Steketee. 2015. Hoarding of animals: An update. http://www.psychiatrictimes.com/addiction/hoarding-animals-update (Accessed April 15, 2017).

Golding, A.M.B. 2002. Domestic violence. *J R Soc Med.* 96:307–308.

Gullone, E. 2011. Conceptualizing animal abuse with an antisocial behavior framework. *Animals (Basel).* 1:144–160.

Hensley, C., Tallichet, S.E., E.L. Dutkiewicz. 2010. Childhood bestiality: A potential precursor to adult interpersonal violence. *J Interpers Violence.* 25:550–567.

Hoffer-Ortiz, J. 2011. Horrendous! Memphis police track disturbing new dog fighting trend—"Trunking." http://www.makeadifferencerescue.org/2011/05/23/horrendous-memphis-police-track-disturbing-new-dog-fighting-trend-trunking/ (Accessed April 1, 2017).

Hollandsworth, S. 2009. Bringing down the dogmen. http://www.texasmonthly.com/story/bring-down-dogmen (Accessed April 10, 2017).

Holsing, E. 2009. What is animal abuse? https://www.mtholyoke.edu/~holsi20e/classweb/worldpolitics/animalabuse.html (Accessed April 1, 2017).

Humane Society of the United States. 2017. Dog fighting fact sheet. http://www.humanesociety.org/issues/dogfighting/facts/dogfighting_fact_sheet.html (Accessed May 2, 2017).

Johnson, O. 2014. Dog fighting and the growing social epidemic of animal cruelty. *J Law Enforc*. 3:1–9.

Lasher, L., M.S. Sheridan. 2004. *Munchausen by Proxy: Identification, Intervention, and Case Management*. Haworth Maltreatment and Trauma Press, Binghamton, NY. P. 353.

Lockwood, R. 2012. Dog fighting: A guide for community action. http://www.aspcapro.org/sites/pro/files/aspca_cruelty_dogfighting_action.pdf (Accessed April 10, 2017).

MacDonald, J.M. 1963. The threat to kill. *Am J Psychiatr*. 120:125–130.

Masoudi, G.F. 1993. Kosher food regulation and the religion clauses of the First Amendment. *U Chi L Rev*. 60:667–696.

McEwen, F.S., Moffitt, T.E., L. Arseneault. 2014. Is childhood cruelty to animals a marker for physical maltreatment in a prospective cohort study in children? *Child Abuse Negl*. 38:533–543.

Merz-Perez, L., Heide, K.M., I.J. Silverman. 2001. Childhood cruelty to animals and subsequent violence against humans. *Int J Offender Ther Comp Criminol*. 45:556–573.

Monsalve, S., Ferriera, F., R. Garcia. 2017. The connection between animal abuse and interpersonal violence: A review from the veterinary perspective. *Res Vet Sci*. 114:18–25.

Mott, M. 2004. U.S. dog-fighting rings stealing pets for "bait". http://news.nationalgeographic.com/news/2004/02/0218_040218_dogfighting_2.html (Accessed May 5, 2017).

Munro, H.M.C., M.V. Thursfield. 2001. Battered pets, Munchausen syndrome by proxy (factitious illness by proxy). *J Small Anim Pract*. 42:385–389.

National Coalition Against Domestic Violence. 2017. Statistics. http://www.ncadv.org/learn-more/statistics (Accessed April 1, 2017).

National Humane Education Society. 2017. Animal fighting. https://nhes.org/animal-fighting/ (Accessed April 11, 2017).

New York Post. 2011. Cockfighting bird stabs, kills man. http://nypost.com/2011/02/06/cockfighting-bird-stabs-kills-man/ (Accessed May 2, 2017).

O'Connor, L. 2013. Animal abuse registry created to track convicted offenders. http://www.huffingtonpost.com/2013/11/01animal-abuse-registry_n_4195903.html (Accessed February 14, 2017).

Overton, J.C., Hensley, C., S.E. Tallichet. 2012. Examining the relationship between childhood animal cruelty motives and recurrent adult violent crimes towards humans. *J Interpers Violence*. 27:899–915.

Patterson-Kane, E.G., H. Piper. 2009. Animal abuse as a sentinel for human violence: A critique. *J Soc Issues*. 65:589–614.

Rollins, B.E. 2007. Cultural variations, animal welfare, and telos. *Anim Welf.* 16:129–133.

Rollins, B.E. 2011. Animal rights as a mainstream phenomenon. *Animals (Basel).* 1:102–115.

Tucker, H., Finlay, F., S. Guiton. 2002. Munchausen's syndrome involving pets by proxies. *Arch Dis Child.* 87:263.

Turner, J. 1980. *Reckoning with the Beast: Animals, Pain and Humanity in the Victorian Mind.* Johns Hopkins University Press, Baltimore, MD.

United States Department of Agriculture. 2013. Animal Welfare Act and Animal Welfare Regulations. https://www.aphis.usda.gov/animal_welfare/downloads/Animal%20Care%20Blue%20Book%20-%202013%20-%20FINAL.pdf (Accessed February 28, 2017).

United States Department of Agriculture. 2017. Humane Methods of Slaughter Act. https://www.nal.usda.gov/awic/humane-methods-slaughter-act (Accessed May 1, 2017).

University of Vermont. 2017. Cruelty to animals acts. https://asci.uvm.edu/equine/law/cruelty/cruelty.htm (Accessed February 28, 2017).

Upadhya, V. 2017. The abuse of animals as a method of domestic violence: The need for criminalization. http://law.emory.edu/elj/_documents/volumes/63/5/comments/upadhya.pdf (Accessed February 14, 2017).

U.S. Constitution Online. 2011. The Constitution of the United States. http://www.usconstitution.net/const.pdf (Accessed May 2, 2017).

Vannemann, B., Bajanowski, T., Karger, B., Pfeiffer, H., Kohler, H., B. Brinkmann. 2005. Suffocation and poisoning—The hard-hitting side of Munchausen Syndrome by Proxy. *Int J Legal Med.* 119:98–102.

Walton-Moss, B.J., Manganello, J., Frye, V., J.C. Campbell. 2005. Risk factors for intimate partner violence and associated injury among urban women. *J Commun Health.* 30:377–389.

Winburn, A.P., Martinez, R., S.K. Schoff. 2017. Afro-Cuban ritual use of human remains: Medicolegal considerations. *J Forens Investig.* 67:1–30.

Wright, J., C. Hensley. 2003. From animal cruelty to serial murder: Applying the graduation hypothesis. *Int J Offender Ther Comp Criminol.* 47:71–88.

2

Crime Scene Investigation

Kevin Parmalee

Contents

Introduction

The scenes of crime are the locations at which a criminal act has taken place (Del Carmen 2010). More specifically, criminal acts involving animals may take place at a variety of locations that are relative to a specific type of animal. Some criminal acts involving domesticated animals may be located at the owner's residence or a common location where the animal is sheltered. Alternatively, criminal acts involving wild animals may include more remote locations that incorporate the animal's natural habitat. Some locations may be much more obvious than others, but while assessing the various locations at which a criminal act took place it is important to consider that there can be multiple locations, or crime scenes, that need to be identified.

The skills and abilities of an investigator to effectively recognize a crime scene can greatly impact the reliability and outcome of a criminal investigation. Therefore, anyone tasked with the duty of investigating a complaint of criminal acts involving an animal should have sufficient training for recognizing, preserving, and documenting a crime scene. This chapter is not intended to take the place of formal training to process a crime scene for evidence; rather it is intended to provide an overview and reference of what is necessary for an effective crime scene investigation of criminal acts involving animals. Since a comprehensive work on crime scene investigations would comprise much more than a single chapter, this chapter will seek to introduce investigators to the common principles of crime scene investigation. Additionally, topics such as interviews, interrogation of witnesses and suspects, and crimes unrelated to animals will not be addressed, but this chapter will provide insight focused on common practices for processing crime scenes involving animals.

An animal at a crime scene can take on three distinct roles in relation to a criminal act. The first, and most common, is that of the *victim* of a criminal act. As a victim, the animal may have been abused and/or neglected in a variety of manners. The next role an animal may have at a crime scene is that of a *suspect*. As a suspect, the animal may be expressing its natural behavior as a predator, or as a tool used by humans to initiate a criminal act. For example, attack dogs can be used by criminals to inflict injury to responding police officers at a residence that is known for drug manufacturing or sales. Alternatively, a hunter may use tracking dogs to aid in the unlawful killing of game animals (Cooper et al. 2009). Finally, an animal may take on the role of *witness* to a criminal act. An animal may bear witness to a criminal act and aid in the investigation by retaining physical evidence in fur, claws, or mouth. Even though the animal will not be able to provide a verbal statement, an animal may bite or scratch an offender thereby providing a transfer of physical evidence that may be used to understand the criminal event. According to Edmond Locard's theory of exchange, when a victim, suspect, and witness interact at a scene there is an exchange of material where each contact leaves a trace (Fisher and Fisher 2012; Gardner 2005). As a result, an animal can potentially possess or contribute to various types of physical evidence at a scene, even though it may not be able to verbally tell you.

Prior to an investigator arriving at a crime scene it is vital that the integrity of the scene is secured and preserved. The actions of the first responder at the onset of the investigation can impact the outcome of a criminal investigation before the investigator even arrives on scene. Therefore, it is imperative that after the first responder secures the scene, steps are taken to prevent any further destruction, damage, or contamination of the scene and evidence.

Actions of First Responders

The first responder to a crime involving an animal will likely be a police officer or animal control officer. The responding officer's performance and decisions at the onset of the investigation will be instrumental in the success of the criminal investigation (Fisher and Fisher 2012; Gardner 2005). When responding to the report of a criminal act involving an animal the first responder must always consider their safety and potential hazards that may be present. In addition to contending with safety issues, such as an irate person and the presence of weapons, the officer will have to consider the safety hazards associated with the type of animal involved. Therefore, the first responder's safety is paramount during any investigation, but to preserve the integrity of the scene that same individual will need to be observant of his or her own actions that may be destructive to the scene and physical evidence.

As early as possible the first responder should take written notes that can later be relayed to the investigator (Fisher and Fisher 2012). The notes should at least include the officer's name, agency, case number, time of call to service and arrival at scene, weather conditions, and observations. More specifically, observations include more than what was viewed and can involve transient events that will not be observed by subsequent investigators. What the responding officer heard, such as a yelping dog, and smelled, such as ignitable liquid, can be useful in furthering the investigation. Furthermore, any actions taken at the scene that may be destructive or impact the interpretation of evidence should be pointedly identified to the responding investigator.

One of the primary methods for a first responder mitigating destruction or contamination of a scene is to consider their entry and exit pathway. A trained first responder should continually be aware of their environment and the impact their presence and actions will have upon the integrity of the scene. While the first responder's safety is paramount, they must also consider the safety of others (Fisher and Fisher 2012). At times medical assistance may be needed, thus requiring the presence of medical personnel such as a veterinarian at the scene. The safety and health of individuals and animals found at the scene is a second major health and safety concern and should be treated expeditiously. Upon the arrival of medical personnel at the scene, the first responder should advise them of the previously designated entrance and exit pathway and direct their attention to any important areas that should be protected from potential destruction or contamination.

Prior to securing the scene for responding investigators, the initial responding officers may conduct a search of the scene. If a search is deemed necessary for safety purposes, such as weapons or suspects, then any actions taken by the responders should be noted. The actions taken during the search should then be relayed to the investigator that will be tasked with investigating the crime scene (Fisher and Fisher 2012). The first responders should make every effort to minimize changes to the scene, but should also refrain from attempting to replace an item or reposition it in a similar position after it was moved. The attempt at staging an item may lead to subsequent misinterpretation of evidence, deterioration of a person's credibility, and a host of other problems in the judicial process. The first responder may be compelled at times to touch or move a weapon for a variety of reasons, but if the weapon can remain in the original location without compromising safety, it should not be handled. During the response and initial containment of the crime scene, all reasonable attempts should be made to reduce the destruction, contamination, or movement of potential evidence by responders (Fisher and Fisher 2012).

Establishing Boundaries

The first responder may secure a scene in a variety of ways, but some of the most common methods include using barrier tape and the presence of uniformed patrol officers (Fisher and Fisher 2012) (Figure 2.1). Other methods may involve using current barriers, such as the front and back doors to a residence, or utilizing alternative barrier systems, such as traffic cones, crowd control devices, and emergency vehicles.

Once the first responder has cordoned off an area that is determined to be the crime scene (Figure 2.2), a designated individual should start an entrance/exit log of personnel that enter and leave the location, which is now deemed the internal crime scene. As observed in Figure 2.2, a second barrier should be established outside the perimeter of the internal crime scene. The second

Figure 2.1 Barrier tape used at a crime scene.

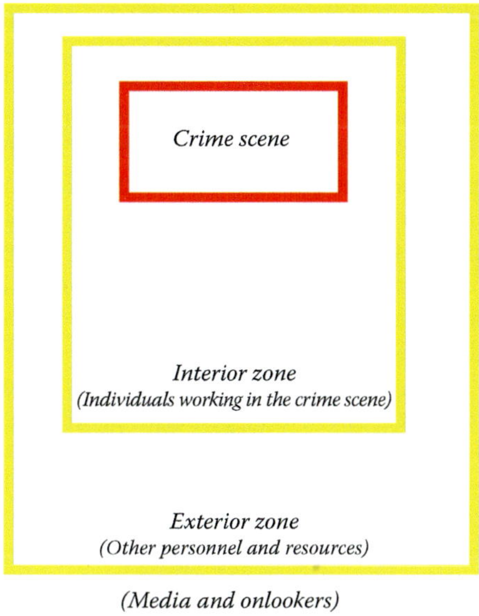

Figure 2.2 Internal and external zones of a crime scene.

barrier will establish a work zone outside the internal crime scene in which various personnel may work without the intrusion of the media and onlookers (Fisher and Fisher 2012; Gardner 2005). The public and media may establish themselves outside the second barrier. It is important to note that when deciding how far to extend the initial barrier, it is easier to reduce the distance of a barrier later than it is to try to extend the barrier once onlookers and the media have established a strong presence. So, when in doubt, make the external barrier large enough so the internal barrier may be expanded and will not require moving the media and public when trying to expand the external barrier. In addition to the logistical problems associated with trying to displace the media to expand a crime scene, it should be noted that the media might use the opportunity to interpret your actions as incompetence.

Response and Arrival of Investigator

Investigating a crime scene requires the trained practitioner to be able to recognize, document, and preserve the scene and physical evidence for the purpose of advancing truth and justice in the criminal justice system (Fisher and Fisher 2012; New Jersey State Police 2012; Saferstein 2007; Swanson et al. 2009). Although the reality of crime scene processing may differ significantly from the celebrated television shows, which aggrandize the capabilities and techniques of crime scene investigators, the work of the crime scene investigator represents a critical role in interpreting how the scene and physical evidence contribute to a criminal case.

An animal's involvement at a crime scene may be significantly chaotic and can provide unique challenges for the investigator. Crime scenes involving criminal acts involving animals should receive at least the same care and attention to detail as scenes of crime that involve humans. As such, much of the same principles and methodologies required to successfully process crime scenes involving humans would also be those utilized for scenes of crime involving animals. Although there are stark similarities in these methodologies, the unique elements that surround crimes involving animals should not be overlooked due to ritualized practices. A greater understanding of various animals, their behaviors, and capabilities, will aid the investigator while analyzing the scene and physical evidence.

With any crime scene, whether involving humans or animals, the investigator's safety is a priority. The use of personal protective equipment (PPE) such as gloves, masks, and protective suits, will aid in the prevention of injury and health concerns, such as cuts and the transmission of biological diseases (Fisher and Fisher 2012; Gardener 2005) (Figure 2.3). The use of PPE will also aid in preventing cross-contamination of evidence. For example, changing gloves between the collection of biological samples will aid in reducing the potential for cross-contamination between the samples.

At times, the crime scene is the only source of information pertaining to a criminal act unlike humans, animals cannot provide additional information or make statements, therefore, animals will not afford the investigator the opportunity for a statement and may not be obviously associated with a human companion. As a result, the crime scene involving animals may be of more value and importance to the investigation when attempting to decipher the information surrounding the crime (Rogers 2016, Personal Communication).

At the onset of the investigation, it may be deemed necessary for specialized personnel to be called to the scene. In cases that involve human death, a

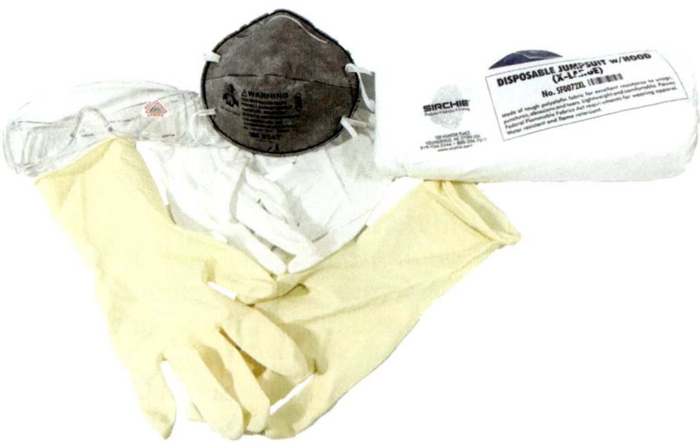

Figure 2.3 Examples of personal protective equipment.

medical examiner's office or coroner may have a medico-legal death investigator respond to the scene and subsequently take custody of the body for later autopsy (Cooper et al. 2009; Merck 2016; Rogers 2013). In cases that involve the death of an animal, it may be determined that a forensic veterinarian is needed to respond to the crime scene. Other times, the situation may warrant the investigator to transport the deceased animal to the forensic veterinarian for a necropsy. In cases that involve animal neglect, abuse, or a suspicious death of an animal, a forensic veterinarian should be consulted. Collaborating with the forensic veterinarian early in the investigation will assist in assuring the animal is collected and preserved in a manner that is optimal for a subsequent forensic necropsy. A forensic veterinarian can provide an investigation with expertise in the areas of medicine, pathology, toxicology, biological, and trace evidence (Cooper et al. 2009; Merck 2016; Rogers 2013).

Developing a Methodology

Prior to entering the crime scene, the investigator should establish a methodical plan of action (Fisher and Fisher 2012; Gardner 2005). The plan should consist of methods that will promote the most efficient and effective tasks for documenting, collecting, and preserving evidence. The main premise for establishing this methodology is to maximize the integrity of the investigation and evidence that may require follow-up analysis. The following concepts will aid in establishing a methodical approach for documenting, collecting, and preserving physical evidence and the crime scene. It should also be noted that although the investigator decides on one approach, there might be situations where the methodology will need to be adjusted or changed to perform tasks more effectively. Processing a crime scene is dynamic and a continually changing environment where changes in weather or new investigatory leads may dictate changes in an investigator's methods to work more effectively (Fisher and Fisher 2012; Gardner 2005).

Establishing a Pattern

Whether performing photography, evidence collection, or searching a scene, the use of an established pattern provides a methodical approach for performing the task. Some of the most common patterns include clockwise, counterclockwise, grid, and spiral (Fisher and Fisher 2012; Swanson et al. 2009). These patterns can be utilized for a diverse number of tasks, but more importantly they offer the practitioner a system of operation that will aid in "telling a story" in a sequential manner. By using these patterns, an individual can convey information with greater ease to a person who was not at the scene. The information will flow more fluidly to others compared to using no pattern method. The flow of the patterns may be utilized in a variety of situations, but are common while searching, photographing, and video recording. Additionally, the use of a pattern can aid in recalling an investigator's actions years later, which is often the situation when an extended period of time exists between a crime occurring and the trial. The use of these patterns will require

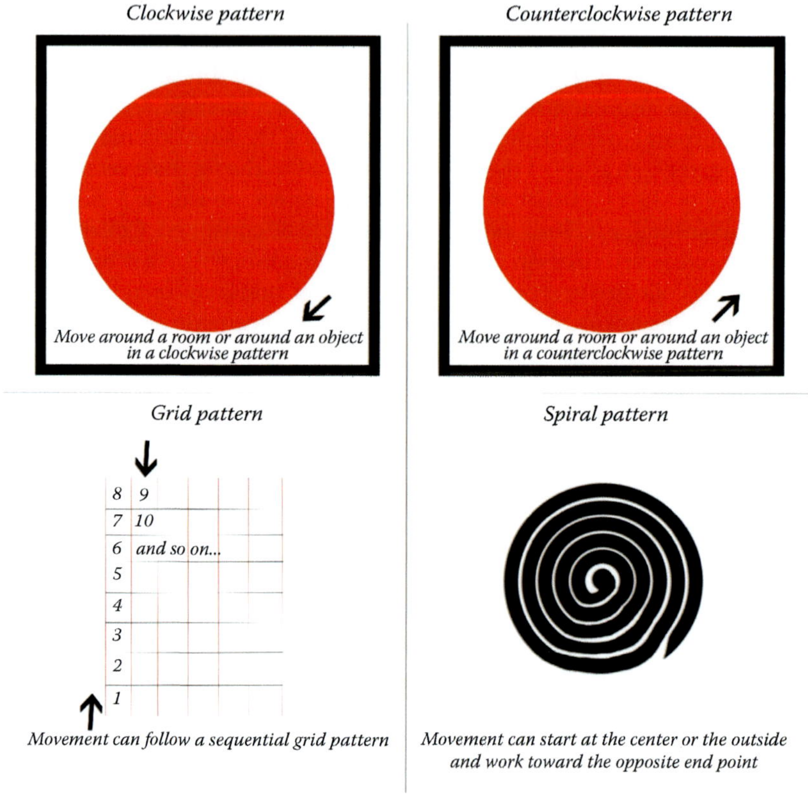

Figure 2.4 Four types of patterns an investigator can use.

a starting area and an ending area that will allow the investigator to work in a systemic pattern while performing a certain task (Figure 2.4).

- *Clockwise pattern*—As the term implies, the pattern follows a left to right circular pattern that corresponds to the rotational pattern of hands on the face of a clock.
- *Counterclockwise pattern*—This term is similar to the clockwise pattern previously described, but the movement follows a right to left circular pattern in a rotational pattern that is opposite to the hands on a clock.
- *Grid pattern*—The grid pattern often incorporates a square or rectangular zone method. Within the larger perimeter area, there are smaller squares or rectangles that are used to create a sequential zone method. Movement from one zone to the next can occur in a variety of ways, such as rows or columns, top to bottom, bottom to top, or a serpentine movement. Some of the common situations that may benefit from using a grid pattern

would include office floor-plans that contain cubical work-spaces, large outdoor scenes, and clandestine graves.

- *Spiral pattern*—The spiral pattern can be used in a circular pattern that starts in the center, or at the perimeter, of the scene and moves in a spiral pattern to the opposite area (Fisher and Fisher 2012; Swanson et al. 2009).

These four patterns can be used often at various crime scenes, but this list is not all-inclusive. There are also other less common methods, such as the use of GPS coordinates, which may be better suited for very large scenes that encompass vast areas. By using GPS coordinates a predetermined sequence of coordinates is established and prioritized to create a pattern.

Alternatively, a scene that presents unique features may require the investigator to utilize those features in developing an effective pattern. An example of this may be the tracking of an injured animal. In this case, a search pattern may be utilized that follows the main tracking trail of the animal, but may also incorporate perpendicular or parallel search patterns in relation to the main trail used for tracking (Figure 2.5). This provides an individual searcher the opportunity to branch off of the trail at a 90° angle to search surrounding areas, then return to the same area of the trail and continue the search along the trail.

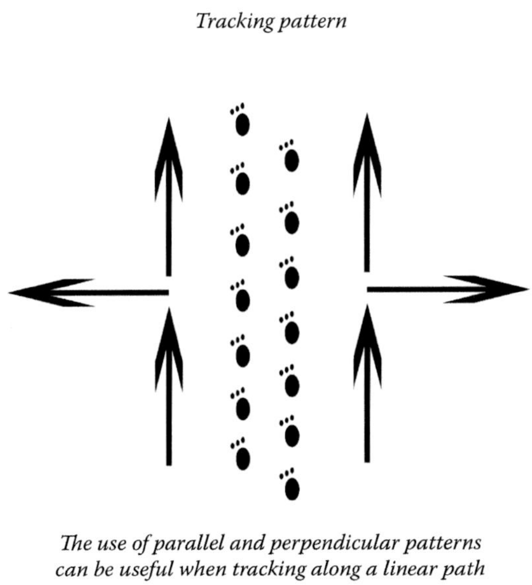

Figure 2.5 Example of a tracking search pattern.

Search Warrants

After the scene has been secured, a determination by law enforcement will likely be made as to whether a search warrant is needed. The Fourth Amendment of the U.S. Constitution protects citizens from unreasonable search and seizure (Del Carmen 2010; Legal Information Institute 2017). Depending on the circumstances surrounding the investigation and the scene, the police department in charge of the scene may seek a search warrant prior to scene processing (Del Carmen 2010). Individuals tasked with working at the crime scene should always consult with the police officers at the scene to make sure there is a valid search warrant or the consent by an owner was obtained. The investigator should notably document whether a warrant or consent to search exists along with the officer's name that provided the information. It is also important to consider the restriction or limitations of the search warrant.

It is important to note that there are exceptions for obtaining a search warrant, such as exigent circumstances. If in doubt, the investigator should continually consult with the law enforcement officers present at the scene. For instance, if an investigator is working at a scene regarding animal cruelty and suddenly comes upon evidence of another crime, such as drugs or arson, no further action should be taken until the police are consulted and the appropriate warrant or amendment to an existing warrant is obtained. Alternatively, if there is an exigent circumstance that the evidence will be destroyed or lost, such as blood on a roadway and heavy rainfall will wash the evidence away, the protection and collection of the evidence is paramount. The law enforcement officer on location will be responsible for guiding the decision as to whether an exigent circumstance exists and should be routinely consulted regarding this issue.

Working the Crime Scene

Prior to documenting the scene or performing other tasks, an investigator should gather an understanding of the scene's environment, safety, and its contents, by performing an initial walk-through. The observations that are noted during the walk-through will provide a more comprehensive understanding of what will be needed to effectively process the scene. Items to note early in the walk-through can include a description of the property or building and labeling the sides. For example, when describing the sides of a building the sides can be referred to by compass coordinates (north, south, east, or west) or by letter designation with "A" assigned to the front of the building and the remaining sequentially assigned to a side, back, and remaining side of the building. A flashlight is a useful tool when walking through the scene because it can easily illuminate dark areas or hiding spaces, but it is also useful as an alternate light source for the searching of latent finger, palm, and animal track or footwear impressions early in the investigation.

During the walk-through of the scene, there may be various indicators of animal neglect (starvation, dehydration, medical problems, and embedded collar), hoarding or types of abuse, such as assault and animal fighting (Fisher and Fisher 2012; Gardner 2005; U.S. Department of Justice and National Forensic Science Technology Center 2013). As a result, the living environment, food and water, medications, and injuries to an animal should be noted. Furthermore, it is important to recognize potential evidence that may be less obvious, transient, or vulnerable to destruction. In addition to documenting what is visually observed, it is equally important to use other senses and document odors and sounds. Recording and photographing detailed observations of the scene can aid investigators in a variety of ways, but is especially useful when attempting to corroborate or refute the statements of people that may be a witness, suspect, or victim (Fisher and Fisher 2012). In addition to the indicators of animal abuse or neglect listed above, the following is a short list of other items of potential evidence:

- Firearms, knives, or other types of weapons and ammunition
- Bullet holes, stab marks, and other indicators of weapons and violence
- Animal and human prescription and illicit drugs, and drug paraphernalia
- Gang-related items such as clothing, patches, photographs, etc.
- Excessive money that may be related to drugs, gambling, or other illegal activities
- Countersurveillance technology, such as video cameras and computers, to watch for police arrival at scene
- If there is a fire scene or abuse using flames; ignitable liquids, other types of fuel, and ignition sources
- Bodily fluids (blood, feces, vomit), blood spatter, bodily tissue
- Fingerprint and footwear impressions or animal tracks

It is always important not to touch or move evidence unless approved by law enforcement to minimize contamination or altering the scene (Fisher and Fisher 2012; Gardner 2005; Saferstein 2007). More specifically, firearms should only be handled by law enforcement until they can ensure the firearm is safe to handle. The investigator may decide that the testing of blood at the scene is beneficial for discriminating whether it is from a human or animal source. As a result, the investigator's relationship and communication with law enforcement at the scene is vital to a successful investigation. Finally, it is important to note that if at any point in the investigation, the investigator observes an item that could potentially be destroyed or damaged, it is appropriate to break from an established method to protect and secure the evidence (De Forest et al. 1983; Fisher and Fisher 2012; Gardner 2005; U.S. Department of Justice and National Forensic Science Technology Center 2013). For instance, if there is blood located on the ground of an outdoor scene and it starts to rain or the animal is tracking through the blood, it is acceptable to break from a predetermined method to document the blood and secure samples. Then, after the evidence is free from potential destruction, the investigator may return to the previous tasks.

After the walk-through of the scene, the investigator may again reassess the plan of action because of new observations that were made. If the investigator will be working with others, tasks should be delegated in a manner that will effectively and efficiently accomplish tasks in a methodical order. Furthermore, the scope of the scene should be determined and the barrier reduced or expanded as needed (Fisher and Fisher 2012; Gardner 2005; Saferstein 2007; U.S. Department of Justice and National Forensic Science Technology Center 2013). If there are multiple scenes and investigators, there may be an option to delegate investigators to each take responsibility of an individual scene, or work as a team processing the scenes in sequence. After the assignments are delegated, the scene should be documented as it was found. The basic methods of documentation consist of note taking, photography, videography, and creating a sketch or diagram.

Notes

It is wise to start taking notes upon being notified and dispatched to the scene. Notes can be as simple or as detailed as necessary and can be written in freehand upon a common notepad or a preprinted form (Figure 2.6).

Keeping notepads, pens, pencils, and markers in the vehicle that will be used to travel to the scene is advantageous. The information gathered for the notes can easily vary, but basic information that should be gathered in notes will consist of the following (Fisher and Fisher 2012):

- Date and time notified
- Individual and contact information of person making notification
- Address of scene
- Time arrived
- Scene description
- Agency in charge of investigation
- Case number
- List of individuals interviewed at the scene and their contact information
- List of evidence gathered at the scene and time it was collected
- Time of completion
- Items for follow-up

As the investigator progresses through tasks at the scene it will be incumbent upon that investigator to record information in the notes that is deemed appropriate or necessary for later recollection. The notes that are generated provide information deemed important by the investigator. As a result, some agencies and states require mandatory retention of notes as evidence. Investigators destroying notes may make themselves susceptible to disciplinary actions or legal action (Dow 2011). It is incumbent upon the investigator to be familiar with procedures and regulations for note retention in their jurisdiction.

Some-Town Police Department
Crime Scene Unit
Crime Scene/Photo Worksheet

Supervisor: ____________ Latent FP: ___ YES ___ NO
Latent palm: ___ YES ___ NO

Department# ____________

SCPO case # ____________ Offense/incident ____________

Investigation officer(s) ____________ ____________

____________ ____________

Date of offense ______ Time of offense ______ hrs Date received ______

Time received ______ hrs Time arrived ______ hrs Time completed ______ hrs

Location of offense ____________

- -

Business/Firm ____________ Address ____________

Victim's name ____________

Address ____________ Phone ______

Victim sex: ☐ Male ☐ Female ☐ Both DOB: ___/___/___ Age: ___ ☐ Emancipated Juvenile?

Race: ☐ Black ☐ White ☐ Asian ☐ Hispanic ☐ Other ____________

Height ______ Weight ______ Occupation ____________

Deceased found by ____________ Time ______ hrs Date ______

Relationship to deceased ____________ Address ____________ Phone# ______

Reported death to ____________ Time ______ hrs Date ______

Deceased pronounced

by: ____________ Time ______ hrs Date ______ Location ____________

Figure 2.6 A preprinted crime scene investigation worksheet.

Photography

One of the most common methods for visually memorializing the observations made by the investigator is with the use of photography (Fisher and Fisher 2012; Miller and McEnvoy 2011; Robinson 2010; Staggs 1997). Photography is an effective tool that allows the investigator to present images to individuals who were not at the scene. Although film photography is still in use, it is common for many investigators to utilize digital photography equipment when capturing images (London and Stone 2012; London et al. 2011; Miller and McEnvoy 2011; Robinson 2010; Staggs 1997) (Figure 2.7). It is beneficial for an investigator to be knowledgeable about the photography equipment and its use prior to deploying it at the scene. Some basic equipment that is used will consist of the following:

- A durable camera bag or case
- Digital single lens reflex (DSLR) camera with interchangeable lenses

Figure 2.7 Camera equipment including tripod, lens, shutter release, flashlight, camera, and flash unit.

- Spare batteries and memory cards
- Tripod
- Flash unit
- Remote shutter release
- Photo card
- Rulers/scales
- Evidence placards

Prior to an investigator ever photographing a scene, it is important to understand the limits of the photographic equipment being used, while also having the skills and knowledge for successfully capturing the images. The images must be effectively captured to provide for a fair and accurate depiction of the subject matter. When an investigator is ready to commence with photography at the scene it is important to review the camera's settings and to have a formatted memory card available. Documentary type images can be captured in the JPEG format, but should be recorded at the camera's optimal resolution (Fisher and Fisher 2012; Robinson 2010; Staggs 1997). The use of a photo card (Figure 2.8), which identifies the date/time, case number, location, and photographer, should be used when capturing images. It is beneficial for the photo card to be the first image captured in the series so connecting the case to the images is easier when reviewing images (Fisher and Fisher 2012; Robinson 2010; Staggs 1997). It is also recommended that the photo card is the last image that is captured so the end of the series of images is established.

Using the previously defined patterns while capturing photographic images can provide an overview, mid-range, and close-up perspective to document the scene and physical evidence in a systematic method (Fisher and Fisher 2012; Robinson 2010; Staggs 1997). The overview images are often taken from farther away and are composed in such a manner as to provide an overview of the scene, its location, and relationship to other locations. The overview image may contain a significant portion of the scene and the items contained within. The images are captured in a consecutive left to right or right to left manner that overlaps the previously captured image. This method allows the images to be placed side-by-side and viewed, without gaps, in a panorama view. After this series of images is captured, the photographer will take position in the corner of the room to the left and capture another series of images (Figure 2.9). This pattern will continue from each corner of the room until the photographer returns to the starting point and has captured the necessary images. If the photographer works in a counterclockwise manner, the following position would be to the right corner of the room, and so on.

After the overview images have been captured, the next series of images are captured from mid-range. Mid-range images provide a perspective and composition that is closer than the overview images and provides an understanding

Figure 2.8 Example of a photo card.

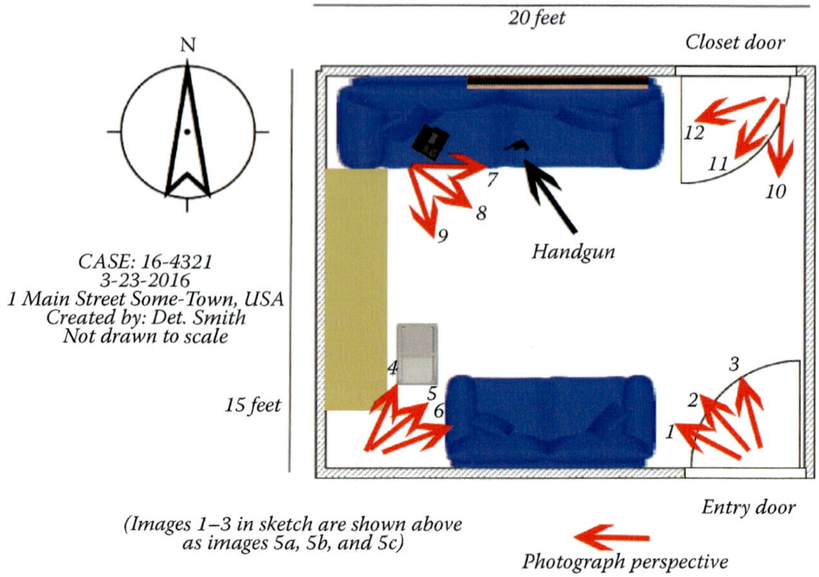

Figure 2.9 Sketch of a room depicting photography using a clockwise pattern to capture overview images.

of relationship among items in the image. Since these images are captured closer to the items of interest, the items may be more distinguishable and their relationship, distance, and orientation may become more discernible.

Finally, the use of close-up images provides the opportunity to capture images that contain more detail and identify information regarding items of interest (Figure 2.10). While capturing close-up images it is important to include

Figure 2.10 A close-up view of a handgun.

images that are captured at a 90° angle. In other words, the lens of the camera should be directed in such a manner that the sensor of the digital camera will be parallel to the surface being captured and the lens is at a 90° angle. This practice will aid in reducing distortion at closer distances.

Maintaining the integrity of the images captured is critical for use in the criminal justice system. Therefore, it is imperative that no images are deleted. If an image of low or poor quality is captured the photographer should adjust settings accordingly and capture another image of optimal quality. The deletion of images provides an area of vulnerability where the integrity of image sequence and missing content can be questioned and the photographer's reasons for deletion perceived as nefarious (Scientific Working Group on Imaging Technology 2009).

Videography

The use of video recorders can provide viewers who were not at the scene an interpretation of images that are fluid and moving. The methods and patterns for capturing video are similar to that of photography, but there are also distinct aspects and equipment that require an investigator to be appropriately trained in capturing crime scene video. There are many types of video recorders, such as tape-based or digital-based recording units. A full evaluation of video equipment goes well beyond the scope of this chapter, but this information provides an overview of how videography fits into the repertoire of a well-trained investigator. Similar to photography, the first image that is recorded using a video recorder should be a photo card that identifies the date/time, case number, location, and videographer (Fisher and Fisher 2012). The photo card should be recorded for approximately 5 seconds, or as long as necessary for an average person viewing the video to read the writing on the card.

The videographer can use the same patterns and methods as the photographer to capture images, but the use of a tripod becomes more essential. For example, whereas a photographer may stand in the doorway of a room capturing a series of overlapping overall images of the room, a videographer would use a tripod from the same perspective, start recording with the video camera stationary for approximately 5 seconds, and then pan the video camera from left-to-right or right-to-left in a deliberately slow motion, and when panning is stopped the recording should continue for approximately 5 seconds before stopping the recording. Recording the images in this slow and deliberate method provides the viewer the time to recognize items in the image and comprehend what is displayed.

One of the most distinct variations between using photography and videography to document the scene is the recording of audio. Audio should not be recorded while capturing video at a scene due to admissibility issues in court (Scientific Working Group on Imaging Technology 2009). Although there may be a switch or menu for turning off the audio on a video camera, the following method is a backup that will further ensure audio will not be recorded. In addition to turning off the audio on the video camera's menu, a ¼ audio jack with the wire cut off may be plugged into the microphone input of the video camera. This method automatically turns off the audio as a backup when there is an oversight to using the audio switch or menu.

The retention of photographs and video footage should be outlined in an agency's standard operating procedures, which outline the appropriate storage and retention process. If no procedures exist, it is recommended that after the last image is captured that the images be downloaded directly to multiple compact diskettes (archive and working copies) using a dedicated copying device or to a dedicated storage device. The archive copies should be secured in long-term storage, while the working copies can be used for day-to-day use.

Evidence Placards

After the series of initial overview, mid-range, and close-up images have been captured and video recorded, the items determined to have evidentiary value should be identified with evidence placards placed near the item (Fisher and Fisher 2012; U.S. Department of Justice and National Forensic Science Technology Center 2013). Photography and videography should then be repeated using the same series of overview, mid-range, and close-up with the evidence placards in the images. If the evidence placard (Figure 2.11) does not contain a ruler/scale, a ruler or scale (Figure 2.12) should be placed next to items of evidence when capturing close-up images.

A dedicated memory card should be used to capture images for one case only, and should not mix images from other cases. This practice eliminates confusion between cases and promotes the integrity of all images being captured. Once the images are downloaded to compact discs the memory cards may be formatted for the next case. The use of a dedicated copy device to download the images from a memory card directly to a compact disc is preferred. This method does not permit for any opportunity to change, delete, or alter images when being copied to a disc. To further increase the integrity of this process rewritable discs should not be used.

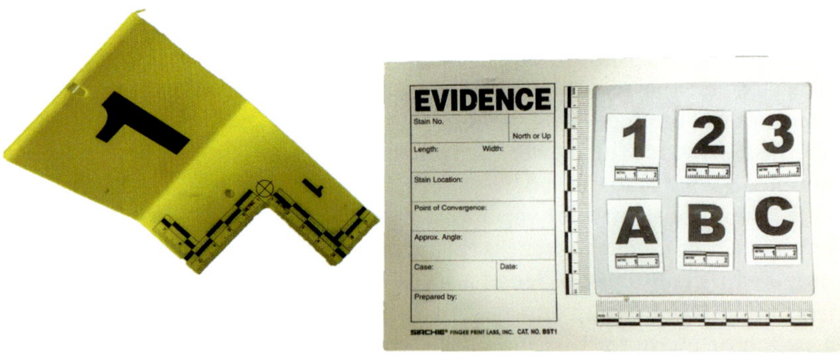

Figure 2.11 Example of evidence placards.

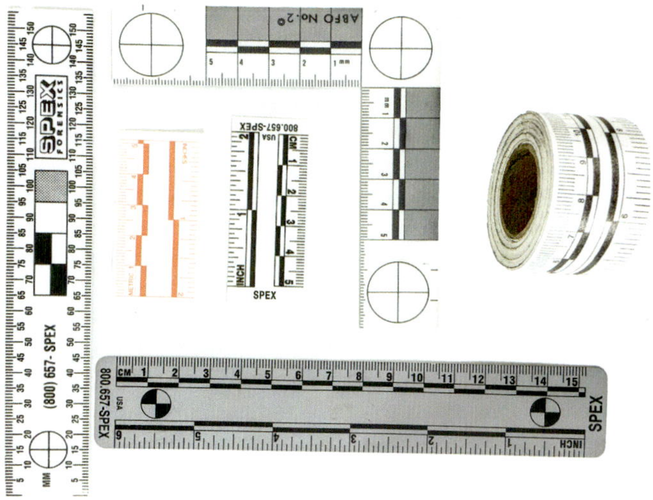

Figure 2.12 Examples of various types of scales.

Sketching the Scene

Sketching the scene is another form of documentation that provides a graphic representation of the scene (Fisher and Fisher 2012; Gardner 2005; U.S. Department of Justice and National Forensic Science Technology Center 2013). Sketching can be accomplished in a variety of methods and from a variety of perspectives, but they can be generally categorized as a rough sketch and a final sketch. Whereas rough sketches are those recorded at the scene and may be incorporated in the notes, a final sketch will be refined for clarity and accuracy afterward and may be made using computer-based programs. A rough sketch at the scene can be accomplished using a pencil, paper, and a measuring device. There are also a variety of vendors that supply plastic templates, containing stencils of common items found at crime scenes. These stencils can be used to aid in drawing a sketch quickly and neatly. Alternatively, if more advanced technology is available, the scene sketch may be recorded using more expensive digital measuring devices, such as laser scanning stations. The benefit of the scene sketch adds to other forms of documentation by providing a tool for a better understanding of spatial and relationship issues at the scene.

A rough sketch may be recorded from a variety of perspectives and used to best depict what the investigator viewed. Common perspectives for sketches include a top-down (bird's-eye) view, elevated, cross-section, and first-person. The top-down view is commonly associated to blueprints of a floor plan used for construction. This perspective offers the viewer an overview perspective that can be used to interpret spatial distance and relationship of items recorded within the sketch. The elevated perspective provides a viewer with similar benefits to those of a top-down sketch, but incorporates a perspective that highlights measurements and spatial relationships vertically. Similarly, the cross-section sketch will incorporate aspects of both the top-down and the elevated to create a sketch that incorporates three-dimensional aspects for a particular section of the scene. The first-person perspective also incorporates both the top-down and the elevated to create a sketch that incorporates three-dimensional aspects, but is visualized from a first-person perspective. The use of computerized software programs may also aid in creating a first-person sketch that can be manipulated so the viewer can change perspectives by moving throughout the scene.

A well-defined sketch will contain detailed information to record the scene, but will also incorporate case-related details, the location and orientation of items, and the identification of the sketch creator. The elements of a good sketch include a compass that will indicate north and provide orientation of the overall sketch. The title will include the case number, date of event, location, individual creating the sketch, and the term "Not to Scale" if the sketch is not a precise scaled representation. Additionally, a sketch may incorporate a key, which provides an area just outside the sketch area that depicts various items from the sketch and identifies what they are in more detail.

The well-trained investigator who seeks to sketch a crime scene may have a variety of equipment, technology, and personnel to choose from. Other times, the investigator may have no additional help and only a pencil, paper, and measuring device. The types of equipment and approaches for sketching crime scenes is too vast to be comprehensive for this chapter, but with appropriate training and experience, sketching crime scenes can assist in providing a more comprehensive understanding of the scene to individuals who were not present.

Search and Seizure

Assuming the Fourth Amendment of the U.S. Constitution was not violated, which protects individuals from unlawful search and seizure, the continuing search for and collection of evidentiary items can assist in understanding the facts surrounding a criminal act (Legal Information Institute 2017). Some items of evidentiary value may be obvious to the investigator during the initial walk-through, while other items of value may be obscured. After the scene has been sufficiently documented, appropriate handling, collection, and packaging can preserve the items that are determined to be of value. The collected items should be secured in a manner that prevents cross-contamination, degradation, or destruction. A more thorough search of the scene may be necessary to reveal obscured or hidden items. As additional items are revealed the appropriate use of notes, photography, and other documentary methods should be made prior to collecting the items.

Evidence Collection

Evidence can have two general categories, one of statements from witnesses, suspects, and victims or one that is a physical item (Fisher and Fisher 2012; Gardner 2005; Merck 2016; New Jersey State Police 2012; Saferstein 2007; U.S. Department of Justice and National Forensic Science Technology Center 2013). It is highly unlikely a deceased or living animal will give a verbal statement as evidence. As a result, physical evidence may be more crucial in crimes involving animals than crimes involving only humans. Physical evidence can be any tangible item that, through analysis and scrutiny, provides data and information surrounding a topic in question. As a result, the proper collection of physical evidence becomes a crucial aspect of the investigation for investigators.

Having the right personnel and tools to do the right job is important. As a result, it is important for the investigator to have other qualified individuals to aid in the investigation, but also be prepared with appropriate tools and supplies. Having additional personnel also enhances personal security while at a scene, but more importantly proves to be very useful when confirming the collection of drugs or expensive items. The lack of this peer review to validate the collection of money, jewels, or drugs at a scene may lead to unnecessary problems if there are later discrepancies in the quantity or amount. Although there are a wide variety of collection supplies to accommodate the vast types of items collected, some are more common than others (Table 2.1).

In conjunction with the collection of items at a crime scene is the appropriate packaging for preservation. There is a wide variety of packaging supplies offered by vendors (Figure 2.13). The investigator should have a substantial supply of various packaging supplies in the vehicle that will be used to travel to the scene. Not having the appropriate supplies will likely create more problems for the investigator at the scene and during subsequent review of the

Table 2.1 List of Common Evidence Searching and Collection Supplies That May Be Utilized during a Crime Scene Investigation

- Flashlight
- Magnifying glass
- Paper bags and envelopes (various sizes)
- Plastic bags (various sizes)
- Tweezers
- Evidence tape
- Rulers and tape measures
- Labels and hang tags
- Zip-ties
- Boxes (various sizes)
- Small plastic containers for liquid samples
- Pipettes, used to obtain liquid samples

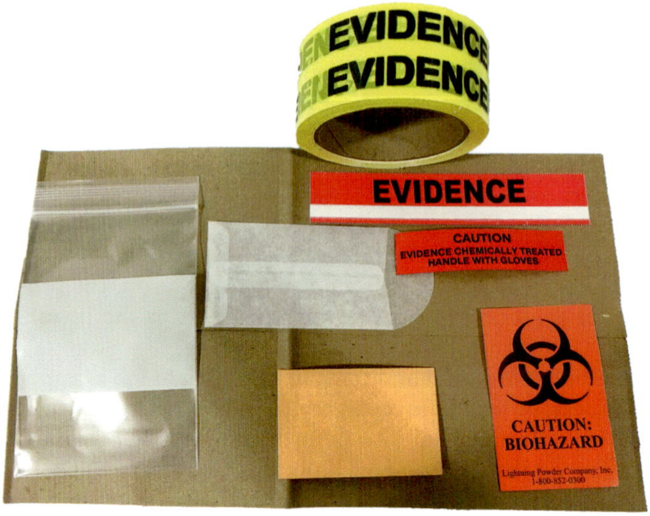

Figure 2.13 Examples of various packaging supplies.

work by scientists and attorneys (Fisher and Fisher 2012; Gardner 2005; Merck 2016; New Jersey State Police 2012; Saferstein 2007; U.S. Department of Justice and National Forensic Science Technology Center 2013).

Table 2.2 provides an overview for the collection and packaging of various items. If an investigator encounters an item for collection that is not common to the following categories on the chart, appropriate discretion should be made to maintain the integrity of the item while minimizing the potential for cross-contamination, degradation, or destruction. When the collection method of an object is in question, the individual should consult with knowledgeable team members, a supervisor, an evidence technician, or the local forensic laboratory.

There are many types of potential evidence that may be observed, and they will vary from scene to scene. Understanding the value of various types of evidence is important. For instance, exculpatory evidence aids in eliminating potential suspects, while inculpatory tends to prove guilt (Swanson et al. 2009). For instance, indicators of maltreatment of an animal may be obtained by evaluating medications, food and water, restraints, feces or urine, disease, injuries, blood or vomit, and available shelter. A thorough evaluation of the scene, the condition, and the contents can provide the investigator with an understanding of the animal's living environment as well as an understanding of the criminal acts. Furthermore, the information gathered may establish a timeline of events.

Nonremovable items may be tested at the scene to recover a variety of potential evidence. Specialized training is needed to effectively develop, record, and preserve impression evidence (Fisher and Fisher 2012). Investigators specifically trained in pattern impression evidence, such as fingerprints, footwear,

Table 2.2 Collection and Packaging Methods for Various Items

Item Type and Collection	Packaging
Blood, saliva, or semen stains • Use two swabs (moisten with distilled water if necessary) and air dry • Stained items may be dried and packaged	• Cap swabs and place in swab box (if available) and place in envelope; Affix biohazard label and seal with tape • Place dried-stained item in paper bag and seal with tape
Teeth and bones (dry with no tissue)	• Individual samples should be placed in paper bags or cardboard boxes, secured against movement in the package, and sealed
Hair/fibers • Use of tweezers • Adhesive side of fingerprint tape lifters as collection method	• Place the hair/fiber sample in a drug-fold, place in envelope, and seal with tape • Fold tape lifters on backing card to secure sample and place in envelope, then seal with tape
Guns and knives • Firearms should be unloaded for safety, but should be clearly marked on packaging if unable to unload • Ammunition should be individually packaged • Sharp edges and points should be wrapped	• The item should be placed in a gun or knife box and secured against movement using zip-ties, or an equivalent • Ammunition should be placed in paper bags or envelopes and sealed with tape
Cords, ropes, leashes, wires, etc. • Do not untie or cut knots • Label any questioned ends and investigator cut ends • Collect entire length	• Items should be individually packaged • Paper bags or cardboard boxes can be used and sealed with tape
Fire debris • Item should be collected using clean tools to avoid contamination	• Clean metal cans should be used and sealed airtight

(*Continued*)

Table 2.2 (Continued) Collection and Packaging Methods for Various Items

Item Type and Collection	Packaging
Deceased animal • Depending on the size of the animal and available supplies the collection method may vary • Legs and head should be bagged using paper bags for potential DNA or trace evidence	• Clean sheets, body bags, and other supplies that are appropriate may be used that will prevent contamination and maintain integrity of the evidence
Medication • If medication is in container, do not open at the scene and package individually • If medication is loose, package individually	• Containers of medication can be placed in paper bags and sealed with tape • Loose medication should be placed in drug folds or small envelopes and placed in larger envelope, then sealed with tape
Animal's food and water • Loose dry food • Loose wet food • Samples of water from bowls can be collected using a pipette	• Dry food may be placed in paper bags • Wet food may be placed in plastic bags or sealed cans for a short time period (caution should be taken as moist samples in sealed containers can cause mold, mildew, and degradation of the sample); Testing should be expedited • Water samples may be placed in sealed plastic containers
Computers, phones, and digital items • Vary in size and weight • Consult with forensic lab or computer analyst before turning an item off	• Paper bags • Faraday bags • Padded secured boxes

(*Continued*)

tire, and tool-marks may proceed in the development and preservation of these items.

An investigator that is alone at a scene and is less skilled in the development of impression evidence will benefit by appropriately collecting the item for subsequent submittal to a forensic laboratory for testing. For a skilled investigator, various development and recovery techniques may be used to

Table 2.2 (Continued) Collection and Packaging Methods for Various Items

Item Type and Collection	Packaging
Chemicals, toxins, and poisons • Can be liquid, solid, or gaseous forms • Can be common household items or for industrial use	• Consult with Hazmat personnel • Document photographically • If safe, may be collected in original packaging and placed in chemically approved collection bags/cans

Sources: 1. New Jersey State Police. 2012. Special and technical services section. *Evidence Field Manual.* New Jersey State Police. 2. U.S. Department of Justice and National Forensic Science Technology Center. 2013. *Crime Scene Investigation: A Guide for Law Enforcement.* Largo, FL. https://www.nist.gov/sites/default/files/documents/forensics/Crime-Scene-Investigation.pdf (Accessed March 29, 2017).

record the impression evidence for subsequent analysis. Additionally, pattern evidence, such as bloodstain pattern evidence, may be located on nonremovable items and require extensive documentation and collection of samples (James et al. 2005). The blood samples may be obtained for subsequent DNA analysis.

Well-trained investigators will have an arsenal of methods and supplies for searching, recording, and testing the scene for potential latent blood, semen, and saliva. Various areas of interest for both human and animal DNA samples will include the mouth and claws of an animal, areas of blood at a scene, and the areas surrounding a wound. In the same manner that a medico-legal death investigator will bag the hands of a deceased human, the paws and mouth/head should be bagged to preserve DNA and trace evidence on deceased animals. The bags should be sealed securely with tape to prevent them from coming loose during transport. After bagging the paws and head/mouth, the remains should be wrapped in a clean white linen sheet and then placed in an impermeable bag (e.g., body bag) (Rogers 2016, Personal Communication). Collection kits for DNA and trace samples may be easily purchased through various vendors. Purchasing kits and supplies from an approved vendor reduces potential arguments that may arise from utilizing inferior products.

Flies and maggots that are present at the scene may provide another source of DNA, but also provide toxicology and time of death information (Merck 2016). The ambient temperature, weather, and location of the flies and maggots should be well documented prior to collecting these samples. To aid a forensic entomologist, the investigator should gather samples of live flies, maggots, and eggs when present at the scene. Many supply vendors sell entomology kits that contain the supplies necessary for the collection and packaging of these samples, but it is important to collect samples at various stages of growth and in sufficient quantity.

Flies may be best captured using an insect net and packaged in clean dry containers. Samples of eggs and maggots can be collected using tweezers. A sample of eggs should be taken from the center of a mass and divided into two separate containers. One will be a jar that contains 75% ethyl alcohol for preserving the sample and the other will be for larval rearing (Merck 2016). Maggots of various sizes may also be present and samples should be collected, but it is important to obtain a sample of the largest (oldest). A sample of the large maggots should be first boiled in hot water for approximately 5 minutes, but if boiling water is not available at the scene the sample may be placed directly into a container with 70–85% isopropyl alcohol. As with the eggs, a second sample of maggots should be packaged in a larvae-rearing container.

Each sample should have a label on the interior of the container as well as one on the exterior. The labels should include case number, date, time collected, location sample was collected, and unique sample number (Merck 2016). Additionally, photography should be utilized throughout the process to include images of the insect environment and flora for postanalysis. Finally, the investigator should take notice of other indicators of a fly's life cycle, such as pupa casings, and then document and collect them. Every effort should be made to expedite case information and samples to the forensic entomologist to aid in successful analysis of the samples.

In addition to using the most appropriate packaging for collecting evidence, it is equally important to use an effective seal to secure the package (New Jersey State Police 2012). Common seals include adhesive evidence tape or a heat-sealing device. Generally, if the item has been sealed in a manner that prevents the items from escaping, the package can be considered sealed. After the seal has been affixed, it is recommended that the individual collecting the item write initials, date, and time over the seal. Furthermore, the packaging should be labeled with appropriate information to identify the contents, a unique identifier (such as the collector's initials and a sequential number, for example, KP-1), the case number, person collecting the item, time it was collected, and location where it was retrieved. In situations that warrant a sealed package to be reopened, efforts should be taken to maintain the original seal and open the package from another location (New Jersey State Police 2012). Upon resealing the package, it should be labeled in the same manner as the original with current date and time. It is encouraged to photograph the package before it is opened and after it is resealed.

At times, it may be convenient to have the number of the unique identifier have the same number as the evidence placard at the scene, but when a numerical deviation exists, and to avoid confusion, the deviation should be noted in the scene notes and subsequent report. A complete list of evidence should be made. This can be included in the notes and should have the unique identifier, a brief description of each item, and the time it was collected. All evidence should be kept in a secure location that has restricted access. At the onset of collecting items it is also imperative to document chain-of-custody.

The chain-of-custody provides a detailed list of individuals that take custody of an item since it was collected (New Jersey State Police 2012). If items are turned over to other personnel or other agencies it will be documented within the chain-of-custody form. A common chain-of-custody receipt includes the date, time, names, and signatures of individuals transferring and receiving items, and also a detailed description of the items. Multiple copies of the chain-of-custody receipt should be made and distributed or filed according to local operating procedures.

Final Walk-Through

After the scene has been documented and the evidence collected, the investigator may conduct a final walk-through before concluding the scene investigation. A methodical search plan should be utilized. The investigator will walk through the scene while re-evaluating the work that had been performed. During this time, the investigator will consider any additional tasks that need to be performed. At this time, the investigator may also perform additional searches for less obvious forms of evidence. For example, the investigator may use a blood reagent, such as Bluestar or Luminol, to potentially visualize unnoticed bloodstains (James et al. 2005). Furthermore, an alternate light source may be used as a technique for aiding in visualizing concealed items such as semen, urine, and blood. After the investigator has performed the tasks that would have visualized concealed evidence, and the investigator is satisfied that if there was evidence it would have been observed by using the techniques, the investigator may conclude the scene investigation.

Follow-Up

In follow-up to the scene investigation, the investigator may be tasked with submitting the collected evidence for analysis. As evidence is tested and returned, the results may confirm or refute statements in contention. Continual evaluation of the information may establish an identity of otherwise unknown participants or a linkage between the scene, participants, and the animal. A constant review of avenues for follow-up will aid in maximizing a more comprehensive understanding of the events surrounding the crime.

Conclusion

Crime scene investigation is a major component of the forensic investigation. The skills and abilities of an investigator to process a crime scene greatly impact the reliability and outcome of a criminal investigation. The veterinary forensic investigator should follow the lead of federal, state, or municipal law enforcement and always approach the crime scene in pairs both for safety and for corroboration of the evidence identified and collected. Processing the scene as well as documenting the scene findings are critical during the investigation. Documentation of the scene includes multiple modalities such as notes, photography, and videography. Additional communication between all members of the investigation team will allow for a superior investigation. Additionally, it should be noted that some of the guidelines may be unique to New Jersey and the investigator on scene should understand the local and state requirements for note retention and investigation of a crime scene.

References

Cooper, J.E., Cooper, M.E., and Budgen, P. 2009. Wildlife crime scene investigation: Techniques, tools and technology. *Endang Species Res.* 9:229–238.

De Forest, P.R., Gaensslen, R.E., and Lee, H.C. 1983. *Forensic science: An introduction to criminalistics.* New York, NY: McGraw-Hill.

Del Carmen, R.V. 2010. *Criminal procedures: Law and practice*, 8th ed. Belmont, CA: Wadsworth.

Dow, P. 2011. Attorney general directive regarding retention and transmittal of contemporaneous notes of witness interviews and crime scenes, Directive #2011-2. http://www.nj.gov/lps/dcj/agguide/directives/dir-2011-2-RetentionTransmittal.pdf (Accessed April 10, 2017).

Fisher, B.J. and Fisher, D.R. 2012. *Techniques of crime scene investigation*, 8th ed. Boca Raton, FL: CRC Press/Taylor & Francis.

Gardner, R.M. 2005. *Practical crime scene processing and investigation.* Boca Raton, FL: CRC Press/Taylor & Francis.

James, S.H., Kish, P.E., and Paulette-Sutton, T. 2005. *Principles of bloodstain pattern analysis: Theory and practice.* Boca Raton, FL: CRC Press/Taylor & Francis.

Legal Information Institute. 2017. Fourth Amendment. https://www.law.cornell.edu/constitution/fourth_amendment (Accessed April 10, 2017).

London, B. and Stone, J. 2012. *A short course in digital photography*, 2nd ed. Upper Saddle River, NJ: Prentice Hall.

London, B., Stone, J., and Upton, J. 2011. *Photography*, 10th ed. Upper Saddle River, NJ: Prentice Hall.

Merck, M.D. Animal CSI: An introduction to veterinary forensics in the investigation of animal cruelty. http://www.dspca.ie/media/AnIntroductiontoVeterinaryForensicsintheInvestigationofAnimalCrueltyArticle1.pdf (Accessed February 12, 2016).

Miller, L.S. and McEnvoy Jr., R.T. 2011. *Police photography*, 6th ed. San Diego, CA: Elsevier.

New Jersey State Police. 2012. Special and technical services section. *Evidence field manual.* New Jersey State Police.

Robinson, E.M. 2010. *Crime scene photography.* 2nd ed. San Diego, CA: Elsevier.

Rogers, E. 2013. The veterinarian as crime scene investigator. *Today's Veterinary Practice.* http://todaysveterinarypractice.navc.com/wp-content/uploads/2015/02/TVP_2013_VeterinaryCSI_References.pdf (Accessed February 12, 2016).

Rogers, E. 2016. Personal Communication. September 2016.

Saferstein, R. 2007. *Criminalistics: An introduction to forensic science*, 9th ed. Upper Saddle River, NJ: Pearson Prentice Hall.

Scientific Working Group on Imaging Technology. 2009. Field photography equipment and supporting infrastructure. https://www.swgit.org/pdf/Section%203%20Field%20Photography%20Equipment%20and%20Supporting%20Infrastructure?docID=47 (Accessed March 29, 2017).

Staggs, S. 1997. *Crime scene and evidence photographer's guide*. Temecula, CA: Staggs Publishing.

Swanson, C.D., Chamelin, N.C., Territo, L., and Taylor, R.W. 2009. *Criminal investigation*, 10th ed. Columbus, OH: McGraw-Hill.

U.S. Department of Justice and National Forensic Science Technology Center. 2013. *Crime scene investigation: A guide for law enforcement*. Largo, FL. https://www.nist.gov/sites/default/files/documents/forensics/Crime-Scene-Investigation.pdf (Accessed March 29, 2017).

3

Videography

A New Tool in Animal Cruelty Investigations

Debra Teachout

Contents

Introduction

During a forensic investigation, video recordings that provide a real-time account of a crime or review of animal behavior may be made available to investigators. Sources of video recordings include closed circuit television systems (CCTV), law enforcement video recorders, and personal video cameras. These videos can be analyzed for authenticity, digitally enhanced, and evaluated for expert testimony. The veterinarian may be presented with a video from a case of suspected animal cruelty and asked to evaluate it within the context of the forensic investigation. The evaluation of videos as evidence has been performed in numerous criminal and civil matters; however, video analysis in relation to animal crimes is less common. Though many veterinarians may be unaware of this form of evidence and its value to the investigation, they certainly possess the knowledge and skills necessary to evaluate the medical aspects, well-being, and treatment of animals captured on video. This chapter will discuss the necessary steps to be used in the assessment of animal welfare from video and the formulation of the expert opinion during an animal cruelty investigation.

Types of Videos Used in Animal Cruelty Investigations

Videos used in animal cruelty investigations can be categorized by format, quality, and continuity. There are numerous formats of videos that can be analyzed for forensic evidence including CCTV (also called video surveillance) and videos recorded from police vehicle dash cameras, body cameras, ATM machine cameras, and cell phone cameras. In some instances these videos are obtained through search and seizure. Undercover and personal/private citizen videos are increasingly being used as the technology for hidden body-worn video cameras continues to improve and as the number of undercover videos successfully used as evidence increases.

Video quality will vary depending on the type of camera used. The recording may be in color or black and white; may range from several seconds to many hours; or may show a single view or multiple views taken from different vantage points. Although beyond the scope of this chapter, video recordings can be submitted to forensic video experts for authentication, audio and visual enhancement, and object comparison techniques (such as comparing an image of a hat at the crime scene with a hat found on a suspect).

Videos can be continuous or discontinuous. Most videos have a time stamp or time clock and if the video is continuous and recorded in a single series, the observer is responsible for ensuring there are no discontinuities in the time clock. Evaluation of the metadata (data about the data) can help to authenticate a digital video file in the forensic setting by distinguishing between original and postprocessed videos (Gloe et al. 2014). However, if the camera recording the event is motion activated, a discontinuous time stamp could occur. The background, subject, and inanimate objects should be assessed for "jumping" or slight movement, which may indicate that the video was edited. Some videos presented to veterinarians for assessment will have several starts and stops in the continuity by design as the videographers may edit or chapter a long video for ease of viewing or to focus on particular events. If the veterinarian should want to view more of the entire video, it should be available upon request.

Handling the Video

Videos and photographs of a crime scene or of victims can serve as essential evidence in court proceedings and both should be processed the same way in the evidence log (Merck 2013). If video is downloaded from the web, it is important to download the original file when possible. Video file metadata can include information such as the title of the video, GPS data, shutter speed, location where the video was filmed, and the date the video was recorded. One should be aware that metadata may not be accurate or even complete. Like other types of evidence, chain of custody should be maintained with appropriate documentation and it begins with the acquisition of the video.

Assessment of the Video

Video evidence can be extremely valuable when taken at the crime scene or when it includes animal victims and a real-time account of the crime. In contrast to the still images of a photograph, videos are particularly useful as they can reveal animal activity and behavior. During a live animal examination, a video may capture and display dynamic conditions such as abnormal behavior (fearful, threatening, dull, unpredictable), vocalization due to pain, nonpurposeful vocalization in cases of brain impairment, weakness, limping or other gait abnormalities from bone and soft tissue injuries, neurologic deficiencies, and initial response to food and water in cases of suspected neglect (Merck et al. 2013). Video that captures interactions of animals with their caretakers can provide valuable information regarding the treatment of the animals. A real-time video recording in nonaccidental injury cases can be used to help focus the veterinary examination of the live animal on specific anatomical areas (Reisman and Lockwood 2014). In nonaccidental injury cases when the animals are deceased or if their bodies are not obtainable for forensic necropsy, a real-time video allows veterinary assessment of animal health, behavior, and welfare during the recorded incident when the animals were still alive.

Within the context of an animal cruelty investigation or civil litigation, the veterinarian may be asked to review video; assess animal behavior, physical condition, and environment; and comment on pain and suffering. The veterinarian may be required to generate a written report and/or present oral testimony in court.

It is important to employ a conceptual and consistent framework for guidance and decision making when assessing animal welfare in a video. This guidance may be provided by the Five Freedoms. The concept of the Five Freedoms was originally developed by the Brambell Commission in the United Kingdom in December 1965, to address livestock welfare. Since that time, they have been refined, updated, and adopted by many veterinary and animal health and welfare organizations throughout the world as relevant for any animal species. They describe the conditions that animals should experience to ensure good welfare and prevent suffering (Table 3.1). Not every video will allow evaluation of every freedom, but the Five Freedoms will serve as a checklist to make

Table 3.1 The Five Freedoms

Freedom from hunger and thirst—By ready access to fresh water and diet to maintain health and vigor
Freedom from discomfort—By providing an appropriate environment including shelter and a comfortable resting area
Freedom from pain, injury, or disease—By prevention or rapid diagnosis and treatment
Freedom to express normal behavior—By providing sufficient space, proper facilities, and company of the animal's own kind
Freedom from fear and distress—By ensuring conditions and treatment which avoid mental suffering

Source: Farm Animal Welfare Council. 2010. *Annual Review 2009–2010.* http://www.fao.org/ag/againfo/themes/animal-welfare/news-detail/en/c/43986/.

sure all aspects of an animal's well-being are considered during the assessment. During the evaluation of videos that show obvious physical abuse of an animal, it is important not to overlook other essential aspects of welfare revealed by examining the animal's surroundings. No one freedom is more or less important than the other; they are all equal (Fraser 2008).

When evaluating a video, regardless of species, it is important to consistently use a step-by-step approach to the evaluation of the animal and scene so that the final assessment is well organized, complete, and clear (Figure 3.1).

Step 1: Watch the video

↓

Step 2: Perform a visual examination of the animal

↓

Step 3: Characterize the abnormalities

↓

Step 4: Formulate the expert opinion

↓

Step 5: Communicate the expert opinion

Figure 3.1 The five steps for assessment of an animal in video evidence.

Watch the Video (Step 1)

The veterinarian should initially simply watch the video in its entirety to establish a general impression of the following: the physical condition/appearance of the animals (Figure 3.2); the behavior exhibited by the animals; the suitability of the housing and environment for the species involved; and the treatment of the animals by caretakers or stockpersons. After the initial review of the video it is important for the veterinarian to analytically watch the video multiple times, often at slower speeds or zooming in to catch details that might be missed at normal speed or distance. Videos may be raw and unedited or in some instances they may be condensed and chaptered by the organization requesting a professional opinion. If the video is expected to be continuous, the reviewer should pay attention to the time stamp and note if a discontinuous time stamp is observed.

Perform a Visual Examination of the Animal (Step 2)

While recognizing the limitations of a visual examination of an animal in a video due to the inability to physically touch the animal, an impression of general health and welfare can certainly be formulated by observing and evaluating how an animal looks, what it does physically, and how it expresses itself dynamically. Visual assessment of an animal in this way is essentially the first part of a routine, standard veterinary physical examination. A typical veterinary physical examination begins before the animal is touched; the animal is simply observed first. This initial visual (and auditory) part of a physical examination is also referred to in veterinary literature as general observation (Defarges 2015), exam at a distance (Roussel 2012), or a hands-off exam (Durham 2013). It revolves around the physical attributes and behavior of the animal (Table 3.2). Additionally, abnormalities such as wounds, draining abscesses, discharge from external organs or orifices, growths, swollen joints, fractures (dangling of limb, bone protruding

Figure 3.2 Screen capture from a severely matted dog that is receiving medical attention. Photo courtesy of Dr. Adam Stern, University of Illinois.

Table 3.2 Some Physical Attributes and Behaviors of an Animal That Can Be Observed during Assessment of Video Evidence
Hair/fur/skin/feather condition
Body condition and contour
Posture
Conformation
Mentation (attentiveness, lethargy, hyper excitation, aggression)
Vocalization
Abnormal behavior
Head shaking
Awareness of surroundings
Facial expression
Teeth grinding
Breathing pattern (respiratory rate, effort and noise, open mouth breathing, panting)
Self-mutilation
Ambulation and gait
Immobility

through skin), lameness, organ prolapses, abdominal distension, and signs of illness or pain may be observed. Eyes may be sunken from dehydration. The whites (sclera) of the eyes may show in cows (Grandin 2015b), horses (Houpt 2005), and dogs (McConnell 2006) secondary to fear. Observations can be made concerning the animal's environment (availability and type of food, water, shelter, bedding, cleanliness, safety), how the animal relates to the environment (calm, inquisitive, frustrated), how the animal interacts with the people present in the video (owners, caretakers, workers, or stockpersons), and how the people interact with the animal. Although the veterinarian reviewing a video is limited by the quality and content of the video as well as by the inability to physically manipulate the animal as would be done during a complete standard physical exam, a problem list of abnormalities observed and a list of differentials or rule-outs ranked in order of probability can be created.

The quality of an animal's experience (contented, anxious, friendly, distressed) can be assessed through their body language (behavior, posture, facial expressions). Video of animals in various circumstances have been used in the development and application of qualitative behavioral assessment (QBA), a scientifically validated method of assessing animal welfare through human examination of animal body language (Wemelsfelder 2007). QBA is a skill that simply requires regarding and relating to animals as sentient beings, being familiar with species-specific behavior, and having experience watching and interacting with animals in different environments and circumstances (Wemelsfelder 2007). It has been applied to the welfare of a range of species including pigs, cattle, horses, poultry, and dogs (Andreasen et al. 2013). QBA can be used for assessing behavioral review of farm animals under field conditions. QBA is especially helpful for assessing how animals react to brief events such as handling (Grandin 2015d). For example, a dog in a shelter may be described as walking confidently and relaxed or fearfully and anxiously when led by a caretaker. The degree or intensity of behavioral expression should also be noted. For example, a sow in a gestation crate may appear not only frustrated, but *extremely* frustrated as she frantically and repetitively chews the metal bars in front of her.

Scales and scoring systems can help in determining the degree of an abnormality and have been developed in various species for directly observable conditions such as body condition, lameness, handling, stunning at slaughter, animal cleanliness, pain assessment, stress levels (Tables 3.3 and 3.4), and panting score for heat stress, to name a few. Behavior, degree of behavior, and scoring systems are essential tools in evaluating the quality of an animal's life as captured on video. The reviewer must take into consideration the audio feed when available.

Characterize the Abnormalities (Step 3)

Upon completion of the visual examination and assessment of the animal and its environment, the veterinarian must describe all abnormalities and record the corresponding video time stamp (if present) or running time reference to allow for later citing. The description and assessment must be based on what is actually seen by the reviewer, not what the reviewer thinks might be happening. Accurate description of the video is paramount, and over-reach must be avoided. If parts of the video are unclear, clarification and additional video (if it exists) should be requested. Definitive comments should not be offered about content for which the reviewer is unsure. Speculation concerning portions of the video that are too blurry, too grainy, too dark, or too light to be seen well should not be attempted.

When assessing the video, the veterinarian may see abnormalities relating to the animal or its environment such as poor body condition, illness, injury, fearful or distressed behavior, isolation, lack of food or water, exposure to temperature extremes, inadequate shelter or bedding, and insufficient space. It is most important to question and report if the animal is experiencing a deficiency in one or more of the Five Freedoms, and the severity of the deficiencies must be described. While all the Freedoms should be addressed, the third Freedom (freedom from pain, injury or disease—by prevention or rapid diagnosis and treatment) particularly applies to the veterinarian's area of expertise. Issues to be addressed include whether a sick or injured animal appears to receive veterinary care and if it does, whether the care is provided in a timely manner. If the animal is in pain (and suffering from chronic

Table 3.3 Seven-Level Cat Stress Score

Score	Body	Belly	Legs	Tail	Head	Eyes	Pupils	Ears	Whiskers	Vocalization	Activity
1 Fully relaxed	i: Laid out on side or on back a: Not applicable	Exposed, slow ventilation	i: Fully extended a: Not applicable	i: Extended or loosely wrapped a: Not applicable	Laid on the surface with chin upward or on the surface	Closed or half-opened, may be blinking slowly	Normal	Half-back (normal)	Lateral (normal)	None	Sleeping or resting
2 Weakly relaxed	i: Laid ventrally or half on side or sitting a: Standing or moving, back horizontal	Exposed or not exposed, slow or normal ventilation	i: Bent, hind legs may be laid out a: When standing extended	i: Extended or loosely wrapped a: Tail up or loosely downward	Laid on the surface or over the body, some movement	Closed, half-opened, or normal opened	Normal	Half-back (normal) or erected to front	Lateral (normal) or forward (normal)	None	Sleeping, resting, alert or active, may be playing
3 Weakly tense	i: Laid ventrally or sitting a: Standing or moving, back horizontal	Not exposed, normal ventilation	i: Bent a: When standing extended	i: On the body or curved backward, may be twitching a: Up or tense downward, may be twitching	Over the body, some movement	Normal opened	Normal	Half-back (normal) or erected to front or back and forward on head	Lateral (normal) or forward	Meow or quiet	Resting, awake, or actively exploring
4 Very tense	i: Laid ventral, rolled, or sitting a: Standing or moving, body behind lower than in front	Not exposed, normal ventilation	i: Bent a: When standing hind legs bent, in front extended	i: Close to the body a: Tense downward or curled forward, may be twitching	Over the body or pressed to the body, little or no movement	Widely opened or pressed together	Normal or partially dilated	Erected to front or back, or back and forward on head	Lateral (normal) or forward	Meow, plaintive meow, or quiet	Cramped sleeping, resting, or alert, may be actively exploring, trying to escape

(*Continued*)

Table 3.3 (Continued) Seven-Level Cat Stress Score

Score	Body	Belly	Legs	Tail	Head	Eyes	Pupils	Ears	Whiskers	Vocalization	Activity
5 Fearful, stiff	i: Laid ventrally or sitting a: Standing or moving, body behind lower than in front	Not exposed, normal or fast ventilation	i: Bent a: Bent near to surface	i: Close to the body a: Curled forward close to the body	On the plane of the body, less or no movement	Widely opened	Dilated	Partially flattened	Lateral (normal), forward or back	Plaintive meow, yowling, growling, or quiet	Alert, may be actively trying to escape
6 Very fearful	i: Laid ventrally or crouched directly on top of all paws, may be shaking a: Whole body near to ground, crawling, may be shaking	Not exposed, fast ventilation	i: Bent a: Bent near to surface	i: Close to the body a: Curled forward close to the body	Near to surface, motionless	Fully opened	Fully dilated	Fully flattened	Back	Plaintive meow, yowling, growling, or quiet	Motionless alert or actively prowling
7 Terrorized	i: Crouched directly on top of all fours, shaking a: Not applicable	Not exposed, fast ventilation	i: Bent a: Not applicable	i: Close to the body a: Not applicable	Lower than the body, motionless	Fully opened	Fully dilated	Fully flattened back on head	Back	Plaintive meow, yowling, growling, or quiet	Motionless alert

Source: Kessler, MR, and DC Turner. 1997. Stress and adaption of cats (*Felis silvestris catus*) housed singly, in pairs and in groups in boarding catteries. *Anim Welf.* 6: 243–254.
Note: a = active; i = inactive.

Table 3.4 A Scale of Behavioral Indicators of Stress in Domestic Stabled Horses

Stress Level	Behavior Score (BS)	Behavioral Indicators
No stress	1	Standing at the front of the stable, looking around or head below wither height, eating. Ears pricked, back or slowly scanning, tail still or gently swishing. Some repetitive oral behavior. *Horse described as:* Horse calm, unconcerned, relaxed, quiet, listening, accepting.
	2	*Behavior exhibited for previous BS plus:* Walking. *Horse also described as:* Horse alert and watching.
Low stress	3	*Behavior exhibited for previous stress level plus:* Occasional weaving behavior, box walking, and repetitive head movements. Ears occasionally flattened. Defecation. *Horse described as:* Listening, interested, alert.
	4	*Behavior exhibited for previous BS plus:* Pacing. Approaching potential stressors, e.g., noise from outside the stable. Repeated tail swishing. *Horse also described as:* Curious, unsettled, barging.
Medium stress	5	*Behavior exhibited for previous stress level plus:* Scratching against stable walls or fittings, pawing at ground with front legs. Nostrils flared. Repeatedly looking around. Tail raised. *Horse described as:* Restless, showing tension in the body, fidgeting when still.
	6	*Behavior exhibited for previous BS plus:* Approaching and retreating away from potential stressors. Stopping eating to focus on potential stressor. *Horse also described as:* Jumpy, easily startled.
	7	*Behavior exhibited for previous BS plus:* Keeping away from potential stressors and remaining still to focus on them. Horse described as for previous BS.

(*Continued*)

Table 3.4 (Continued) A Scale of Behavioral Indicators of Stress in Domestic Stabled Horses

Stress Level	Behavior Score (BS)	Behavioral Indicators
High stress	8	*Behavior exhibited for previous stress level plus:* Repeated performance of stereotypic behavior, e.g., weaving, box walking, repetitive head movements. Stamping of hind feet. Snorting. *Horse described as:* Very unsettled and alert.
	9–10	*Behavior as exhibited for previous BS.* *Horse also described as:* Agitated, fidgety, anxious, active, aggressive, uncomfortable.

Sources: 1. Young, T., Creighton, E., Smith, T., and Hosie, C. 2012. A novel scale of behavioural indicators of stress for use with domestic horses. *Appl Anim Behav Sci.* 140:33–43. 2. McDonnell, S.M., Freeman, D.A., Cymbalaluk, N.F., Scott, H.C., Hinchcliffe, K., and Kyle, B. 1999. Behaviour of stabled horses provided continuous or intermittent access to drinking water. *Am J Vet Res.* 60:1451–1456. 3. Strand, S.C., Tiefenbacher, S., Haskell, M., Hosmer, T., McDonnell, S.M., and Freeman, D.A. 2002. Behaviour and physiological responses of mares to short-term isolation. *Appl Anim Behav Sci.* 78:145–157.

neglected illness or injury), it is important to address if and how the animal is euthanized. Evidence of neglect or of inhumane euthanasia practices should be documented and referred to by time in the video. When assessing the third Freedom in video content, the absence of a veterinarian or a veterinary pen does not mean veterinary care does not exist. However, if, for example, a rectal prolapse is observed in a pig and the prolapse is necrotic and covered by maggots, these findings would support the fact that adequate veterinary attention has not likely occurred, and this should be noted. In some videos, large numbers of animals may be observed. In such cases, it is important to attempt to identify individual animals; however, the animals may be assessed as a group rather than as individuals if abnormal findings such as cases of severe illness/injury, overly rough handling, or animals housed in a poorly sanitized environment are widespread and individual animals are difficult to identify.

The best method for accurately identifying pain in animals is by observing their behavior (Epstein et al. 2015), or by witnessing acts or procedures done to animals that are known to be painful, such as routine livestock management procedures (beak trimming, tail docking, castration) when performed without the benefit of anesthesia or analgesia (Grandin 2015e). Any type of disease or tissue injury can produce pain and subsequent emotional suffering (Merck and LeCouteur 2013). Video enables veterinarians to infer from behavior that an animal might be in pain by capturing abnormalities such as distorted facial expressions, change in vocalizations, trembling, and restlessness (Gregory 2004c; Merck and LeCouteur 2013) (Table 3.5). Veterinarians should remember that some animals will lie quietly while in pain (Gregory 2004c). Pain assessment can be made easier and more precise by the use of pain scoring systems such as the Colorado State Pain Charts for dogs (Hellyer et al. 2006a; Hospital, Colorado State University, Veterinary Teaching 2016), cats (Hellyer et al. 2006b; Hospital, Colorado State University, Veterinary Teaching 2016), and horses (Blossom et al. 2007); the Glasgow Short Form for dogs (Reid et al. 2007); and the Grimace Scales for horses (Dalla Costa et al. 2014), rabbits (Keating et al. 2012) or mice (Langford et al. 2010). The World Small Animal Veterinary Association's publication *Guidelines for Recognition, Assessment and Treatment of Pain* contains helpful descriptions and pictures for recognition of pain in dogs and cats. It also recommends that numerical rating scales be used due to improved sensitivity over simple descriptive scales (no pain, mild pain, moderate pain, severe pain) or visual analog scales (a mark on a line running from no pain to maximum pain) (Matthews et al. 2014). Although palpation of the painful area is included in some pain scoring systems such as the Colorado Pain Scale, visual assessment of animal behavior, body tension, posture, and facial expressions provide adequate evidence for evaluating the presence and severity of pain.

Table 3.5 Ways to Observe the Expression of Pain in Animals
Facial expressions
Vocalizations
Trembling
Lameness
Abnormal posture
Unsteady gait
Reluctance to move
Reluctance to get up or lie down
Restlessness
Poor response to handling
Hiding
Licking at painful area
Absence of behaviors indicating comfort (grooming, eating, drinking, normal social interaction, normal ambulation)

Sources: 1. Gregory, N.G. 2004c. Pain. In *Physiology and Behaviour of Animal Suffering*, by N.G. Gregory, pp. 94–130. Ames, IA: Blackwell Publishing. 2. Merck, M.D., and R.A. LeCouteur. 2013. Special considerations in animal cruelty cases. In *Veterinary Forensics: Animal Cruelty Investigations,* 2nd ed., by M.D. Merck, pp. 69–96. Ames, IA: Wiley-Blackwell.

During the assessment of the animal, as previously mentioned, a visual examination may reveal gait abnormalities, open wounds, and/or poor body condition. It is imperative that when describing the observed abnormalities they are recorded in a manner similar to documenting information in a veterinary medical record. For example, it would be incorrect to simply state that an animal is emaciated; rather, it would be more accurate to describe the animal as showing decreased musculature, protruding boney prominences (ribs, vertebral spinous processes, pelvic bones) evident from a distance, a markedly prominent abdominal tuck, and include the time in the video for easy reference. To indicate severity, this animal should be assigned a number based on appearance using an appropriate body condition scoring system, and that particular scoring system should be referenced. Body condition scoring charts have been published by various governmental, professional, and private organizations. The U.S. Department of Agriculture (USDA) Animal and Plant Health Inspection Service (APHIS) National Veterinary Accreditation Program training materials as well as the USDA APHIS Animal Welfare Inspection Guide contain numerous visual body condition score charts that feature demonstrable criteria for the assessment of body condition of animals including horses, cattle, pigs, small ruminants, cats, cougars, dogs, elephants, leopards, lions, and tigers (USDA 2013; USDA APHIS 2016).

After identification of any abnormalities (behavioral or physical), a problem list should be created. This list will be used during the formulation of the veterinarian's opinion for the case.

Formulate the Expert Opinion (Step 4)

After the evaluation of a video and the creation of a problem list, the veterinarian must formulate and explain his or her conclusions in the expert opinion written report or during testimony in court. Deficiencies in the Five Freedoms, severity of the deficiencies, and consequences to the animal's physical and mental well-being should be discussed with particular attention given to any injury, illness, and/or pain resulting from animal maltreatment. If the veterinarian concludes that animals are suffering, the reasons for that conclusion must be substantiated.

It is always helpful, when formulating an opinion about the findings in a video, to be able to review police reports, witness reports, or other crime scene or local area data before drawing any conclusions or providing a report. This additional data may prove useful in allowing full interpretation of the video content.

Maltreatment, Injury, Illness, and Pain

Identification of the signs of injury, illness, and/or pain, especially if resulting from maltreatment, will likely be the most important findings in the video. There are four general classifications of animal maltreatment: physical abuse, emotional abuse, physical neglect, and emotional neglect (Merck and LeCouteur 2013). Physical abuse injuries, also termed nonaccidental injuries, will occur in cases of obviously violent actions against animals such as physical assault, burning, shooting, stabbing, hanging, choking, drowning, dragging, throwing, kicking, and mutilation (Reyes 2013). In animal sexual abuse cases, video of the assault may be found on the suspect's phone or computer, and the veterinarian may be asked to assess the animal's behavior and comment on pain and suffering (Merck and Miller 2013). More passive offenses toward animals include neglect or abandonment, and hoarding (Reyes 2013). In these situations not only will the animals appear physically abnormal (poor body condition score, unkempt, dirty, untreated injury or illness), but also often animals will be observed living within a plethora of environmental deficiencies.

When assessing neglect, a critical and accurate assessment of the animal's living conditions should be undertaken. Shelter suitability, enclosure safety, comfort level, and access to appropriate edible food and clean drinkable water should be intensively evaluated. It must be especially noted if food and water are available to all animals within their enclosures or if there is evidence of food and water in any other areas of the premises that were recorded. If animals are observed as unable to walk or move due to injury or disease, it is important to comment on suffering if food and water access are impossible for those individuals (Figure 3.3). Other abusive environmental conditions that may be observed in the video include overcrowding, manure/urine buildup, temperature extremes, filthy housing, broken cages, and unsafe conditions that cause animals to fall frequently and become injured (wet, dirty floors) (Grandin 2015a).

The animal's environment and living conditions include the presence of caretakers/stockpersons. The attitude of these individuals critical to good welfare and the revealed relationship between the caretaker/stockpersons and the animals is often a fundamental element in the video that should be addressed. Some may argue that evaluation of human behavior is difficult and beyond the purview of the veterinarian; therefore, limit the evaluation to the observed actions and consequences to the animal. Avoid assessing or assigning intentions to the humans committing the actions. Fear and stress

Figure 3.3 Screen capture showing an injured/ill chicken unable to walk and therefore unable to access food or water. Photo courtesy of Mercy for Animals.

may occur when animals are handled or restrained, but it increases greatly if animals are handled with excessive roughness or shocked multiple times with electric prods (Grandin 2015e). Aversive behaviors toward the animals such as shouting, hitting, kicking, stomping, punching, stabbing, choking, or otherwise tormenting would, in addition to bodily suffering, cause suffering from fear and should be documented as abuse. Fear behavoir will vary by species. For example, cats will hiss and arch their backs (Gregory 2004a), grazing animals such as horses and cattle may switch their tails quickly, defecate, lay their ears back and hold their heads up high, and chickens may freeze (Grandin 2015b).

Suffering

A prime function of the veterinarian is to recognize and relieve suffering in animals. This duty requires the clinical ability to recognize signs of suffering and to identify possible sources such as hunger, thirst, pain, fear, or frustration. The ability to diagnose the physical and emotional causes of suffering is essential in veterinary forensic cases. If suffering is identified the veterinarian has the responsibility to provide a clear record of evidence to indicate what has caused the animal to suffer and why, especially in cases of direct animal cruelty or neglect (Webster 2012). Degree of suffering is important to document in that it can influence charges filed and affect sentencing (Merck and LeCouteur 2013).

Suffering, an experience that is both unpleasant and extreme, can result from inadequate food and water, temperature extremes, injury, disease, boredom, extreme confinement, and/or social isolation (Dawkins 2005). If suffering or abuse is persistent and especially harsh, animals may display learned helplessness. Learned helplessness (Seligman 1972) is a behavioral phenomenon where an animal is repeatedly subjected to an averse stimulus from which it cannot escape. Eventually the animal will stop trying to avoid the stimulus and behave as if it is helpless as it has learned it has no ability to improve or change its condition. If the animal is given a chance at escape it will not try (Merck and LeCouteur 2013). In other situations, if anxiety, fear, frustration, emotional numbness, and deprivation (social isolation, barren environments) are relentlessly experienced, sterotypies and neurotic behaviors may be observed (Gregory 2004b). Severe deficiencies in environmental enrichment and food choices can lead to abnormal behaviors such as bar-biting, pacing, and repetitive behaviors (Grandin 2015c).

Ultimately, when evaluating video evidence, the veterinarian must go beyond simply identifying and describing the abnormal behavior, physical findings, and/or abusive events. A professional opinion must be provided as to how the animal is injured/ill, how it is reacting to that injury/illness, and what the animal is experiencing in terms of pain and suffering.

Communicate the Expert Opinion (Step 5)

The final report should be well-written, clear, organized, complete, and concise. A strong opening statement that summarizes the veterinarian's opinion of the video's content and a strong conclusion that emphasizes the same are important. Explanatory comments should be descriptive and should focus on specific events or abnormalities identified in the video. For example, if a worker is observed kicking a live turkey like it was a football, the incident should be described in those words as they convey a clear description of the action. In contrast, it is too ambiguous for the reviewer to merely state that a worker handles turkeys roughly.

Expert statements should explain what might be beyond the grasp of the average viewer of the video. For example, anyone can see that a worker is kicking a turkey. The veterinarian's responsibliity is to explain why kicking a turkey like a football will negatively impact it. One could explain that based on a reasonable degree of certainty the turkeys that were kicked could sustain physical injuries such as bruising, lacertions, joint dislocations, broken bones, and/or internal injuries. These physical injuries as well as the experience of being kicked would cause turkeys to suffer greatly from pain, fear, and distress. It should also be noted that turkeys possess a range of physical and mental capabilities very similar to mammalian species; therefore, turkeys are capable of feeling pain, fear, and distress. Law enforcement relies on experts to report if the animals are harmed or if they experience injury, pain, and suffering from the actions on the video. It is helpful to them to explain that turkeys can, in fact, suffer from being kicked since possibly some law enforcement officers or others involved in the case may believe that turkeys, as animals raised for food, do not feel pain like dogs or cats do.

Comments about whether a particular practice or activity shown in a video is standard or accepted in industry or veterinary practice should be offered with references to support each statement. If possible, expert statements should mention any alternative practices or activities that could have or should have been used. For example, if a video of a dog being drowned for euthanasia purposes was analyzed, it would be important to explain that it is not standard or accepted veterinary practice to euthanize dogs by drowning. The report should state that according to the current American Veterinary Medical Association's Guidelines for Euthanasia of Animals, dogs should be euthanized by intravenous injection of a barbiturate. Drowning is considered an inhumane and unacceptable means of euthanasia (Leary et al. 2013).

It is important for the veterinarian to maintain objectivity in the report. Based on his or her veterinary medical education and experiences, the veterinarian should state the primary rule-out and/or explanation how an injury or illness came to be. It is important for the reviewer to understand (and perhaps state) that his or her opinion could change if there becomes more information available that previously had not been provided (such as additional video footage).

It is helpful to understand and have a sense of the language used in laws prohibiting cruelty to animals within the relevant jurisdiction and for some of that language to be employed if applicable in the assessment. For example, if the legal statute states it is illegal to "cause undue suffering to an animal" it is helpful to law enforcement if the expert opinion statement contains similar wording such as, "kicking a turkey like a football causes undue suffering in that animal."

Sometimes expert statements will be shared with the general public. In the case of undercover video work it is possible that the organization requesting the expert opinion may make some or all of it available to the media.

Conclusion

Video is an important tool in revealing violations of animal cruelty laws. It not only provides for a real-time recording of events that transpired, but it also may be the only documented evidence of a potential crime not witnessed by a member of law enforcement or the general public. Veterinary analysis of a video can play a major role during the forensic investigation by identifying and characterizing behaviors, reactions, injuries, and illnesses of an animal; documenting unsatisfactory or cruel environmental conditions; and reporting animal suffering. Undercover videos are often critical to exposing animal abuse in settings that are hidden from the general public such as in puppy mills, factory farms, circuses, horse training facilities, and research laboratories.

In today's society, cameras are everywhere and constantly record many aspects of daily life. With these recordings, new evidence can be analyzed to support or refute charges brought against a person, organization, or institution. The strength of the video analysis will depend on the quality of the video and thoroughness of the evaluation. Regardless of the species of animal in the video, a step-by-step approach to evaluation of the animal in the video is imperative in order to perform a visual examination of the animal, identify problem areas, and formulate an expert opinion.

References

Andreasen, S.N., F. Wemelsfelder, P. Sandoe, and B. Forkman. 2013. The correlation of qualitative behavior assessments with welfare quality protocol outcomes in on-farm welfare assessment of dairy cattle. *Appl Anim Behav Sci.* 143:9–17.

Blossom, J.E., P.W. Hellyer, P.M. Mich, N.G. Robinson, and B.D. Wright. 2007. *Equine Comfort Assessment Scale.* Colorado State University Veterinary Medical Center.

Dalla Costa, E., M. Minero, D. Lebelt, D. Stucke, E. Canali, and M.C. Leach. 2014. Development of the horse grimace scale (HGS) as a pain assessment tool in horses undergoing routine castration. *PLoS ONE.* 9.

Dawkins, M.S. 2005. The science of suffering. In *Mental Health and Well-Being of Animals*, by F.D. McMillan, pp. 47–56. Ames, IA: Blackwell Publishing.

Defarges, A. 2015. The physical examination. *Clinician's Brief.* September 73–80.

Durham, H.E. 2013. Cardiovascular physical examination. *Western Veterinary Conference 2013 Proceedings.* Las Vegas, NV: Veterinary Information Network. http://www.vin.com/members/cms/project/defaultadv1.aspx?id=6000969&pid=11371&.

Epstein, M., I. Rodan, G. Griffenhagen, J. Kadrlik, M. Petty, S. Robertson, and W. Simpson. 2015. 2015 AAHA/AAFP pain management guidelines for dogs and cats. American Animal Hospital Association. https://www.aaha.org/public_documents/professional/guidelines/2015_aaha_aafp_pain_management_guidelines_for_dogs_and_cats.pdf (Accessed July 25, 2016).

Fraser, D. 2008. How do the different measures relate to each other. In *Understanding Animal Welfare*, by D. Fraser, pp. 222–240. Ames, IA: Wiley-Blackwell.

Gloe, T., A. Fischer, and M. Kirchner. 2014. Forensic analysis of video file formats. *Digit Invest.* 11:S68–76.

Grandin, T. 2015a. An introduction to implementing an effective animal welfare program. In *Improving Animal Welfare: A Practical Approach*, 2nd ed., by T. Grandin, pp. 1–14. Boston, MA: CABI.

Grandin, T. 2015b. How to improve livestock handling and reduce stress. In *Improving Animal Welfare: A Practical Approach*, 2nd ed., by T. Grandin, pp. 69–95. Boston, MA: CABI.

Grandin, T. 2015c. Implementing effective standards and scoring systems for assessing animal welfare on farms and slaughter plants. In *Improving Animal Welfare: A Practical Approach*, 2nd ed., by T. Grandin, pp. 49–68. Boston, MA: CABI.

Grandin, T. 2015d. Successful technology transfer of behavioral and animal welfare research to the farm and slaughter plant. In *Improving Animal Welfare: A Practical Approach*, 2nd ed., by T. Grandin, pp. 313–327. Boston, MA: CABI.

Grandin, T. 2015e. The importance of measurement to improve the welfare of livestock, poultry, and fish. In *Improving Animal Welfare: A Practical Approach*, 2nd ed., by T. Grandin, pp. 15–34. Boston, MA: CABI.

Gregory, N.G. 2004a. Anxiety and fear. In *Physiology and Behaviour of Animal Suffering*, by N.G. Gregory, pp. 22–31. Ames, IA: Blackwell Publishing.

Gregory, N.G. 2004b. Emotional numbness and deprivation. In *Physiology and Behaviour of Animal Suffering*, by N.G. Gregory, pp. 32–45. Ames, IA: Blackwell Publishing.

Gregory, N.G. 2004c. Pain. In *Physiology and Behaviour of Animal Suffering*, by N.G. Gregory, pp. 94–130. Ames, IA: Blackwell Publishing.

Hellyer, P.W., S.R. Uhrig, and N.G. Robinson. 2006a. *Feline Acute Pain Scale.* Colorado State University.

Hellyer, P.W., S.R. Uhrig, and N.G. Robinson. 2006b. *Canine Acute Pain Scale.* Colorado State University Veterinary Medical Center.

Hospital, Colorado State University Veterinary Teaching. 2016. How we assess your canine's pain level. *IVAPM.* https://ivapm.org/for-the-public/animals-and-pain-articles/how-we-assess-your-canines-pain-level/ (Accessed August 7, 2016).

Houpt, K.A. 2005. Horses: Behavior management and well-being. In *Encyclopedia of Animal Science*, by W.G. Pond and A.W. Bell, pp. 531–533. New York: Marcel Dekker.

Keating, S.C.J., A.A. Thomas, P.A. Flecknell, and M.C. Leach. 2012. Evaluation of EMLA cream for preventing pain during tattooing of rabbits: Changes in physiological, behavioural and facial expressions. *PLoS ONE.* 7.

Langford, D.J., A.L. Bailey, M.L. Chanda, S.E. Clarke, T.E. Drummond, S. Echols, S. Glick et al. 2010. Coding of facial expressions of pain in the laboratory mouse. *Nat Methods.* 7:447–449.

Leary, S., W. Underwood, R. Anthony, and S. Cartner. 2013. AVMA guidelines for euthanasia of animals. *American Veterinary Medical Association.* https://www.avma.org/KB/Policies/Documents/euthanasia.pdf (Accessed February 1, 2016).

Matthews, K., P.W. Kronen, Lascelles, D., Nolan, A., Robertson, S., Steagall, P., Wright, B., K. Yamashita. 2014. Guidelines for recognition, assessment and treatment of pain. *J Small Anim Pract.* 55:E10-E68.

McConnell, P. 2006. *For the Love of a Dog.* New York: Random Publishing House.

Merck, M.D. 2013. Crime scene investigation. In *Veterinary Forensics: Animal Cruelty Investigations*, 2nd ed., by M.D. Merck, pp. 17–35. Ames, IA: Wiley-Blackwell.

Merck, M.D. and D.M. Miller. 2013. Sexual abuse. In *Veterinary Forensics: Animal Cruelty Investigations*, 2nd ed., by M.D. Merck, pp. 233–241. Ames, IA: Wiley-Blackwell.

Merck, M.D. and R.A. LeCouteur. 2013. Special considerations in animal cruelty cases. In *Veterinary Forensics: Animal Cruelty Investigations*, 2nd ed., by M.D. Merck, pp. 69–96. Ames, IA: Wiley-Blackwell.

Merck, M.D, D.M. Miller, and P.C. Maiorka. 2013. CSI: Examination of the animal. In *Veterinary Forensics: Animal Cruelty Investigations*, 2nd ed., by M.D. Merck, pp. 37–68. Ames, IA: Wiley-Blackwell.

Reid, J., A.M. Nola, J.M.L. Hughes, D. Lascelles, P. Pawson, and E.M. Scott. 2007. Development of the short-form Glasgow Composite Measure Pain Scale (CMPS-SF) and derivation of an analgesic intervention score. *Anim Welfare.* 16:97–104.

Reisman, R. and R. Lockwood. 2014. Street cameras, security cameras, cell phones and other unconventional sources of evidence in animal cruelty cases. *International Veterinary Forensic Sciences Association Annual Conference.* Orlando, FL.

Reyes, C.L. 2013. Statistics and measurement of animal cruelty. In *Animal Cruelty: A Multidisciplinary Approach to Understanding*, by M.P. Brewster and C.L. Reyes, pp. 109–123. Durham, NC: Carolina Academic Press.

Roussel, A.J. 2012. Physical Examination in Ruminants I. *ABVP Symposium 2012.* San Antonio: Veterinary Information Network. http://www.vin.com/members/cms/project/defaultadv1.aspx?pId=11351&meta=Generic&id=5329649.

Seligman, M. 1972. Learned helplessness. *Annu Rev Med* 23:407–412.

USDA. 2013. *USDA Animal Welfare Inspection Guide.* Washington, DC.

USDA APHIS. 2016. *National Veterinary Accreditation Program.* https://www.aphis.usda.gov/aphis/ourfocus/animalhealth/nvap (Accessed July 28, 2016).

Webster, J. 2012. Educating veterinarians in animal welfare. *Veterinary Information Network, Australian Veterinary Association Proceedings 2012.* May. http://www.vin.com/members/cms/project/defaultadv1.aspx?id=6308029&pid=11355& (Acccessed July 26, 2016).

Wemelsfelder, F. 2007. How animals communicate quality of life: The qualitative assessment of behaviour. *Anim Welfare.* 16:25–31.

4

Bloodstain Pattern Analysis

Anita Zannin

Contents

Introduction

Is bloodstain pattern analysis (BSPA) a science or an art? That question is asked in courtrooms across the country, especially after the 2006 National Academy of Sciences (NAS) report. The answers to this question have been as varied as the types of BSPA practitioners. Some say science, some say art, some say a little of both. My typical answer to this question is that it is a "discipline based on scientific principles." While BSPA is not a "hard" science, it is based on the principles of the hard sciences of physics, mathematics, biology, and chemistry. There is an element of subjectivity, and the analysis rendered is ultimately an opinion—as is the case with several other forensic science disciplines. Reproducibility is an important concept in the sciences. When a fluid is acted upon by a force, it will behave in a predictable manner. This predictability and reproducibility is what allows BSPA to be taught repeatedly. Bloodstain pattern analysis is not serology, or DNA; it is the analysis and interpretation of the size, shape, distribution, and location of bloodstains in order to determine the events which gave rise to their origin. It is the study of the static aftermath of a dynamic, blood-shedding event. BSPA is used, in conjunction with other forensic disciplines, such as forensic pathology and DNA analysis, to assist in reconstructing a scene to determine the most likely scenario. This chapter introduces the animal forensic investigator to the basic tenets of blood pattern analysis. The complexity of this subject will relegate the investigator to only the recognition of important bloodstain evidence, the proper documentation, and appropriate collection of bloodstain evidence. Most will not be able to draw a conclusive interpretation of same, rather will help the investigator to know when to contact a bloodstain pattern analysis expert.

History of Bloodstain Pattern Analysis

Often, it is thought that BSPA is a relatively new discipline in forensic science. However, the reality is that BSPA has a long history, dating back to the 1800s, in Europe.

- 1895—Dr. Eduard Piotrowski produced a book; complete with color plates, entitled *Uber Entstehung, Form, Richtung und Ausbretung der Blutspuren nach Hiebwunden des Kopfes* (Concerning Origin, Shape, Direction and Distribution of the Bloodstains following Head Wounds Caused by Blows). This appears to be the first truly scientific study of BSPA, including the understanding and application of the scientific method.
- 1939—French scientist Dr. Victor Balthazard et al. presented their paper, *Des Gouttes De Sang Projete* (Research on Blood Spatter) at

> the 22nd Congress of Forensic Medicine. Page one of this paper states, "This research paper was to pinpoint characteristic elements of a bloodstain which might give decisive hints as to its origin." This original research included study of trajectories, the trigonometric relationship (the ratio between width and length of a bloodstain), an awareness of target surface considerations, and the understanding that the dynamics of a blood-shedding event could not always be copied under laboratory conditions.

The first significant documentation of BSPA in the United States came from Dr. Paul Kirk, a professor at the University of California at Berkeley. In 1953, Kirk published a book entitled *Crime Investigation—Physical Evidence and the Police Laboratory* with a section called "Blood: Physical Investigation," which included examination of angular and velocity effects on bloodstains. In 1955, Dr. Kirk authored a lengthy affidavit in the case of *Ohio v. Sheppard* (the case upon which the movie *The Fugitive* was based). In this affidavit, Kirk reviewed the investigation, drying times, and adopted a "whole scene" approach and established the relative positions of the victim and attacker at the time of the beating. This was a significant milestone for bloodstain evidence in the legal system. Dr. Kirk encouraged Herbert L. MacDonell to continue with bloodstain pattern research and to apply for a grant from the Law Enforcement Assistance Administration (LEAA). MacDonell did apply for and receive that grant, resulting in the 1971 publication of *Flight Characteristics and Stain Patterns of Human Blood* (MacDonell 1973).

The parallels between Balthazard and MacDonell's work truly speak to the reproducibility of this discipline. One should remember that, in the late 1960s and early 1970s, the Internet, as we know it today, did not exist, so previous research on the subject was not as easy to find as it is today. This means that the work of Balthazard and MacDonell were completed independently of one another.

In March 1973, the first BSPA course (Institute on the Geometric Significance of Human Bloodstain Evidence) was taught by MacDonell (MacDonell 2005). This was the beginning of the development of BSPA as a recognized field in the legal system in the United States. Since then, many 40-hour basic BSPA courses have been taught, and many of those students, too numerous to name here, have gone on, conducted additional research and now teach the discipline themselves. MacDonell revised his initial research publication as more literature was located, research conducted, cases evaluated, and court decisions rendered, with his last publication, *Bloodstain Patterns*, Second Revised Edition, in 2005. In 2004, MacDonell was awarded an honorary ScD for his many contributions to the field of forensic science. The professional organization for bloodstain pattern analysts, the International Association of Bloodstain Pattern Analysts (IABPA), was founded in 1983 and today has over 900 members worldwide. Each year, a U.S. and European IABPA conference is held. This is by no means a complete history of BSPA, but meant to give a brief evolution of the discipline.

The Role of Bloodstain Pattern Analysis

BSPA can be used to reveal many different significant facts of evidentiary value about a scene. It is important to understand that not all the items listed below may be able to be ascertained from all scenes. Some things BSPA can reveal include:

- What type of event occurred (e.g., a stabbing or beating vs. a shooting)?
- How many blows were struck (a minimum number of blows)?
- Did the victim move after the injury was inflicted?
- The relative position of the participants.
- The duration of the attack (this can be a factor in charging the accused or at sentencing).
- Was the attacker injured?
- Which stains should be analyzed?
- Support or refute witness, victim, and/or suspect statements.
- Sequencing of the events.

In *some* cases, all the above might be able to be determined. In other cases, only a few of these items can be ascertained, whereas in some cases *none* of the above items may be ascertained with scientifically defensible conclusions. Sometimes there may be very complex, overlapping patterns, limited available information, or extensive alteration of the scene. Also, there may be contamination of the scene by first responders including: medical technicians, law enforcement or firefighters, animals and family/friends/passersby who discover the scene. In these types of scenarios, it may be that the most responsible opinion to have is to *not have an opinion*. It is critical for an analyst to understand the limitations of the discipline and not render an opinion that cannot be scientifically supported.

Biology/Physiology/Anatomy

Blood is an incompressible fluid. This means that blood doesn't reduce in volume with an increase in pressure. The main functions of blood are transportation of gases, nutrients, removal of metabolic waste, and defense (James et al. 2005). The defense function includes fighting infection and clotting.

Human blood is composed of both liquid and solid (cellular) portions (Figure 4.1). The liquid portion of the blood is called plasma and constitutes approximately 55% of the total blood volume and 90% of plasma is water. Also in solution with the plasma are salts, hormones, proteins, lipids, ABO antibodies (blood typing system), glucose, fibrinogen, and clotting factors. Once clotting has occurred, the liquid portion is referred to as serum. White blood cells (WBC) and platelets are found in a layer called the buffy coat seen when

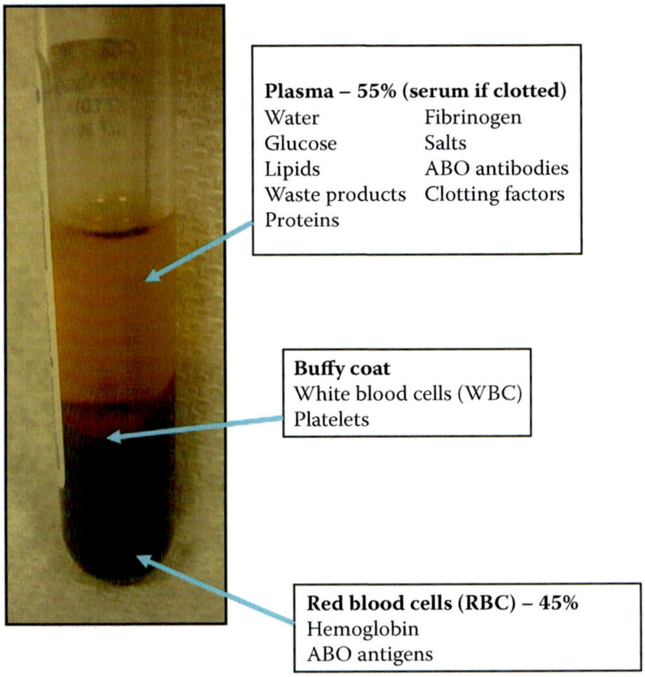

Figure 4.1 Components of blood in blood tube after centrifugation.

separated by centrifugation. This constitutes less than 1% of the total blood volume; therefore, it is included in the total cellular percentage, at approximately 45%.

The bulk of the cellular component of blood is comprised of the red blood cells (RBC), where hemoglobin and ABO antigens are located. Mature RBCs have the shape of a biconcave disc and lack a nucleus. Each RBC contains approximately 280 million hemoglobin molecules (Sears 1999), and each hemoglobin molecule can carry up to four oxygen molecules. Therefore, hemoglobin's primary function is the transportation of oxygen from the lungs to the tissues and of carbon dioxide to the lungs for gas exchange. RBCs are small and flexible enough to be able to pass through capillaries (approximately 3 to 10 microns in diameter) single file (Secomb 1991).

WBCs contain a nucleus and are therefore the cells in the blood which are utilized for nuclear DNA analysis. There are several types of WBCs; however, generally speaking, their main function is fighting infection. WBCs are significantly larger and less plentiful than RBCs.

The body contains three categories of blood vessels: veins, arteries, and capillaries. In general, arteries carry blood away from the heart, while veins carry blood to the heart. Arteries are thick-walled vessels that contain smooth muscle. These vessels pulse in the same cadence as an individual's heartbeat. The smooth muscle contractions are what propel the blood through arteries

Table 4.1 Estimated Circulating Blood Volume in Various Species

Species	Estimated Circulating Blood Volume (mL/kg)
Human—Adult	65–75 (females typically have less)
Human—Children	80
Human—Neonates	100
Dog	85
Cat	55
Pig	70
Sheep	60
Cow (nonlactating)	60
Horse	76
Rabbit	55

and create significant pressure in these vessels. Veins are comparatively thin-walled vessels that have valves within to prevent backflow. Skeletal muscle movement is what propels the blood through veins and they have significantly less internal pressure than arteries. Capillaries are predominantly microscopic vessels that act as a sort of "bridge" between veins and arteries. It is in these vessels that gas and nutrient exchange takes place.

The amount of blood in a body is related to body weight. Estimated circulating blood volume for various species is found in Table 4.1.

There are many medical conditions that can cause bleeding, both internally and externally. This is important to remember when evaluating a scene—not all scenes are criminal in nature. Bloodstained scenes may be the result of homicidal or assaultive behaviors, but they may also be due to suicide (in humans), accidental trauma, or natural causes or medical complications. It is imperative that the analyst approach the scene with an open, observant, and analytical mind.

Scene and Evidence Precautions

A bloodstained scene can be a dangerous environment for many reasons; items such as hypodermic needles, loaded firearms, broken glass, knives, and so on may be present. Human blood can carry many infectious diseases (including, but not limited to HIV, hepatitis B, and hepatitis C). In some cases, there are animal diseases that may be transmitted to humans via blood (or other body fluids) that may be present on the scene. Therefore, it is important to approach each scene as though it is infectious as blood at a scene may be of human or nonhuman origin and utilize the proper personal protective equipment (PPE). Gloves should always be used when dealing with blood evidence to protect the investigator from the blood, and the blood from contamination by the investigator. Tyvek suits®, or protective disposable lab coats, should be used to protect the analyst's clothes from becoming contaminated with blood. Masks, protective eyewear, and hair coverings should be utilized when there is a chance of splashing or aerosolized blood and to protect from inadvertent contamination of the scene with the analyst's own DNA. Shoe covers should always be utilized, both to protect footwear and to protect the scene from contamination by items that may be transferred from the tread of the analyst's footwear. In general, in a complex or confusing crime scene, the veterinary forensic investigator is cautioned to assess the species source of bloodstain evidence, utilizing a presumptive test like Hexagon OBTI. Should the veterinary investigator identify the presence of human blood, retreat and notify law enforcement since a human trauma/death scene will take priority over an animal scene.

Categories of Bloodstains

Depending on whose terminology one uses, the overall categories may differ. For the purposes of this writing, the categories used will be those outlined by James, Kish, and Sutton (2005). Those categories are passive, spatter, and altered, under which are several subcategories (Table 4.2). Also, the Scientific Working Group on Bloodstain Pattern Analysis (SWGSTAIN) compiled a list of recommended terminology that the IABPA has adopted.

Generally, bloodstains included in the passive category are those that are under the influence of only gravity, slow movement, or transfer stains. Transfer stains occur when a blood-bearing object transfers liquid blood onto another surface. Examples include blood dripping from a finger, a victim who is lying on the ground whose blood is "seeping" out of wounds, creating an area of pooling (if on a nonabsorbent surface) or saturation (absorbent

Table 4.2 Categories and Subcategories of Bloodstains

Passive	Spatter	Altered
Contact	Impact mechanism	Clotted
Drop(s)	Secondary mechanism	Diluted
Flow	Projection mechanism	Dried
Free-falling volume		Diffused
Saturation/pooling		Insects
		Sequenced
		Voids

surface), and a bloody hand or paw touching another surface and depositing a print or swipe.

Spatter patterns include impact such as occurs in a beating or shooting, "secondary" (also known as satellite spatter), and projected patterns. Projected patterns are those which are acted on by a force greater than that of gravity and occur because of forces other than impact, such as arterial gushing and expirated bloodstain patterns. Altered bloodstain patterns are those that have undergone some sort of physiological, physical/mechanical, and/or chemical change, such as diluted bloodstains, or patterns created by insects. While the word "altered" may seem to imply a negative connotation or deliberate change to deceive, however, that is not the context in bloodstain categorization. While patterns in this category can include deliberate changes to the bloodstains, in this context, it simply means that there has been some change. These categories will be examined in more detail below.

The volume of an "average" drop of passively falling blood has been reported to be 0.05 mL with a diameter in the air of 4.56 mm. There are several factors that influence the volume and diameter of a blood drop including: the nature of the surface from which the blood falls (e.g., dripping from the end of a baseball bat vs. the tip of a knife), the rate of bleeding, the distance fallen (to a point), and the effect of a force (such as impact) acting on the blood. There are several resources available that document many of these factors based on experimentation.

Blood exhibits cohesive forces to achieve the most stable configuration by reducing the exposed surface area. This creates surface tension that is resistant to penetration—like a "skin." A common experience that most people have had is watching water bugs walk across the surface of the water. This is possible because of the water's surface tension. The surface molecules have unequal molecular attractive forces acting on them—air on one side and other water molecules on all other sides. A drop of blood will fall when the gravitational attraction, or some other force, overcomes its surface tension. There are many potential reasons that a stain may exhibit certain characteristics—for example, you could have a small drop of blood that, size-wise, is consistent with impact spatter, but may have simply dripped off of something with a small surface area, or dripped close to the surface. Blood does not spontaneously "break up"; a force has to influence the blood (such as an impact) for this to happen.

The nature of the target surface is of utmost importance. Generally, when blood strikes a smooth, hard, nonporous surface, the drop will be smooth and round (Figure 4.2). If a drop of blood strikes a soft and porous surface, spines, satellite spatter, and/or scalloping may be observed (Figure 4.3). This occurs because the fibers or other microscopic projections penetrate the surface tension and rupture the drop. Blood (or any other liquid) does not fall in the shape of a teardrop as is often seen in drawings, paintings, advertisements, and even weather maps. Once a drop of blood breaks free, it organizes into the most efficient possible configuration, which is that of a sphere. Some oscillation from spherical to "egg-shaped" may be observed, the degree of which appears to be dependent on drop size/volume (James et al. 2005). Spines are

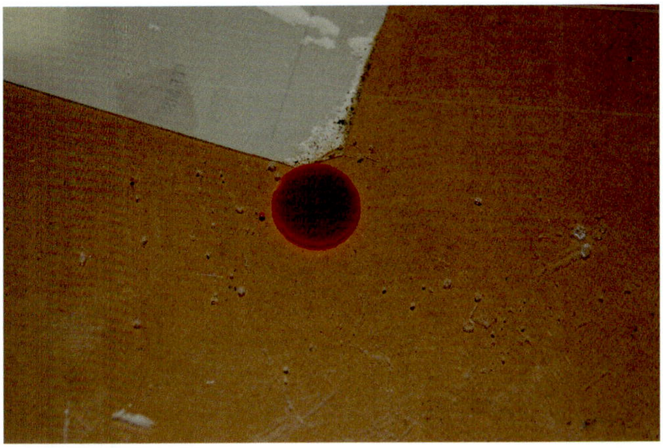

Figure 4.2 Glass—smooth edges, accompanying drop seen to the left.

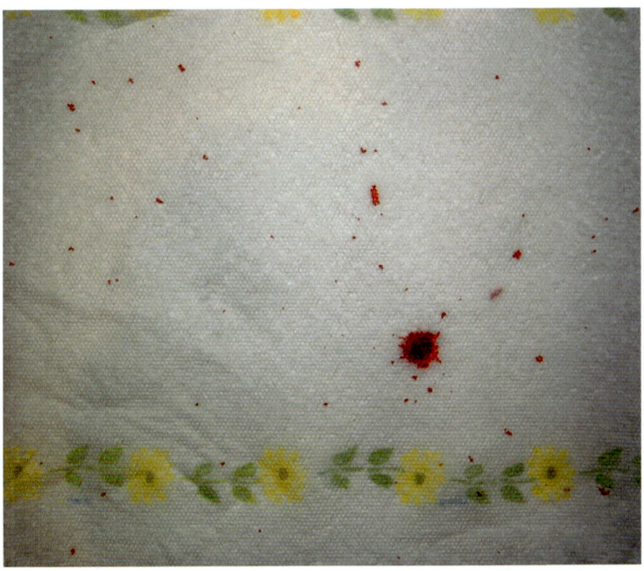

Figure 4.3 A drop on a paper towel; note the spines and satellite spatter.

fine projections that are still attached to the parent drop. Satellite spatter is disconnected from the parent drop (seen radiating circumferentially around the parent drop) (Figure 4.3). Scalloped edges have a "wavy" appearance.

When blood strikes a surface at 90°, the resulting stain is round in appearance (absent distortion caused by the target surface). As the angle of impact becomes more acute, the stain becomes more elongated (Figure 4.4). The angle of impact is the internal angle between the flight path of the blood drop and

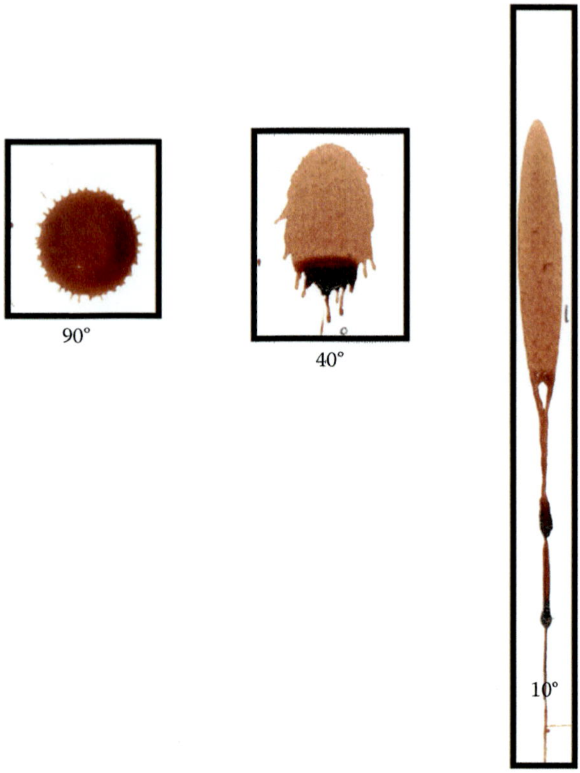

Figure 4.4 Blood drops at decreasing angle of impact.

the surface it strikes. There is a trigonometric relationship between the length and width of a bloodstain. To calculate the angle of impact, the width (at the center, widest part of the bloodstain) and length ("rounding" distortion at the terminal edge where necessary) are measured. The width is divided by the length, providing a ratio of 1 or less. This ratio is the sine of the internal angle. To find the angle, a scientific calculator is utilized to find the $\sin^{-1}$ (inverse sine). Each calculator is a little different, but buttons labeled "inv," "2nd," "function," and so on and the sin key will result in the angle of impact. A passive 90° drop will have a ratio of 1 because its length and width are equal. A drop whose width is half its length will result in a ratio of .5, and a 30° angle of impact.

For example, when W = 5 mm and L = 10 mm:

$$\text{Angle of Impact} = (\text{Width/Length})^{\sin-1}$$

$$\text{Ratio}: (5\,\text{mm}/10\,\text{mm}) = .5$$

$$\text{Angle of Impact} = (.5)^{\sin-1} = 30°$$

It is important to note that the units of measurement must be the same for the width and length (e.g., both in millimeters, or both in inches, etc.) so that they cancel out to reveal a unitless ratio.

The area of convergence is the place, in two dimensions, where the bloodshedding occurred. In other words, the location on the surface (wall, floor, etc.). This is determined by drawing a line, or using string on-scene, from the leading edge (this is where the blood drop impacts the surface) of the bloodstain, projecting it backward following the line of its long axis. This is done for several stains from within the pattern, to achieve a representative sampling. Where the lines or strings cross is the area of convergence. The area of origin is the three-dimensional location where the bloodshed occurred. One method to find the area of origin is after finding the area of convergence and calculating the angle of impact as described above, each line or string is raised, with the use of a zero baseline protractor, to its calculated angle, revealing the location of the surface from which blood was shed.

It is important to note that the area of origin will be the height/distance past which the event could not have occurred because the "stringing" method does not take into account the effects of gravity and air resistance. BSPA is not a precise discipline—these methods will not reveal *exactly* where the blood source was located, but it can give an idea of whether the victim was lying down, sitting, or standing, which is then compared against the statements of suspects, witnesses, and victims (if living). For example, an individual claims that he or she shot a large dog as it was lunging at him or her. After analysis, the vast majority of the bloodstains on the floor are determined to fall between a 10° and 20° or smaller angle of impact. This would indicate that the statement is not consistent with the physical evidence—the blood source was on the ground, not lunging, either in the air or from a typical height of a standing large dog. Computer software has been developed to produce "virtual" stringing known as directional analysis of bloodstain patterns.

Passive Bloodstains

Contact Patterns

Contact patterns are generally referred to as transfer patterns, of which there are many types. A transfer pattern requires contact between two items, at least one of which is wet with blood. Sometimes, a transfer pattern may have recognizable features that may provide information about the object that created it such as a potential weapon shape, hair, footwear, and fabric. It is not uncommon to see a mirror image of the object that created the pattern, when blood is transferred from one part of the body to another, or with the folding over of fabrics. Fingerprints, palm prints, paw or nose prints, foot and/or footwear transfer patterns may be transferred with sufficient detail that an identification is possible, if there are features with discernable uniqueness contained within the paw or nose print, depending on the target surface.

Hair compression transfer patterns and hair/fur swipes are often easily recognized by the fine, wispy nature of the pattern. Sometimes, hair or fur may be present within the pattern.

Figure 4.5 Wall exhibiting both swipe and wipe patterns.

Swipe patterns are included in the category of passive patterns. Swipe patterns result from the contact of a bloody surface with a nonbloody surface exhibiting relative motion between the two. As a general rule, the feathered end of a swipe pattern reveals the direction of travel (Figure 4.5). James et al. (2005) include wipe patterns in the passive category, but acknowledge that wipe patterns may also be included in the altered category. The SWGSTAIN definition of a wipe pattern is: "An altered bloodstain pattern resulting from an object moving through a preexisting wet bloodstain." Wipe patterns are common in clean-up efforts and are also seen in sequenced patterns.

When a bloodstained object first makes contact with a surface, which is generally where there will be the most pressure applied, it may exhibit a nonspecific stain. As the bloody object travels along and eventually departs from the surface, the amount of pressure lessens, producing the feathered edge characteristics. The wipe stains are those which have passed through the existing spatter on the wall, removing the centers and/or altering the edge characteristics. Although the drying time of blood is subject to many variables, wipe patterns may assist in reconstructing a sequence of events.

Flow Patterns

Flow patterns occur when there is a great enough volume of blood that it is unable to adhere to the target surface. Gravity and object topography/contour dictate the direction of flow patterns. These patterns are useful in determining if a victim (or bloodstained item) moved or was moved after bleeding started (e.g., important in determining a sequence of events and potentially helping to determine the primary vs. secondary/tertiary crime scenes). When a flow pattern is still wet, a flow line's direction will change with the position of the body/object. For instance, if flow patterns are identified on an individual's leg with directionality from the knee to the foot, but the individual is found lying down on the ground, it can be determined that the victim was in a seated or standing position for a period of time to allow the blood to dry sufficiently such that no change in directionality is exhibited, before moving or being moved to the ground.

Drops and Free-Falling Volumes

Passive drops are usually fairly easily identifiable on glass (Figure 4.2). Passive drops on carpet appear to have much smaller diameters due to their absorption into the carpet. Often seen are drip trails when the blood source moves between two or more places, such as an individual walking away with a dripping weapon, or a bleeding victim walking around the scene. Directionality is not always evident, however, with sufficient velocity, sometimes edge characteristics and wave cast-off can help determine the direction of travel. Directionality is determined by examining the shape of the bloodstain. The tapered end, or tail, indicates its forward direction of travel. Wave cast-off is a smaller blood drop thrown from the parent drop upon impact (Figure 4.6). When there are overlapping stains, it may be difficult to match the parent stains with their wave cast-off. However, if a line is drawn through the long axis of the wave cast-off, similar to what is done for area of convergence, and projected back, it is often possible to assign the wave cast-off to the appropriate parent stain. A word of caution: if a wave cast-off stain is seen without its parent stain, one might determine its directionality to be opposite its actual direction of travel due to the amount of blood at its "head" and thin tail. However, wave cast-off is discernable from a parent stain in its geometry. The parent stain has an elliptical shape with a tapered end, again, with the tapered end indicating the drop's forward direction of travel, whereas wave cast-off has a more rounded end and a straight "neck" (as opposed to tapering to a point).

When a passively dripping blood source does not move, and blood drips into itself, it creates a discernable drip pattern that creates small (usually around 1 mm in size), round to oval satellite spatter in a radiating pattern around the parent stain (Figure 4.7). Typically, there is not a great deal of obvious directionality as compared to projected patterns discussed later. The satellite spatter or secondary spatter is formed when drops continue to strike

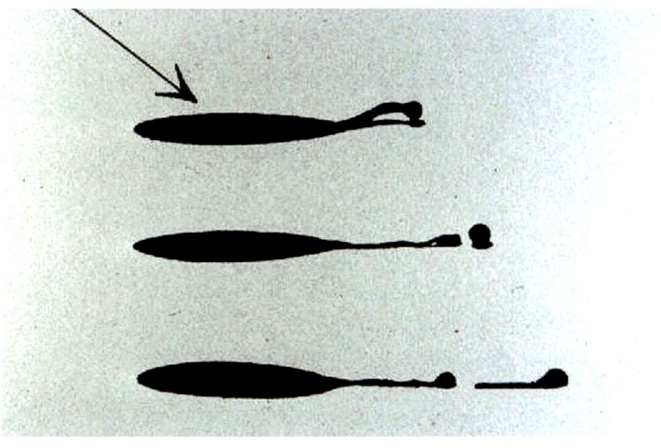

Figure 4.6 Mechanism of wave cast-off formation by high-speed photography. The arrow indicates the drop's direction of travel/impact angle. Photo courtesy of Herbert L. MacDonell.

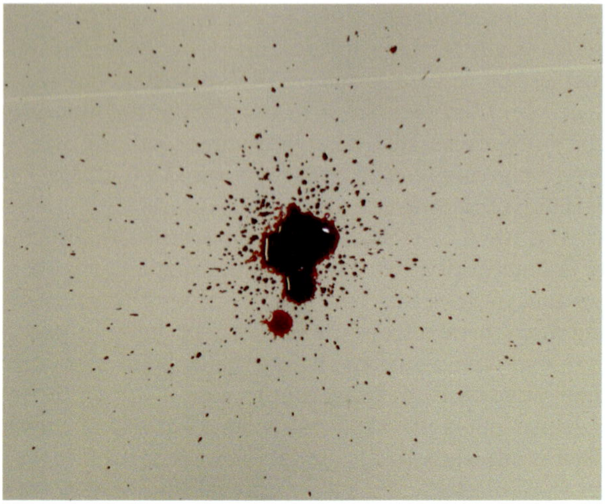

Figure 4.7 A drip pattern.

each other; the small stains are formed and are spattered into the air, out and away from the forming pool. Large, free-falling volumes are those of ~1 mL or more falling all at once as opposed to drop by drop. This is also referred to as splashed blood.

Saturation/Pooling

Saturation and pooling are often misused interchangeably as they both refer to an accumulation of blood. The SWGSTAIN definitions of saturation and pooling are as follows:

> *Saturation stain*: A bloodstain resulting from the accumulation of liquid blood in an absorbent material.
>
> *Pool*: A bloodstain resulting from an accumulation of liquid blood on a surface (Figure 4.8).

Spatter Bloodstains

Impact Spatter

The old classification of bloodstains was based on the velocity at which the blood source was impacted and the size of the bloodstains that resulted. However, there is enough overlap between the categories as they relate to bloodstain size, that new classification and terminology has been proffered. The old terminology referring to impact spatter was low velocity impact spatter (LVIS), medium velocity impact spatter (MVIS), and high velocity impact spatter (HVIS). The new method of referring to these categories still relies on the sizes of the stains; however, it focuses more on the overall size, shape, distribution, and location in the context of specific case information, instead of a strict classification based on size alone. For instance, if a person had a bloody

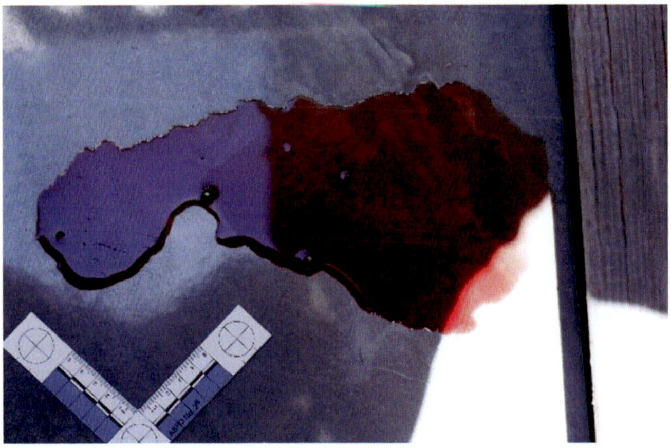

Figure 4.8 Pooling of blood on a nonabsorbent surface.

nose that gushed onto the floor and another person was standing next to him or her, we might find stains around 1 mm in size on the pant leg of the innocent bystander. The resulting pattern may be incorrectly classified as impact spatter without case-specific information, instead of satellite spatter from a free-falling large volume of blood.

Impact spatter, which is consistent with a beating or stabbing, tends to have the preponderance of bloodstains with a diameter of approximately 1–3 mm. However, there can be a wide variation from 1–3 mm based on type of weapon, amount of exposed blood, and several other factors. The velocity of the force that impacts the blood source is generally between 5 and 25 feet/second. There must be blood exposed before it can be spattered. This means that in the absence of something extraordinary, like a crushing head blow, it would not be surprising not to see any blood spatter resulting from a single blow to the head. An individual who administers a beating or stabbing may or may not become spattered with blood themselves.

There are many factors that determine whether an assailant becomes spattered with blood, including, but not limited to: the length, weight, and shape of the weapon, the direction of force, the number of blows, and the relative positions and movements of the victim and attacker. An absence of blood spatter on an assailant does not prove nonparticipation for several reasons. Research by MacDonell and Kish has coined the axiom in bloodstain pattern analysis that "absence of evidence is not evidence of absence" (MacDonell and Kish 1996). This means that simply because a suspect has little or no blood on his or her person or clothing does not mean that he or she was not involved in the incident. There are many factors that determine whether an assailant becomes spattered with blood, as mentioned earlier, including but not limited to:

- The nature of the weapon (length, mass, arc of swing) utilized
- Direction of the blows or sharp force trauma

- Number of wounds and if covered by clothing or hair/fur
- Duration of assault
- The assailant discarded clothing worn during assault and cleaned themselves up
- Assailant committed the assault while naked and subsequently cleaned up
- Assailant utilized outer protective clothing

There are, however, areas that assailants often overlook when cleaning up. Items like socks, shoelaces, and jewelry are good places to look for bloodstains that may have been overlooked, or not easily cleaned. Conclusions about bloodstains on clothing should be rendered cautiously as the weave of the fabric may distort the shape of the original bloodstain; where, for example, a 90° impact angle may appear more ovoid in shape, or vice versa. This phenomenon may also be observed on unfinished wood as the grain may distort the stain. The distribution of bloodstains in a beating often appears in a radiating pattern around the origin, not unlike a sunburst, on either vertical or horizontal surfaces. In many cases, calculating the angle of impact and stringing is not critical as the victim's location at the time of bloodshed can be ascertained by observation. This may not be the case with multiple victims and complex, overlapping patterns.

Impact spatter consistent with gunshot wounds (GSW), explosions, and high-speed machinery is generated by a force impacting the blood source at greater than 100 feet per second. In these patterns, there is also a range of spatter sizes that may be seen, from 0.01 mm to 3 mm or greater. The defining feature of this type of spatter is that the preponderance of stains is less than 1 mm and has been described as mist-like or aerosolized in appearance. Two types of spatter may result from a gunshot wound; forward spatter and back spatter. Forward spatter is what comes out of the exit wound with the projectile in a perforating GSW. Back spatter is what comes out of the entrance wound back toward the muzzle of the firearm and shooter (James et al. 2005). If the GSW is a penetrating wound, there is no exit wound, therefore no possibility of forward spatter. Generally, forward spatter is greater in volume and travels significantly farther than back spatter, because of the energy transfer from the projectile.

Research by Dr. Martin Fackler suggests that collapse of the temporary wound cavity in contact or close range GSWs is responsible, at least in part, for spatter production (James et al. 2005). Gases, heat, and a projectile exit the muzzle of a firearm when fired. These gases, and therefore the resulting pressures, are transmitted to the body tissues when a projectile is fired at contact or close range. The permanent cavity is that space produced by the projectile passing through the body. The temporary cavity is a significantly larger cavity, because of the transferred gases and energy, which is much like a balloon, surrounding the permanent cavity. The tissue of the temporary cavity collapses after the passage of the projectile. It is this collapsing that is proposed to force blood out of the entrance and/or exit wounds, creating spatter.

In actual casework, due to the dynamic nature of violent assaults and the proximity, color, and texture of surface on which the blood is deposited, the mist-like stains may never be identified. Additionally, these very small stains typically only travel approximately 1 to 4 feet (with some exceptions) due to air resistance and dry almost immediately. If there is an object close enough to the blood source to receive the mist type spatter, the stains may be easily disturbed or destroyed with normal actions of investigators, depending on the nature of the surface. To assist with understanding why the small stains do not travel very far, an analogy would be the difference in trying to throw a handful of flour versus a handful of rocks—the bigger, heavier rocks will go significantly farther. The blocking effects of hair or fur and clothing must also be taken into account, as they can easily block the very small stains from depositing on surrounding objects. With a single shot to the chest of a clothed victim or furry animal, one might not expect to see spatter on surrounding objects. The amount of spatter depends on several factors including but not limited to:

- Wound location
- Type of ammunition
- Caliber of firearm
- Muzzle to target distance
- Number of shots fired
- Presence or absence of clothing, hair, or other intermediate objects

If there is nothing nearby on which the mist can deposit or is blocked, the only observed pattern might be more similar to that seen with a beating or stabbing. Case specific information is always important to help narrow down the possible mechanisms that caused the pattern. The barrels of firearms should always be examined for the presence of blood. This can be especially important in investigations where range of fire and firearm orientation may be important factors to discern. There is a "drawback" effect produced by the rapid contraction of gases within the barrel of a firearm that creates a partial vacuum. In contact and near contact wounds, blood can be drawn into the barrel, up to several inches, depending on factors like type of firearm, ammunition, and distance from the wound (MacDonell and Brooks 1977). It is important to note that lack of blood in a barrel of a firearm does not exclude its involvement in the shooting.

Projected

Cast-Off

There are two types of cast-offs, not to be confused with wave cast-off. The first type is cessation cast-off. Cessation cast-off occurs when a bloody object comes to a sudden stop and blood is projected off the end of an object. Frequently, cessation cast-off is obscured by impact spatter and may be difficult, or impossible, to differentiate.

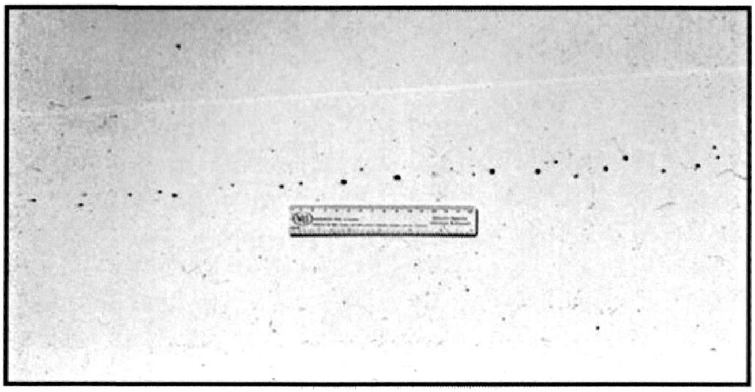

Figure 4.9 Cast-off—note the linear configuration, round stains in the middle and the right to left directionality on the left side of the photo. Photo courtesy Herbert L. MacDonell.

The second type of cast-off is usually simply referred to as "cast-off." This type of cast-off refers to blood that is released from an object due to its motion. This is usually seen in beatings and stabbings on walls and ceilings when the bloody object is swung vertically. If the object is swung in a horizontal manner, as in a baseball swing, cast-off may be present on the walls in a horizontal configuration. Cast-off is identifiable by its linear nature and changing directionality through the arc of the swing (Figure 4.9). Stains will be round at any area where the object is positioned at 90° from the target surface throughout the arc of the swing. For example, when a person is swinging a bloodied weapon in a vertical, overhead swing, you may see round stains (indicating a 90° angle of impact), on the ceiling directly overhead, when the weapon is perpendicular to the ceiling.

There are many factors that determine the configuration of cast-off patterns. Some of these include the number of blows struck, the material of which the weapon is made, shape and length of weapon, the amount of blood available to be cast-off, and the force of the swings. The overall size can be consistent with that of impact spatter, but may also be larger. While the stain sizes often remain similar throughout a cast-off pattern, the "downswings" may produce somewhat smaller stains as the force of the downswing can be greater than the upswing, and there may be less blood available on the object. Cast-off patterns may be found on ceilings, walls (side swing), or even floors, depending on the relative positions of the assailant and victim. Cast-off patterns may also be seen on clothing. Sometimes, cast-off stains are found on the shoulder, back, and/or back of the leg of the assailant. Cast-off patterns on the front of clothing should be carefully considered as this may indicate proximity to the event, even without participation.

Expirated

Expirated bloodstains are those which are created because of air pressure. This may be due to blood in the nose, mouth, or airways, air mixed with blood in the chest or abdominal wounds, or positioning of the victim, such as with his or her head in and breathing into a pool of blood. The size of such bloodstains varies greatly and will depend on how forcefully the blood was expelled. As previously seen in impact spatter, the greater the force, the smaller the bloodstains. As a result, expirated patterns may be confused with impact spatter—either that which is seen with a beating/stabbing, or what is seen with gunshot wounds. One must be very cautious and consider all possibilities when examining cases where both impact spatter and expirated blood may be present.

There may be some characteristics that allow differentiation of the patterns. For instance, air bubbles may be present. The presence of air bubbles is essentially conclusive that there is some sort of airway injury. However, the absence of air bubbles does not mean that the pattern cannot be expirated. There are several variables, such as the origin of the expirated blood (from mouth, nose, wound), the nature of the injury causing the bleeding, the nature of the target surface, and the force with which blood is expirated that may affect whether air bubbles may be present and/or seen. In some cases, when blood with air bubbles dries, there are bubble rings that remain. A bubble ring is the outline within a bloodstain that remains where the bubble had been before it ruptured and/or dried (James et al. 2005). While the description may sound similar to that of a perimeter stain (discussed in the section on altered bloodstains), they are visually different from one another. The outline of a bubble ring may be thicker, thereby creating what look like little vacuoles or craters, where the perimeter stain is generally flat and is the outline of a stain that has been wiped through before it was dry.

Bilateral patterns may be identified if blood is projected from both nares, by, for example, sneezing with blood in the nasal cavity. Additionally, sometimes mucous strands are identified with blood projected from the nose or mouth. Expirated blood may appear lighter in color due to dilution from saliva when blood is expirated from the mouth. It is important to keep in mind that a lack of dilution and/or air bubbles does not eliminate a pattern from being expirated. There are field tests for salivary amylase (an enzyme found in saliva) that may assist investigators with determining the origin of the blood. Analysts must remain objective and open-minded when evaluating bloodstain patterns in a case. There will be times when it is impossible to determine whether a pattern is impact spatter or expirated. If, for example, there is a victim who has had a perforating GSW to the head, both forward and back spatter are possibilities. Therefore the victim may have blood coming out of his/her nose and mouth. Bloodstains that are approximately 1 mm in size are found on the wall near the victim and salivary amylase testing is negative. The best conclusion that the analyst could come to is that the pattern could be either impact spatter or expirated blood because there are no other factors to confirm that one or the other is more likely. If there are factors that allow the analyst to form an opinion that one mechanism is more likely than another, they must be scientifically defensible.

Arterial Bleeding

As previously mentioned, arteries have a large smooth muscle layer, which contracts in the same cadence as an individual's heart rate; this is how medical

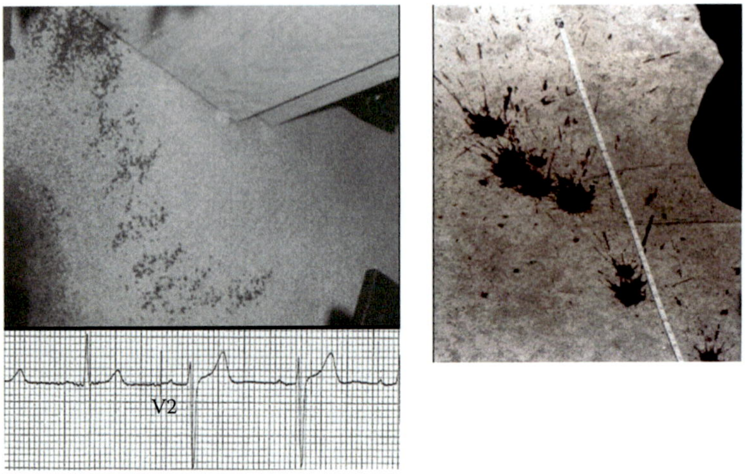

Figure 4.10 Note the arterial "spraying" (left image) with comparison to the EKG strip, illustrating the contraction/relaxation cycles of the heart. Distinct "pulses" of the victim with the cut carotid artery crawling (right image). Photo of arterial "spraying" and "pulses" courtesy of Herbert L. MacDonell.

professionals are able to count their patients' pulses—anywhere there is a palpable pulse. This also makes arteries more resistant to collapsing than veins and they have tension in them, somewhat like a taut rubber band. If an artery is completely severed, it is common for the ends to retract under the skin, subcutaneous fat, and muscle, resulting in a "spraying" type of pattern (Figure 4.10, left). A crushed artery may also produce this type of pattern. It is not uncommon to also see the overall "peaks and valleys" in the pattern, corresponding to the contraction and relaxation of the heart—much like an electrocardiogram strip that is also seen in Figure 4.10 for comparison purposes. As the individual's blood pressure drops, the relative height of the "peaks" will diminish.

If an artery is partially severed or is superficial, where the cut ends are exposed to the external environment, the resulting bloodstain patterns appear as distinct "pulses" where individual heartbeats can be counted (Figure 4.10, right). In some cases, it is possible to see features of a combination of the two types of arterial bleeding outlined here, where distinct pulses can be seen in addition to the overall "peaks and valleys;" however, they may appear more rounded "hills" as opposed to sharp "peaks."

Altered Bloodstains

Clotted Blood

When an individual suffers a bloodletting injury, there is a complex clotting cascade that takes place to stop the bleeding and form a scab. However, blood will clot when it is outside the body as well. This can be observed rather quickly (within minutes) in a blood tube that does not have an anticoagulant in it when one has blood drawn for medical testing. When clotting occurs in a pool of blood, serum separation will be seen (Figure 4.11, right).

The length of time required for clotting and serum separation is affected by many variables. These include the initial volume of blood, temperature, humidity, substrate on which blood is located, and source of blood. The source of blood is important because wounds that involve the head or otherwise breach the spinal canal may result in the mixing of cerebrospinal fluid (CSF) with the blood, which is known to significantly accelerate the clotting process. Serum separation can also occur on an absorbent surface such as bedding or carpet.

When clotting or clotted blood continues to be impacted, small clots or pieces of larger clots can be spattered. Generally, when fresh blood is spattered, it will dry before a clot can form. Therefore, if clotted spatter is seen, this may give an indication of how long an attack continued, which, in some areas may be a factor in what charges are sought against a defendant. The length of an attack can also be a significant factor in sentencing, when the prosecution is attempting to show the particularly heinous, atrocious, and cruel nature of the attack. If a time lapse estimate is requested by investigating agencies or counsel associated with a case, this should be done very conservatively due to the large number of variables involved. Sometimes the best an analyst can report is a sequence of events, without assigning specific time frames.

Drying time estimates should also be addressed very conservatively as many of the same variables (temperature, humidity, substrate, amount, etc.) will affect drying time as well. Additionally, it is not uncommon for an attorney to ask a question like, "How long would it have taken for the victim's hair (shirt, pants, etc.) to become saturated with blood?" This too should be approached very cautiously and conservatively if the analyst wasn't at the scene when the injuries and subsequent bleeding occurred, which is usually the case. For example, a GSW to the head may cause blood to gush out of the nose like a faucet, whereas a similar GSW to the head in another case may cause only a few drops of blood to drip out of the nose. Although both examples have a GSW to the head, the first victim's clothing would become saturated in a matter of seconds, where the second victim's clothing may not

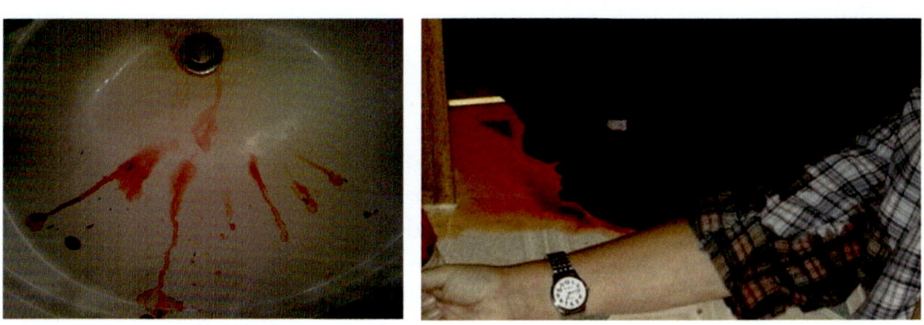

Figure 4.11 Diluted bloodstains around the drain, the right side and just left of the center of the photo. Note darker periphery (left image). Clotting, serum separation, and capillary diffusion (right image).

become saturated at all, or would take many minutes. Similar principles can be applied to an animal's fur. Once again, it cannot be overstressed that the only proffered opinions should be those that are defensible.

Diluted Bloodstains

Diluted bloodstains are those that have been altered by addition of a liquid (Figure 4.11, left). This may be environmental, such as snow or rain, physiological, such as tears, perspiration, or saliva, or deliberate, such as seen in clean-up efforts. Diluted blood is generally darker around the periphery. It is important to note that bathrooms (including sinks, showers, bathtubs, and drains) should always be examined as assailants may go there to clean up after committing a crime. In veterinary cases, the assailant may also attempt to clean the animal victim.

Bloodstains that are found in places where the stains may be further altered by a change in temperature/humidity, such as a walk-in freezer, should be dealt with first and thoroughly photographed (be sure photographs are acceptable) and presumptive testing completed if necessary prior to permitting a significant change in the environment (such as leaving the freezer door open for prolonged periods of time).

Dried Bloodstains

As has been discussed previously, environmental factors, target surface, and amount of blood are important when considering the drying times of blood. Under "room temperature" conditions, small spatter stains, thin/light transfer stains, and flow patterns with a small volume of blood can dry within a few minutes on nonporous surfaces. Larger volumes of blood will take longer to dry, and surfaces that can be saturated (e.g., carpet, bedding, etc.) usually take longer than the same volume of blood on a nonporous surface. Generally, drying time is decreased with elevated temperature and lower humidity. Conversely, drying time is increased with lower temperature and increased humidity. Increased airflow, such as produced by fans, wind, and breezes from open windows, will affect drying times. Casework will often present features of both aforementioned generalities. For example, in areas closer to the equator, one may find a situation with increased temperature and increased humidity. Experiments may need to be performed in cases where drying times are a significant issue. In these cases, the size of the bloodstains, temperature, humidity, target surface, and air flow should be replicated as closely as possible.

Bloodstains dry from the periphery toward the center. If a stain has been wiped through prior to complete drying, the peripheral rim will remain intact, but the center of the stain will be removed (Figure 4.12). This is referred to as a skeletonized stain, or a perimeter stain. This drying principle holds true with all types of stains, pools, saturation, flow patterns, and so on. In some instances, the center of the stain may dry and begin to flake away. This is often seen on smooth and varnished type surfaces or on surfaces with a greasy film.

Dried bloodstains on different types of skin may appear very different from one another. Blood in a uniform layer that has dried relatively quickly and

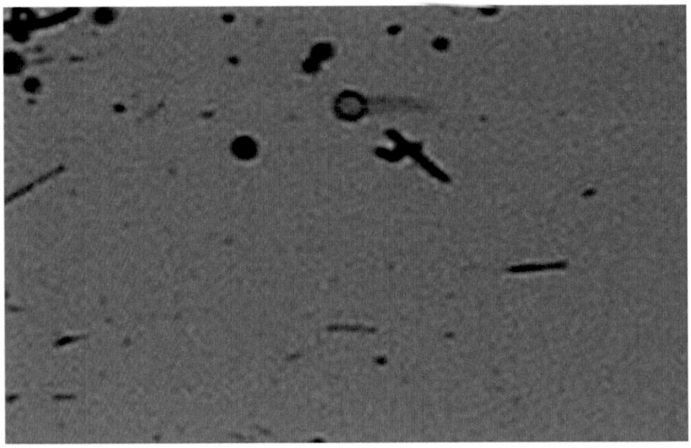

Figure 4.12 Bloodstain wiped through after 4 minutes, leaving a peripheral rim intact.

without disturbance may have a "crazed" or cracked appearance. This phenomenon can be seen on several other types of target surfaces as well. Blood that is deposited in thicker, smaller drops or spatter can appear "puckered." Still others may appear more as most people without experience in the discipline might expect—somewhat of a "crusty" appearance. Dried bloodstains on different compositions of animal fur (e.g., a water-resistant coat vs. a downy coat) may appear different from one another, but are nonetheless normal.

It is important to note that the type of skin (ethnicity, age, medical conditions, etc. in humans) in addition to the use of products along with the usual environmental factors on the skin can affect the appearance of the bloodstains. In veterinary cases, while bloodstains on a hairless cat or short-haired dog belly may behave similarly to those on human skin, the same type of stains would look markedly different on a wire-haired dog, which would also be different from an Angora-type cat. Spatter patterns and expirated patterns exhibiting directionality may remain intact on extremities or other body areas that may assist with positioning in reconstruction, if needed.

The aging of bloodstains (time from when the blood was deposited) has been an elusive task. There has recently been work published using hyperspectral imaging in the aging of human bloodstains that may have more promise than previous aging attempts (Edelman et al. 2012). It is commonly thought that bloodstains darken, from red to a rusty type color to black, as they age. While bloodstains do tend to darken as they age, attempting to estimate age of a bloodstain by its color, without experimenting with replicate conditions particular to that case, is not scientifically defensible. Extrapolation of drying times from human bloodstains for use in other animal species is cautioned against as it can be a matter of speculation and requires a scientific reference and/or experimentation for confirmation.

Bloodstains deposited on a piece of glass and a piece of wood at the same time and subsequently examined a week later may show surprising results.

The one on the wood may appear much darker while the one on glass may still appear red due to the light that is transmitted through the glass. Consider bloodstains on two identical light bulbs in lamps with blood deposited at the same time. One lamp was never turned on, while the other remained on for an hour before being shut off. Once law enforcement arrives, in both instances, the bulb will be cold, but the stains on the two light bulbs may look very different. Depending on when law enforcement arrives, the amount of blood deposited, temperature, and so on, the bloodstains on the bulb that was never turned on may still be "tacky" or even wet, while the bloodstains on the bulb that had been on may be dry, darker, and perhaps even starting to flake off. Absent case specific experiments (whose estimates should still be conservative as not every variable can be replicated), it is best to be conservative—if the blood was still wet upon arrival, then it can be concluded that it was recently deposited. If the blood is dry upon arrival, then it can be concluded that some time has passed since it was deposited. Epstein and Laber published data in *Experiments and Practical Exercises in Bloodstain Pattern Analysis*, taking into account several environmental factors, surfaces characteristics, and volumes of blood up to 10 mL that can be used as a general guide/reference (Laber and Epstein 1983).

Diffused/Capillary Action Bloodstains

Diffusion is defined as the net movement of a substance from an area of high concentration to an area of low concentration. Capillary action refers to the ability of a liquid to flow in small/narrow spaces in defiance of gravity and without the assistance of external forces. This occurs when the adhesive forces, which are the forces between two dissimilar substances, between the liquid and the container, are greater than the cohesive forces within the liquid. Cohesive forces are those forces between like substances. Therefore, conversely, if the cohesive forces are greater than the adhesive forces between the liquid and container, a reverse flow will occur. It is capillary action that is the principle at work when using paper towels or sponges when cleaning up a liquid. Diffusion because the movement is from an area of high concentration (Figure 4.13—the blood pool on the floor) to low concentration, and capillary action because the liquid portion of the blood is being drawn up the shirt—from the floor/back of the body to the front of the body, in defiance of gravity. Some individuals may be familiar with the term "wicking" which is often used to describe capillary action. The rate at which this phenomenon may occur is highly dependent on the surface, weave, or "grain" involved, in addition to the adhesive forces.

Capillary action is the principle at work in thin layer chromatography, where there is a solid and a mobile phase. In bloodstain cases, the mobile phase is the liquid portion of the blood and the solid phase is the porous material on which it travels (Figure 4.13). Caution should be exercised when evaluating bloodstains/spatter patterns related to directionality determinations as the weave of the fabric can distort the shape of the stain—what was dropped at a 90° angle and should appear round may appear somewhat elliptical and vice versa, an elliptical stain may appear more rounded. Additionally, with some fabrics, it can be extremely difficult to determine on which side of the fabric the

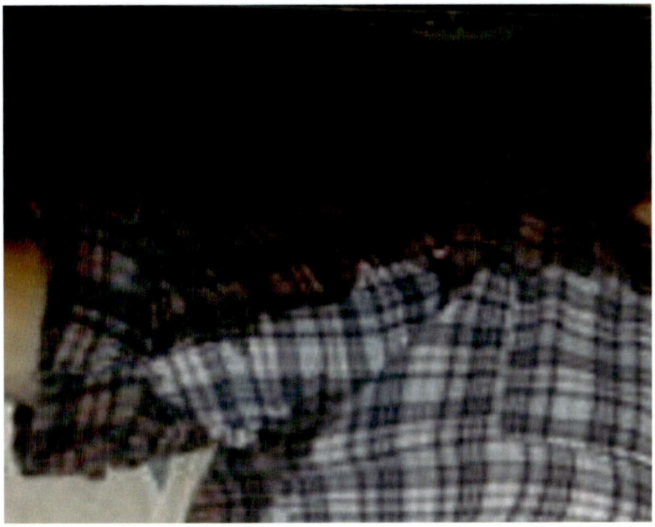

Figure 4.13 Diffusion and capillary action.

blood was deposited. This author has seen this issue in several types of material and experimentation may be required on unusual or unfamiliar materials.

Insects (and Other Animals)

Not uncommonly, a victim or victims, whether by homicide, suicide, or accidental or natural deaths, are not discovered until they are significantly into the decomposition process. Indeed, sometimes the first indication of a dead body may be extensive fly activity around the trunk of a car or around a garbage can, for example, or vultures circling an outdoor area. Maggots can ingest up to approximately 95% of a body's mass, who will then turn into flies. Flies can create very small stains that may be confusing to the analyst at a scene where other small stains may be present, such as a beating or shooting. The appearance of these artifacts may differ from dome shaped, because of the sucking action of their proboscis (sometimes characterized as "lappers and suckers" as opposed to "biters" like a horsefly), to a swiped appearance as a result of defecation, or transferred from walking through liquid blood.

These stains are often seen concentrated around light sources, windows, and ceilings and may also be found on a variety of surfaces including on the deceased's body and clothing. One of the defining features of these "patterns" is that there is no pattern—there is no defined area of convergence (Figure 4.14). Some additional items to consider when evaluating if the stains are related to the mechanism that caused death include:

- Is there a lack of edge characteristics that would be expected on a given surface?
- Is there evidence of fly activity (live or dead flies present)?

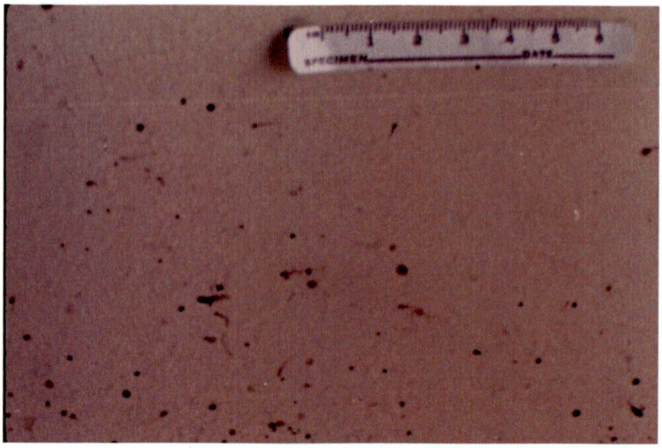

Figure 4.14 Close-up of fly artifacts on a ceiling. Photo courtesy of Herbert L. MacDonell.

- Are there stains in other rooms that do not appear to be connected to the incident? Compare stains in other rooms to those near the body.
- Do they look like known fly artifacts?

Sequenced

It is not uncommon to find multiple and/or overlapping bloodstain patterns at the scene of a death or assault. This may occur for a variety of reasons, from an injured party simply moving around, to a prolonged struggle or assault to staging efforts. Sometimes, the sequence of pattern deposition can be ascertained and, therefore, can be utilized to help to corroborate or refute statements.

For example, at the scene of a beating, as seen in Figure 4.15, the victim's husband said that he found his wife beaten when he arrived home. However, looking closely at the bloodstain shows that the sequence of events was

- Impact spatter deposited on the wall.
- Palm print, confirmed to be the husband's, in blood, transferred to wall, and created the perimeter stains seen as his palm wiped out the center of the impact spatter on the wall.
- Additional impact spatter deposited on top of the palm print.

Can the husband's statement be true? It can be concluded that the person who deposited the bloody handprint (the husband) was present after the beating began and before it ended. Therefore, his statement that he came home and found his wife at some point later is not consistent with the physical evidence.

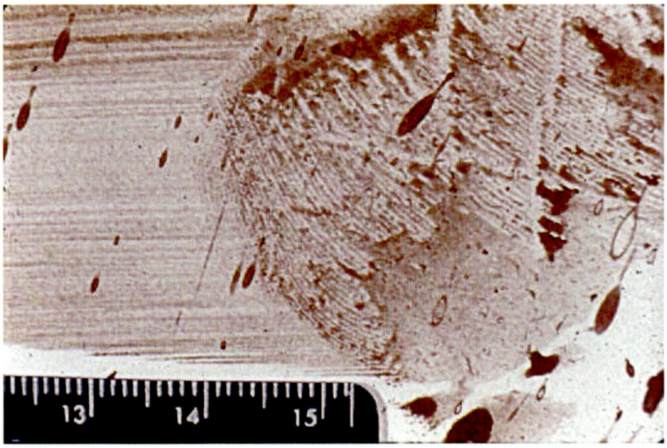

Figure 4.15 Sequenced impact spatter, palm transfer creating perimeter stains, then additional impact spatter. Photo courtesy of Herbert L. MacDonell.

By examining the edge characteristics of overlapping swipes, the order of deposition may be able to be determined. The "newest" swipe will disrupt the edges of the previously deposited swipe if it is still at least partially wet. Another example to consider is a scene where a clean-up was attempted and the body present at the scene. If the body does not disrupt the wiping pattern, it can be deduced that the body was placed there after the wiping occurred. Further, with a significant amount of blood, if no disrupted clots are present, this would indicate that the wiping occurred while the blood was still quite fresh which may help confirm or refute suspect or witness statement regarding a timeline of events.

There are several more types of sequencing stains that may be observed that can answer different types of questions. When determining sequence from photographs, the analyst should be conservative, because in certain circumstances, the determination may not be as straightforward as previously discussed.

Void Patterns

The currently accepted definition of a void pattern is "an absence of blood in an otherwise continuous bloodstain or bloodstain pattern." Voids can help to place an object and/or individuals within a scene.

A void may reveal a recognizable pattern, or it may only show that something blocked the deposition of blood in that particular area (Figure 4.16). Voids are commonly seen in between transfer patterns on the extremities of a victim, which may assist with victim positioning. Likewise, voids on the clothing of suspects or victims may indicate how it was worn (buttoned or unbuttoned), folded, or creased at the time of blood deposition.

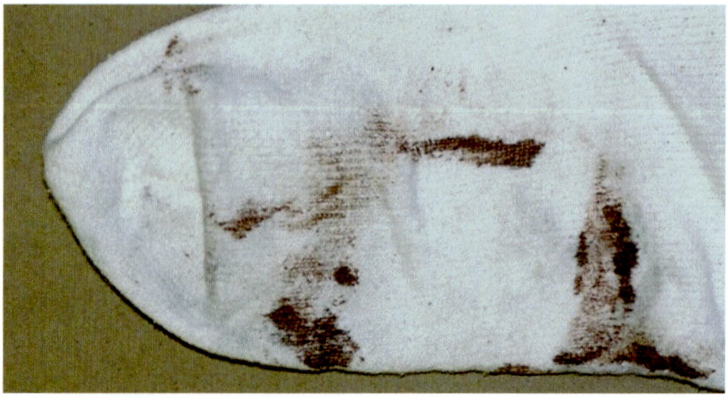

Figure 4.16 Void within a transfer pattern on a sock.

Estimating the Volume of Blood Loss

It is not uncommon for blood to be present at a scene in the absence of a body. Therefore, a common question asked is, "Is this amount of blood loss sufficient to have caused death?" Because there are so many variables, especially with the variety of target surfaces on which blood is found, estimation of blood loss should be approached cautiously and conservatively. This also highlights the importance of obtaining sufficient control samples from crime scenes. As an investigation progresses, it is not uncommon for additional issues or questions to arise that may necessitate experimentation. It is best to be able to utilize material from the scene that is the same age, wear, has been subjected to the same conditions, and so on as opposed to attempting to locate the closest possible material for this experimentation.

Estimation of blood volume loss can be performed on scene or from photographs if appropriate photographs have been taken, including scaled photographs, although available scale may also be utilized. The best way to illustrate this is with an example. In this case, during a robbery, the family dog was stabbed. The knife was left at the scene, but the dog was removed. The major areas of pooled and transferred blood were in the bathroom (Figure 4.17). The question posed was, "Is this a fatal amount of blood loss for the dog?" To make this determination, we must determine the dog's total blood volume. From veterinary records, the dog was reported to weigh 33 lb (15 kg). With a reported canine blood volume of 85–90 mL/kg, the dog has a total blood volume of 1275–1350 mL. As per the literature, a 40% blood loss is fatal for a dog.

Figure 4.18 shows how the measurements of the partial tile and full tile were obtained. It was determined that the tiles were 18 square inches. In this case, it was necessary to request that the crime scene unit return to the scene to take additional measurement photographs. If we imagine accumulating the entire large transfer stain (drag mark) on the floor into the nearly full tile, we can picture that it may cover the tile relatively

Figure 4.17 Overall views of major blood volumes.

Figure 4.18 Obtaining measurements for the triangle and square shaped tiles for determination of amount of blood loss.

uniformly. Therefore, we need to calculate the area of a triangle and the area of a square.

$$\text{Area of a Triangle} = (\text{Base} \times \text{Height})/2$$

$$\text{Area of a Square} = \text{Length of a Side}^2$$

Inserting the previously determined measurements to determine the area of a triangle, $(15.5 \times 7.5)/2 = 58.125$ (rounded down to 58) square inches. The area of the square tile in this case is $(18)^2 = 324$ square inches. Adding 324 and 58 results in a total bloodstained area of 382 square inches.

Figure 4.19 is an experimentally produced graph of blood volume versus area. With this guide as a reference, it can be seen that an area of 382 square inches corresponds to a blood volume of approximately 250 mL. Referring back to the estimated blood volume of the dog (1275–1350 mL), it is necessary to calculate what percentage to which a 250 mL blood loss equates. The appropriate formula to utilize is:

$$\text{Percent} \times \text{Whole} = \text{Part}$$

After rearranging to solve for percent: Part/Whole = Percent (must multiply by 100 to obtain percentage). Inserting the calculated numbers: 250/1275 = .196(100) = 19.6% and 250/1350 = .185(100) = 18.5%. Therefore, a blood loss of approximately 250 mL is equivalent to an approximately 18.5%–19.6% loss in a 33 lb (15 kg) dog, less than half of the 40% required to be considered fatal. It is important to remember that this is a "quick and dirty" maximum estimate of blood available at the scene. Certainly, if the dog was removed in a sheet or blanket, which also may have been saturated with blood, it would increase the amount of blood loss. However, while all possibilities must be considered, one can only work with volumes of which there is actual evidence.

Some important items to remember are that the blood volume versus area graph was created utilizing nonporous surfaces. Therefore, these estimates

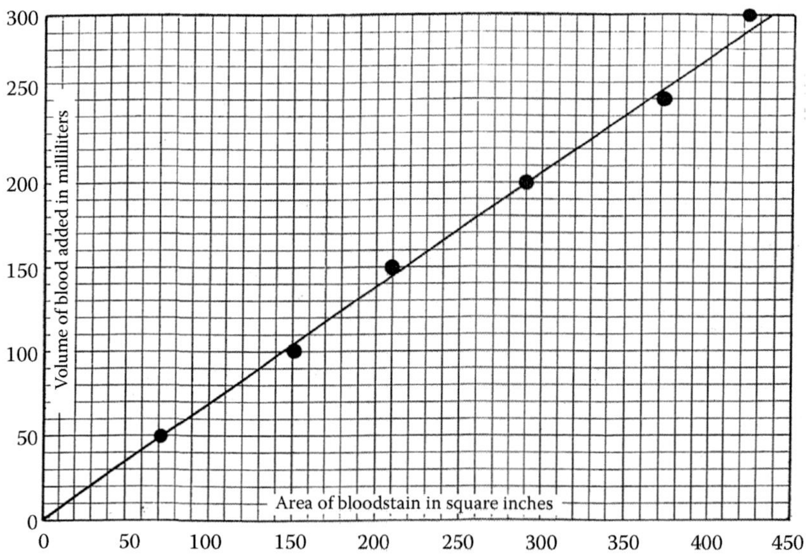

Figure 4.19 Graph of experimentally produced blood volume versus area. Photo courtesy of Herbert L. MacDonell.

can be done, related to this graph, on nonporous surfaces and assumes an even distribution ("thickness") of blood on the surface. There are methods to assist in determining the volume of blood loss in porous/absorptive surfaces; however, they are more complex and are not appropriate for a quick, on scene estimate.

Documentation

It is not uncommon for BSPA to be performed "remotely" from photographs and other case documentation. Sometimes, the analyst's conclusions regarding the significance of particular bloodstains is compromised as a result of incomplete or not appropriately gathered documentation.

Photography is critically important for BSPA. Photographs should be taken with the standard overall, mid-range, and close-up (preferably macro, where very small stains are involved) protocol. After the initial "as found" scene photography is complete, markers may be placed to assist in showing the orientation of the pattern in a particular photograph. This may be accomplished in many ways, depending on the nature and size of the area being photographed. Photographs should be taken in a manner such that the close-up photographs can be easily related to the overall scene. Some methods utilized are gridding off a large area such as a wall with either painter's tape, stick-on scales (Figure 4.20), or markers. Individual stains may be circled to show the overall distribution from a distance. Scales should be utilized when photographing bloodstains, and they should be photographed at 90° from the surface whenever possible to minimize any distortion. Videography is also useful in documenting the spatial relationships among objects and stain patterns that may be difficult to discern from two-dimensional photographs.

Bloodstains on clothing may be highlighted in different ways as well. Some methods include ring reinforcers (with the paper backing still on), stick-on arrows, triangles created from masking tape, and so on. Clothing should be photographed prior to the placement of any marking devices. Consideration must also be given if there is going to be, or is likely to be, DNA testing.

Written documentation should accurately describe the overall pattern as well as the size, shape, distribution, and location of individual stains. The condition of the blood should also be described (wet, dry, partially dry, crazed, etc.). Areas of bloodstaining can also be indicated on the scaled scene diagram using measurements from triangulation.

Collection of items with bloodstain patterns of interest or that may be difficult or questionable should be collected in their entirety when possible. When considering bloodstaining on flooring, both the bloodstained sample and a control flooring sample (without visible bloodstaining) should be collected for evidence and possible experimentation. If carpeting, the carpet and padding should be collected and notation made as to the underlying surface (hardwood, cement, etc.). Additionally, these samples should be labeled to indicate what their positions were within the carpet/flooring. Compass directions and measurements via triangulation may be useful in achieving this. The control

Figure 4.20 Door and wall with a stick-on ruler grid.

sample(s) should be sufficient in size/quantity so that both prosecution and defense analysts have adequate material on which experiments can be conducted if necessary. Each person maintains their floors/carpets differently, so the best way to carry out case specific experiments as closely as possible to the actual conditions is to use flooring from that particular scene. If flooring cannot be collected for logistical or storage reasons, it should be described as thoroughly as possible (e.g., marble tile with apparently sealed grout, linoleum with a hazy appearance, etc.). This will allow experts to reconstruct as closely as possible if the case requires a reconstruction. Swabs of wet or dry stains (collected with a swab wet with sterile water) should be collected from a representative sample of each discrete area of bloodstain patterns and from those stains which appear "out of place" (e.g., a passive stain on the back of a single victim found face down) for presumptive and DNA testing to assist in placing participants in their relative positions in reconstruction efforts, if necessary.

Multiple methods should be utilized to thoroughly document a scene. There may appear to be some overlap in documentation, but it is better to have redundancy instead of a gap that may turn out to be critical. When documenting a scene, the investigator should ask, "Could someone unfamiliar with this scene review my documentation and reconstruct this scene?" If the answer is "no," then there must be a gap in documentation that should be revisited.

Presumptive Testing and Chemical Enhancement

The definition of "presumptive" according to Merriam Webster Dictionary (2017) is "giving grounds for reasonable opinion or belief." Therefore, when conducting presumptive testing either on scene or in the laboratory, a positive result does *not* mean that the suspected stain/sample is, in fact, blood. A positive presumptive test gives the analyst grounds for reasonable belief that the substance is blood and can continue with their investigation as if it were blood, pending confirmatory or DNA testing.

Historically, the chain of testing was as follows: presumptive → confirmatory → species determination → DNA. Today, however, it is very common that the intermediate steps are not performed and a sample is sent for DNA testing after a positive presumptive test is obtained.

There are many presumptive tests available, catalytic color tests, such as phenolphthalein (PTH) (also known as Kastle-Meyer or KM), leucocrystal violet (LCV), Hemastix, leucomalachite green, tetramethylbenzidine (TMB) as well as chemiluminescent and fluorescent preparations. Hexagon OBTI is currently the only presumptive test available that can make the analyst more confident that a suspected sample is, in fact, human blood. While false positives have occurred with some primate, weasel, and badger blood samples, it did not react with blood from animals including cat, dog, rabbit, cattle, pig, sheep, and horse, among others (SEIDDEN identificación 2017).

It is good practice to collect at least two swabs of a stain and utilize one for presumptive testing and one to submit for DNA testing as many of the color tests can render the sample useless for DNA testing. Catalytic color tests are tests that function by utilizing a chromogen solution (color) that is oxidized, usually by a 3% hydrogen peroxide, which is catalyzed by the presence of hemoglobin, and results in a visible color change. These tests should be read within a few seconds of the completion of the application of solutions to the swabs or the results are not reliable.

Examples of tests that produce light instead of color are chemicals such as Luminol. BlueStar Forensic and Fluorescein are luminescent and fluorescent, respectively. These chemicals are typically used to identify areas of bloodshed after a clean-up or enhance bloodstains that may be on a substrate where visualization of bloodstains is difficult. Investigators should be properly trained before attempting to utilize these methods to ensure proper application to avoid distortion of patterns, proper photographic documentation, and to ensure viable sample collection for DNA testing. Because these are typically used on latent bloodstains, there is a limited amount of blood available for testing and over-application can degrade the specimen. When photographing chemiluminescent or fluorescent reactions, it is preferable to use a technique that reveals both the reaction and the surrounding location. This can be achieved by either "painting with light" or rear curtain sync techniques.

Some agencies will take a photograph of the area in normal light conditions, followed by the chemical enhancement of the same area (that typically looks like areas of light on a black background) and then layer the two photographs in a photo editing program. While this technique is not impermissible, there are a few steps that should be taken to ensure admissibility. First, once the image of the "normal" lighting conditions is obtained, a tripod must be used. Second, a scale should be placed for the normal light conditions, photographed and left in place for the chemical reaction photographs. The scale will serve as proof that the camera was not moved from its original position and provide an "anchor" to utilize when the photos are layered in the photo editing program. Unscaled photos, or one scaled photograph with one unscaled photograph, should not be used for layering purposes. Additionally, each step in the photo editing process should be documented, whether within the software program, in writing, or both so that the composite image can be deconstructed and reconstructed following the documented steps by a third party.

All presumptive tests are subject to some false positive results—which is a positive reaction from a substance other than blood, such as vegetable peroxidases and chemical oxidants (e.g., cleaning agents). There are several studies available that examine the specificity (how likely the test is to react to materials other than blood) and sensitivity (how low of a concentration of blood will the test detect). For color tests, if there is an apparent color reaction before the addition of the oxidizing agent, this is also considered a false positive. Positive and negative controls should be performed immediately prior to use in casework to assure that the chemicals are functioning properly. It should be noted that this is a very brief overview of presumptive testing to acquaint the reader with some of the commonly used chemicals. A great deal of literature exists that covers additional testing and enhancement methods.

Evaluating a Bloodstain Case

A bloodstain pattern analyst may be asked to conduct an analysis at various points in the criminal justice process—from responding to a fresh crime scene to evaluating a cold case. This section will also be an overview to provide a very brief outline of issues to consider when evaluating a bloodstain case, regardless of where it is within the process, rather than a comprehensive reference manual.

At a fresh scene, a preliminary walk-through should be conducted, initial observations noted, and assessment of what PPE, equipment, and personnel will be necessary. The reconstruction of a bloodstained scene requires the input from other disciplines and information sources, such as the autopsy/necropsy report, hospital records, witness statements, DNA, and other laboratory testing.

Initially, patterns should be identified and described based solely on their size, shape, distribution, and location, without attempting to attribute a specific event that created the pattern—this will be done later. For example, a pattern consisting of small, round stains, between 1 and 3 mm in diameter, are located on a wall approximately 30 cm above the floor. The "differential diagnoses" based on this information could be: impact spatter, satellite spatter, or expirated bloodstains. If there is no pooling of blood nearby, nor evidence that one was cleaned up, or that an object onto which dripping may have occurred had been removed, satellite spatter may be ruled out. After review of EMS, hospital/veterinary hospital, autopsy/necropsy reports, scene and autopsy/necropsy photographs, there is no documentation of blood in the nose, mouth, airway, airway injury, or positioning of the victim such that an expirated pattern is possible (such as breathing into a pool of blood), then expirated bloodstains may be ruled out. This would leave impact spatter the most likely pattern and would then be correlated with the injuries. Once DNA testing results are obtained, it may be possible to place individuals in their respective positions. This is especially important when multiple victims are involved.

Each case will have different information available for review. It is important to note that the analyst may find him or herself in the position of not having sufficient information on which to base an opinion, or many overlapping, complex, and/or altered patterns that make rendering an opinion difficult or impossible. It is critical that the analyst recognizes this and only reports conclusions that can be supported by the available evidence.

Several examples of worksheets are available to ensure that examinations are systematic and thorough, whether it is of a scene, clothing, vehicle, or other items of evidence. It is not an uncommon defense of an accused to be something like "look at all the blood at this scene. No blood was found on Mr. Jones' person, clothes, or vehicle. Mr. Jones could not have been involved in this crime and not gotten any blood on himself!" Always remember: "absence of evidence is not evidence of absence!" However, case-specific information must be taken into account when considering the potential validity of such a statement. For example, in a stabbing case, there were copious amounts of blood all over the floor, and witness statements offered that blood was flowing from the very first stab wound. A friend of the accused was reported to have held the victim down during the attack on multiple occasions, yet no traces of blood were found on any of his clothing, and the clothing tested matched the description of witness accounts of his clothing. Defense counsel inquired as to whether it was likely that could be true, assuming witness accounts were correct. In this case, while it is *possible* that the friend may not have gotten blood on his clothing, with the copious amount of blood and indications of a significant struggle, it is not *likely* that the friend held the victim down on multiple occasions after blood was flowing.

Conclusion

Bloodstain pattern analysis can be a valuable investigative tool. If crime scene investigators and detectives participate in a basic bloodstain pattern analysis course, while it will not make them instant "experts," it will assist them in identifying, understanding, and preserving valuable bloodstain evidence for evaluation by an expert that might otherwise be overlooked and lost. Proper documentation is critical for a useful bloodstain pattern analysis.

It should be remembered that bloodstain pattern analysis can be utilized as another "tool" in the investigative toolbox. Because several stain patterns can appear similar to one another although caused by different mechanisms, one should be critical of an analyst or expert that concludes that a given pattern could have only occurred by one particular mechanism. For instance, in the aforementioned example of the 1–3 mm sized pattern on the wall 30 cm from the floor, if blood was found in the nose and/or mouth of the victim, then the best opinion that can be rendered is that the pattern is *either* impact spatter *or* expirated. For this reason, bloodstain pattern analysis is frequently better utilized in identifying what *could not* have happened.

It is better to be conservative in one's opinion rather than reporting or testifying to opinions that cannot be supported by the physical evidence and scientific references. The analyst may want to keep in mind, "Would I want to be convicted based on this evidence?" when forming their conclusions. If an analyst is unable to be objective, the case should be referred to another analyst. Case-specific experimentation may need to be performed, and if evidence and control samples are properly collected, this will allow the analyst to render the best opinions.

Finally, this chapter on bloodstain pattern analysis is not all inclusive, but meant to assist with understanding some of the basic tenants, procedures, and challenges that exist in this discipline.

References

Edelman, Gerda, van Leuwaan, T. G. Aalders, M. C. G. 2012. Hyperspectral imaging for the age estimation of bloodstains at the crime scene. *Forensic Sci Int.* 223:72–77.

James, S., Kish, P., and Sutton, T. P. 2005. *Principles of Bloodstain Pattern Analysis, Theory and Practice.* Boca Raton, FL: CRC Press/Taylor & Francis.

Laber, T. L. and Epstein, B. P., 1983. *Experiments and Practical Exercises in Bloodstain Pattern Analysis.* Minneapolis, MN: Callan Publishing Inc.

MacDonell, H. L. 1973. Flight characteristics and stain patterns of human blood. In *National Institute of Law Enforcement and Criminal Justice,* 77 pages, U.S Government Printing Office.

MacDonell, H. L. 2005. *Bloodstain Pattern,* 2nd revised ed. Elmira, NY: Golos Printing.

MacDonell, H. L. and Brooks, B. 1977. Detection and significance of blood in firearms. In *Legal Medicine Annual.* Wecht, C., Ed. New York: Appleton-Century-Crofts, pp. 185–199.

MacDonell, H. L. and Kish P. E., 1996. Absence of evidence is not evidence of absence. *J Forens Identi.* 46:160–164.

Merriam Webster Dictionary. 2017. Presumptive. http://www.merriam-webster.com/dictionary/presumptive (Accessed April 4, 2017).

Sears, D. W. 1999. Overview of hemoglobin's structure/function relationships. *Biochem Mol Biol Educ.* 30:208.

Secomb, T. W. 1991. Red blood cell mechanics and capillary blood rheology. *Cell Biophys.* 18:231–251.

SEIDDEN identificación. 2017. *Hexagon OBTI.* http://www.seidden.com/Hexagon_ing.htm (Accessed April 2, 2017).

5

Forensic Physical Examination of the Cat and Dog

Jennifer Woolf and Julie Brinker

Contents

Introduction

Any time animal abuse or neglect is known or suspected to have occurred, it is important to perform a thorough examination and document all normal and abnormal findings. The examination may take place wherever it is convenient and safe to do so: a clinic, a shelter, or, in some large-scale cases, at the scene, specifically documenting any injury or illness which may be important to the legal case (Munro and Munro 2008). The most important aspect of the forensic examination is that all lesions and areas of the body, regardless of perceived significance, should be observed, described, photographed, and then interpreted. Whenever reasonable, the description should include historical information about the duration of the problem and accurate measurements. In this chapter, we will discuss a forensic examination for a single cat or dog and include information specific to large-scale cases with multiple animals from a single crime scene.

The Forensic Examination

History

A veterinarian may be presented with an animal for a forensic examination under a multitude of situations, including criminal, civil, and insurance investigations. In some instances, the owner of the animal will present it for an examination, whether there is an expressed concern for abuse. The owner could be the abuser, but it is also possible that the owner is unaware of the abuse or the owner could also be a victim, such as a domestic violence victim presenting a pet for injuries sustained by the same abuser (Woolf 2015). At other times, animal control or law enforcement agents may present an animal for injuries, to determine whether those injuries are considered nonaccidental. Finally, an animal might be presented by a good Samaritan who may or may not know what has occurred. It is best to indicate in the record who presents an animal each time it is seen, including the names of everyone present for the examination.

In many instances, an animal comes in without a history and that should be indicated in the record. If any information about the animal is available, note specifically who it is that provides the history as well as what is said.

If more than one person in the room is giving information, indicate who said what, preferably using specific names or initials. Also, note in the medical record the demeanor and interactions of the people in the room with the pet and each other. Be sure to use objective terms to describe people's behavior. Realize the person being interviewed may be the abuser and hence prone to violence or mental instability. It is always advisable to contact law enforcement if one is concerned about the client's behavior, regardless of any client confidentiality laws. It is also possible that the person being interviewed is unaware of the abuse and may be alarmed to hear of any suspicions. Finally, because the person being interviewed may be a victim of the same abuser, care and compassion for that person's welfare and safety are necessary.

When obtaining a history, ask open-ended questions such as: What happened? Were there any witnesses? Has anything like this ever happened in the past? It is also important to be aware of assumptions people make. For instance, a person may assume an animal was the victim of a motor vehicle accident because it was found outside and injured. However, upon asking questions, the veterinarian may learn that the person did not actually see the animal get injured. Making assumptions to fill in unknown details is a common human reaction and should not be construed as an automatic indication of a person deliberately lying (Kahneman 2011).

Every contact with an owner should be written in the medical record and signed and dated by the person making these notes. This includes phone calls and digital communication such as email or texts with an owner even if the animal is not seen. In some cases, a pattern of calls and/or office visits can develop suggesting abuse (Munro and Thrusfield 2001a). These patterns include when the story does not fit the clinical signs seen, when the animal is seen for injuries repeatedly (Figure 5.1), when injuries of varying ages are observed during a single visit (Figure 5.2), when another animal in the home has also been seen for injuries or death, and when there is a delay in seeking veterinary care. In some instances, a specific person may even be identified as the abuser (Arkow and Munro 2008; Munro and Munro 2008). Sometimes this is blatant, for example, "My dog pooped on the floor again so I kicked him, but it wasn't that hard." Other times it may be subtler, for example, "Ever since my boyfriend moved in with us, Smokey keeps getting hurt."

Signalment

The record should start with the signalment. Always scan the animal for a microchip and note if one is found. If a name is given for the pet, that may be used; otherwise, a unique identification number should be assigned. In many cases, both names and identification numbers are included. Whatever system is used, it is vital that the identification is unique to that animal.

Be aware that certain signalments are more often associated with abuse than others. Male dogs are more often abused than female ones, and intact dogs and cats of either sex are at greater risk than their spayed and neutered counterparts. Young animals are at higher risk than older animals, perhaps

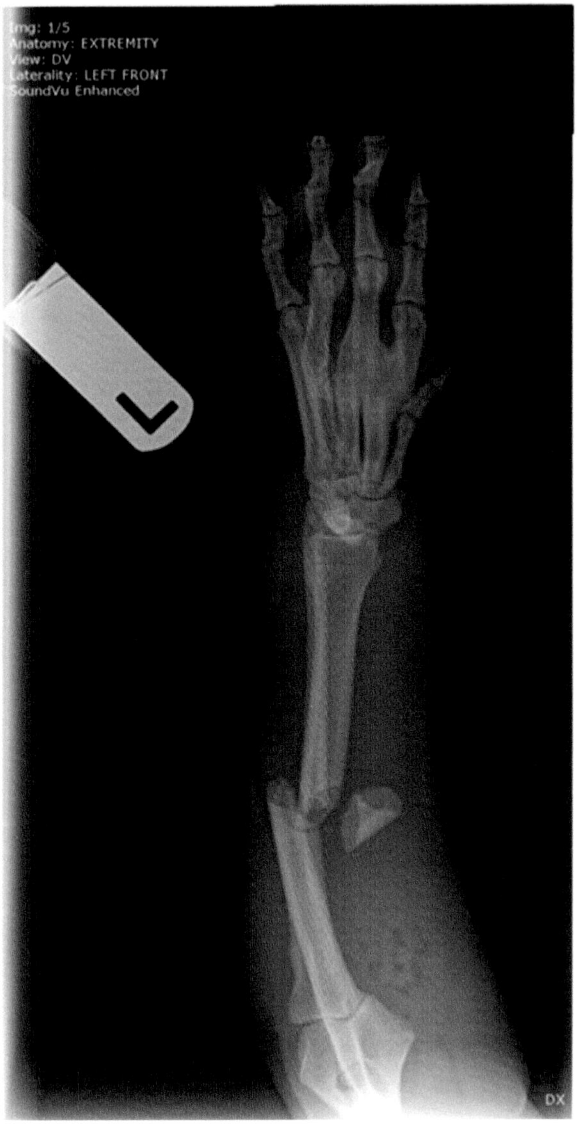

Figure 5.1 Dog, left antebrachium: Radiograph showing an acute, open, comminuted fracture of the radius and ulna. Also note the healed fractures of metacarpals 2–4.

because people develop a stronger bond over time. Pit-bull type dogs, mixed breed dogs, and domestic shorthair cats are also at increased risk of abuse (Munro and Thrusfield 2001b).

Note the species and breed in the record, if known. If the breed is not known, an estimate may be made based on how the animal looks, but state

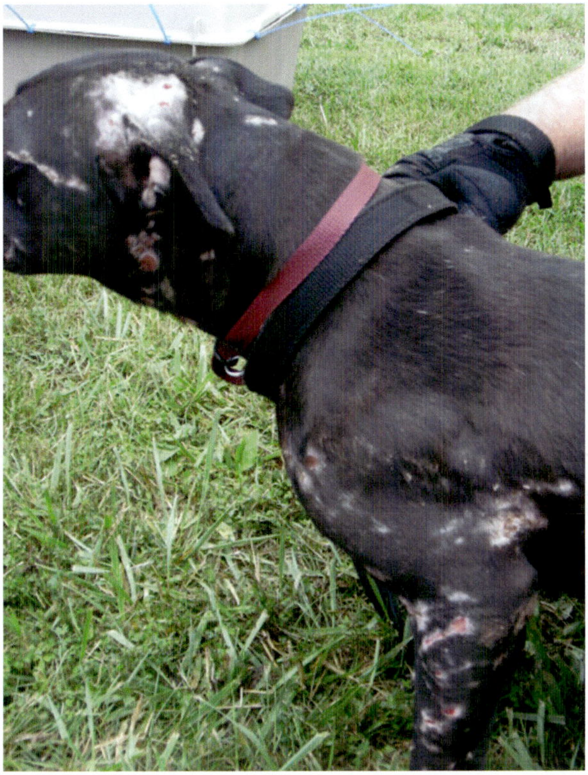

Figure 5.2 Numerous fresh and healed scars on the head, neck, and front legs of a pit bull removed from an organized dog-fighting situation. Photo courtesy of the Humane Society of Missouri.

this in the record, for example, "Breed-type" or "Phenotype." Note the sex and the reproductive status, if known. If a female is noted as spayed, include what made that determination, such as it was known from previous medical history, suspected based on a spay tattoo or tipped ear, or it was decided based on a ventral midline scar that is consistent with a prior spay surgery. This way, should it come into question later, it can be established if this was a known fact or an educated guess. This may be documented using photographs or video.

The specific age of the animal can be stated if it is known via medical records. If the age of a puppy or kitten is unknown, the dental eruption pattern may be used to provide an age range as long as the record states this was estimated. Otherwise, it is best to keep to general terms such as neonate or nursing young, juvenile, young adult, adult, and senior or geriatric. Table 5.1 provides guidelines to allow for age estimation for dogs and cats.

Table 5.1 Age Estimation for Dogs and Cats

Stage of Life Term	Estimated Age Range[a]	Signs and Physiological Processes Associated with Stage of Life
Neonate or nursing young	Birth to 6 weeks	• Still nursing or in the process of weaning. • Deciduous teeth erupting or present (1). • Eyes and ears are closed at birth then open during this phase, learning to walk (2). • Most ossification centers appear (2). • Minimal exploration of the environment (3).
Juvenile	6 weeks to 6–9 months	• Weaned (4). • Dentition changing from deciduous to adult (1). • If adult dentition present, teeth are clean and white. Has not yet reached puberty (3). • Most ossification centers closed (2). • Growth plates on long bones still open (5). • Environmental exploration is extensive (3). • Play behaviors develop (4).
Young adult	7–9 months to 2 years[a]	• All adult teeth are present (1) with minimal wear and calculus build-up. • Growth plates on long bones close (5). • Puberty occurs (3). • Develops social maturity (6).

(*Continued*)

Table 5.1 (Continued) Age Estimation for Dogs and Cats

Stage of Life Term	Estimated Age Range[a]	Signs and Physiological Processes Associated with Stage of Life
Adult	2 years to 8 years[a]	• Fully mature physically, all growth plates are closed (5). • No longer has the appearance of a puppy or kitten, but does not have typical physical signs of an elderly dog/cat. • Dental calculus, periodontitis, and tooth wear become evident. • Secondary sex characteristics are present if intact or altered postpuberty.
Senior or geriatric	8 years[a] and older	• Developing signs of old age such as arthritis, lenticular sclerosis of the eyes, tumors, metabolic diseases, poorer coat, and more severe dental disease.

Sources: 1. DeBowes, L. Dental disease and care. *Veterinary Pediatrics: Dogs and Cats from Birth to Six Months*, 2nd ed. J. Hoskins, Ed. Philadelphia, PA: W.B. Saunders Company, 1990, 125–132. 2. Greco, D. and B. Partington. The physical examination and diagnostic imaging techniques. *Veterinary Pediatrics: Dogs and Cats from Birth to Six Months*, 2nd ed. J. Hoskins, Ed. Philadelphia, PA: W.B. Saunders Company, 1990, 1–21. 3. Olson, P. and T. Nett. Reproductive endocrinology and physiology of the bitch. *Current Therapy in Theriogenology*, 2nd ed. D. Morrow, Ed. Philadelphia, PA: W.B. Saunders Company, 1986, 453–457. 4. Beaver, B. Behavior development and behavioral disorders. *Veterinary Pediatrics: Dogs and Cats from Birth to Six Months*, 2nd ed. J. Hoskins, Ed. Philadelphia, PA: W.B. Saunders Company, 1990, 22–32. 5. Muhlbauer, M.C. and S.K. Kneller. *Radiography of the Dog and Cat: Guide to Making and Interpreting Radiographs.* Ames, IA: Wiley-Blackwell, 2013, 128–129. 6. Landsberg, G.M., W.L. Hunthausen, and L.J. Ackerman. *Behavioural Problems of the Dog and Cat*, 3rd ed. Edinburgh: Saunders, 2013, 13–28.

[a] These are generalities that will vary depending on species and breed. Large and giant breed dogs tend to mature later but age earlier than cats and smaller dogs.

Subjective

For any medical examination, it is important to note the subjective findings. Is the animal bright, alert, and responsive or is it quiet, depressed, or lethargic? Does it appear to be adequately hydrated? How is the behavior of the animal? What body postures is the animal offering that might indicate its emotional state? While these are subjective observations, care must be made to use words that describe what is actually seen rather than interpretations. Table 5.2 provides examples of objective descriptions for common subjective terms of behavior.

Behavior

Some behaviors demonstrated by the patient may suggest or result from abuse or neglect. For example, an emaciated animal that eats or drinks voraciously when food and water is provided indicates that the ability and desire to eat or drink are present. Behaviors that indicate guarding of a specific body part may indicate localized pain (Hellyer et al. 2007), and behavioral observations are a large part of the dataset used to assign a pain score to an animal as discussed below. Signs of extreme fear may be the result of inadequate socialization (Landsberg et al. 2013). Behaviors that indicate severe dog-aggression are often observed in dogs trained to fight (Capra et al. 2009). When recording behavioral observations in the examination record, be careful to utilize only objective terms as opposed to subjective conclusions. For more information about animal behavior, the reader is referred to Chapter 12 (Animal Behavior for the Forensics Specialist).

Table 5.2 Examples of Objective Descriptions for Common Subjective Terms—Behavior

Subjective	Objective
Fearful	Crouched down, leaning back, pupils dilated, looking away, ears back, paw lifted, shaking, licking lips, tail low or tucked, body and face tense
Fear aggressive	Leaning back, pupils dilated, eyes wide, ears back, shaking, growling, barking, tail low and wagging stiffly, body and face tense
Aggressive	Moving forward, brows down, staring directly at target, lips retracted exposing only front teeth, ears forward, growling, barking, tail high and wagging stiffly, body tense
Playful	Ears forward to neutral, eyes soft, body loose, tail high (or level with spine), wags tail loosely with wide movements, mouth open, tongue hanging out, corners of mouth pulled caudally exposing all the bottom teeth, bounces front end up and down, play bows
Depressed	Ears neutral, eyes soft, looking down, moves slowly, tail neutral, slow to respond to handling

Body Condition Scoring

Body condition scoring is used in veterinary medicine to approximate body composition (amount of body fat and muscle) and to give some objectivity to otherwise subjective terms such as "overweight" and "thin." A body condition score (BCS) should be assigned to all live animals examined. There are multiple systems available for this purpose including an article published by the American Animal Hospital Association (AAHA) (Baldwin et al. 2010), two charts, one for cats and one for dogs, widely distributed by Purina® (Laflamme 1997a,b), and the Tufts Animal Care and Condition scale (Patronek 1998). The scoring system chosen should be identified, utilized uniformly throughout the case, and cited in the report.

Of the various body condition scoring schemes published, there are two different methods of arriving at a specific BCS for an individual animal. The charts most commonly used by veterinarians in clinical settings involve either a 1- to 5-point scale or 1- to 9-point scale with 1 as emaciated (Figure 5.3) and 5 or 9 as grossly obese, respectively, with 3 or 5 as ideal, respectively. These can almost be interchanged if you add half-steps to the 5-point scale as demonstrated by AAHA's chart (Baldwin et al. 2010). The advantage of this method is that each integer on the 1–9 scale (or half-integer on the 1–5 scale) represents a change of approximately 5–15% of body weight with a median of 10% (German et al. 2009). This information can be used to formulate a nutritional program to return the animal to an ideal body composition and indicate to the courts how far the animal deviates from the accepted clinical ideal conformation.

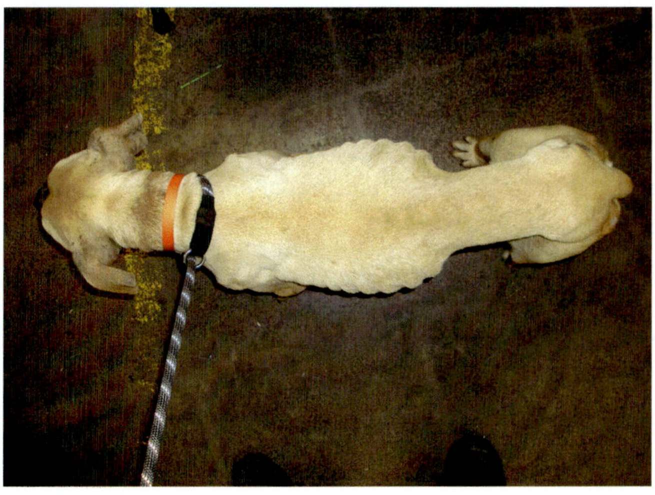

Figure 5.3 This dog with a BCS 1/9 on the Purina scale exhibited hematemesis and hematochezia due to gastric rupture the morning after removal from the owner. Foreign material was found in the stomach at necropsy. Photo courtesy of the Humane Society of Missouri.

The Tufts Animal Care and Condition (TACC) scale is designed as a tool to help identify the presence and severity of neglect of an animal. To that end, the TACC uses four separate 1–5 scales for (1) body composition, (2) weather, (3) environmental health, and (4) physical care, where 1 is ideal and 5 is the worst condition for each scale. The BCS aspect of this scheme is different from the others discussed in this chapter in that it places an emaciated animal at a 5 and the ideal weight animal at a 1, with no consideration made for overweight and obese animals. All available data regarding the animal and its environment can be used to obtain a score for as many of the four scales as possible. The final result is the highest score on any one of the scales utilized (Patronek 1998). The biggest advantage for the TACC is it gives an overall gauge of "how bad" a situation is. The disadvantage is that it can result in conflicting or confusing information. For example, a mildly thin dog would receive a 2 on the TACC Body Condition Scale. If this dog were found in a cage piled with weeks of feces, it would receive a score of 5 on the TACC Environmental Health Scale. Since that Environmental Health score is higher than the Body Condition score, it would give the dog a final TACC score of 5. Writing the report to explain this would require much additional verbiage whereas simply describing the environment thoroughly and providing a simple BCS is easier for the court to understand.

Pain Scoring

Similar to body condition scoring, pain scoring is an effort to take subjective observations of painful behavior and give them objectivity. Several pain scoring systems are available which can provide a consistent method for use within the organization, and can quantify acute (Brondani et al. 2013; Hellyer et al. 2006a,b; Reid et al. 2007) or chronic pain (Brown et al. 2008; Hielm-Björkman et al. 2009). The majority of acute pain scoring systems were developed to monitor post-surgical pain, but are still useful for abuse cases as they typically utilize direct observation of the animal. Conversely, most of the chronic pain scales center around an owner questionnaire, which may make their utilization in an abuse or neglect case less useful due to the decreased potential of obtaining an accurate history from the owner or caretaker, provided it is possible to obtain a history at all.

Not all of the observations needed to obtain a pain score may be possible in every case of an abused or neglected animal. At times, fear, stress, and poor socialization can cause behaviors which mimic painful behavior, and at other times these issues hide painful behavior. Despite these limitations, a pain score should be assigned to an animal whenever a painful condition is identified or suspected and the report should indicate and provide a reference to the specific pain scale utilized in the case. If no pain is suspected, this should be noted as well.

Objective

As one would for any medical examination, it is important to get vital signs during a forensic examination. The temperature, pulse, and respiratory rate should be obtained or noted as to why they were not obtained. Note the color of the mucus membranes as well as the hydration level and the capillary refill time. Get an accurate weight and be sure to include a body condition score in the subjective section. Remember, only objective descriptions belong in the *Objective* section of a forensic examination (Table 5.3). In the *Assessment* section, diagnoses can be included if they are adequately supported by the examination, radiographs, and diagnostic test findings. Colloquialisms can be used to help clarify a diagnosis into layman's terms in the report.

Ensure that as many systems of the body are examined as possible. If this cannot be done for any reason, state that for the record. It is just as important to document the lack of abnormal findings as it is to document those which are abnormal. The phrase *no significant findings* is preferred to *within normal limits*, since the former is easier to explain in court than the latter if there is a discrepancy in judgment between two veterinarians. A standard form for recording physical examination findings is useful for forensic purposes as it contains a checklist of organs or body systems to ensure a complete examination. When appropriate an outline drawing of a cat or dog will allow for recording external lesions to better illustrate their location. These forms are part of that animal's medical record, so the original must be kept safe as part of the evidence related to the case. Information on these forms can be utilized as notes to formulate a forensic report for legal purposes.

Eyes, Ears, Nose, and Throat

In neglect cases, findings of a chronic nature are commonly observed. When these findings involve the eyes, the problems often seen may include untreated corneal ulcers, keratoconjunctivitis sicca, glaucoma, entropion/ectropion (Figure 5.4), and prolapsed gland of the third eyelid (Thompson 2013). Signs of an extended lack of care, especially when accompanied by a clinical appearance of secondary or end-stage pathological changes because of these conditions, may be an indication that these diseases have not been appropriately treated prior to presentation. An owner claiming to have attempted treatment without success should have medical records to support this claim. In large-scale cases where many of the animals exhibit these conditions, this may be a sign that the animals have not received appropriate medical care.

Upper respiratory signs are also quite common in large-scale cases of abuse or neglect such as animal hoarding situations and poorly managed commercial breeding facilities regardless of the species being bred, for example, puppy mills (Figure 5.5). Stress and poor air quality cause or contribute to upper respiratory inflammation and infections in dogs and cats. Poor air quality can damage the respiratory epithelium and increase susceptibility to viral and bacterial infections. Chronic stress decreases the body's immune response which also increases susceptibility to disease (Dinnage et al. 2009; Polak et al. 2014; Pruett 2003).

In the ears, chronic signs of neglect may include severe otitis externa secondary to yeast, bacteria, or parasite infections. In extreme cases, these can move down the canal through the tympanic membrane to cause otitis media or otitis interna. In these instances, in addition to the outward signs of excessive discharge, inflammation, scabbing, scaling, and crusts, there may also be

Table 5.3 Examples of Objective Descriptions for Common Subjective Terms—Examination Findings

Subjective	Objective	Diagnosis	Colloquialism
Wound	3 cm × 4 cm oval superficial ulceration with serous discharge, erythema, and alopecia	Pyotraumatic moist dermatitis	Hot spot
Eye boogers or runny eyes	Mucoid ocular discharge with a dry appearance, Schirmer tear test results 3 mm in 60 seconds	Keratoconjunctivitis sicca	Dry eye
Ear discharge	Large amount of dark brown discharge in the ear canal occluding the tympanic membrane with moderate erythema of the ear canal wall and crusts on the concave surface of the pinna	Otitis externa	Ear infection
Corneal pigmentation	Cornea exhibits black pigmentation covering approximately 50% of the cornea oriented over the central and lateral regions of the globe	Pigmentary keratopathy (note: there are many causes of this which can be named specifically if definitively diagnosed, this is not always associated with a disease process)	Not applicable
Runny nose and cough or tracheobronchitis	Bilateral mucoid nasal discharge and spontaneous coughing	Canine infectious respiratory disease	Kennel cough

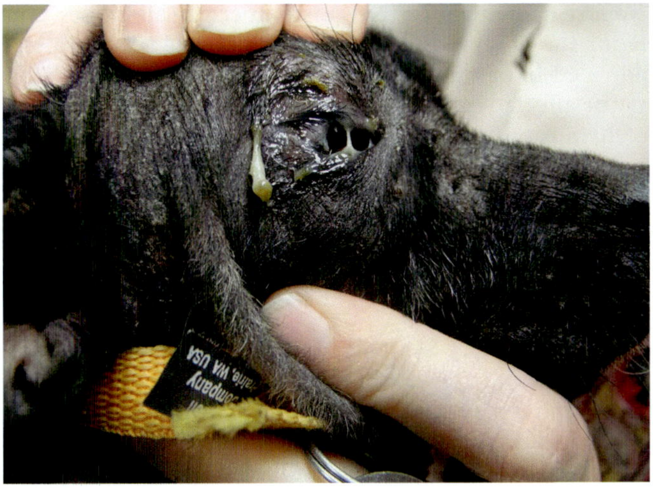

Figure 5.4 Chronic demodicosis, keratoconjunctivitis sicca, and entopion in a dog removed from a hoarding situation. Photo courtesy of the Humane Society of Missouri.

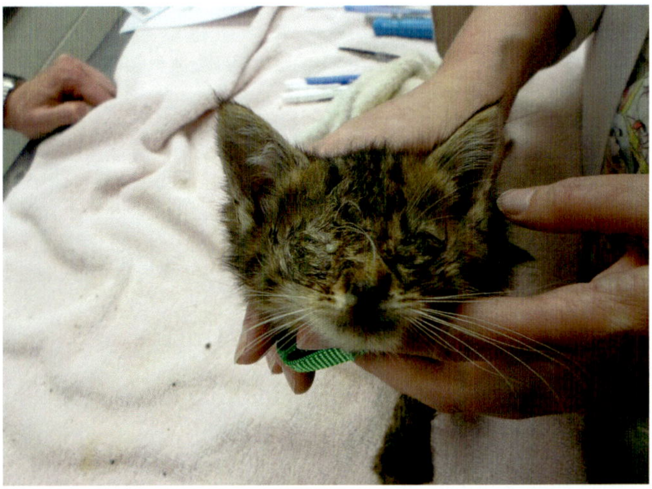

Figure 5.5 This kitten came from a home with over 60 other cats. Most had upper respiratory disease and smelled like ammonia and feces. Photo courtesy of the Humane Society of Missouri.

neurological signs such as a head tilt, ataxia, or nystagmus (Thompson 2013). While some well-cared-for dogs do have chronic otitis, when there is a lack of medical care for this condition, criminal neglect becomes a concern. As with upper respiratory diseases, in large-scale cases of abuse or neglect it is the number of infections observed that contributes to the array of potential evidence of neglect or abuse due to inadequate provision of medical care.

When nonaccidental injury (NAI) is suspected, all causes that may be responsible for the observed physical insults should be considered, investigated, and ruled in or out. When blunt force trauma (BFT) is identified, the eyes may be affected in more subtle ways with chemosis, hyphema, petechiae, or ecchymosis affecting the sclera and conjunctiva. Other suspicious injuries could include proptosis or globe rupture, with or without skull fractures. Incomplete asphyxiation, whether due to hanging, drowning, or crushing, may cause petechiation or scleral injection, although asphyxiation is a diagnosis of exclusion and has no pathognomonic signs (Prahlow and Byard 2012).

Cardiovascular/Respiratory Systems

Neglect cases involving the cardiovascular and respiratory systems may involve upper respiratory tract infections which can advance to a lower airway pathology if allowed to progress. The clinical signs can be severe, especially in cat hoarding situations (Polak et al. 2014). It is not unusual to find large amounts of ocular and nasal discharge, sometimes with changes to the corneas and even ocular rupture. In many regions, heartworms are endemic and dogs not on heartworm preventatives can be infected. While the presence of heartworm disease alone does not necessarily indicate abuse or neglect, advanced stages of heartworm disease that are causing clinical signs such as coughing and exercise intolerance can be a sign of neglect due to lack of medical care. This can be particularly important in large-scale cases as it may demonstrate general neglect of numerous dogs.

NAIs may result in cardiovascular or respiratory signs depending on the type of abuse involved. For example, epistaxis, hemoptysis, and dyspnea can be secondary to BFT and there may not be any other outward signs of injury on the exam. However, pulmonary contusions, pneumothorax, and fractured ribs, among other findings, may be evident on radiographs. If there are bilateral fractured ribs, then there must have been at least two instances of force against the animal (Intarapanich et al. 2016).

Gastrointestinal System

Some of the more common neglect cases affecting the gastrointestinal (GI) system involve dental disease, starvation, and parasitism. All physical examinations should include evaluation of the teeth and oral cavity as thoroughly as can be done safely. Injuries due to BFT to the head can be observed in the oral cavity such as a torn labial frenulum, fractured teeth, bruising, palatal fractures, and lacerations inside the buccal and labial mucosa from impacting the teeth. Petechiae and ecchymosis are frequently visible. Dental fractures can be caused by chewing hard objects and other BFT, whether accidental or nonaccidental. From personal observation of one of the authors (J.B.), shearing forces such as the use of break sticks in fighting dogs can also result in tooth fracture. Abnormal tooth wear can result from attrition or abrasion (American Veterinary Dental College 2016). Abnormal tooth wear in an individual animal does not by itself indicate abuse or neglect, but when similar wear patterns are observed in a large percentage of animals from a single source, it can indicate the presence of a detrimental husbandry issue such as severe incisor wear from feeding a group of dogs on the ground or other abrasive surface (Figure 5.6). Periodontal disease is commonly found in dogs and cats as they age, but an animal should receive veterinary care to correct the problem. Significant calculus deposits, periodontitis, gum recession, dental abscesses, and oronasal fistulas are all indicative of inadequate dental care.

Starvation is a form of emaciation, defined as severe muscle wasting and loss of fat reserves due to an inadequate caloric intake, usually from a cause external to the animal such as a lack of quality or quantity of food or an inability to access food. These animals often want to eat if given the opportunity (Gerdin et al. 2016). Cachexia is another form of emaciation, but the cause is internal to the animal, for instance a disease process such as neoplasia. These animals often choose to not eat (Gerdin et al. 2016). Whenever possible, diagnostic testing should be performed on animals suspected to have been starved to rule out the various natural diseases that can cause cachexia. An animal that is emaciated due to starvation will gain weight when fed appropriately whereas a cachexic animal will maintain or continue to lose weight despite adequate and appropriate feedings (Gerdin et al. 2016).

If there is gastrointestinal ulceration secondary to starvation, parasites, foreign material, intussusception, or infection with bacteria or viruses, there may be vomiting of fresh or digested blood and/or there may be melena (Thompson 2013). Animals that have been starved may also exhibit pica.

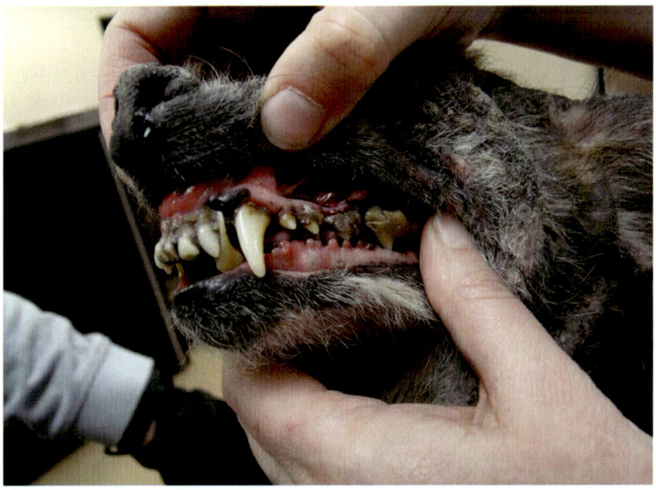

Figure 5.6 Maxillary and mandibular incisor wear due to abrasion. Mandibular canine tooth wear due to attrition from malocclusion and contact with the maxillary third incisors. Severe periodontal disease due to inadequate dental treatment. This dog was removed from a property where dozens of dogs were fed by pouring dog kibble on a sheet of plywood. Photo courtesy of the Humane Society of Missouri.

Radiographs and other imaging modalities such as ultrasound can be helpful to look for foreign material and abnormal structures in the gastrointestinal tract (Gerdin et al. 2016; Stern 2013).

Neglected animals may also have an excessive number of internal parasites. This is particularly common in animal hoarding (Polak et al. 2014), illegal dog fighting, and high-density breeding cases. The parasite burden can be so extreme as to cause severe illness or death. Puppies and kittens are more susceptible to the effects of parasitism (Overgaauw and Nederland 1997). It is for this reason that a fecal analysis and, at a minimum, a PCV/TP is recommended upon intake of any neglected animal. It is important to document any internal parasites and related parasitic anemia that may be a part of the animal's total health picture. Similarly, it is important to note if any vomiting or diarrhea resolved after antiparasitic medications were administered.

NAIs may affect the GI system of cats and dogs in a number of ways. BFT such as kicks to the abdomen may lead to lacerations of the liver or spleen, bruising of the intestines or bleeding within them, or rupture of the stomach or intestines. Injuries that penetrate the body wall such as a sharp force trauma (SFT) from a stabbing, a gunshot wound (GSW), or other projectiles can also penetrate the gastrointestinal tract leading to peritonitis and hemorrhage. Some of these injuries may be difficult to find under the hair coat. Poisoning may lead to emesis, diarrhea, and/or hemorrhage depending on the toxin used. If caustic chemicals are forced into an animal's mouth or are on the fur and are licked off, there may be ulceration of the mouth and esophagus (Thompson 2013).

Musculoskeletal System

Neglect can affect the musculoskeletal system in many ways. Starvation can cause varying degrees of muscle atrophy depending on the degree of calorie restriction and the amount of time involved. In growing individuals, improper nutrition can also lead to improper bone development (Greco 2014). Loss of muscle mass due to starvation can sometimes be distinguished from other causes of orthopedic and neurological disease by a combination of distribution and general clinical picture. In starvation, the muscle atrophy is generalized, not focal, and will often resolve with proper nutrition. On radiographs, the bones of starved animals can appear more translucent than expected and in severe cases, there may be malformation or pathological fractures (Kumar et al. 2008).

Fractures can be a result of NAI. It is important to take radiographs of both the area of immediate concern as well as the rest of the body to look for signs of other healing or healed fractures (Tong 2014). Fractures due to NAI can be caused by BFT, SFT, GSW, or other projectile weapons. It is important to determine if the mechanical forces necessary to cause a fracture fit the story that is given. For instance, many cats fall off tables, beds, or shelves, but fractures are not common injuries in these scenarios. One study found that repetitive fractures, transverse fractures, fractures located in more than one region of the body, and fractures with signs of healing are all more common in NAI in dogs (Tong 2014). For more information about radiology, the reader is referred to Chapter 9 (Veterinary Forensic Radiology and Imaging).

Studies have reviewed and compared differences in injuries caused by motor vehicle accidents (MVA) versus those caused by NAI (Intarapanich et al. 2016; Munro and Thrusfield 2001b). As has been noted previously, repetitive injuries are more common in NAI. In instances of repetitive injury, victims may have injuries in different stages of healing or in different locations on the body indicating multiple applications of force. Additionally, animals suffering from NAI are more likely to have injuries to the front halves of their bodies than the back halves (Intarapanich et al. 2016; Munro and Thrusfield 2001b). This may be because animals who are victims of motor vehicle injuries to the cranial halves of their bodies are more likely to die from their injuries prior to being seen by a veterinarian. Also, it is likely that those who wish malice on an animal intend to cause harm to the front part of the body: the head, face, and thorax (Intarapanich et al. 2016). Fractures of the skull (Intarapanich et al. 2016; Munro and Thrusfield 2001b), teeth, and ribs (Intarapanich et al. 2016) were more common in NAI than MVA.

Urogenital System

While neglect cases may affect the urogenital system (e.g., chronic uroliths that are ignored, hematuria blamed on behavior rather than a medical issue, growing tumors), this is often secondary to ignorance or embarrassment and these situations usually call for client education.

NAI may affect the urogenital system in a multitude of ways. If the kidneys or urinary bladder are affected by BFT, there may be hematuria, retroperitoneal hemorrhaging, or uroperitoneum, for instance (Munro and Munro 2008; Ressel et al. 2016). Ethylene glycol is a common toxin which causes acute kidney injury, whether the exposure is accidental or intentional (Newman 2012).

Animal sexual abuse, like with humans, may have no clinical signs or it may be very severe and can lead to death (Beirne 1997). Assault may occur directly on the genitalia or the anus. Dogs are more likely than cats to be victims of this particular form of abuse (Munro and Thrusfield 2001c). A sexual assault kit like the one used with humans may be beneficial for collecting evidence for veterinary cases as well (Munro and Munro 2008). A Wood's lamp or alternative light source may be useful for locating evidence (Nelson and Santucci 2002; Santucci et al. 1999; Stern and Smith-Blackmore 2016). When possible, document any injury with photographs in addition to written notes in the record. It is important to look for and collect evidence aseptically as soon as one is suspicious of sexual assault so as to not risk losing or contaminating evidence (Bradley and Rasile 2014; Stern and Smith-Blackmore 2016). If an animal is sexually assaulted, there may be signs on the skin of the genitalia. Because the animal may have been restrained during the abuse, it is important to also look for lesions associated with restraint such as tape residue or fibers from a rope around the legs and muzzle. The ears and tail may also be used for leverage or restraint so there may be injuries to these locations, such as petechiae, ecchymosis, abrasions, joint injury, and fractures (Figure 5.7). For more information about animal sexual abuse, the reader is referred to Chapter 14 (Animal Sexual Abuse).

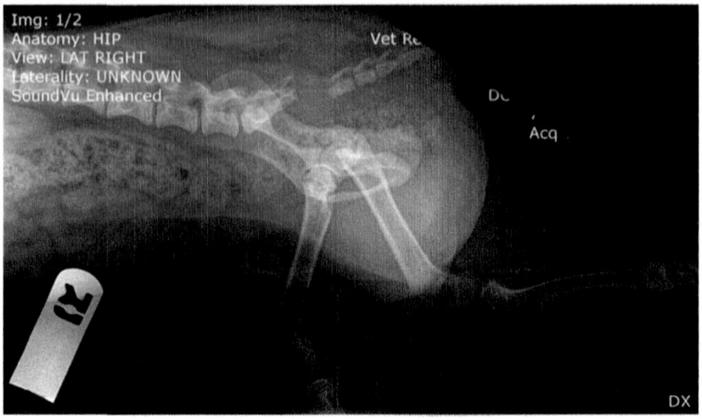

Figure 5.7 Dog, pelvis: Right lateral radiograph of the pelvis showing a severe sacrocaudal fracture with significant displacement and a large amount of soft tissue swelling.

Integumentary System

Abnormalities of the skin are a very common finding during physical examinations of small animals. Severity and chronicity, as well as failure to comply with education and treatment recommendations, are some common factors that distinguish abuse and neglect from uncomplicated medical problems found on well-cared-for animals. External parasites, pruritus, and self-trauma can be found on pets. Severe infestations of fleas and ticks, especially when anemia is a concurrent finding, can be indicators of abuse or neglect due to failure to provide adequate medical care. Demodectic and/or sarcoptic mange are also not unusual in dogs, but severe cases that involve chronic changes to the skin such as hyperkeratosis, hypertrophy, hyperpigmentation, and secondary pyoderma can be the result of neglect (Figure 5.4). The coat may be generally unkempt or severely matted with secondary dermatitis underneath the mats. When hair mats encircle extremities for an extended period of time, the felted hair may constrict around the appendage and may result in damage to the underlying tissues (Figure 5.8). Nails may be overgrown in neglected animals (Figure 5.9); in severe cases, they may tear or may grow into the skin or pad of the animal causing infection and pain.

Other neglect issues can include embedded collars and other foreign bodies that affect the skin. Embedded collars occur most commonly when a collar is placed on a young animal and, as the pet grows, the collar is not adjusted accordingly. These can lead to serious infections and the collars may need to be surgically removed from the neck. Always cut the collar off instead of unfastening it to preserve its actual circumference once removed. Be sure to measure and photograph the collar and the neck before and after removal. Other objects such as rubber bands, tape, rope, and hair elastics can act similarly on different parts of the body such as the legs, tail, and muzzle (Figure 5.10). Wounds and damaged skin are susceptible to secondary myiasis (maggot

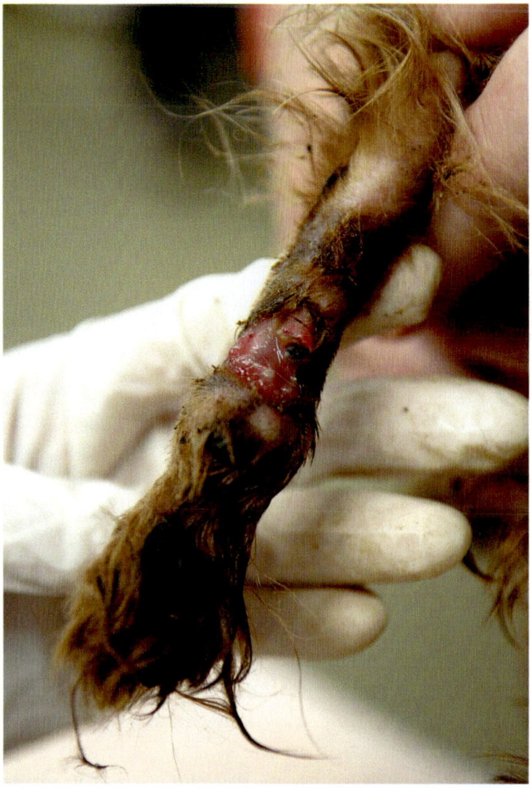

Figure 5.8 Full-thickness ulceration, hyperpigmentation, and scarring of the skin on the caudal aspect of the left front leg found beneath a circumferential mat of fur on an 8-year-old Yorkshire terrier removed from a substandard commercial breeding facility. Photo courtesy of the Humane Society of Missouri.

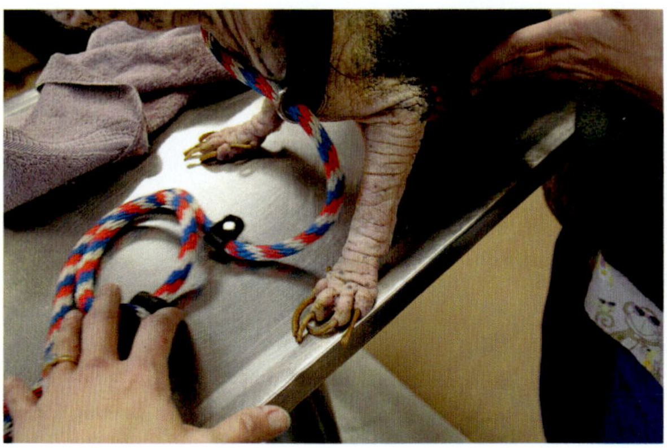

Figure 5.9 Severely overgrown toenails, chronic demodicosis, with alopecia and hyperkeratosis in a dog removed from a hoarding situation. Photo courtesy of the Humane Society of Missouri.

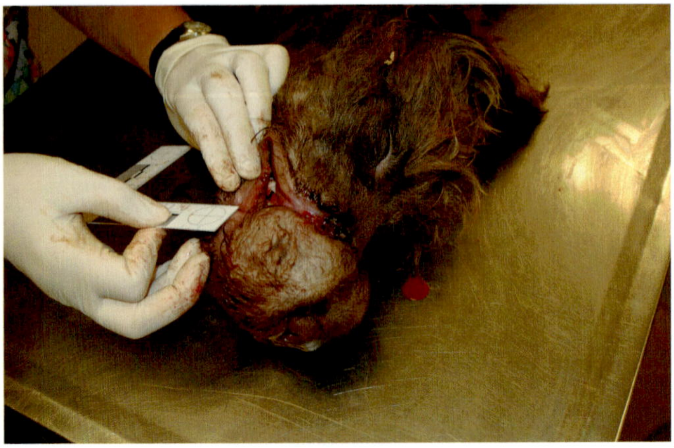

Figure 5.10 Circumferential full-thickness laceration of the muzzle with rostral edema due to an embedded ligature and resulting restriction of venous and lymphoid return. Photo courtesy of the Humane Society of Missouri.

infestation) when the animal is unable to clean the wound properly either due to debilitation or lack of access (Figure 5.11) (Anderson and Huitson 2004).

Many forms of NAI may also affect the skin. In cases of sexual assault, marks on the skin either to the genitalia or on locations such as the ears and tail may be due to restraint. BFT may leave bruising, but the fur, pigmentation, and deeper vascularization of the skin of cats and dogs compared to humans both protect the skin and hide injuries. Shaving an area of concern

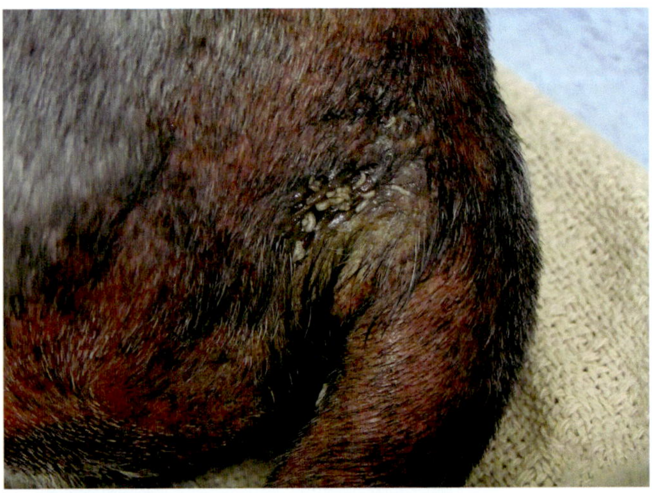

Figure 5.11 Dermatitis and myiasis found beneath extensively matted hair coat. Second and third instars of *Chrysomya* spp. and *Phaenicia* spp. were identified. Photo courtesy of the Humane Society of Missouri.

and utilizing an alternative light source may make bruises more visible (Merck et al. 2013b). This difference in vascularization also means that increased force may be necessary to cause visible bruising if the vessels beneath the skin are more damaged than those within the dermis. It may be necessary to view an area of concern over a few hours or days to appreciate the full extent of the bruising. BFT can also cause lacerations which are commonly found over bony prominences. SFT (Figure 5.12) and projectile injury can damage the skin as well. Sometimes the pattern of the injury can indicate the type of weapon used (de Siqueira et al. 2016). For instance, a two-pronged meat fork used repeatedly to stab an animal will leave injuries with paired holes.

When describing the location of any lesion on the skin, two details are particularly important to include in the record. The first should be measurements of the lesion. These should be taken with a ruler or similar instrument and recorded with either two-dimensional or three-dimensional measurements. In other words, a flat lesion will have two measurements, one for the length and one for the width, whereas a dermal mass or a stab wound will have three measurements, one for the length, one for the width, and one for the height or depth.

The second detail for describing a lesion is its location, which should be measured accurately from landmarks on the body or perpendicular to anatomical baselines such as the dorsal midline so a reader can picture where it is. When possible, measure the distance from the lesion to three different points on the body to triangulate its location. For instance, a lesion on the dorsum between the shoulder blades may be described as having its cranial-most edge being located 10 cm caudal to the base of the right ear, 15 cm caudal to the base of the left ear, and 0.5 cm to the right of the dorsal midline. Use of photographs and body charts are imperative to augment the understanding of the location of lesions.

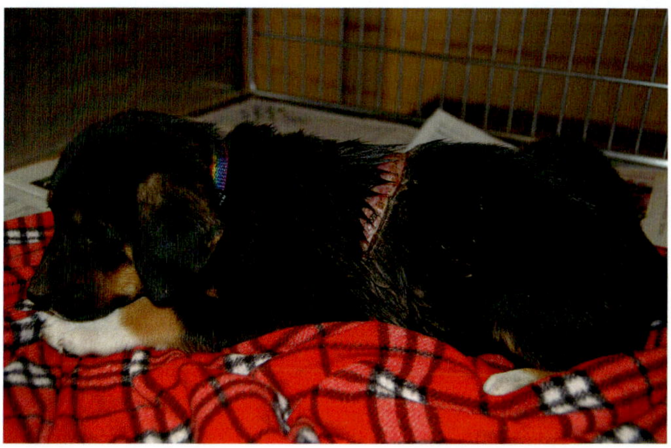

Figure 5.12 Sharp-force injury (chop wound) on the dorsal aspect of a puppy that was struck with a machete. Photo courtesy of the Humane Society of Missouri.

Gunshot Wounds

Entrance and exit wounds have subtle differences that should be noted to determine the trajectory of the projectile. The entrance wound may have residue and stippling if the distance between the muzzle of the gun and the animal is close enough, usually less than a few inches. As the distance away from the weapon increases, these are less likely to occur. Most entrance wounds have a margin of abraded skin (abrasion rim). There may also be hair dragged into the wound. Look for signs of gunshot residue or singed hair. Be aware that projectiles may form very small wounds that are hard to see beneath the fur and may not bleed much externally. When the edges of an entrance wound are apposed, there may be a piece of skin that appears to be "missing." Exit wounds, if present, may be larger than entrance wounds due to the projectile tumbling inside the body and becoming deformed by the forces exerted upon it by the body. The edges of an exit wound will usually come together when apposed (Figure 5.13), and subcutaneous tissues may protrude from the wound (Bradley-Siemens and Brower 2016). In addition, a projectile can go completely through one part of the body, for instance a leg, and then re-enter at another location such as the thorax. Where this happens, the second entrance wound is more likely to have the characteristics of an exit wound as described above except hairs and skin edges may still be pulled into the wound opening.

Radiographs are important when evaluating puncture wounds. Sometimes GSW are mistaken for bite wounds (Bradley-Siemens and Brower 2016). Radiographs may help differentiate the two because they allow the veterinarian to evaluate for the presence or absence of foreign bodies and projectile fragments, identify skeletal trauma, and potentially show signs of air or fluid

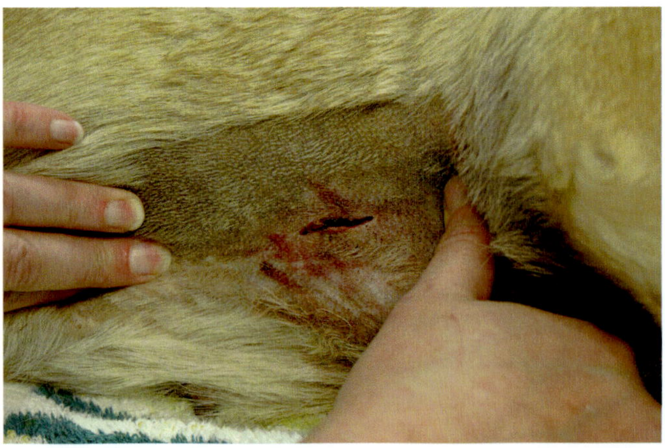

Figure 5.13 Exit wound from a bullet that entered the point of the right shoulder, passed through the proximal humerus to exit caudal to the right axilla. Note that gentle retraction applied to the ends of the wound causes apposition and tissue edges are everted. Photo courtesy of the Humane Society of Missouri.

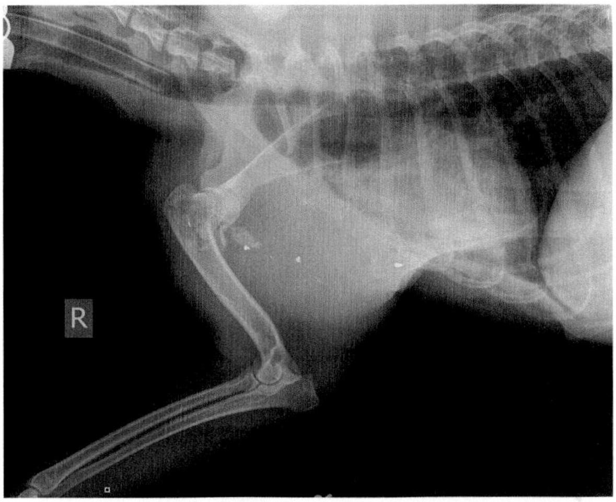

Figure 5.14 Lateral radiograph of dog from Figure 5.13, right forelimb: gunshot wound where bullet entered the proximocranial humerus and exited distomedially. Metallic fragments (from projectile) and pieces of bone visible in the caudal aspects of the wound tract. Photo courtesy of the Humane Society of Missouri.

(blood or urine) in the body cavity involved (Figure 5.14) (Bradley-Siemens and Brower 2016). As always, do not forget to photograph the area of concern and collect samples for evidence. Whenever possible, try to describe the trajectory of the projectile when writing the forensic report. Describing a trajectory does not have to be complicated; stating "the projectile entered the cranial aspect of the left shoulder, passed through the proximal humerus, exited through the caudal aspect of the left shoulder, then grazed the left lateral thorax horizontally for 4 cm" is sufficient. However, when describing the entry and exit wounds themselves, specific locations of the wounds should be described in detail.

Burns

Sometimes animals are set on fire (Figure 5.15). Often an accelerant such as gasoline, kerosene, or lighter fluid is used and the odor of such material can be detected during the exam. If burns of this nature are suspected, it is important to try to collect the accelerant if any is still present. The best place to collect samples of accelerant is from the margins of the burns or at a dependent location where the accelerant may have pooled, such as around the paws in a standing animal. The fur containing the accelerant should be removed using scissors, not electrical clippers. If the animal is wearing a collar or other material, it may have been in contact with the accelerant and will be a good source to collect. Place the material, be it a collar, clothing, or fur, into an arson can or unlined paint can leaving at least half of the can empty, then seal and sign it for evidence (U.S. Department of Justice and National Forensic Science Technology Center 2013) and submit with a chain of custody form.

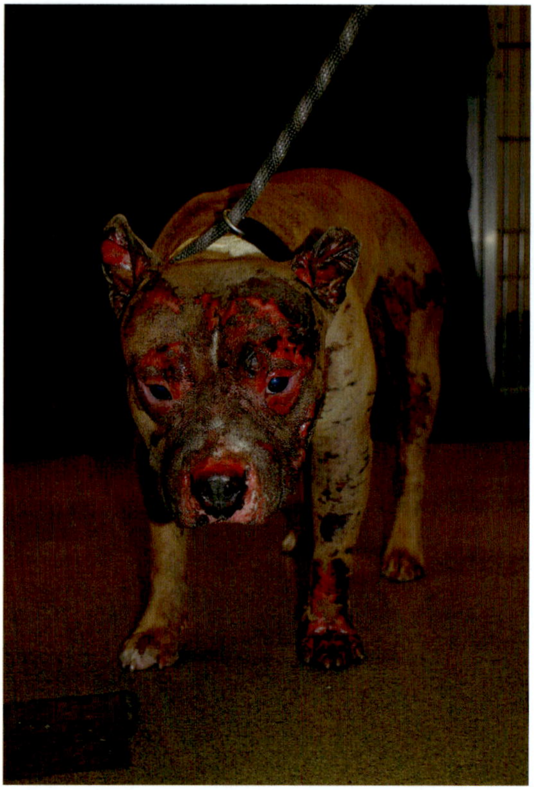

(a)

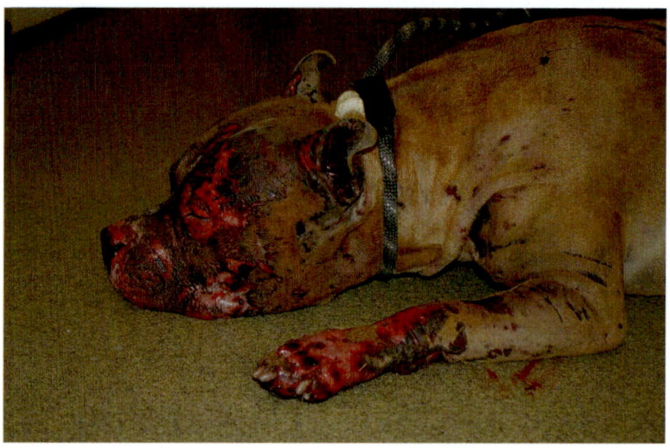

(b)

Figure 5.15 An adult pit bull that was splashed in the face with gasoline and set on fire. (a) Note the splash pattern on the left legs and deeper burns on the left front foot where the gasoline dripped down and the dog stood in it. (b) Left lateral view with splash marks visible on the neck, left shoulder, and left front leg. Photos courtesy of the Humane Society of Missouri.

Burns may also occur if a hot liquid or caustic chemical is poured on an animal (Figure 5.16). When this happens, drip lines may be seen along with splash marks. These can help indicate the position of the animal as well as the direction of the fluid (Wohlsein et al. 2016).

Immersion burns, where an animal is dunked into excessively hot water or other liquid, can also occur. Signs of this include a watermark line indicating where the liquid was and where it was not (Wohlsein et al. 2016). Folds in the skin can lead to striping, like a zebra or a tiger, between areas of normal skin and areas of burned skin (Greenbaum et al. 2004).

It is important to note what degree the burns are; first, second, third, or fourth. First-degree burns are superficial, like sunburns, and only affect the epidermis; they are painful. Second-degree burns involve the epidermis and part of the dermis; they, too, are painful. Third-degree burns extend into the subcutis, whereas fourth-degree burns extend to the skeletal muscle and/or bone. Because the pain neuroreceptors are damaged, third and fourth degree burns are not painful (Wohlsein et al. 2016). The Rule of Nines, adapted from human burn victims, gives some objectivity to the amount of surface area that has been affected by second, third, and fourth degree burns. The thorax and abdomen are considered 18% each of the total body surface as is each hind leg. Each front leg is 9%, the head is 9%, and the neck is 1% of the total body surface as well. Together, all the parts equal 100% of the body surface area (Wohlsein et al. 2016). By utilizing this in the notes to document the extent of the animal's body that is affected by the burns, it helps to give a better picture of the burn pattern and severity.

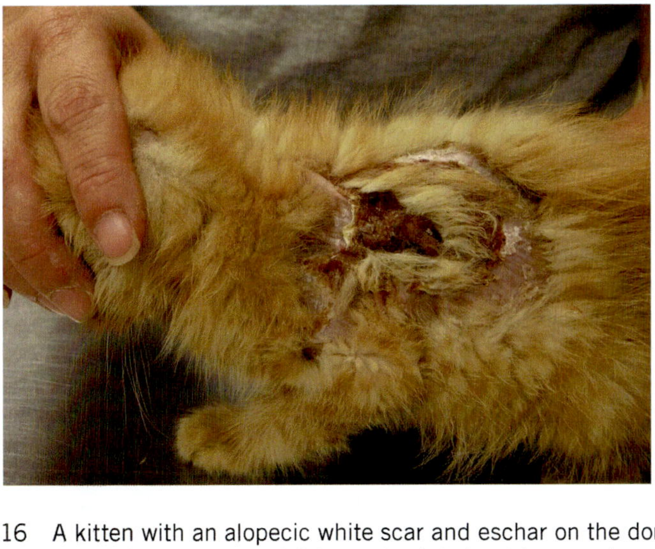

Figure 5.16 A kitten with an alopecic white scar and eschar on the dorsal neck and left shoulder. Drip marks are visible on the left front leg causing suspicion that the healing wound is from a caustic chemical. Photo courtesy of the Humane Society of Missouri.

Assessment

A list of all the issues found, both on the animal and in the environment where applicable, can help the veterinarian see the total picture for the animal. From that problem list, the veterinarian can form a list of differential diagnoses. Along with possible forms of abuse, it is necessary to consider other differentials for the problems identified. Then the veterinarian can analyze the differentials to assess which ones best explain the clinical signs and consider which diagnostics may need to be performed to narrow the list (Lorenz 2009). For certain forms of abuse, for example, starvation and asphyxia, it is the ability to rule out other causes that allows the practitioner to state with any certainty that neglect or abuse are the reasons for the condition in which the animal is found.

It is important to remember that there is no pathognomonic sign of animal cruelty. It is the totality of the case including the history, witness statements, law enforcement documentation, digital evidence such as social media, along with the examination and diagnostic findings which determine whether the injuries are consistent with abuse or neglect. It is not the responsibility of a veterinarian to make the final declaration of animal cruelty; that is the responsibility of law enforcement, prosecutors, and the court system. Rather, the veterinarian's role is to use medical science to identify cases in which abuse or neglect are *reasonably suspected* and then take appropriate steps to properly document the findings and report those concerns to an appropriate authority (Woolf 2015).

Accidents and Diseases That Mimic Animal Cruelty

Motor Vehicle Accidents

As was mentioned in the *Musculoskeletal System* section, animals involved in MVA may mimic animal abuse. The story given by the person presenting the animal is important. Ask if the person actually saw the animal get hit by a car or if this was an assumption. If the person saw it, ask what was seen: the speed of the car, the type of car, what part of the animal was hit, and was the animal rolled under the car, for instance. Then assess whether the story fits with the injuries seen on the animal. In one study, MVA were more commonly associated with abrasions, pulmonary contusions, pneumothorax, and pelvic/sacral fractures (Intarapanich et al. 2016).

High-Rise Syndrome

High-rise syndrome describes the typical injuries, such as head and facial injuries including palatal fractures; pneumothorax, pulmonary contusions, and other thoracic injuries; and fractures of the forelimbs (Gordon et al. 1993; Whitney and Mehlhaff 1987), that occur when an animal falls, generally greater than two stories from a multistory building. These falls can result in multiple fractures and/or internal injuries that may mimic abuse. The history and any witness statements may help guide a veterinarian in the diagnostic process. Animals will more commonly fall if a window is open or when chasing a toy or other object. Realize that it is unlikely that the examination alone will be able to differentiate between an animal that fell from a building and one that was thrown from a building. However, signs of chronic abuse in addition to the acute signs of injury should be cause for an investigation.

Hemorrhage and Coagulopathies

Various accidents, diseases, and toxins can lead to unexpected bleeding, whether internal or external. Obviously, sometimes animals are poisoned intentionally, but accidents can occur as well. Many rodenticides and excessive use of nonsteroidal anti-inflammatory drugs cause bleeding. Bleeding may also be secondary to congenital disorders such as von Willebrand's disease and hemophilia, or due to acquired diseases such as immune-mediated thrombocytopenia (Thompson 2013). Diagnostic tests combined with the history and evidence found on the scene should help differentiate disease from abuse in many cases.

Fractures

While fractures can certainly occur with abuse, they may also occur with accidents or natural disease. As always, ask questions to see if the story fits the injuries that are found on examination. Consider if the forces that would be necessary for the type of fracture present could have occurred as described. At the same time, be aware that pathological fractures may require minimal force to happen, so look at the radiographs carefully for any signs of structural weakness of the bone. Certain diseases such as osteogenesis imperfecta, malnutrition causing calcium and phosphorus imbalances, and hyperparathyroidism, to name a few, may also lead to brittle bones susceptible to fracturing (Thompson 2013). Additional diagnostics should be utilized to determine if the signs are more consistent with natural disease or abuse.

Plan

The forensic examination needs to include a medical plan and follow-up as appropriate, just like any other clinical veterinary medical record. Whenever possible, perform diagnostics to rule in/out causes for the clinical signs other than abuse. If a person has knowledge of, or has directly witnessed events, that history may provide a story and timeline explaining the observed injuries and other signs. It is mandatory that the practitioner document the findings of the clinical examination, whether they confirm or contradict the story presented. In this way, if the case does get charged as a cruelty case, the veterinarian can show objective reasoning while limiting bias.

The plan should also include any needed follow-up examinations to monitor the condition. Records for each examination should be generated as carefully as the initial one. These follow-up examinations may document improvement with minimal care, such as an animal that is emaciated but gains weight being fed a basic diet and receiving standard care such as a monthly dewormer. By showing an improvement in weight and body condition score, and further documenting visible changes with photographs, one can demonstrate how difficult or easy it was to care correctly for the animal. If a great deal of effort and care is necessary to return the animal to a normal state, that information can be important as well.

Ancillary Testing

Radiographs

As discussed under *Musculoskeletal System*, radiographs are a must if fractures or projectile injuries are suspected. They can also be quite useful to look for old, healed, or healing injuries that are not currently causing clinical signs. Therefore, in any case where abuse or neglect is under investigation, radiographs of the entire animal are recommended (Merck et al. 2013b). Including a commercially available scale within the exposed image aids in identifying the size of radiographic lesions. When obtaining radiographs in cases that may involve abuse or neglect, it is especially important to ensure that all positioning markers are placed appropriately and that all data related to the patient is correct. This avoids the risk of images being eliminated as evidence in court. Writing on the radiograph after the image is obtained (either with a marker on a film or with digital manipulation) is also not acceptable as this can constitute tampering with evidence. Other imaging modalities such as ultrasonography, computed tomography (CT), and magnetic resonance (MR) imaging can also be used. For more information about radiology, the reader is referred to Chapter 9 (Veterinary Forensic Radiology and Imaging).

Laboratory Tests

There are a large variety of diagnostic tests available that can be used to help determine the cause of an animal's condition at the time of examination. The choice of tests performed should reflect the needs of the individual animal's diagnostic plan as well as the needs of the case. The results of the tests can and should be used to document the extent of any medical problems present at the time of the examination, help determine the prognosis for recovery, and direct future care of that animal. Some tests can be performed in-house with minimal supplies or quality control (QC) measures; other tests require specialized equipment that is available for in-house use but needs significant QC efforts. A myriad of additional specialized tests as well as the more commonly utilized tests can be performed at reference laboratories. Documenting the performance of each test in a test log (containing the date, person performing the test, and test result) is vital, as is ensuring that test procedures are appropriate, standardized, and effective for their purpose. Where possible, the creation of photomicrographic images can be performed when any results are found under microscopic examination. If a test involves equipment that requires QC measures, they should be performed on a regular basis and records of such should be maintained (Tvedten and Willard 2012). If a test is performed at an outside laboratory, ensure chain of custody protocols are followed. It is best to contact the laboratory ahead of time to discuss this.

Documenting Evidence

Photography and Videography

Photographic documentation of the animal being examined and the lesions that are identified is one of the ways to corroborate your physical examination findings. Because living beings change with time (wounds heal, weight is gained or lost, etc.), photographs and video can provide a visual record of the evidence at the time of the examination.

Using a digital camera allows collection of many more images than film cameras. It also allows users to ensure the desired image is captured in the frame properly. A digital single lens reflex (SLR) camera often provides better ability to focus on specific objects of interest and utilize multiple photographic modes such as macro and zoom options. Choose a camera that utilizes secure digital (SD) cards that can be removed. The images from the cards can be transferred to a read-only device such as a CD or read-only protected section of a secured hard drive to avoid manipulation of original images (Blitzer et al. 2008). Be sure the SD card is reformatted prior to use and that the date and time are correctly set on the camera (Marsh 2014).

At a minimum, the whole animal should be photographed starting with an identifier that links the animal in the photographs with the written records attached to it (a "mug shot"). In many cases, this is done with a *case board* photograph where the various identifications of that animal, case numbers, the date of the exam, location of the exam, the photographer's name, as well as any other relevant identifiers are written on a card or white board. That board or card is photographed with the animal itself at the start of the series of photographs of that individual. These are clinical images and should not be manipulated or framed in any way to dramatize the lesion or animal (Figure 5.17). Never delete photographs from the series (U.S. Department of Justice and National Forensic Science Technology Center 2013). This avoids argument that exculpatory evidence—evidence that would release the defendant from blame or refute the existence of a crime—was removed.

Photographs that should be included in the visual record include images of the entire animal from both sides (left and right lateral), a dorsal view (taken from the top), a caudal view (taken from behind), the face and cranial part of the body (taken from the front), and a ventral view (the underside of the animal—usually taken by bracing the animal so it stands on its hind legs). Following these overall images, any visible lesion or area of concern that is identified should be photographed several times, starting with a mid-range image to allow the viewer to orient where the lesion exists on the body, then a close-up image of the lesion, and a second close-up image that contains a photographic measurement scale (Marsh 2014; U.S. Department of Justice and National Forensic Science Technology Center 2013). In a pinch, anything of consistent scale, such as a coin, can be utilized. If desired, one or more of the animal identifiers can be included in the close-up images as well. Do this "forest-to-tree" approach for each lesion so as to make sure the viewer knows when you have changed to a new lesion, even if it is in the same general location. As much as possible, the subject of the photographs should be at right angles to the camera and centered so there is no distortion. Also, consider taking multiple photographs of the same view but on different settings (e.g., with the flash, without the flash, using the macro setting, etc.). Keeping a log of photographic images taken can help identify individual images that may be later taken out of context from the series, or help locate specific

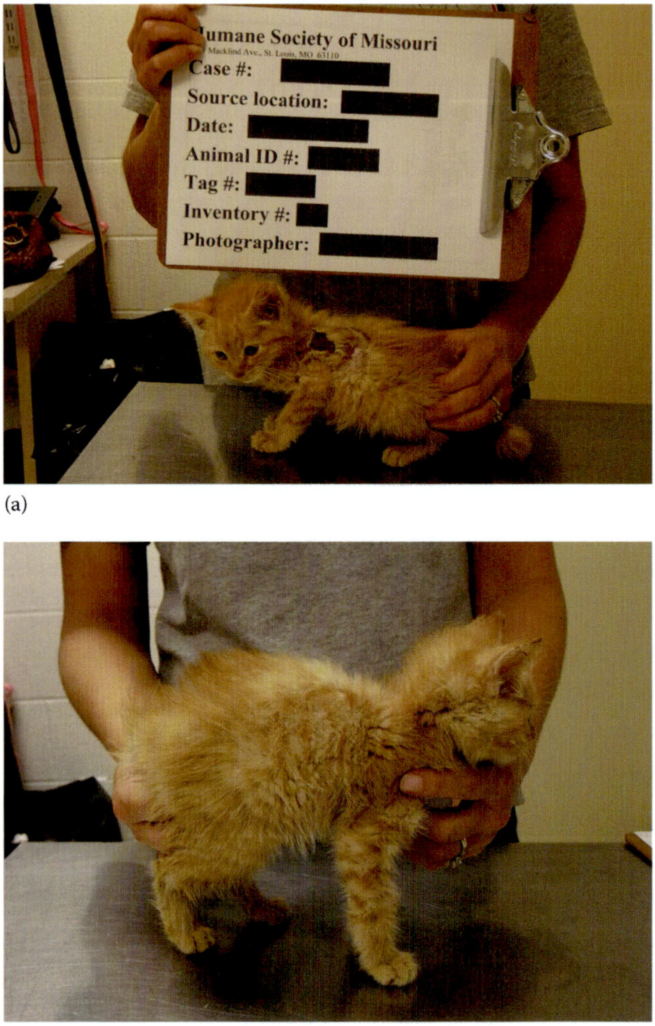

(a)

(b)

Figure 5.17 Series of evidence photographs for a kitten with suspected chemical burn from Figure 5.16. (a) Case board at the start of the photograph series showing the kitten in left lateral view. This is the "mug shot." (b) Right lateral view. *(Continued)*

images without searching through potentially hundreds of individual image files (U.S. Department of Justice and National Forensic Science Technology Center 2013).

Videography can be particularly useful for documenting large scenes or for documenting animation or sound. It should not be used to replace photographs

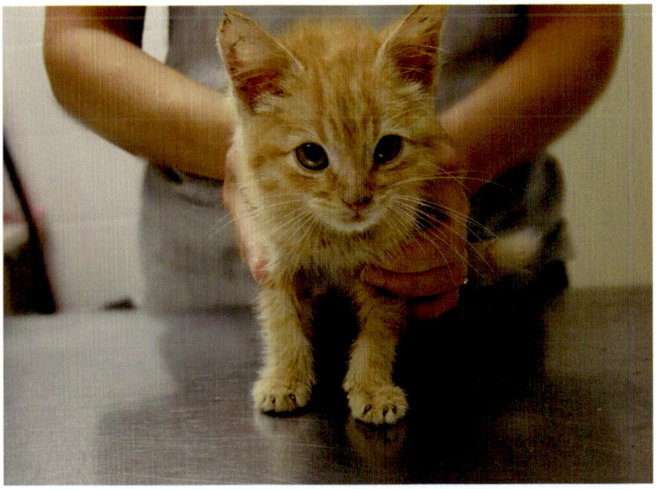

(c)

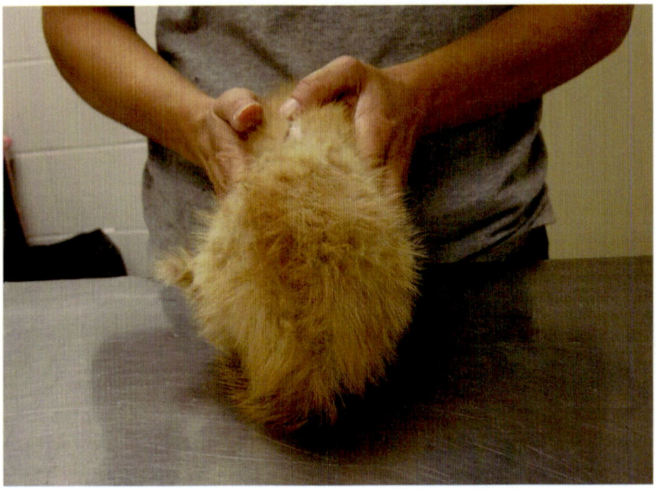

(d)

Figure 5.17 (Continued) Series of evidence photographs for a kitten with suspected chemical burn from Figure 5.16. (c) Face and cranial portion of the body. (d) Caudal view. *(Continued)*

but may augment them. Dynamic events such as behavior can be better documented using a video to show, for instance, a stereotypy, lameness, neurological abnormalities, or the vigorousness with which a starving animal ate once provided with food. Video can also be used to capture sounds, or the lack of them, in a given situation. A dog that screams, for example, when a certain part of the body is palpated, or the lack of barking in a room of dogs who are

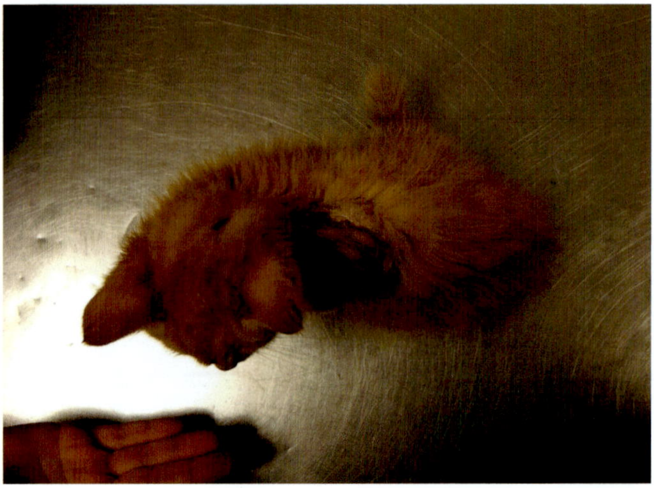

(e)

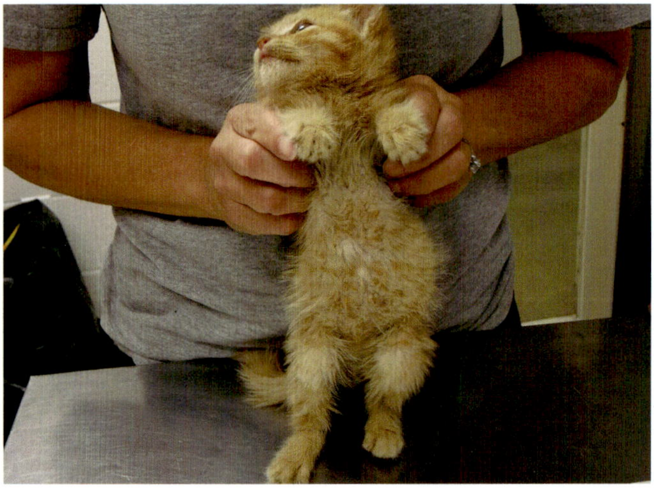

(f)

Figure 5.17 (Continued) Series of evidence photographs for a kitten with suspected chemical burn from Figure 5.16. (e) Dorsal view. (f) Ventral view.

(Continued)

cowering can be very powerful evidence. Just remember when recording video that the surrounding voices will be recorded as well, so either everyone needs to be mindful of what they are saying or the camera's microphone should be muted (U.S. Department of Justice and National Forensic Science Technology Center 2013). For more information about videography, the reader is referred to Chapter 3 (Videography: A New Tool in Animal Cruelty Investigations).

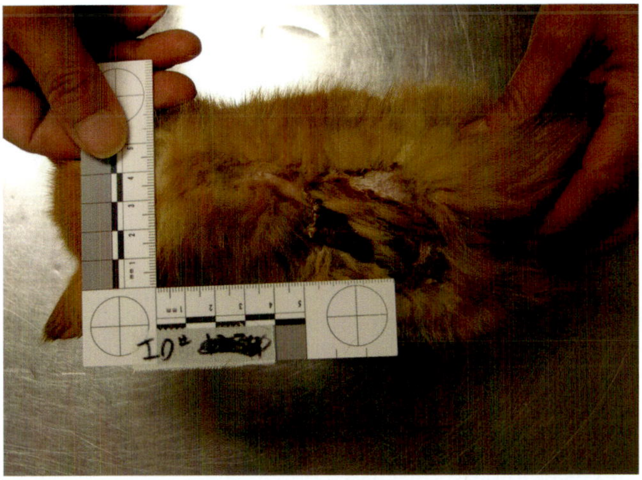

(g)

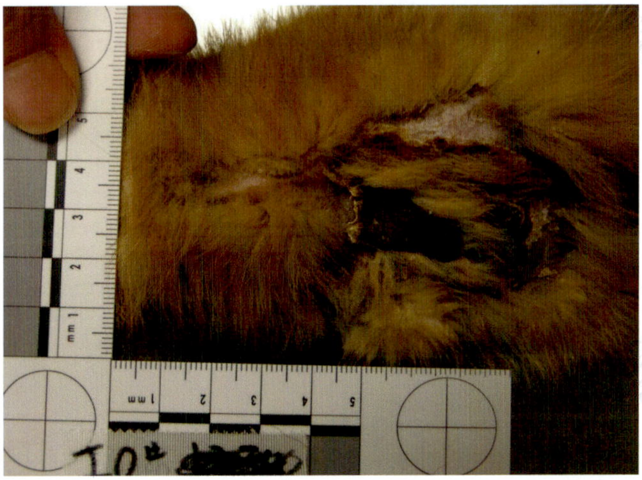

(h)

Figure 5.17 (Continued) Series of evidence photographs for a kitten with suspected chemical burn from Figure 5.16. (g) A mid-range view with an ABFO photographic scale held on the plane of the wound. (h) Same view as (g), but close-up and including the scale (a close-up photo without scale should be taken as well). Photos courtesy of the Humane Society of Missouri.

Evidence Handling

In the case of animal cruelty or neglect, evidence begins with the animal itself, and includes all documentation and notes, previous medical records, physical examination findings, test results, radiographs, photographs, video footage, samples of hair, collars/leashes/ropes/chains attached to the animal, and any relevant materials found in the environment. In order to use evidence in a court of law, the prosecution must be able to show that it has not been altered except in documented ways. Every time any piece of evidence changes hands it must be logged in a chain of custody document that follows that item from the time it is collected until the time it is presented in court or disposed of as directed by the courts (U.S. Department of Justice and National Forensic Science Technology Center 2013).

In addition to maintaining the chain of custody, the various materials must be packaged and stored properly. Items contaminated with bodily fluids should be dried and packaged in paper envelopes to decrease degradation (U.S. Department of Justice and National Forensic Science Technology Center 2013). Collars and other items attached to the body should be cut, leaving the fastener untouched to allow for collection of DNA or trace evidence from buckles, clips, or locks. Small samples of hair should be folded into a paper bindle (also called a druggist's fold) then sealed in a paper envelope unless volatile chemicals are suspected to be present, in which case an accelerant collection should be followed as discussed previously.

If potential DNA evidence needs to be collected, for example in sexual assault, fighting dogs, or other bite wounds, a minimum of two samples needs to be taken. The first sample should be a swab used to collect a control sample from the animal; often a buccal swab is used for this. The second sample should be taken from the material of concern. If it is no longer moist, use sterile saline solution to dampen a swab, then rub it on the area of concern, then use a dry swab to collect the now-moistened sample. All swabs should be air dried (no heat added and no UV light) prior to packaging in paper envelopes (U.S. Department of Justice and National Forensic Science Technology Center 2013). It is also good practice to consult with the laboratory prior to collection. For more information about DNA testing, the reader is referred to Chapter 11 (DNA Evidence Collection and Analysis).

Large-Scale Cases

Large-scale cases are any situation where multiple animals are involved, often with one or a few perpetrators, and law enforcement is investigating it as one incident even if there may be multiple charges. Common types of large-scale cases include poorly managed commercial breeding facilities (Figure 5.18), hoarding situations, and organized dog fighting. In these situations, a veterinarian's expertise can assist the investigation in many ways.

Planning

When faced with many animals suspected to have been abused or neglected, planning is paramount. Search warrants may need to be obtained stating what parts of the property may be searched, above- and belowground. Investigators need to know as much as they can about the location and terrain involved as possible. This will allow for identification of hazards to the health and safety of the people and animals at the site, determination of the number of people

Figure 5.18 One room of a commercial breeding kennel. The excessive amount of organic matter including hair, feces, and dirt indicate that it had not been cleaned appropriately for an extended period. These dogs were severely matted, smelled of ammonia, and several had wounds from mats constricting around their extremities. Pododermatitis, conjunctivitis, otitis, and dental diseases were also common findings in these dogs. A close-up image of two of the dogs can be seen in Figure 5.20. Photo courtesy of the Humane Society of Missouri.

and equipment necessary on-scene and at the shelter, and decisions on the best ways to get necessary equipment into and out of the location. As accurate an estimate of the number and species of animals as possible is vital to avoid surprises and ensure that any unusual situations can be handled appropriately (Figure 5.19).

Figure 5.19 An emaciated tiger was found in a cage among the buildings of a poorly managed commercial breeding facility that had 208 dogs. While unexpected, a good working relationship with a local zoo allowed for proper tranquilization, examination, removal, and care of the tiger. Photo courtesy of the Humane Society of Missouri.

Consultation with a veterinarian during this stage can help fine-tune these decisions and how the case should be handled if animals are confiscated. A vital part of the planning stage involves securing appropriate housing and care for the animals should impoundment be necessary. In some cases, the investigators may choose to care for the animals at the location for a period of time due to health or safety concerns, or until better arrangements can be made. This is often called impoundment on-site. Not all shelters can handle an influx of dozens to hundreds of animals in a single day, and no facility can do this at a moment's notice because cages must be prepared, vaccines and laboratory test kits must be ordered, and additional personnel must be scheduled.

Triage/Survey/Walk-Through

Once on a large-scale crime scene, the initial survey of the entire scene is the time to visually triage the animals and document them in their environment with photographs, video, and written notes/drawings. This is when investigators and veterinarians can identify hazards in the environment that may cause medical problems for the animals such as wire flooring (Figure 5.20) that can injure feet (Merck et al. 2013a) or husbandry practices that could harm the animals such as improper feeding practices. It is also important to note any potential hazards for the responders such as needles and signs of zoonotic diseases.

One of the most important parts of a veterinarian's on-scene involvement at this stage is triage of the animals. Singling out individuals that need immediate care and either providing that care or arranging for it to be handled appropriately is a vital part of any cruelty or neglect investigation. While always

Figure 5.20 Two Yorkshire terriers on wire flooring in a commercial breeding facility. Feces and shed hair has built up in their cages and they are visibly unkempt and matted. These two dogs are from the situation seen in Figure 5.18. Photo courtesy of the Humane Society of Missouri.

keeping in mind the welfare of the animal, it is necessary to document every animal, especially the critical ones, *in situ* as much as possible prior to removing it from its environment. Additionally, identifying possible contagious diseases and taking steps to minimize any further spread is important as there may be regulatory issues related to the transport of ill or injured animals.

Examination

Just as in smaller cases, the physical examination is the center of proving illness or injury caused by abuse or neglect of animals in a large-scale case. Every individual animal must receive a complete physical examination. These examinations can take place at the scene or at another appropriate location such as a shelter. Some may choose to do a quick physical examination at the scene after the visual triage but prior to a lengthier full medical and forensic examination at a different location. The choice of locations and procedures will often vary based on facilities, equipment, personnel, and individual situation. Always consider the safety of the animals and the people involved when deciding what is best. Once it is time to do a full examination, it should proceed much as it would for any individual animal. All forensic examinations should take place as soon as feasible after law enforcement has secured the scene and given permission to begin.

Data Collection

Large-scale cases often benefit from diagnostic testing just like smaller-scale cases. However, a large-scale case produces a lot of information. The results of all examinations and tests will provide information that leads to a diagnosis and treatment plan for each individual animal, but this information also provides data on the whole group of animals. For example, if one dog in a group of 50 healthy dogs has evidence of chronic skin and ear infections, it may have severe atopic dermatitis; criminal neglect may not be present. But if 30 out of 50 dogs have severe alopecia, hyperkeratosis, excoriations, hyperpigmentation, and otitis externa, these findings are more likely related to chronically untreated, possibly contagious skin disease due to neglect or abuse.

Assessment/Data Analysis

When documenting large-scale cases, each animal is treated both as an individual with its own medical and behavioral problems that must be addressed, but also as part of a larger group that has collective problems. This allows for better understanding of how there can be a few apparently healthy individuals in a case where the group as a whole had been experiencing abuse or neglect. Review all the physical examination findings, diagnostic test results, and diagnoses of each individual animal and identify how many animals share common problems.

Create a list of the problems identified in each of the individual animals and determine the number and/or percentage of individuals that exhibit that problem. In this way, the reader can quickly identify that 14 out of the

16 animals had fleas, for instance, or 70% of the animals from the property exhibited hair loss, without going through each individual animal's report to find a single abnormality. Combine the common abnormalities found in this manner and compare them to the environmental situation from which the animals were taken. These common findings may correlate to abusive or neglectful practices experienced by most of the animals in the case.

Some individual animals in a group experiencing abuse or neglect may not show lesions. However, if they were found in the same situation as affected individuals, it is possible that they were also abused or neglected but had individual traits that minimized the consequences from those situations such as a shorter exposure time, a different metabolic rate, ability to avoid aggressive humans, or a more competent immune system.

Conclusions/Report of Findings

The forensic veterinarian's report is the compilation and interpretation of all veterinary medical aspects involved in the case. This is the primary document that will be used in court when dealing with the medical findings; it is an essential part of any case that may be required in legal proceedings. When writing reports for large-scale cases, individual animal write-ups are required as part of the overall final report. However, the comments and some of the assessment information will apply to all the animals in the group and can be left off that specific subsection of the individual animal reports, as they will be included in the larger case summary. For more information regarding the forensic report, the reader is referred to Chapter 17 (Expert Witness Testimony and Report Writing).

Case Summary Document

The case summary document can be organized similarly to a report for a single animal, but it refers to the group of animals almost as its own entity. It is essentially an "executive summary" from which the court can easily survey the overall findings in the case. The report should contain minimal medical jargon because many different people will need to read and understand it. Instead, use medical verbiage only to clarify lay terminology when necessary to be sure that it is clear to all readers. The headers should be identical to an individual animal's report and should be signed and dated as usual, but the body of this summary will include the following sections:

- History
- Overall objective findings
- Assessments or analysis
- Conclusions and comments

The history section covers the overall history that can be obtained and describes the environment in which the animals were found. Any information from other people or sources such as; police reports it is preferable to document and acknowledge the original source of the information.

The objective findings section consists of the list of the problems identified in the individual physical examinations and the number of animals affected. This was previously compiled to facilitate the assessment of the case. Results of diagnostic testing are summarized here as well. A table such as the one shown in Table 5.4 can be used as a visual aid to summarize the large quantity of information found in large-scale cases. Bulleted lists may also be useful in some situations. This section, along with the history and environmental findings, provides the supporting information for the next two sections and allows the court to quickly access basic data as it applies to the group as a whole. Photographs throughout the report can augment with pictures what the veterinarian is indicating with the written words.

The assessment or analysis section of the case summary will refer to the information listed in the objective and history sections to provide possible causes or rule-out lists to explain why so many of the animals exhibit the same problem. Environmental causes of the identified medical problems are supported or refuted here.

Finally, the conclusions and comments section in the case summary will provide an explanation for the findings common to many of the individual animals, the related science, and how any causes that were identified in the assessment section may or may not represent abuse/neglect. It is here that the veterinarian can offer opinions on the condition and care of the animals, the environment in which they were found, and support the conclusions with references. This is also the place where the veterinarian can point out what an average person in the community should have seen and/or could have done to identify and address the problems found in the animals for the case. When writing the conclusions, select wording that reflects the applicable legal statutes which were or may have been violated.

Table 5.4 Example of a Table Summary for Large-Scale Cases

Animal ID	BCS (Purina)	URI Signs	Dental Disease (Score 3 or 4)	Ear Mites
2016-10-009	3	Yes	No	Yes
2016-10-010	6	No	No	No
2016-10-011	3	Yes	Yes	Yes
2016-10-012	2	Yes	Yes	Yes
Total	BCS ≤ 4: **3**	**3**	**2**	**3**

Note: In this example, 75% of the cats had a BCS ≤ 4 out of 9, 75% had signs of URI, 50% had high dental disease scores, and 75% had ear mites.

Legend: BCS = body condition score utilizing the Purina Scoring Chart; URI = upper respiratory infection.

Conclusion

When approaching a clinical forensic examination for a potential abuse, neglect, or insurance fraud case, the veterinarian should perform a medical examination like any other with the added emphasis of thoroughly describing and carefully documenting any lesions or conditions that could be related to the case. All systems should be examined and notes should indicate the findings, whether abnormal or no significant findings. Documentation needs to include written notes and photographs; diagrams and videos may also be useful. Be cognizant of proper evidence collection and chain of custody. Write a complete report comprised of the objective physical examination findings with opinions and interpretations of those findings in the conclusions.

References

American Veterinary Dental College. 2016. Nomenclature—Teeth AVDC—American Veterinary Dental College. AVDC.org. http://222.avdc.org/Nomenclature/Nomen-Teeth.html (Accessed October 19, 2016).

Anderson, G.S. and N.R. Huitson. 2004. Myiasis in pet animals in British Columbia: The potential of forensic entomology for determining duration of possible neglect. *Can Vet J.* 45:993–998.

Arkow, P. and H. Munro. 2008. The veterinary profession's roles in recognizing and preventing family violence: The experiences of the human medicine field and the development of diagnostic indicators of non-accidental injury. In *The international handbook of animal abuse and cruelty: Theory, research and application*, ed. F.R. Ascione, pp. 31–58. West Lafayette, IN: Purdue University Press.

Baldwin, K., J. Bartges, T. Buffington, L.M. Freeman, M. Grabow, and D. Ostwald. 2010. AAHA Nutritional Assessment Guidelines for Dogs and Cats. *J Am Anim Hosp Assoc.* 46:285–296.

Beirne, P. 1997. Rethinking bestiality: Towards a concept of interspecies sexual assault. *Theor Criminol.* 1:317–340.

Blitzer, H.L., K. Stein-Ferguson, and J. Huang. 2008. *Understanding forensic digital imaging.* Burlington: Academic.

Bradley, N. and K. Rasile. 2014. Recognition and management of animal sexual abuse. *Clinician's Brief.* 73–77.

Bradley-Siemens, N. and A.I. Brower. 2016. Veterinary forensics: Firearms and investigation of projectile injury. *Vet Pathol.* 53:988–1000.

Brondani, J.T., K.R. Mama, S.P.L. Luna et al. 2013. Validation of the English version of the UNESP—Botucatu Multidimensional Composite Pain Scale for assessing postoperative pain in cats. *BMC Vet Res.* 9:143.

Brown, D.C., R.C. Boston, J.C. Coyne, and J.T. Farrar. 2008. Ability of the canine brief pain inventory to detect response to treatment in dogs with osteoarthritis. *J Am Vet Med Assoc.* 233:1278–1283.

Capra, A., L. Marazzina, and M. Albertini. 2009. Are pit bulls different? Behavioral evaluation within a rehabilitation program of ex-fighting dogs. *J Vet Behav.* 4:76.

de Siqueira, A., S.E. Campusano Cuevas, F.A. Salvangi, and P.C. Maiorka. 2016. Forensic veterinary pathology: Sharp injuries in animals. *Vet Pathol.* 53:979–987.

Dinnage, J.D., J.M. Scarlett, and J.R. Richards. 2009. Descriptive epidemiology of feline upper respiratory tract disease in an animal shelter. *J Feline Med Surg.* 11:816–825.

Gerdin, J.A., S.P. McDonough, R. Reisman, and J. Scarlett. 2016. Circumstances, descriptive characteristics, and pathologic findings in dogs suspected of starving. *Vet Pathol.* 53:1087–1094.

German, A.J., S.L. Holden, T. Bissot, P.J. Morris, and V. Biourge. 2009. Use of starting condition score to estimate changes in body weight and composition during weight loss in obese dogs. *Res Vet Sci.* 87:249–254.

Gordon, L.E., C. Thacher, and A. Kapatkin. 1993. High-rise syndrome in dogs: 81 cases (1985–1991). *J Am Vet Med Assoc.* 202:118–122.

Greco, D.S. 2014. Pediatric nutrition. *Vet Clin North Am Small Anim Pract.* 44:265–273.

Greenbaum, A.R., J. Donne, D. Wilson, and K.W. Dunn. 2004. Intentional burn injury: An evidence-based, clinical and forensic review. *Burns.* 30:628–42.

Hellyer, P., I. Rodan, J. Brunt, R. Downing, J. Hagedorn, and S. Robertson. 2007. AAHA/AAFT pain management guidelines for dogs and cats. *J Fel Med Surg.* 9:466–480.

Hellyer, P.W., S.R. Uhrig, and N.G. Robertson. 2006a. Canine acute pain scale. http://www.csuanimalcancercenter.org/assets/files/csu_acute_pain_scale_canine.pdf (Accessed October 21, 2016).

Hellyer, P.W., S.R. Uhrig, and N.G. Robertson. 2006b. Feline acute pain scale. http://www.csuanimalcancercenter.org/assets/files/csu_acute_pain_scale_feline.pdf (Accessed October 21, 2016).

Hielm-Björkman, A.K., R. Hannu, and R. Tulamo. 2009. Psychometric testing of the Helsinki Chronic Pain Index by completion of a questionnaire in Finnish by owners of dogs with chronic signs of pain caused by osteoarthritis. *Am J Vet Res.* 70:727–734.

Intarapanich, N.P., E.C. McCobb, R.W. Reisman, E.A. Rozanski, and P.P. Intarapanich. 2016. Characterization and comparison of injuries caused by accidental and non-accidental blunt force trauma in dogs and cats. *J Forensic Sci.* 61:993–999.

Kahneman, D. 2011. *Thinking, fast and slow.* New York: Farrar, Straus and Giroux.

Kumar, K., I.V. Mogha, H.P. Aithal et al. 2008. Determinants of bone mass, density and growth in growing dogs with normal and osteopenic bones. *Vet Res Commun.* 33:57–66.

Laflamme, D. 1997a. Development and validation of a body condition score system for dogs. *Canine Pract.* 22:10–15.

Laflamme, D. 1997b. Development and validation of a body condition score system for cats: A clinical tool. *Feline Pract.* 25:13–18.

Landsberg, G.M., W.L. Hunthausen, and L.J. Ackerman. 2013. *Behavior problems of the dog and cat*, 3rd ed. Edinburgh: Saunders/Elsevier.

Lorenz, M.D. 2009. The problem-oriented approach. In *Small animal medical diagnosis*, 3rd ed., ed. M.D. Lorenz, T.M. Neer, and P. DeMars, pp. 3–12. Ames, IA: Wiley-Blackwell.

Marsh, N. 2014. *Forensic photography: A practitioner's guide.* West Sussex: John Wiley & Sons, Ltd.

Merck, M.D., D.M. Miller, and R.W. Reisman. 2013a. Neglect. In *Veterinary forensics: Animal cruelty investigations*, 2nd ed., ed. M.D. Merck, pp. 207–232. Ames, IA: Wiley-Blackwell.

Merck, M.D., D.M. Miller, R.W. Reisman, and P.C. Maiorka. 2013b. Blunt force trauma. In *Veterinary forensics: Animal cruelty investigations*, 2nd ed., ed. M.D. Merck, pp. 97–121. Ames, IA: Wiley-Blackwell.

Munro, H.M.C. and M.V. Thrusfield. 2001a. "Battered pets:" Features that raise suspicion of non-accidental injury. *J Small Ani Pract.* 42:218–226.

Munro, H.M.C. and M.V. Thrusfield. 2001b. "Battered pets:" Non-accidental physical injuries found in dogs and cats. *J Small Ani Pract.* 42:279–290.

Munro, H.M.C. and M.V. Thrusfield. 2001c. "Battered pets:" Sexual abuse. *J Small Ani Pract.* 42:333–337.

Munro, R. and H.M.C. Munro. 2008. *Animal abuse and unlawful killing: Forensic veterinary pathology.* Edinburgh: Elsevier.

Nelson, D.G. and K.A. Santucci. 2002. An alternate light source to detect semen. *Acad Emerg Med.* 9:1045–1048.

Newman, S. 2012. The urinary system. In *Pathological basis of veterinary disease*, 5th ed., ed. J.F. Zachary and M.D. McGavin, St. Louis, MO: Elsevier Mosby.

Overgaauw, P.A.M. and V. Nederland. 1997. Aspects of *Toxocara* epidemiology: Toxocarosis in dogs and cats. *Crit Rev Microbiol.* 23:233–251.

Patronek, G.J. 1998. Issues and guidelines for veterinarians in recognizing, reporting, and assessing animal neglect and abuse. In *Recognizing and reporting animal abuse: A veterinarian's guide*, ed. P. Olson, pp. 25–39. Denver, CO: American Humane Association.

Polak, K.C., J.K. Levy, P.C. Crawford, C.M. Leutenegger, and C.A. Moriello. 2014. Infectious diseases in large-scale cat hoarding investigations. *Vet J.* 201:189–195.

Prahlow, J.A. and R.W. Byard. 2012. *Atlas of forensic pathology.* New York: Springer.

Pruett, S.B. 2003. Stress and the immune system. *Pathophysiology.* 9:133–153.

Reid, J., A.M. Nolan, J.M.L. Hughes, d. Lascelles, P. Pawson, E.M. Scott. 2007. Development of the short-form Glasgow composite measure pain scale (CMPS-SF) and derivation of an analgesic intervention score. *Anim Welf.* 16:97–104.

Ressel, L., U. Hetzel, and E. Ricci. 2016. Blunt force trauma in veterinary forensic pathology. *Vet Pathol.* 53:941–961.

Santucci, K.A., D.G. Nelson, K.K. McQuillen, S.J. Duffy, and J.G. Linakis. 1999. Wood's lamp utility in the identification of semen. *Pediatrics.* 104(6):1342–1344.

Stern, A.W. 2013. Starvation due to neglect: A canine case series. *J Vet Sci Technol.* 4(1).

Stern, A.W. and M. Smith-Blackmore. 2016. Veterinary forensic pathology of animal sexual abuse. *Vet Pathol.* 53:1057–1066.

Thompson, M.S. 2013. *Small animal differential diagnosis: A book of lists*, 2nd ed. St. Louis, MO: Elsevier.

Tong, L.J. 2014. Fracture characteristics to distinguish between accidental injury and non-accidental injury in dogs. *Vet J.* 199:392–398.

Tvedten, H. and M.D. Willard. 2012. *Small animal clinical diagnosis by laboratory methods*, 5th ed. St. Louis, MO: W.B. Saunders.

U.S. Department of Justice and National Forensic Science Technology Center. 2013. *Crime scene investigation: A guide for law enforcement.* https://www.nist.gov/sites/default/files/documents/forensics/Crime-Scene-Investigation.pdf (Accessed October 21, 2016).

Whitney, W.O. and C.J. Mehlhaff. 1987. High-rise syndrome in cats. *J Am Vet Med Assoc.* 191:1399–1403.

Wohlsein, P., M. Peters, C. Schulze, and W. Baumgartner. 2016. Thermal injuries in veterinary forensic pathology. *Vet Pathol.* 53:1001–1017.
Woolf, J.A. 2015. How can veterinarians be reporters of animal abuse when they are not taught to recognize it? *J Am Vet Med Assoc.* 247:1363–1364.

6

Forensic Physical Examination of Large Animals

Janice Kritchevsky

Contents

Introduction

This chapter will discuss the considerations one should make when examining live large animals as part of a forensic investigation. The topics that apply to all common species of domestic large animals will be covered first, followed by specific considerations for individual animal species. As is the case more generally, neglect, either due to caretaker incompetence or ignorance, is much more common than outright acts of cruelty. The rural farming population is aging, and lack of care due to dementia or other incapacity of caretakers is often found to be behind incidences of neglect in traditional farm species. In contrast, the livestock that are considered "nontraditional" such as pot-bellied pigs, South American Camelids (SAC), and backyard chicken flocks often suffer due to the inexperience and ignorance of their owners.

The Brambell Commission's Five Freedoms (excellent guidelines for all animals) are a good guide when evaluating any individual animal's circumstances. If the conditions outlined by the Five Freedoms are met, one can assume that the animal's welfare needs have been achieved (Broom 1988). Those freedoms are

1. Freedom from hunger and thirst.
   - There should be potable water and adequate amounts of appropriate feed available.
2. Freedom from discomfort.
   - There should be adequate housing that includes a dry place to rest and shelter from the elements.
3. Freedom from pain, injury, or disease.
   - Appropriate and timely veterinary care as well as adequate husbandry measures including vaccination and parasite control.
4. Freedom to express most normal behaviors.
   - Animals should be housed in a manner that they can express many of their normal behaviors and move normally.
5. Freedom from fear and distress.
   - In the forensic context, this includes being free from deliberate acts of cruelty and housed in a manner that prevents predation.

Assessment of the Physical Environment in Forensic Investigations

Open Air Enclosures

The "outside in" principle applies to forensic examinations of large animals. Before focusing on the individual animals, one should evaluate their living conditions and the overall environment in which the animals reside. Knowledge of normal husbandry practices is extremely helpful, and consulting a producer or veterinarian familiar with the species in question will help ensure that key details are not missed and that situations are not misinterpreted. Sufficient quality and quantity of appropriate feed and potable water should be on the premises. The environment should be free of hazardous materials, and fencing for pastures or other enclosures should be of sufficient size and durability to secure livestock inside the enclosures and limit predator access to commonly predated species such as poultry and small ruminants. Pastures or other fenced areas that contain livestock should be free of trash, farm equipment, and other hazards (e.g., holes and other obstacles, toxic flora). This is particularly important where cattle or horses are housed. Cattle are not particularly picky eaters and are also extremely curious. They will ingest a large variety of toxic or dangerous substances ranging from battery acid to nails. Horses are easily injured on objects that protrude from the ground or from walls or fencing.

There is a great deal of data available on the housing and nutritional needs of production animal species and horses. An excellent resource when evaluating the physical premises is the USDA's *Guide for the Care and Use of Agricultural Animals in Research and Teaching* (2010), often referred to as the "Ag Guide" and the Universities Federation for Animal Welfare (UFAW) *Handbook on the Care and Management of Laboratory and Other Research Animals* (Hubrecht and Kirkwood 2010). Although they are written as resources for institutions, they are clear references that provide minimum space requirements in square feet, specific feed requirements, transportation guidelines, and other husbandry resources including humane euthanasia guidelines for most farm animal species. Unfortunately, guides to the housing and care of SACs are extremely difficult to come by and are usually not based on peer-reviewed literature.

Fencing

Fencing should be in good repair and appropriate for the species. It should represent enough of a visual barrier that animals can see it easily and avoid it. Fencing should be evaluated not only in its ability to keep livestock contained, but also for its ability to prevent predators from entering. This is particularly important with small ruminants and poultry as these species are particularly vulnerable to dog and coyote attacks. If there is standing water or mud there should also be areas that animals can access that are relatively dry, and a shelter to allow animals to avoid the elements should be available. In pastured or range situations, tree copses and other natural windbreaks can take the place of a man-made shelter. If animals are on pasture, it is important to determine whether the pasture represents the sole source of forage or if it is used for exercise and supplemental feeding. If the pasture is the sole source of forage, the stocking density guidelines should be followed for the species in question (Cowlishaw 1969; Jones and Sandland 1974; Singer et al. 2002). Bear in mind that drought or other environmental conditions may alter stocking density and one should always evaluate the animal's body condition score when assessing whether feed intake is adequate. Extremely short cropped pasture with prominent weeds indicates that the pasture is overgrazed, and additional forage in the form of hay should be made available. At times, one might be confronted with a situation where one or two animals are in extremely poor condition while the majority of their herd mates are fine. Potential reasons for this are that the animal is lowest on the totem pole and thus is not allowed access to feed, that it has different metabolic requirements due to breed or life stage, or that it suffers from a disease that causes weight loss.

Indoor Housing

Indoor housing enclosures should be large enough for animals to move freely. The floor should be even and dry. The indoor environment should be well ventilated and have no ammonia odor. If there is an odor or one experiences irritation to the eye or other discomfort, the ammonia content in the air should be measured using a commercial ammonia detector. One should be sure to place the measuring devices at "animal level" so that the inhaled concentration can be estimated. Inhaled ammonia concentrations 5 ppm or less are desirable, and concentrations over 50 ppm can cause respiratory damage and increase an animal's susceptibility to disease. Stall floors should be dry and there should be adequate space for animals to stand and lie down. When in a group housing situation, all animals should be able to access feed and water sources.

Feed

Hay should have no visible mold and a pleasant, neutral odor (Figure 6.1). Round bales which are exposed to the elements may develop a crust of discolored, spoiled hay, but should contain good quality forage on the inside where animals can reach it. When a bale is opened up, one should not see a large amount of dust or particulate matter released. The hay should consist of grass and/or legume with few visible weeds. If there is a question about the plant makeup of a hay bale, several core sections can be sent to a USDA or other diagnostic laboratory or feed testing service for analysis (Clarkson 2012). Grain and other nutritional supplements should be secured in rodent-proof containers, kept in a dry location, and have no visible evidence of mold or spoilage. If grain smells like a musty basement or is spoiled, it should not be fed to animals. Avoid exposure, as is possible, to vermin housing in the bedding and feed.

Figure 6.1 Visible mold on hay. Picture courtesy of Dr. Laurent Couëtil, Purdue University.

Individual Animal Identification

Unless one is dealing with an extremely large herd or flock, animals should be examined individually with a separate medical record generated for each animal. One should attempt to identify the animal using any permanent identification if that is present. The USDA APHIS supplies permanent ear tags and published guidelines on their use in animals that move across state lines or are sent to slaughter (USDA APHIS 2017).

Photographs of each animal and body condition scoring using published guides are part of the minimum database that should be included in the medical notes and forensic investigation documents. If possible, a hands-on, complete physical examination should be performed as well. White markings, scars, hair whorls, and any other identifying characteristics should be noted. The presence of halters, collars, leg bands, and plastic ear tags should be noted although these are not considered a permanent identification (Neary and Yager 2002). In horses, llamas, and alpacas, implanted microchips are commonly used (various placement locations in the body for each species) for permanent identification and a detector should be used to check for their presence. A microchip may be placed in any animal, so scanning an unknown animal of another species should be considered as well. Microchips are inserted in the rostral neck or within the nuchal ligament in horses and at the base of the ear or the tail in camelids (Canadian Llama and Alpaca Association 2016), so scanning for their presence should concentrate on those areas. The nose prints in ruminant species can be as individual as a fingerprint in a human. Nose printing is often used to identify sheep and cattle, particularly if they are entering exhibitions or sales. Newer computerized pattern recognition software is being developed which greatly facilitates nose print analysis, which in turn may lead to a wider application of this technique (Noviyanto and Arymurthy 2013). Breed registries often require purebred sheep, goats, and cattle to be tattooed on the inside of the ear (location varies with the species). Some producers of nonregistered stock also elect to tattoo their animals for record-keeping purposes. Horses that have raced may be tattooed on their inside upper lip. Freeze branding is performed on cattle and horses. Finally, hot branding is still performed in cattle and horses although its use is discouraged for humane reasons.

Plastic ear tags (some with radio frequency identification [RFID] chips) are the most common form of identification for cattle, sheep, goats, and swine. Larger tags are easier to read, but are prone to being ripped out. Small metal ear tags can be considered a form of permanent identification, but are difficult to read unless the animal is well restrained. Metal leg bands are considered permanent identification in poultry although there is some evidence they alter normal behavior (Dennis et al. 2008). Swine are often identified by ear notching. Notches are taken out of the skin of the ear in a pattern that is unique for that animal. Ear notching can theoretically be used in cattle and other species, but it is only commonly performed in commercial swine (Neary and Yager 2002).

Temporary identification can be made via paint sticks, marking crayons, or the application of tags using glue designed for this purpose. Marking animals within a herd can greatly facilitate evaluation of larger groups of animals. Finally, definitive identification of an individual animal can be made through DNA testing (Cassidy and Gonzales 2005).

Body Condition Score

External evaluation of any animal begins with the assessment of whether it is too thin, too fat, or in the proper condition. Body condition scoring should only be performed on a live, standing animal. The abdomen of an animal in lateral or sternal recumbency is often displaced, which can be extremely misleading. To aid in this assessment, body condition scoring (BCS) charts have been developed. Although they differ somewhat between species, the overall premise is the same in all (Table 6.1). BCS evaluates how well the skeleton is covered by subcutaneous fat and muscle on key points of the body (Cabiddu et al. 1999; Henneke et al. 1983; Herd and Sprott 1969; Maes et al. 2004; Russel et al. 1969; Van Saun 2009; Wildman et al. 1982). These areas are the rib cage, the tail head or pelvis, the loin or crease down the back, and the neck. Most often BCS are given in a 9-point scale although some 5-point scales exist. A condition score of 1 is the thinnest an animal can be on most scales, although some may rate 1 as most conditioned and 5 or 9 as the least (Figures 6.2 through 6.4). For that reason, when reporting an animal's BCS, the overall numbers in the scale, what the number means in lay language, and which BCS scheme being used should be specified. For example, an extremely thin horse that has been assigned a BCS score of 2 would be reported as: "The horse has a body condition score of 2 out of 9. A BCS of 2 is considered very thin." Ideal condition is

Table 6.1 Body Condition Score

Body Condition Score	Description	
1	Poor, emaciated	No fat and minimal muscle, all skeletal structures easily visible
2	Extremely thin	Minimal fat and muscle, all skeletal structures visible
3	Thin	All ribs visible, prominent spinal processes but some fat and muscle along spine
4	Slightly thin	Some ribs visible, slight fat cover, spinous processes not visible but can be palpated. No muscle loss
5	Moderate	Right amount of fat cover, no muscle loss Just last ribs can be seen, spinal process can be palpated but not seen
6	Moderately fleshy	Ribs not visible, hindquarters smooth and rounded. Visible fat around tail head
7	Fleshy	Spine and ribs felt with firm pressure. Fat cover over entire body
8	Obese	Ribs difficult to feel, spinous process lowest point on back, tail head covered by fat
9	Extremely obese	No visible skeletal or muscle definition, patches of fat subcutaneously

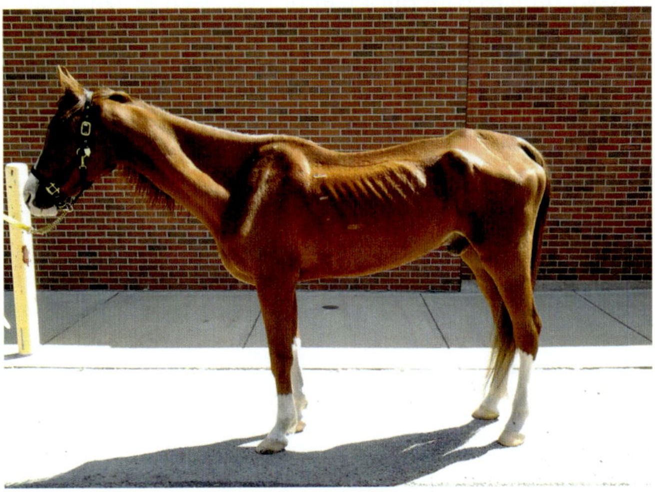

Figure 6.2 Extremely thin (BCS 1.5) horse. Note that one can appreciate most skeletal structures including cervical vertebrae.

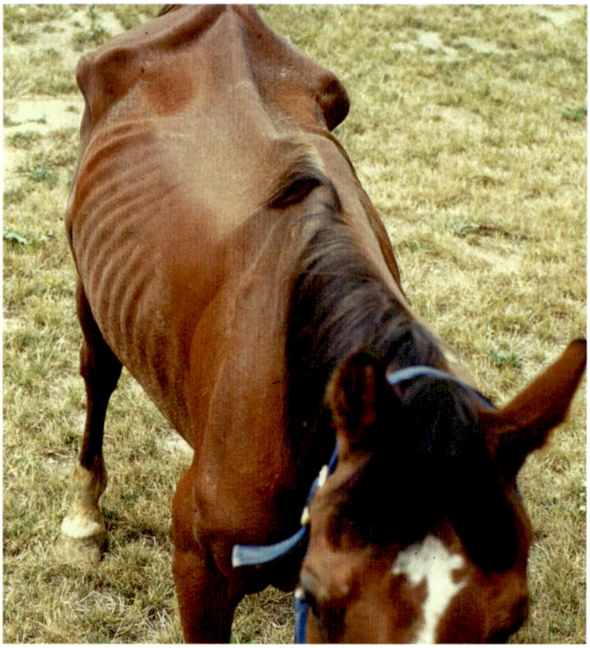

Figure 6.3 Extremely thin horse (BCS 1.5) as viewed from above. Vertebral spinous processes are easy to appreciate.

between 4.5 and 6.5 on a 9-point scale, where an animal's bony prominences can be felt upon palpation but they are covered by muscle or fat and not easily visualized. In animals with thick hair or wool such as llamas, alpacas, and sheep, one must physically palpate the animal to determine a BCS as the coat obscures all other features.

The advantage of a BCS system is that it is semiquantitative and thus removes subjective impressions from the process. One person's "good dairy character" is another one's "painfully thin," and that difference in opinion can be difficult to explain to a third party. The second advantage is that it helps concentrate the evaluation of condition to the musculoskeletal system. Animals with distended abdomens, subcutaneous edema, or extremely thick fleece or hair coats may be judged to be fat by a person not familiar with the species. By evaluating the cover over the ribs, backbone, and pelvis, a better estimate of the animal's condition can be made. Assigning a BCS score should be part of the record of any animal that is being examined for forensic purposes. Determining a BCS of an animal with a short hair coat from photos or videotape can be done with the same degree of accuracy and agreement between observers as from a live inspection (Ferguson et al. 2006). It is not possible in a heavily fleeced animal such as an unshorn sheep or camelid, or in a horse with a heavy winter hair coat or the hypertrichosis that is found with pituitary pars intermedia dysfunction.

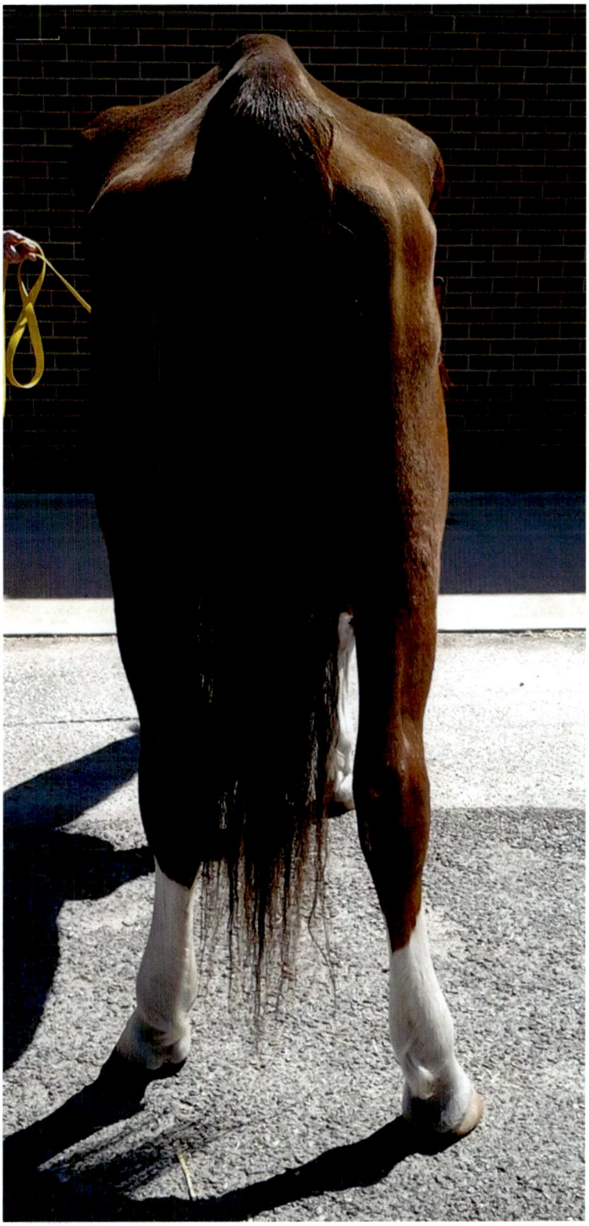

Figure 6.4 Back view of a thin horse (BCS 1.5). Note that the sacrum is the tallest part of the silhouette.

Medical Record

As is the case in small animal practice, an accurate, complete medical record is essential for a successful prosecution of animal neglect or cruelty. It is a legal document, and the record should be clear, timely, and accurate. The record needs to definitively identify each individual animal examined, including the age, breed, reproductive status, color, markings, and any other distinctive features. Unless the age, weight, and breed are definitively known, it should be clearly stated in the record that these are estimates. For example, a black beef cow that looks like an Angus should be referred to as an "Angus-type" unless the registration has been documented. The number and condition of other animals on the premises should also be noted. A careful history should be obtained, and any prior medical records should be located and attached. The person giving the history and their relation to the animal should be noted. In addition to the physical examination findings, the animal's behavior, attitude, and awareness of its surroundings should be recorded. All entries in a written record should be legible, written in ink, and the person making the entry should sign and date their work. In the case of an error, the correction should be made by placing a line through the words that should be struck and initialing the correction. One should never erase or completely obscure the original wording.

A written medical record should be secured in a locked area until all the legal issues surrounding the case have been resolved. Medical and forensic records will be made available for reciprocal discovery (the other side can review original notes and all documentation); therefore, it is important to avoid personal notes and nonprofessional comments within the records. Laboratory results, radiographs, and photographs should be clearly labeled with the case and time obtained and included with the rest of the record. An electronic medical record should be password protected, and saved in a way that ensures control of access. They must remain available throughout the entire legal process.

Refeeding Syndrome

Rehabilitating starved herbivores is extremely difficult and requires a great deal of time. Even with the best of care, it can take 3 to 5 months to bring a starved horse back to its original condition (Whiting et al. 2005). Managing an animal that is too weak to stand is particularly difficult, and being down is associated with a poor prognosis as is being less than 50% of normal body weight. Recumbency in an animal over 500–600 pounds often results in pressure sores, muscle compression injury, and/or impaired ventilation. One may find that using a sling to assist the animal to rise and help them support their weight is extremely helpful. Unless the sling is designed to support the animal via the skeleton without putting pressure on the viscera, it should only be used to assist the animal to rise and then taken off (Ishihara et al. 2006). Hip lifters in cattle can cause a great deal of soft tissue trauma and should be used as infrequently as possible. In addition to the morbidity attendant with being down, herbivores are quite susceptible to refeeding syndrome. Refeeding syndrome is the term given to the metabolic and physiologic derangements associated with caloric repletion of the starved human patients (Solomon and Kirby 1990). Refeeding syndrome has been documented in horses (Witham and Stull 1998). Chronic starvation results in the breakdown of muscle tissue, including cardiac muscle, shrinking of the circulating plasma fluid volume, and atrophy of the gastrointestinal tract. Starvation also results in the depletion of whole body stores of phosphorus and magnesium (Marinella 2003). To maintain homeostasis, the serum concentration of phosphorus remains constant at the expense of intracellular stores. If a starved animal is given a high-carbohydrate meal, the sudden increase in serum glucose concentration stimulates insulin secretion. The high insulin facilitates the entry of glucose into cells, along with the phosphorus needed to generate ATP and energy as well as potassium and magnesium. This can result in a sudden decrease in serum phosphorus, which in turn can cause respiratory failure, seizures, red blood cell lysis, and cardiac arrhythmias or arrest. Serum phosphate concentrations less than 0.50 mmol/L can produce the clinical features of refeeding syndrome (Marinella 2003).

Prevention of refeeding syndrome can be best accomplished by being aware that any animal that has been starved with a BCS of 2 or less is at risk. In addition to documenting emaciation, a complete physical examination including blood testing for serum electrolyte concentrations and fecal analysis for parasite burden should be performed to rule out an underlying medical problem contributing to the animal's emaciated state.

The first 10 days of rehabilitation is the most critical period, and most problems arise within 5 days of feeding. It is best avoided by slowly reintroducing low-carbohydrate feed and supplementing magnesium and phosphorus. In small animals and humans, supplementing with omega-3 and -6 fatty acids and glutamine is believed to be beneficial as well. The best way to provide a high protein and mineral, low carbohydrate feed in an herbivore is to offer alfalfa hay. It was found that alfalfa hay alone produced better results when rehabilitating starved horses than feeding a complete diet or grass hay (Witham and Stull 1998). The initial amount fed must be limited in horses, as they will eat more quickly than their stomach can empty, leading to megaesophagus. Initially horses should be fed 1 pound of alfalfa hay every 4 hours, which can be gradually changed to 4 pounds hay every 8 hours in 7 days, which, in turn, can be increased to free choice alfalfa at 2 weeks (Witham and Stull 1998). Grain and fat can be added to the diet at 1 month in low amounts and then gradually increased. One can expect an increase in energy and strength within 2–3 weeks, but it may be several months before appreciable weight gain occurs. Although death by starvation in ruminants is well documented, there are no published reports of refeeding syndrome in ruminants that were near starvation and then rehabilitated. However, the same principles of providing high protein feed applies. Giving the affected animal rumen fluid from a healthy animal may help speed return to normal gastrointestinal function in ruminants and camelids.

Tachycardia is extremely common in animals that are being refed. It does not mean that they are in pain or distress. It will resolve as cardiac mass increases and extracellular fluid volume stabilizes. Similarly, refeeding increases carbon dioxide production and oxygen consumption. The animal is not able to compensate easily by increasing their ventilation because the respiratory musculature has atrophied due to starvation. The consequence is an increase in minute ventilation causing tachypnea (Solomon and Kirby 1990). Again, as muscle mass improves, the respiratory signs will resolve.

Nonaccidental and Other Forms of Traumatic Injury

There is a paucity of literature on nonaccidental injury in large animals. There are some case reports of individual acts of abuse, but it has not been evaluated in a systemic fashion. In addition to injury by humans (including gun and arrow projectiles) (Figure 6.5), large animals are prey species that can

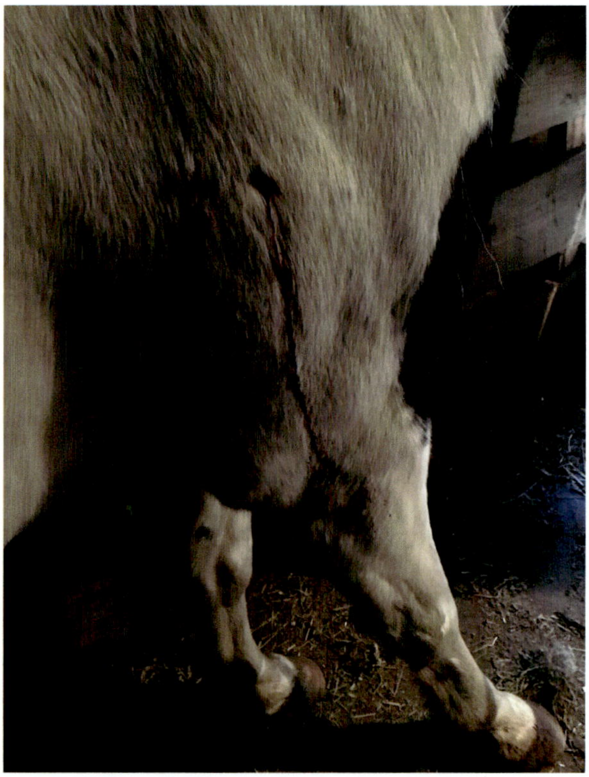

Figure 6.5 Bullet wound (entry site) found in a horse's shoulder. Picture was taken immediately after the injury was found.

be attacked by domestic dogs and wild predators. The principles that apply in the diagnosis and treatment of traumatic injury in other species such as cats and dogs, however, also apply to large animals. Except for some horses, most pastured animals maintain a minimum distance from humans, termed their flight zone, and will not allow themselves to be caught easily. This may help prevent being directly struck by objects or weapons. Pastured animals are quite susceptible to missiles in the form of rocks, pellets, bullets, and arrows. At times, they are hit not as deliberate acts of cruelty but because they are mistaken by hunters as game species.

A complete physical examination including ancillary diagnostics such as radiographs is needed to assess the degree of primary injury and secondary complications in instances of traumatic injury (Figure 6.6). Once this has occurred, a medical plan for treatment and supportive therapy should be made if possible. If the injury is to a limb so that the animal is nonweight bearing, humane euthanasia should be considered unless recovery is likely.

The injuries suffered should be well documented in the medical record. This includes a written description of the number and type of wounds as well as photographic evidence. The animal's identification data and a scale such as a measuring stick should be added to each photograph. Additionally, the time and date the photograph was taken should be recorded (be aware that most digital images contain metadata that may include date, time, and sequential photo number) and photographs should not be deleted even if they are of poor quality. Each wound should be photographed from a distance so that its location on the animal's body is clear, then at closer and closer ranges down to a close-up view of the wound.

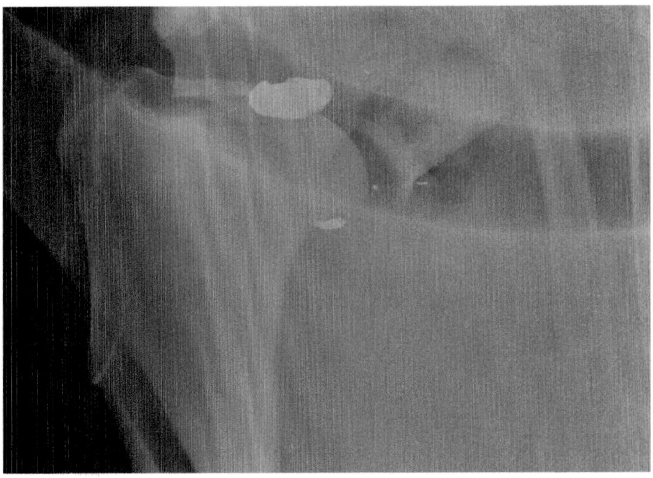

Figure 6.6 Lateral view of the scapula from the horse in Figure 6.5. Note the presence of a single, large bullet fragment and several small bullet fragments, and fracture of the scapula at the shoulder joint.

Predator Attacks

Surveys of small animal emergency room admissions have found that dog attack is the second most common cause of traumatic injury reported (Hall et al. 2014). The precise numbers have not been compiled in large animals, but it is an extremely frequent occurrence, and easily one of the most common types of traumatic injury. Different species of carnivores attack prey in different ways and thus leave different patterns of wounds. To document the attacking species or individual, the area surrounding and within wounds can be swabbed for the predator's saliva and submitted for DNA analysis. For more information regarding DNA testing, the reader is referred to Chapter 11 (DNA Evidence Collection and Analysis). Additionally, all wounds should be photographed as described above.

Coyotes and wild Felidae such as lynx, cougars, and bobcats are selective, attacking one animal at a time. They kill animals with either one or a small number of bites, most often to the neck. Eagles and hawks (birds of prey) grab prey from the top, often over the back, and may leave puncture wounds and lacerations.

Predator aggression is a normal behavior in canines, and most dogs can never be safely kept with prey species (Borchelt 1983). Some dog breeds such as the Akbash and Great Pyrenees are excellent livestock guardian dogs and stay with the herd they are to protect. Dogs do not set out to efficiently kill livestock. They purse and chase fleeing animals, biting them and then letting go. Because of this behavior pattern, most victims of dog attacks suffer from multiple bites to the legs and rear quarters (Figure 6.7). This results in many puncture wounds and lacerations. In addition to bite trauma, many bite wound victims have additional medical problems. Shock occurs due to extensive tissue injury or blood loss. Myositis resembling capture myopathy may be present if animals are chased/over-exercised before and after being bitten. Animals may also suffer injures while running to avoid pursuing dogs. In one survey, 11 of 15 large animals that presented with dog bites had multiple puncture wounds, lacerations, and areas of missing skin on their rear legs, thighs, perineal region, and a tail (Sojka 1995) (Figure 6.8). Poultry and waterfowl can also present with similar injuries due to dog attacks (Figure 6.9). Two presented with wounds that were on the cervical area without hind limb involvement. One horse suffered lacerations when it ran into a fence, and one llama suffered lumbar spinal cord damage as it jumped to avoid an attack. Complications included nerve damage resulting in inability to walk normally, jugular vein thrombosis, myoglobinuria, and clostridial myositis (Sojka 1995). Usually, the dogs were owned by the livestock owner or known by the livestock owner. Because the bite wounds are contaminated and are accompanied by surrounding crush injury, victims of dog attack tend to have prolonged recoveries, even with prompt treatment.

Exposure to Toxic Substances

There are many different classes of toxic substances that are used in agricultural production, and thus have the potential to cause injury or death in large animals that are inadvertently exposed. These include insecticides, herbicides,

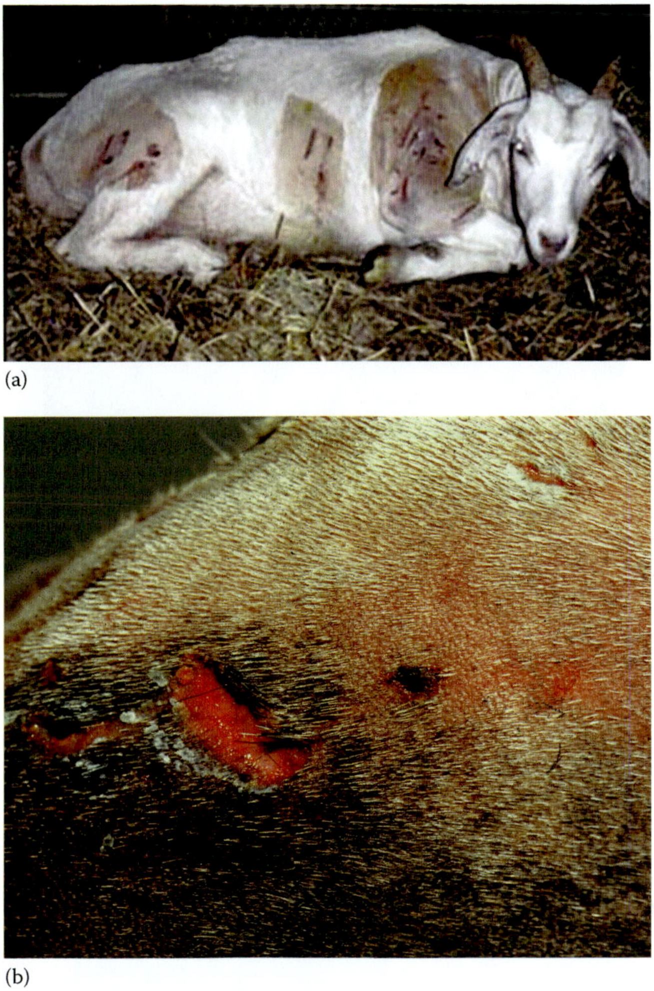

Figure 6.7 (a) A goat that has been attacked by dogs. The goat presented with multiple puncture wounds and myositis. (b) Close-up of the bite wounds.

and petrochemicals, as well as toxic plants, which may be present on pasture or mold or poorly maintained feed, incorporated into hay or silage. Calculation or mixing errors may result in feed additives and/or supplements being incorporated into diets in toxic concentrations. An example of this is the deaths of several valuable polo ponies due to an improperly compounded vitamin/mineral supplement resulting in acute selenium toxicity. In addition to accidental exposure to toxic substances, animals may also be the victims of deliberate poisoning. In the case of deliberate intoxication, the ensuing legal action would be pursued in criminal or civil courts. Inadvertent toxicity that results in animal loss may lead to legal claims in civil court or require expert analysis

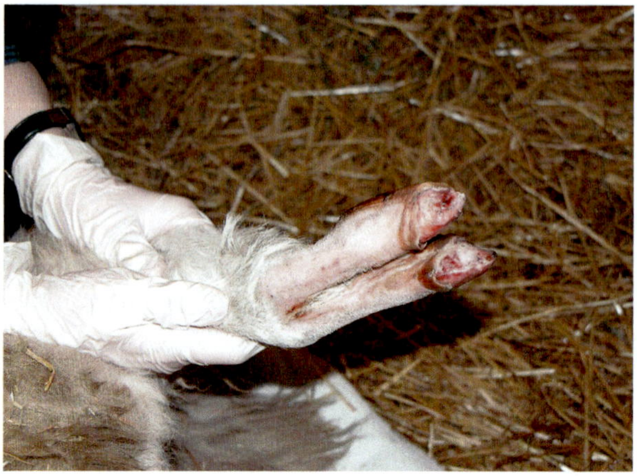

Figure 6.8 De-gloving injury in an alpaca that was attacked by dogs resulting in the loss of the rear claws.

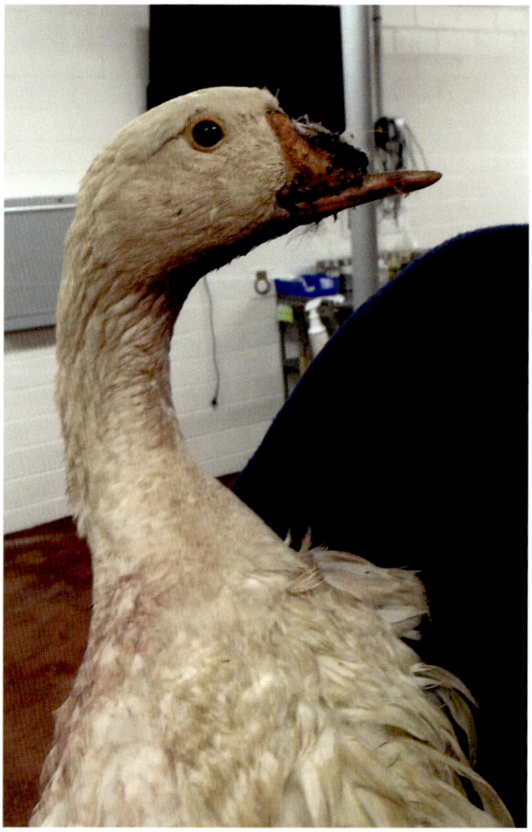

Figure 6.9 A goose with an avulsed upper beak due to a dog attack.

for insurance purposes. In all instances, an accurate diagnosis, supportive blood analysis, feed analysis, and stomach contents should be collected and sent to the appropriate laboratories considering the chain of custody. Finally, all physical evidence should have proper chain of custody documentation.

In a case of acute illness or death in a single group or multiple groups of animals, the means to a successful prosecution is to gather all forensic information in a coordinated and well-documented method. If allegations cannot be supported by the physical and medical evidence or there are reasonable differential diagnoses possible, one must question whether the case should proceed (Murphy 2007). In general, this decision would be made either by the prosecutor, in a criminal case, or by the plaintiff in a civil case.

Unfortunately, often diagnostic samples and other evidence are not secured because there was no initial index of suspicion that the animal suffered from a toxic insult when first examined. At times this cannot be avoided, but these occurrences will be minimized if a careful, complete history is obtained and correct chain of custody procedures observed if there is even a limited suspicion that the case will become part of a legal proceeding. Any laboratory used for diagnostic purposes should be told that submissions are potentially evidence and one should receive assurances that the laboratory is able to handle them in an appropriate manner (chain of custody). Often a rapid turnaround time and minimal cost must be sacrificed to achieve accurate, precise results, and one should not be surprised if analytic reports come more slowly than usual.

Historical items that might lead one to suspect a toxicity include a recent change of feed or moving into a new environment, having more than one previously healthy animal in a group suffer from similar clinical signs simultaneously, animals that suffer from disease or failure in more than one organ system, and clinical signs that are highly suggestive of a specific toxin exposure. For example, even though there is more than one cause for hemolytic anemia in horses, the development of hemolytic anemia in a herd of horses shortly after a storm has caused branches from surrounding red maple trees to fall into their pasture is close to absolute evidence of red maple toxicity. Similarly, the sudden development of cardiac failure in a group of previously healthy cattle that have recently been switched to a monensin-containing feed should make one extremely suspicious of a mixing error or miscalculation and that too much monensin was added when the feed was formulated.

Samples that should be obtained if possible from a live animal in cases of a suspected toxicity include: 20–30 mL blood submitted in heparinized tubes, urine, and vomit in the case of swine. If possible, at least 2 kg of wet or fermented feeds and 1 kg dry feed should be submitted when one suspects an ingested toxin. Wet feeds, forage, and plants can wilt rapidly and will ferment if placed in plastic bags, so they should be shipped to the laboratory in sealed paper evidence bags. If possible, the entire plant may be sent including samples to an agriculture college for identification. If the plants are too large to be sent as the entire specimen, complete leaves wrapped in newspaper, and any distinguishing parts such as flowers and seedpods or fruits should be included. Dry feeds such as grains, straw, and hay should be sent in sealed plastic bags. Samples of hay and straw should be taken from several bales or areas within a bale if only one bale is available. Hay samples from the middle, outer layer, and in between position should be submitted from a round bale. Any discolored or moldy portions of feed should be sent with a description of their location within the bale. Silage or other fermented feeds should be placed in airtight plastic bags with as much of the air removed as possible before shipping. Finally, if water contamination is suspected, at least 2 L of water should be submitted (Lorgue et al. 1996). The pasture or other areas where the animals were housed should be inspected by a person who knows what toxic plants are indigenous to the area and how to identify them in all stages of growth. For more information about toxicology, the reader is referred to Chapter 13 (Veterinary Forensic Toxicology).

Horses

A horse's temperament is defined by genetic predisposition, training, and experience. Until one handles an individual horse, there is no way to estimate how it will react in a given situation. For that reason, one should be aware of a horse's body language and other cues it may be sending before performing an examination. For more information about equine behavior, the reader is referred to Chapter 12 (Animal Behavior for the Forensics Specialist). Horses may develop aversions to situations or events that are associated with painful or frightening associations or that the horse finds inherently frightening. Many horses are averse to dark, enclosed spaces, which makes them difficult to load onto trailers. A horse's aversion to a situation should not be indicative of past abuse. Donkeys and mules are more stoic than horses but can be more difficult to examine. One should always be sure that a donkey or mule is well restrained before proceeding with an examination.

When possible, it is best to have a complete physical examination including dental evaluation and relevant blood testing performed by a veterinarian. In the case of neglect, blood would be submitted for routine chemistry and complete blood count to assess organ function and whether anemia is present. If drug administration or toxicity is suspected, it may be submitted to a veterinary diagnostic laboratory. It is important to contact the laboratory prior to submitting samples from suspected cruelty cases. Failure to follow laboratory guidelines may result in rejection of the requested analysis. Prior to that, however, a general visual examination can be performed by anyone familiar with normal equine behavior and appearance. A horse in good physical condition acts aware of its surroundings and reacts to movement and noises. They should walk or trot willingly when led and place equal weight on all limbs. Horses normally spend most of their waking hours eating, and a lack of interest in food is abnormal. Horses should be able to ingest, chew, and swallow without dropping any food or saliva from their mouths. Horses ingest 1–2% of their weight in dry matter per day. Thus, a 1000-pound horse should be fed between 10 and 20 pounds of hay daily (University of Maine 2016). Normal horse manure is formed into approximately fist-sized fecal balls with little or no additional fluid. Normal heart rate in adult equids is between 28 and

44 beats per minute and body temperature is 99–101°F. A horse that is excited, frightened, or has just exercised may have a higher heart rate and body temperature. If the vital signs remain elevated once the animal appears calm and rested, one can suspect a medical problem. A horse that has been starved loses cardiac muscle and has a decreased cardiac output when compared to a normal animal. As it is being refed, the circulating fluid volume increases and the only way the heart can compensate is by increasing its rate. Thus, tachycardia in a horse that is being refed does not necessarily indicate pain or distress, but is an expected reaction. Heart rates as high as 100 beats per minute may be found in a horse as it is being successfully rehabilitated. Tachypnea is also common in horses that are being refed as atrophied respiratory muscles accommodate an increase in oxygen consumption and carbon dioxide production. Respiratory rate should return to normal as muscle mass returns. The eyes should be clear and held open. Any nasal or ocular discharge except for a small amount of clear fluid is abnormal. The horse should be willing to have each hoof picked up, although a horse that has not been trained to do this may not. The legs should be symmetric and the joints should not be swollen or painful to the touch. A horse that is unwilling to move or will not bear weight on a leg requires immediate veterinary attention. Any equipment the horse is wearing should be assessed for tightness; it should be loose enough to move freely and not cause pressure, but not so loose that it may entangle a hoof. Tack that is too tight can cause sores, pressure necrosis, and/or skeletal deformities. Sway back or lordosis is a genetic defect that becomes more pronounced as a horse ages and it *is not* a sign of malnutrition or overuse.

Careful examination of the mouth is a part of a physical examination. While a speculum is required to inspect every back molar, one can do a fair assessment by unassisted visual inspection. Permanent incisors erupt annually, so that a horse up to the age of 5 can be aged by counting the number of permanent versus deciduous incisors. After 5 years, alterations in the appearance of the teeth can be used to determine the age, although the nature of the forage a horse eats has a bearing on how quickly the teeth are worn. Thus, the older a horse becomes, the more unreliable the teeth become to determine the exact age. The table surface of the molars should be smooth, and the breath should not be fetid or otherwise smell bad. The hair coat should be uniform and free from areas of hair loss or breaks in the skin. Rain rot, caused by *Dermatophilosus congolensis*, is characterized by firm clumps of hair over the topline. It is a common finding in horses that are not groomed frequently and spend most of their time outdoors. It is difficult for full thickness skin wounds over the distal extremities to heal by contraction and epithelization (second intention), particularly if they are over high-motion areas. Untended wounds can be prone to become covered with excess granulation tissue and may remain in a static, nonhealing state for months or years.

Hooves should be normal shape and symmetric. Normally, the weight of the animal is born by the walls and frog of the hoof, the sole should not touch the ground. Abnormal growth rings indicate a time when the metabolism of cells at the coronary band have altered by a physiologic event (Figure 6.10).

Figure 6.10 Hoof ring in a horse that had recovered from infectious disease and transient laminitis. The change in the hoof wall coincides with a time when there was abnormal growth at the coronary band.

One can roughly time the event by measuring the distance from the coronary band—hooves grow an average of 8 mm/month. Thus, an abnormal growth ring that is 32 mm away from the coronary band occurred 4 months earlier. The time between hoof tissue being formed on the coronary band and then reaching the ground is approximately 1 year's time. If a horse is examined and has abnormal growth evident in the entire hoof, it is fair to say that this defect has been present for a year or more. Abnormal hoof growth is the hallmark of laminitis. Horses with chronic laminitis that do not receive proper hoof care develop extremely elongated hooves, sometimes referred to as "sled" or "ski jump" hooves (Figure 6.11). Their presence is a sign of neglect.

Horses are herd animals with defined social hierarchies. Dominance is asserted through biting and kicking, and horses can inflict serious and even life-ending injury to each other (Figure 6.12). Injuries are most common when animals are first introduced before dominance hierarchies have been established. Injury can occur either through direct trauma or when a submissive animal is chased into fences or other hazards. Geldings and mares can be mixed safely, but stallions are usually pastured individually to prevent injuries to other animals and must be carefully handled by experienced equine staff.

How a horse manifests pain depends on the body systems involved. If pain is due to a visceral problem such as colic, pain will manifest as rolling, kicking at the flanks, and looking at its side. Musculoskeletal pain is manifest by reacting when the painful area is touched, and not bearing weight on the painful area. A horse that has extreme pain in more than one leg may be reluctant to move or spend most of the day lying down. Nonspecific indicators of pain in horses include an increased heart rate and respiratory rate, decreased appetite, swishing the tail, grinding teeth, and a "sour" disposition.

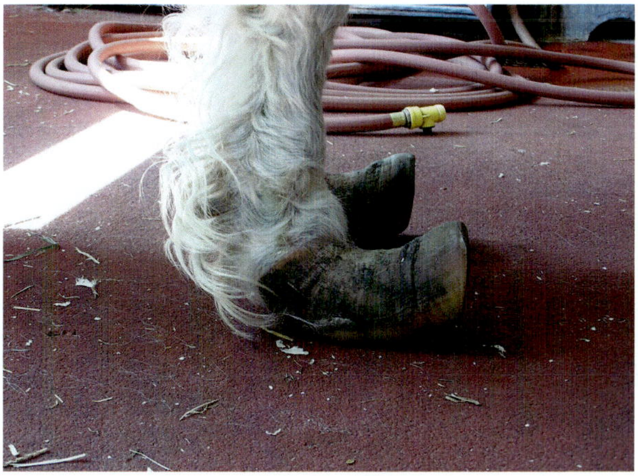

Figure 6.11 Severely overgrown "ski jump" hooves in a pony with chronic laminitis.

Special Circumstances

In addition to nonaccidental injury and neglect, there are specific instances where horses that are otherwise well taken care of can be considered abused. In most instances, these occur in an attempt to alter a horse's appearance or performance for showing or racing reasons.

Soring

Soring, the practice of placing irritating substances on the pastern, heel bulbs, and coronary band area of Tennessee Walking Horses, was made illegal through federal legislation in 1970 (American Veterinary Medical Association 2013). It has been deemed a cruel and unethical practice by the American Veterinary Medical Association and most, if not all, state abuse statutes. A horse that is sored produces an exaggerated gait which is desired in the show ring. Often affected areas are covered by bandages or other materials to mask the open wounds and scar tissue that occurs. Other methods to cause pain in the front feet are the application of heavy chains on the pastern or adding pressure-causing devices to the shoes. To determine if a horse is sored, one must examine the skin of the pastern for areas of alopecia, scar tissue, and open wounds. The shoes should be removed to make sure they are not applying pressure to the sole. Tennessee Walking Horse shoes can be extremely thick due to the practice of adding stacks of material and may require a trained farrier to remove safely. Unfortunately, the pain associated with soring cannot always be readily distinguished from naturally occurring reasons for bilateral front limb lameness such as navicular disease.

Because soring is illegal under federal law, the USDA is charged with ensuring that it does not take place. They certify horse industry organizations, which in turn certify inspectors to examine horses before and after they are shown. Inspectors examine the horse, particularly the lower front limbs, and observe them at a walk for signs of lameness. Because Tennessee Walking

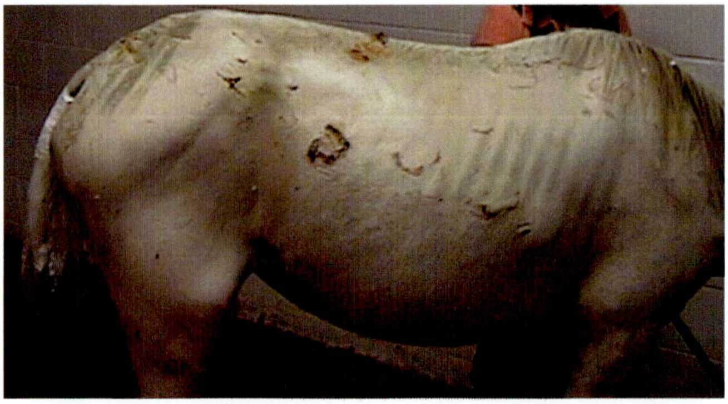

(a)

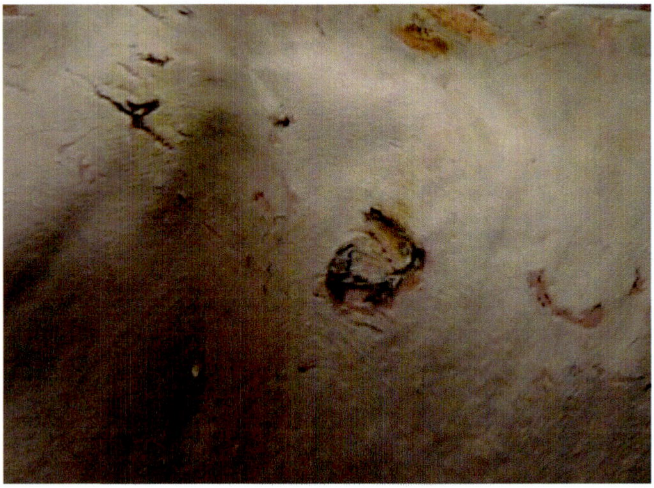

(b)

Figure 6.12 (a) Traumatic injury in a yearling that was turned out in the same pasture as an older stallion. Note the multiple kick marks and bruising. (b) Close-up of the injuries.

Horses have a 4-beat gait and do not trot, it is extremely difficult to evaluate lameness in the breed compared to other show horses. Inspectors may use chemical detectors to evaluate swabbed samples from the coronary band area. They are forced to do this because subtle forms of soring are impossible to detect any other way.

Gingering

To achieve a very animated disposition and an elevated tail in breeds such as Hackneys, Saddlebreds, and Arabians, substances are placed in the rectum or perineal region prior to entering the show ring. The practice is called "gingering" because the original substance used in this manner was ginger. Many other irritating and caustic substances have been used including cayenne, iodine, and turpentine. Over time, dermatitis and scarring of the perineal area can occur. The practice is strictly illegal, and "ginger testing" is sometimes performed at shows by taking swabs for chemical testing. Thermography can also be used to detect changes in skin and anal temperature associated with the practice (Turner and Scoggins 1985). Because many horses resent manipulation of the tail and perineal regions, one cannot assess whether an irritating substance has been placed in the area by virtue of the horse's behavior alone.

Alcohol Epidural

A horse that is kicked by its rider will often twitch its tail in response. This is considered a fault in horses that are exhibited in Western pleasure classes. To prevent any tail movement, some dishonest individuals will administer an alcohol epidural, which causes prolonged or permanent paralysis of the tail (American Veterinary Medical Association 2012). This practice is most common in Quarter Horses, but can also be seen in other breeds that exhibit in Western pleasure classes such as Paint and Appaloosa. An alcohol tail block should be suspected in a Western pleasure horse that appears to have partial or complete loss of voluntary movement of the tail. Additionally, ascending myelitis and other neurologic problems that occur in horses that are exhibited in Western pleasure classes should raise the index of suspicion that the horse received this procedure. Most horses will reflexively clench their tails when they are elevated and the perineal area is stimulated. A block can be definitively diagnosed by performing an EMG on coccygeal muscles.

Drugs and Other Banned Substances

All pari-mutuel racing jurisdictions, American Quarter Horse Association, and U.S. Equestrian Federation–sanctioned events have clear laws prohibiting the use of drugs and other banned substances. Most other governing bodies that sanction horse shows or exhibitions have similar prohibitions on their books as well. Random drug testing is performed to ensure compliance with these laws. The most common type of infraction identified are overages, where a permitted substance is detected in a blood concentration that is over a predefined limit. There are times when illegal substances are knowingly given with the intent of altering the animal's performance. To detect illegal drug use in horses, postperformance testing is conducted regularly in the case of race horses or randomly in the case of show horses. This usually means securing blood and urine although saliva or hair samples are collected occasionally. Once the samples are collected, they are sealed and strict chain of custody is observed as they are sent to a testing laboratory. Blood is collected into serum separator tubes so that serum can be obtained without opening the tube or disturbing any materials that are sealing the tube. If administration of a banned substance is suspected (based on performance, postrace symptoms, or the presence of unexplained injection sites) outside of a racing or show jurisdiction, multiple blood samples should be collected into evacuated plain, ethylenediaminetetraacetic acid (EDTA), or citrate tubes for analysis (consult the testing laboratory for the most appropriate sample). In all instances, multiple blood tubes are collected and at least one is frozen for confirmatory or reciprocal defense analysis at a later date.

Cattle

Cattle and other food animals have a defined flight zone, and generally will not allow humans to walk up to them without attempting to escape. This trait doubtlessly protects cattle from direct attack by humans, but can make examination difficult. Normal behavior for a cow is for it to be aware of its surroundings and extremely curious about new objects, but to maintain a definite distance between itself and humans. They normally stand up hind end first, and can look quite awkward. This should not fool an examiner to think they cannot stand up extremely quickly when motivated. They should walk or trot easily without lameness. Before attempting to examine anything but the youngest calf, one should assure that the animal is adequately restrained. This will prevent injury to both the examiner and the animal.

Neck tags, leg bands, and ear tags should be noted and recorded. Additionally, the inner ear should be examined for tattoos. Female cattle, particularly dairy cows, may have an ear tattoo indicating that they were vaccinated against Brucellosis when they were calves. The normal pulse and temperature for calves are 101–103°F and 100–140 beats per minute, respectively. Cows have normal temperatures of 100–102°F and heart rates of 50–80 beats per minute. Both will increase if the animal is excited or has recently exercised. Gastrointestinal health is best determined by assessing rumen contractions. These can either be auscultated or palpated on the left paralumbar fossa. During a rumen contraction, the rumen pushes up against the skin, and this motion can be detected when one's hand is resting lightly on the space. Healthy ruminants will experience 1–2 rumen contractions per minute. If the animal is extremely stressed or agitated, rumen contractions may be absent. If normal cud chewing is observed, one can assume that rumination is occurring normally. A cow will normally eat 2.5–3% of its body weight per day in dry matter intake (United States Department of Agriculture 2016). They will not eat if water is not available, and when faced with an anorexic cow, one should first ensure that it has access to water. Normal cow manure is unformed and has the consistency of custard. Ruminants have no upper incisors, cattle ingest food by pushing their lower incisors against a dental pad. Permanent incisors can be differentiated from deciduous teeth, and a new pair of permanent incisors erupts annually from the ages of 1 to 4. Thus, a cow's age can be accurately determined until all their permanent incisors have erupted and are in wear. Animals should have no swellings or pain over any joint and should walk easily bearing weight on all four hooves evenly. A cow that is reluctant to stand when approached is not normal. In female animals, the udder should be uniform in size and be free of skin ulceration. The teats should appear symmetrical and the orifice should not be ulcerated or discolored. Dairy cattle are more angular than beef breeds, and there are separate BCS charts for dairy and beef cattle (Herd and Sprott 1969; Wildman et al. 1982). When evaluating the condition of an individual, the appropriate body condition scoring chart (beef or dairy) should be used.

The hair coat should be smooth and without disruptions in the skin. Many cattle in muddy or dirty environments have caked mud on their legs, underbelly, and brisket. This indicates the amount of dirt in the environment, but does not represent a welfare concern unless it inhibits animal movement. The claws should be symmetric and the interdigital space clean and free of ulceration. Cattle resent being handled closely, and in most instances special equipment such as a squeeze chute or tilt table is needed to carefully examine hooves and interdigital spaces. Like horses, cattle can develop laminitis, which is evident by prominent rings and abnormal growth of the hoof.

In general, cows of different sizes and gender will coexist on pasture with less friction than horses. However, smaller animals will be pushed away from limited food sources by larger cows which may result in under-condition or even starvation. If there is not adequate feeder space, animals should be separated or a second food source should be provided. Younger smaller animals may be ridden by bulls, which can cause considerable trauma and pregnancy in heifers younger than recommended for safe calving. For these reasons, bulls are usually housed separately unless they are being used to breed cows.

Cattle are quite stoic, and may mask pain. Musculoskeletal pain is manifest by limping and spending most of the time in sternal recumbency. A cow experiencing severe musculoskeletal pain may refuse to stand, and this should be considered a cause of being a "downer cow." Nonspecific signs of pain include vocalization, anorexia, teeth grinding, grunting, and depression or dullness.

Small Ruminants: Sheep, Goats, South American Camelids

Sheep, goats, and South American camelids (llamas and alpacas) are prey species that are notoriously stoic. Additionally, many have fleece or extremely long hair coats, making visual examination difficult. A thorough physical examination always requires putting hands on and palpating the animal. Because most have a highly defined flight distance, this usually requires catching and then restraining the animal in some way. Normal temperature and heart rate for sheep, goats, and SAC are 102–103°F, 101–104°F, 99–102°F, and 60–90, 70–80, and 60–90 beats per minute, respectively. Small ruminants are extremely poor at thermoregulation, and body temperatures as high as 105°F can be observed after a small amount of exercise or if the animals have been housed in direct sunlight during hot days. Body condition scoring sheets are available for all species (Cabiddu et al. 1999; Russel et al. 1969; Van Suan 2009). Unless the animals have been recently shorn, it is imperative that BCS scoring be done in conjunction with palpation.

Camelid claws and sheep and goat hooves should be symmetric and not overlong. In most animals, this requires at least annual trimming. Overgrown hooves or claws predispose to hoof rot and can cause distortion in the weight bearing surfaces, which may lead to lameness. Permanent incisors erupt annually in a manner similar to cattle, and thus sheep and goats' ages can be accurately determined up to the age of 4. Camelid canine teeth erupt at 5 years of age, and they can be aged up to that point. Small ruminant and camelid feces are normally pelleted and dry. Alpacas and llamas will defecate and urinate in a single location within an enclosure in piles called latrines. Despite this behavior, internal parasites are a common finding and a large source of morbidity in camelid species.

Good fencing is exceedingly important for small ruminants. Goats are good climbers and jumpers, and can be difficult to keep inside enclosures. They often will not attempt to escape if they have companions, but go to lengths to get close to other animals. Except for those animals pastured on federal lands, predator attacks by dogs is by far the most common cause of traumatic injury. In addition to secure fencing, adding a guard animal such as a purpose-bred dog or donkey can discourage predation.

Small ruminants and camelids are extremely social animals that are stressed when not in the company of others of their species. All ages and sexes can be mixed although intact males are generally kept separate unless there is a specific desire to have offspring. Lambs and bucks can attain sexual maturity at a very young age, and they should be castrated while quite young or separated from females to prevent misbreeding.

Signs of pain in sheep and goats are generally similar to cattle although they are notoriously stoic and can show little pain even after having suffered from severe injury. Camelids rest in a cushed state with their front and rear legs tucked under their body. An alpaca or llama that is experiencing abdominal discomfort may sit with both its rear legs thrust to the side.

Swine

There are two distinct populations of pigs that might require a forensic examination. These are commercial hogs, those that are raised to go through marketing channels for food, and miniature pet pigs such as pot-bellied pigs and other similar breeds.

Commercial Pigs

By and large, commercial hogs are owned by experienced farmers who are familiar with their nutritional and husbandry needs. The breeds of swine used in commercial operations are fast growing and only boars and sows used for breeding reach adult sizes. There are numerous resources available that describe humane handling and treatment of pigs in the context of a commercial swine operation including space and other environmental needs in swine at all stages of growth (Lammers et al. 2007; Purdue University Cooperative Extension Service 2010).

Physical examination of swine is often limited by their reluctance to be handled in any way. Healthy animals should have a moderate BCS (4 or 5 out of 9) and bright eyes with no ocular or nasal discharge. Pigs should be able to get up and walk and trot easily with no obvious lameness or gait abnormality. The skin should be clean and free of any ulceration or other lesions. Pigs, particularly those that are recently mixed, will fight to establish dominance. This may result in bruising, abrasions, and lacerations.

Miniature Pigs

In contrast to commercial hogs, pigs that are kept as pets are often owned by individuals with no prior experience with swine care or husbandry. They are kept in their owner's dwellings in urban or suburban areas, their humane care in some instances might be assured by animal control or local humane societies. Finding reputable information can be difficult as most swine professionals do not concern themselves with miniature pet pigs. As one might expect, the vacuum of information has resulted in a plethora of Internet sites and "experts" that offer dubious information. Whenever possible, guidelines taken from the peer-reviewed and scientific literature should be referenced (Braun and Casteel 1993; Hubrecht and Kirkwood 2010; Tynes 1999). From a regulatory standpoint, miniature pigs are swine, and subject to all the vaccine, testing, and pharmaceutical restrictions of commercial animals. Antibiotics and other substances that are banned in food-producing animals are technically illegal in pet pigs, although there is little mechanism to enforce this directive. Many mini-pigs are well socialized and submit to being picked up and otherwise handled. When stressed, such as when being examined by a stranger or after having suffered an injury, they revert to the tendency to resent handling and to object by squealing extremely loudly. A screaming pig is not necessarily in pain, and if one is not familiar with normal swine behavior, their resistance to restraint can be misinterpreted as a painful reaction to an injury. Pigs often mask their pain, but may appear lethargic, separate from other individuals in their litter, or lie with a huddled appearance. Pigs will vocalize when they want to be fed, no matter what their nutritional status, and squealing when they anticipate feeding is not a sign of starvation. A pig that anticipates food will often make chewing motions and experience increased salivation, which can be misinterpreted as frothing at the mouth.

Most miniature pigs, even those labeled "micro" or teacup, usually reach adult weights between 80 and 100 pounds. The actual adult size is extremely difficult to predict; one should not assume that a smaller adult pig has been starved or mistreated. Any sized pig should be of at least average body condition score and have some degree of subcutaneous fat. Commercial swine feed, dog food, cat food, and horse sweet feed is too nutrient-dense to be fed to pet swine. Many pet pigs become grossly overweight, which can lead to musculoskeletal problems such as degenerative joint disease and the ultimate result of an animal unable to rise. Miniature pigs of any type should receive 1.5–3% of their body weight daily in a stage-appropriate mini-pig feed supplemented with low caloric density greens (Tynes 1999).

Signs of musculoskeletal pain include limping and reluctance to stand. Extreme musculoskeletal pain can result in a pig that is completely unwilling to rise. Nonspecific signs of pain include lethargy, hiding under bedding, anorexia, and resenting handling in any form.

Poultry

Like swine, commercially raised poultry are unlikely to be the subject of forensic investigations. They are raised in protected systems by individuals that have familiarity with the husbandry needs of the species. Only in cases of malicious intervention or gross negligence would they become a subject of investigation. There are many resources available that deal with the proper humane care of poultry in a wide range of management systems, providing guidance for individuals who do not work with the species daily (Jacob 2015; Ross Industries 2014).

With the rise of the backyard chicken and an increased interest in local sourcing of eggs and poultry, there are increasing numbers of birds kept by individuals with little prior poultry experience. Chickens are the most popular backyard bird, but ducks are gaining in popularity as well. The temperament and size of geese and turkey serve to limit their appeal. First and foremost, chickens require secure housing as they are susceptible to a wide range of predators, both wild animals and domestic pets. Additionally, allowing the mixing of chickens with wild birds such as sparrows and starlings may lead to the spread of avian diseases. A coop that has one small opening may permit a weasel or other small land predator to enter. If the top of the coop is not covered, hawks or eagles can predate domestic birds. Locking poultry inside during the night helps decrease their susceptibility to attack. The forensic veterinarian must be aware of the rise of avian flu in domestic fowl and the implications for agroterrorism. Concerns are heightened when human travelers have completed travel to areas with endemic foreign animal disease.

There are BCS scoring systems (Gregory and Robins 1998) available for birds, which are concentrated on evaluating the muscling and subcutaneous fat over the keel. Because of overlying feathering, the keel must be physically palpated to gain a body condition score (Gregory and Robins 1998). The keel should be palpable, but the muscle of the breast should protrude beyond it. The eyes and nostrils should be clear and the head and feet free of sores or other lesions. The feathers should be clean and lie smoothly against the bird, and the vent should be clean and dry. In addition to there being a secure enclosure, poultry should be provided a place to get out of the elements and to perch if they are a perching species. There should be clean food and nonsoiled water available. Feed should be appropriate for the species and life stage. This is particularly important for egg-layers as producing shells requires a great deal of calcium, and the dietary calcium requirements for laying birds is quite high. If the calcium needs are not met, birds are susceptible to osteoporosis and bone fractures. The keel and legs are the bones most often affected.

Birds engage in aggressive behaviors toward each other, and dominant animals can kill less aggressive flock mates. This may be improperly assessed

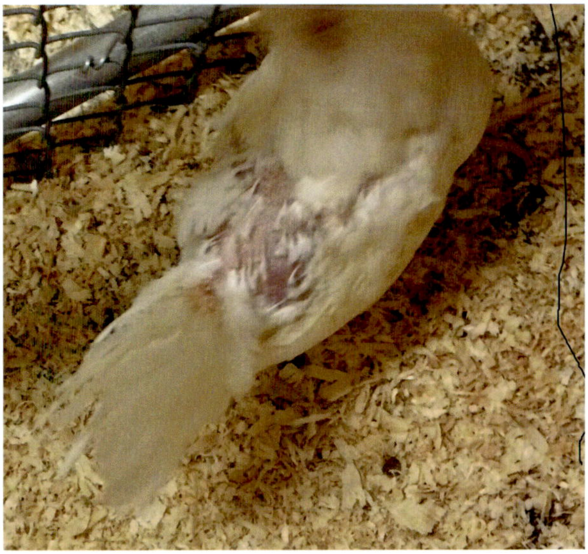

Figure 6.13 Loss of feathers in a hen that was housed with a rooster.

as animal cruelty. Providing adequate housing space and forms of environmental enrichment such as dirt baths can minimize inter-bird aggression. Loss of feathers on a bird, anywhere on its body and at any stage of life, can be due to pecking by another bird (Sedlackova et al. 2004). Often birds are attracted to a damaged area on the picked-on bird, so injured animals should be removed from the flock quickly to prevent further trauma. Roosters can be aggressive breeders and will harass hens. Loss of feathers on the back is seen in hens that are being over-bred by roosters (Figure 6.13). Housing the sexes separately or adding more birds to improve the hen to rooster ratio usually improves the situation. There should be 8–10 hens for every rooster in the flock. Unfortunately, in most instances other types of traumatic events result in the death of the bird or in animals that are so badly injured that humane euthanasia is required.

Cockfighting

Cockfighting occurs when two roosters from aggressive breeds are allowed to fight each other, usually until one of the birds is dead. It is illegal in many industrialized countries and it is banned in all 50 states in the United States. Breeds used for cockfighting are Bantam type birds such as the Shamo, Asil, Tuzo, or Old English Game Bantam. Like fighting dogs, roosters go through several weeks to months of training prior to a scheduled fight. During this time, they may be fed specialized diets, vitamin and mineral supplements, given anabolic steroids, and conditioned on treadmills or over courses (The American Society for the Prevention of Cruelty to Animals 2016). They can be put into practice fights with less aggressive roosters. Before fighting, their wattles and comb will be cut off to prevent them from injury, and most of their feathers may be plucked off as well. During a fight, knives or artificial spurs, called gaffs (dagger-like attachments), are often placed over the bird's natural spurs. These weapons increase the severity of injury when two birds fight. In some instances, the natural spur is sharpened and no additional weapons are used.

What separates a premise with birds designed for cockfighting from other poultry housing is their unique method of maintaining individual roosters on tethers or in individual cages. One should be suspicious of fighting if one sees birds housed individually, the presence of fighting breeds, the presence of gaffs and other fighting paraphernalia, first aid materials, and specialized feeds and medicine. One might also observe large numbers of dead birds on the premises, and postmortem examination would show traumatic injury as the cause of death in many of these animals.

Conclusion

Examination of the living animal is of utmost importance in any investigation of animal cruelty. Documentation of abnormal findings such as wound and body condition scores is of value and would provide information that may support or refute case findings. Use of other forensic modalities such as DNA testing may be of value and sample collection during the time of examination may be warranted. Evaluation of a large animal in cases of neglect will be of value to rule out underlying natural disease as a cause of the emaciated condition of an animal. In addition to the clinical examination of an animal, any laboratory findings should be complete and recorded in the medical record.

By far the most common intervention of a forensic veterinarian in large animal medicine is monitoring an animal for abuse or lack of good husbandry practices. These poor practices can lead to classic signs of animal abuse, "starvation," or "poor doer." There are active abuse situations that can exist and must be investigated with an open mind-set to ensure a complete, appropriate, and thorough case conclusion.

References

American Veterinary Medical Association. 2012. Literature review on the welfare implications of horse tail modifications. https://www.ams.usda.gov/rules-regulations/organic/handbook/5017-1 (Accessed September 27, 2016).

American Veterinary Medical Association. 2013. Soring: Unethical and illegal. https://www.avma.org/KB/Resources/Reference/AnimalWelfare/Documents/soring_in_horses_factsheet.pdf (Accessed September 27, 2016).

Borchelt, P. L. 1983. Aggressive behavior of dogs kept as companion animals: Classification and influence of sex, reproductive status and breed. *Appl Animal Ethology.* 10:45–61.

Braun, W. F., and S. W. Casteel. 1993. Potbellied pigs: Miniature porcine pets. *Vet Clin North Am Small Anim Pract.* 23:1149–1177.

Broom, D. M. 1988. The scientific assessment of animal welfare. *Appl Anim Behav Sci.* 20:5–9.

Cabiddu, A., Branca, A., Decandia, M., Pes, A., Santucci, P. M., Masoero, F., and L. Calamari. 1999. Relationship between body condition score, metabolic profile, milk yield and milk composition in goats browsing a Mediterranean shrubland. *Livestock Prod Sci.* 61:267–273.

Canadian Llama and Alpaca Association. 2016. http://www.claacanada.com/microchip_information.php (Accessed September 27, 2016).

Cassidy, B. G., and R. A. Gonzales. 2005. DNA testing in animal forensics. *J Wildlife Management.* 69:1454–1462.

Clarkson, N. 2012. Horse hay: How to identify the good stuff. http://www.horsetalk.co.nz/2012/11/04/horse-hay-how-to-identify-the-good-stuff/#axzz48XlDHdMe (Accessed September 27, 2016).

Cowlishaw, S. J. 1969. The carrying capacity of pastures. *Grass Forage Sci.* 24: 207–214.

Dennis, R. L., Fahey, A. G., and H. W. Cheng. 2008. Different effects of individual identification systems on chicken well-being. *Poultry Sci.* 87:1052–1057.

Ferguson, J. D., Azaro, G., and G. Licitra. 2006. Body condition assessment using digital images. *J Dairy Sci.* 89:3833–3841.

Gregory, N. G., and J. K. Robins. 1998. A body condition scoring system for layer hens. *N Z J Ag Res.* 41:555–559.

Hall, K. E., Holowaychuk, M. K., Sharp, C. R., and E. Reineke. 2014. Multicenter prospective evaluation of dogs with trauma. *J Am Vet Med Assoc.* 244:300–308.

Henneke, D. R., Potter, G. D., Kreider, J. L., and B. F. Yeats. 1983. Relationship between condition score, physical measurements and body fat percentage in mares. *Equine Vet J.* 15:371–372.

Herd, D. B., and L. R. Sprott. 1969. Body condition, nutrition and reproduction of beef cows. Texas A &M University Agricultural Extension Service B-1526. http://oaktrust.library.tamu.edu/bitstream/handle/1969.1/87723/pdf_62.pdf?sequence=1&isAllowed=y (Accessed September 27, 2016).

Hubrecht, R. H., and J. Kirkwood. eds. 2010. *The UFAW Handbook on the Care and Management of Laboratory and Other Research Animals*, 8th edition. Hoboken, NJ: Wiley-Blackwell Publications.

Ishihara, A., Madigan, J. E., Hubert, J. D., and R. S. McConnico. 2006. Full body support sling in horses. Part 1: Equipment, case selection and application procedure. *Equine Vet Edu.* 18:219–222.

Jacob, J. 2015. Raising chickens for egg production. http://articles.extension.org/pages/71004/raising-chickens-for-egg-production (accessed September 27, 2016).

Jones, R. J., and R. L. Sandland. 1974. The relationship between animal gain and stocking rate: Derivation of the relation from the results of grazing trials. *J Agric Sci.* 83:335–342.

Lammers, P. J., Stender, D. R., and M. S. Honeyman. 2007. Niche pork production. https://pdfs.semanticscholar.org/5b70/080a78846de6fadf6451a96dd6d13fb80470.pdf (Accessed September 27, 2016).

Lorgue, G., Lechenet, J., and A. Riviere. 1996. Samples for laboratory analysis. In: *Clinical Veterinary Toxicology*. Cambridge, MA: Blackwell Science, pp. 19–29.

Maes, D. G. D., Janssens, G. P. J., Delputte, P., Lammertyn, A., and A. de Kruif. 2004. Back fat measurements in sows from three commercial pig herds: Relationship with reproductive efficiency and correlation with visual body condition scores. *Livestock Prod Sci*. 91:57–67.

Marinella, M. A. 2003. The refeeding syndrome and hypophosphatemia. *Nutr Rev*. 61:320–323.

Murphy, M. J. 2007. *Toxicology and the Law. In Veterinary Toxicology: Basic and Clinical Principles*. R. C. Gupta, Ed. pp. 110–128. New York: Academic Press.

Neary, M., and A. Yager. Methods of livestock identification. Purdue University Extension AS-556-W, 2002. https://www.extension.purdue.edu/extmedia/as/as-556-w.pdf (Accessed September 27, 2016).

Noviyanto, A., and A. M. Arymurthy. 2013. Beef cattle identification based on muzzle pattern using a matching refinement technique in the SIFT method. *Comput Electron Agric*. 99:77–84.

Purdue University Cooperative Extension Service. 2010. *The Pork Industry Handbook*. Purdue University Press, West Lafayette.

Ross Industries. 2014. *Broiler Management Handbook*. http://en.aviagen.com/assets/Tech_Center/Ross_Broiler/Ross-Broiler-Handbook-2014i-EN.pdf (Accessed September 27, 2016).

Russel, A. J. F., Doney, J. M., and R. G. Gunn. 1969. Subjective assessment of body fat in live sheep. *J Agric Sci*. 72:451–454.

Sedlackova, M., Bilcik, B., and L. Kostal. 2004. Feather pecking in laying hens: Environmental and endogenous factors. *Act Vet Brno*. 73:521–531.

Singer, J. W., Bamka, W. J., Kluchinski, D., and R. Govindasamy. 2002. Using the recommended stocking density to predict equine pasture management. *J Eq Vet Sci*. 22:73–76.

Sojka, J. E. 1995. Epidemiology and treatment of dog attack. The 13th Annual American College of Veterinary Internal Medicine (ACVIM) Forum. 693–695.

Solomon, S. M., and D. F. Kirby. 1990. The refeeding syndrome: A review. *J Parenter Enteral Nutr*. 14:90–97.

The American Society for the Prevention of Cruelty to Animals. 2016. Cockfighting. http://www.aspca.org/animal-cruelty/other-animal-issues/cockfighting (Accessed September 27, 2016).

Turner, T. A., and R. D. Scoggins. 1985. Thermographic detection of gingering in horses. *Eq Vet Sci*. 5:8–10.

Tynes, V. V. 1999. Potbellied pig husbandry and nutrition. *Vet Clin North Am Exot Anim Pract*. 2:193–207.

United States Department of Agriculture. 2017. Animal Disease Traceability. https://www.aphis.usda.gov/aphis/ourfocus/animalhealth/SA_Traceability (Accessed April 3, 2017).

United States Department of Agriculture. 2016. 5017-1: Calculating dry matter intake from pasture. https://www.ams.usda.gov/rules-regulations/organic/handbook/5017-1 (Accessed September 27, 2016).

University of Maine. 2016. Cooperative Extension Bulletin #1006, Pasture and hay for horses. https://extension.umaine.edu/publications/1006e/ (Accessed April 3, 2017).

USDA. *Guide for the Care and Use of Agricultural Animals in Research and Teaching.* 2010. http://www.fass.org/docs/agguide3rd/Ag_Guide_3rd_ed.pdf (Accessed September 27, 2016).

Van Saun, R. J. 2009. Nutritional requirements and assessing nutritional status in camelids. *Vet Clin Food Anim.* 25:265–279.

Whiting, T. L., Salmon, R. H., and G. C. Wruck. 2005. Chronically starved horses: Predicting survival, economic, and ethical considerations. *Can Vet J.* 46:320–324.

Wildman, E. E., Jones, G. M., Wagner, P. E., Boman, R. L., Troutt, H. F., and T. N. Lesch. 1982. A dairy cow body condition scoring system and its relationship to selected production characteristics. *J Dairy Sci.* 65:495–501.

Witham, C. L., and C. L. Stull. 1998. Metabolic responses of chronically starved horses to refeeding with three isoenergetic diets. *J Am Vet Med Assoc.* 212:691–696.

7

The Forensic Necropsy

Adam W. Stern and Mee-Ja Sula

Contents

Introduction

The external and internal examination of the body (by dissection) of an animal following death is known as a necropsy or postmortem examination. The forensic necropsy is similar to the forensic autopsy, as both have a more specific focus compared to the standard diagnostic necropsy and autopsy, respectively. For all postmortem examinations, the cause of death may be determined; however, in the forensic necropsy in addition to determination of the cause of death, one may also determine the manner of death, the postmortem interval, and/or collect evidence. In some instances, the postmortem examination may be inconclusive whereby a cause of death is not determined. All findings identified during the forensic necropsy should be documented utilizing notes and photographs. Upon completion of the forensic necropsy the pathologist will generate a report that integrates the pathological findings with any specialized tests performed.

During the forensic necropsy there may be documentation of different types of injuries and/or natural diseases. In many instances, the forensic necropsy is performed in cases of sudden and unexplained death or when a violent death is suspected. Sudden death is defined as death that occurs within seconds to minutes of the onset of clinical signs, traumatic injury, or with no warning (Panella and Hodge 2013). The forensic necropsy should also be performed in cases of suspected neglect, as in the case of suspected starvation (Gerdin et al. 2016; Stern 2013). In such cases, evidence of natural disease with a protracted course should be sought out (e.g., cancer cachexia, gastrointestinal disease) as it may explain the emaciated condition of the animal.

Cause and Manner of Death

Determination of the cause of death is one of the primary goals of the forensic necropsy. The cause of death is defined as the etiologically specific disease or injury that initiated the train of events that lead to death (Centers for Disease Control and Prevention 2003; Gerdin and McDonough 2013). The cause of death is divided into the underlying (or proximate) cause of death and immediate cause of death. The proximate cause of death is that in which, in a continuous sequence, unbroken by an efficient intervening cause, produces the fatality and without which the end result would not have occurred. The immediate cause of death is the complication(s) and sequela of the underlying cause.

Manner of death is defined as the category which the individual's death best fits into and is based on the circumstances of how the injury or disease occurred (Illinois Coroners and Medical Examiners Association 2007). Manner of death is divided into two types (natural and non-natural) and further broken down into five standardized categories: natural, accident, suicide, homicide, and undetermined. The category of undetermined is used when information pointing to one manner of death is no more compelling than one or more alternative manners of death, when all available information is considered (Illinois Coroners and Medical Examiners Association 2007). There is no established definition regarding manner of death for veterinary forensics; however, some authors use a similar classification scheme dividing deaths into natural and non-natural (Merck et al. 2013a; Rogers and Stern 2013). The subcategories of accidental and nonaccidental can be used to further classify non-natural manners of death. Some authors feel that manner of death appears to be of little use in veterinary forensics (Gerdin and McDonough 2013). In veterinary medicine, animals with severe injuries and/or disease are often euthanized prior to dying because of the process for which they are euthanized. This must be taken into consideration during the forensic necropsy (Gerdin and McDonough 2013). In such cases, the immediate cause of death would be euthanasia, whereas the underlying cause of death should be the reason for euthanasia (such as a gunshot injury to the chest).

The Forensic Necropsy Procedure

Prior to performing the forensic necropsy, information regarding the animal's previous medical history including diagnostic tests, medical intervention (treatments, procedures), and information regarding euthanasia method (if applicable) should be reviewed. Information about the crime scene including available law enforcement and witness reports, photographs, and/or videos, detailed information with regard to circumstances of how the animal was recovered, stored (such as refrigerated or frozen), and transported, should be made available to the pathologist for review prior to commencing the forensic necropsy. The forensic necropsy is broken down into two main components: the external examination and the internal examination (Table 7.1).

Table 7.1 Suggested Procedures to Be Performed during the Forensic Necropsy
Obtain photographs of the body of the animal including the face, oral cavity, left and right sides, dorsum and ventrum. If the animal is clipped, repeat previous photographs
Obtain trace evidence as required (oral swabs, nail cuttings, etc.)
Photograph and document any external lesions
Remove the skin to visualize the subcutaneous tissue
Open the thoracic and abdominal cavities and examine all organs and structures
Collect formalin-fixed tissues. Consider collecting samples for microbiological studies and/or toxicology testing
Perform histopathology
Determine the cause of death
Determine the manner of death

The external examination provides information such as animal identification including a scan for a microchip, evidence collection, and assessment of patterns of injury. The internal examination includes dissection of the body and assessment of internal organs and structures. If not already begun, chain of custody should commence upon receipt of the animal. The identity of the animal should be verified before accepting the remains for examination.

External Examination

Upon receiving an animal for a forensic necropsy, the bag should be opened and the body of the animal should be immediately photographed inside the bag. The identification of the animal should again be verified with the chain of custody form and case ID# (such as police department case number, unique laboratory identification number). The animal is then placed on the necropsy table at which time the external examination begins. The body should be examined for identifying features such as collars, tattoos, and/or ear tags as well as be scanned for a microchip. The sex of the animal should be documented. At this point swabs of the oral cavity and/or nails should be performed, along with removal of the nails, if required. These samples should be preserved as they may be used at a later date for DNA analysis. Upon collection of any evidence (such as swabs for DNA, projectile recovery), appropriate documentation on a chain of custody form should be completed for each item of evidence. If possible, duplicate samples (i.e., DNA swabs) should be collected. For more information about DNA sample collection, the reader is referred to Chapter 11 (DNA Evidence Collection and Analysis). Radiological studies can be performed at this time. Photographs should be taken throughout the postmortem examination. Personal protective equipment should be worn by anyone performing the postmortem examination of an animal.

In all cases, the animal should be evaluated for rigor and lividity and sites affected should be documented. Odors emitted by the body should also be noted. The body should be examined in both an uncleaned and subsequently cleaned state. The fur of a dog or cat can easily be clipped using electric clippers, and although in large animal species clipping of the entire body might not be practical, if a specific area of interest is identified, clipping is recommended. The entire body should be examined both visually and through palpation. In some cases, the head and/or distal limbs may be submitted wrapped in white linen sheets or with bags over them in an attempt to prevent evidence loss and/or contamination (Merck et al. 2013a). In these instances, when the bags are removed they should be examined for loose evidence and preserved for future analysis.

Photo documentation of patterned injuries and lividity patterns is completed next. Injuries that can be identified during the external examination include gunshot injuries, sharp force injuries, injection sites, burns, and blunt force trauma. For example, if during the external examination multiple puncture wounds are identified and confined to the head, pectoral area, and forelimbs of a dog, this pattern might be suggestive of injuries often encountered in cases of organized dog fighting (Merck 2013). If patterned injuries such as puncture wounds (suggestive of injuries from teeth) are identified, clip the fur around the wound while avoiding areas with visible blood as this would be a good source of potential saliva to be used for DNA analysis (Veterinary Genetics Laboratory 2016). If a gunshot injury is identified, this pattern of injury would support the use of radiological studies to ensure that a more accurate forensic necropsy is performed. Gunshot residue testing may also be used to support the projectile injury being from a bullet rather than a sling-shot projectile or an arrow with a bullet-type point.

Additionally, during the external examination, evidence of medical intervention should be documented. Commonly encountered findings include indwelling IV catheters, injection sites, shaved areas, and/or the presence of electrocardiography electrodes.

Internal Examination

The internal examination begins by placing the body into left lateral recumbency. A full thickness cutaneous incision extending from the ramus of the mandible the entire length of the animal to the pubis is made, circumnavigating the penis and prepuce in male dogs. The skin and limbs are reflected back to expose the musculature of the right lateral abdomen and chest. Soft tissues of the right axilla, extending between the medial aspect of the scapula and lateral chest wall, including the brachial plexus are cut, releasing the forelimb to lay flat. The axillary and prescapular lymph nodes are examined and collected. The joint capsule of the right hip is incised and the joint space evaluated. The ligament of the head of the femur is severed and the hind limb laid flat. The quantity and quality of subcutaneous fat and musculature is documented (Figure 7.1). Large joints including both the femorotibial (stifle)

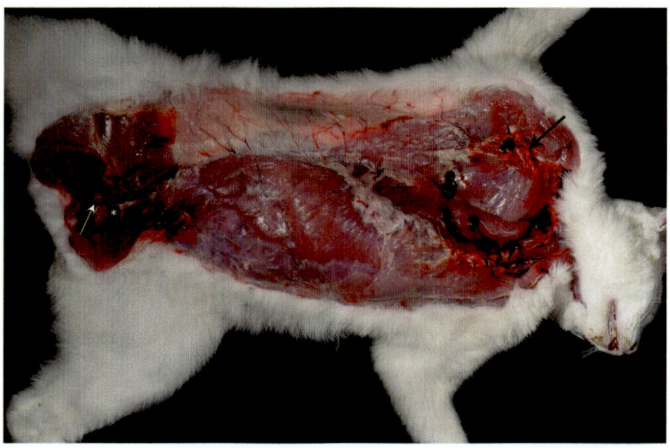

Figure 7.1 Initial approach, whole cat. The animal is left-side down with its right fore and hind limb reflected to reveal subjacent subcutis and musculature. Brachial plexus (black arrow), acetabulum (asterisk), and head of the femur (white arrow).

and scapulohumoral (shoulder) are opened and the character and quantity of the joint fluid and the articular surfaces are evaluated. Additional joints are examined if necessary.

In forensic necropsies, particularly those in which either blunt or penetrating force trauma is possible, complete reflection of the skin, to include the length of the limbs, over the dorsal midline, and the entirety of the down (left side) is required. More extensive reflection allows for ready identification of soft tissue edema and blood accompanying bruising or small lacerations which may be difficult to identify from the haired side of the body. In affected areas, surrounding soft tissues as well as the underlying musculature is explored to determine extent of involvement and to search for foreign objects. Foreign objects may carry hair into the deeper soft tissues, which can be helpful to identify areas of interest for further examination (Figure 7.2).

Foreign objects, such as fragments of bullets or ball bearings (BBs), plastic rifle pellets, arrows, bolts, broken knife blades, and so on may be more readily identified at the time of skin reflection. A projectile traveling through the body will progressively lose momentum, which may prevent it from exiting the body through the tough, highly elastic skin of many animals. This should particularly be suspected when hemorrhage without a cutaneous perforation is identified on the side opposite a puncture wound (Wobeser 1996); keeping in mind that deflection from an otherwise linear trajectory is common when a projectile encounters bone. If a projectile type wound is suspected, attempting to identify the course of trajectory is important to aide in determining the relationship between the shooter and the animal at time of impact. The trajectory cannot often be clearly delineated until all body cavities are opened. If foreign material is identified, photographs are taken of the object in situ and then removed from the body and placed against a neutral background. If

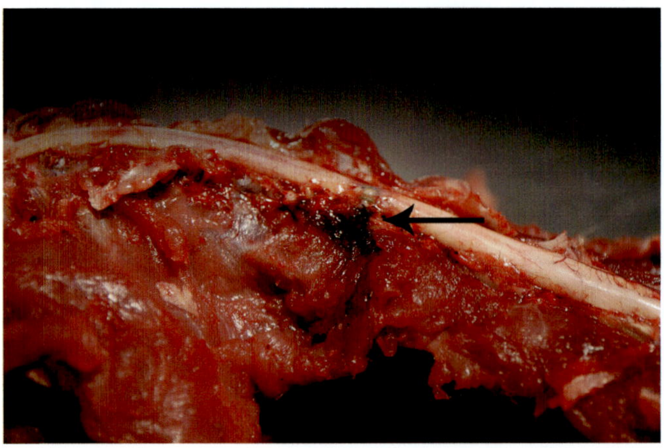

Figure 7.2 Spinal column, cat. Minimal hypaxial intramuscular hemorrhage with embedded hair tuft (black arrow). Note the ball bearing (BB) pellet in the spinal cord just above.

the foreign material appears to be metallic, nonmetallic instruments or fingers should be used during collection to prevent alteration of any identifying marks.

Next, the abdomen is opened just caudal to the last rib by penetrating through the external and internal abdominal oblique muscles and the peritoneum, taking care not to puncture internal organs. The abdominal cavity is evaluated for fluid, adhesions, or foreign material which, if present, is collected and measured. The position and orientation of abdominal organs as well as organ size (Table 7.2) and/or volume, color, contour, and texture are assessed. The quantity and character of omental and perirenal fat are documented. Abdominal fluid/blood should be collected and measured in a graduated cylinder or other calibrated measuring device. Identification of the source of free blood may be possible by localization of an area of hemorrhage and/or a lightly adherent blood clot on or around the area of interest (Figure 7.3). In blunt trauma, significant hemorrhage may expand tissues as a hematoma. If hematoma/free blood clot formation is extensive, volumes should be estimated. For blood clots, a reasonable estimate of volume can be made based on weight; approximately 1 gm = 1 mL of fluid blood. Fluids collected from the abdomen may need to be sifted in cases where foreign material is suspected, such as a perforated bowel, or in cases of potential surgical error where suture or other material may become free floating in the abdomen.

The muscular diaphragm is punctured at the dorsal most aspect (relative to positioning at necropsy). The normal negative pressure present in the thorax should result in visual expansion of the rib cage, outpouching of the diaphragm, and in larger animals, an auditory sound of air movement into the thorax. Failure of one or more of these changes may indicate a loss of negative pressure and further examination of the thoracic cavity for penetrating trauma is warranted. The thoracic cavity is evaluated for fluid, adhesions, or foreign material which, if present, are collected and measured. The right lateral ribcage is removed by cutting with rib cutters along the dorsal and ventral

Table 7.2 Liver and Heart Weights as a Percentage of Lean Body Weight[a]

Species	Heart (%)	Liver (%)
Dog	0.7–1.2	3–3.5
Cat	0.3–0.45	3–3.5
Ox (cow)	0.37	1
Horse	0.25	1.1
Sheep/goat	0.48/0.51	1.88/2.01
Bird (psittacine)	1.21	1.76

[a] Weights are those routinely used at the University of Tennessee College of Veterinary Medicine, Department of Biomedical and Diagnostic Sciences, Pathology Section.

Figure 7.3 Liver, chicken. Blood clot over a hepatic fracture. Note the postmortem lacerations made in the ventral portion of the liver are not associated with an adhered blood clot.

aspects of the right lateral rib cage. The pericardial sac is incised and the pericardial space evaluated for fluid, adhesions, or foreign material. The position and orientation of thoracic organs, as well as organ size and/or volume, color, contour, and texture are assessed (Figure 7.4).

At this time, any tissue samples for bacteriology are ideally collected with sterilized instruments and placed into clean petri dishes or Whirl-Pak® sample bags. Alternatively, a variety of commercially available microbiology swabs for both aerobic and anaerobic bacteria can also be utilized if storage and transport of larger tissues is an issue. Collection of bacteriology samples prior to significant handling decreases the chance of contamination from instruments or the examiner.

Special Considerations for the Internal Examination

Autolysis and Decomposition

Decomposition is best defined as the breaking down of tissues as the combined result of autolysis and putrefaction; where autolysis is the process of self-digestion by the body's internal cellular enzymes, and putrefaction is the

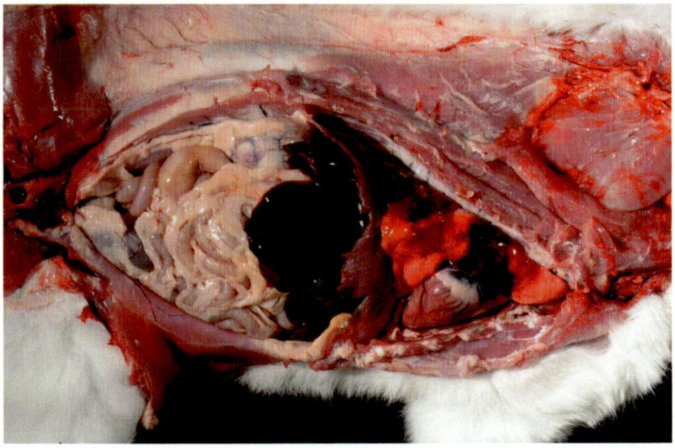

Figure 7.4 Fully opened cat allowing for examination of the thoracic and abdominal cavities.

result of bacterial, fungal, protozoal, and insect action on tissues (Miletich 2010; Zhou and Byard 2011). Autolysis begins as soon as cellular respiration ceases and toxic metabolites accumulate resulting in cell death and release of cellular enzymes. Autolysis occurs at different rates in different tissues and occurs more rapidly in tissues such as the liver with high inherent enzyme activity or the brain with high water contents (Miletich 2010). Putrefaction occurs as microorganisms proliferate within autolyzing tissue—and typically occurs most rapidly in tissues containing large numbers of bacteria in life (e.g., gastrointestinal tract). Ambient temperatures, body condition of the animal, hair coat density and length, underlying disease, and storage conditions of the body, among many other factors, can significantly alter the rate of decomposition. As such, detailed information about the circumstances surrounding the death and the condition of the body prior to necropsy is useful in interpreting the extent of decomposition at the time of necropsy. For more information regarding postmortem changes observed in animals, the reader is referred to Chapter 8 (Postmortem Changes and the Estimation of Time Since Death).

Imbibition of Hemoglobin

Imbibition of hemoglobin refers to the red discoloration of soft tissues that occurs with advanced autolysis. In the normal process of decomposition, red blood cells break down and release hemoglobin. This hemoglobin is then taken up by tissues resulting in a dark pink to red discoloration. Imbibition of hemoglobin, which is a postmortem event, must be differentiated from congestion, which can also give the tissues a dark red hue.

Postmortem Tears/Ruptures

It is not uncommon for tissues as they autolyze to lose tensile strength. Bodies in transport may be subjected to forces which can result in a postmortem tear, fracture, or rupture of internal organs which can be difficult to differentiate from antemortem lesions. When in doubt, identification of vital tissue reaction such as hemorrhage, edema, and fibrin are supportive; the area in question should be evaluated histologically for definitive determination.

Organ/Tissue Analysis and Special Collection Procedures

Once the initial inspection of the thorax and abdomen is completed, individual organs are removed en bloc or individually from body cavities. In general, the heart is left attached to the lungs, trachea, and tongue until completely dissected to facilitate examination of the great vessels. The liver should not be removed from the rest of the gastrointestinal tract until the proximal duodenum is opened and the gall bladder is squeezed to confirm patency of the bile ducts.

Tissues are examined for any evidence of inflammation, neoplasia, necrosis, or variation in anatomy, along with general color, texture, size, shape, consistency, and changes in contour. Normal weights of some organs have been established in multiple species, and at minimum, the liver and heart are weighed (Table 7.2). Many organs contain multiple anatomic and physiologically distinct areas that may undergo concurrent or distinct pathologic processes which should be considered during examination and sampling.

Although there are many factors that affect the quality of tissues for microscopic examination, proper formalin fixation likely plays the most significant role. For necropsy specimens, the ideal tissue sample is less than 1 cm in thickness allowing for penetration and fixation in approximately 12 hours at 25°C (Thavarajah et al. 2012). To ensure proper fixation, total formalin to tissue ratio should be at least 10:1. A complete set of tissues should be collected for histopathology (Table 7.3). Although all collected tissues may not be examined histologically, particularly in cases of obvious trauma, necropsy is the only opportunity to collect tissue samples, and a complete formalin-fixed set is recommended.

Tubular Organs

Tubular organs such as the gastrointestinal tract, trachea, and some reproductive organs are opened along their length, taking care not to disturb the mucosal surfaces. Luminal contents are evaluated and collected if indicated. After initial sampling, mucosal surfaces may be gently washed with water under very low pressure to allow for better visualization of the mucosa, and additional samples taken if additional changes are identified. Intestinal contents should be retained frozen for possible toxicology testing if necessary. Fecal samples can be saved for parasitology testing.

Solid Parenchymal Organs

Solid organs are at a minimum bisected and the cut surfaces examined. Larger organs including the liver and spleen are examined by serial, parallel slices (bread loafing) (Figure 7.5). All cut surfaces should be closely examined.

Table 7.3 Recommended Sample Collection and Examination Procedures

Organ	Examination	Sampling
Head and Neck		
Brain and pituitary	Examine whole	Entire brain intact *Toxicology*: One-half of one cerebral cortex saved frozen
Eyes	Examine whole Submerge in water to view tapetum/retina	Entire globe intact *Toxicology*: Aspirate vitreous and save in glass vial
Tongue	Bread loaf	1 representative section
Tonsils	Examine whole	Intact (small) 1 representative section (large)
Thyroid and parathyroid	Examine whole	Submit whole (small) 1 representative section (large)
Trachea	Open dorsally entire length and cut down mainstem bronchi	1 circumferential section
Esophagus	Open dorsally entire length	1 circumferential section
Lymph nodes and salivary glands	Bisect	1 representative section of each
Thoracic Cavity		
Lungs	Bread loaf, taking care to note distribution of changes	3 sections from 3 different lobes, closer to hilus
Heart	As outlined in text	3 sections including left papillary muscle, right ventricular free wall, and interventricular septum with left outflow track (aortic valve) **Submit whole in animals <5 kg
Thymus	Bread loaf	1 representative section Tissue from suspect area of mediastinum if thymus is not apparent
Mediastinal lymph nodes	Bisect if prominent	1 representative section

(*Continued*)

Table 7.3 (Continued) Recommended Sample Collection and Examination Procedures

Organ	Examination	Sampling
Abdominal Cavity		
Liver	Bread loaf	3 sections from 3 different lobes, closer to hilus: One should include gall bladder *Toxicology*: 100 or more grams, saved fresh
Spleen	Bread loaf	2 representative sections from different regions
Pancreas	Bread loaf	1 representative section attached to duodenum
Adrenals	Bisect	1-half of each
Kidneys	Bisect and remove capsule	At least 1 section of each kidney, ensuring inclusion of full thickness cortex, medulla, and renal pelvis *Toxicology*: One-half of one kidney
Urinary Bladder	Open	1 representative section *Toxicology*: Aspirated urine collected into glass
Gastrointestinal Tract		
Stomach	The gastrointestinal tract should be opened along its entire length and the mucosa examined Closed loops of bowel from grossly abnormal areas can be collected fresh for *bacteriology/virology*	1 full thickness representative section of fundus and pylorus *Toxicology*: All gastric contents, frozen
Duodenum		1 representative section with attached pancreas
Jejunum		2 representative sections from different regions
Ileum		1 representative section
Cecum		1 representative section
Colon		1 representative section from each portion of colon *Parasitology*: 10 or more grams, fresh, chilled immediately

(*Continued*)

Table 7.3 (Continued) Recommended Sample Collection and Examination Procedures

Organ	Examination	Sampling
Reproductive Tract		
Ovaries	Bisect	1-half of each
Uterus	Opened along entire length	1 representative section from each horn and the uterine body *Bacteriology*: One representative section (or swab), fresh
Testicles	Bisect	1-half each (small) 1 representative section each (large)
Prostate	Bisect	1 representative section
Abdominal lymph nodes including mesenteric and sublumbar should be incised and collected if abnormal		
Other		
Skin		1 representative section including panniculus muscle
Mammary glands	Incise all mammary glands	1 representative section
Skeletal muscle		1 representative section if needed
Sciatic nerve		1 representative section if needed
Abdominal fat		*Toxicology*: 10 grams or more, frozen
Bone marrow	Femur cracked or band sawed	1 section from metaphysis submitted in cassette or attached to bone—ensure bone is fragmented so marrow can be removed *Bone marrow evaluation*: One intact femur or humerus, fresh or frozen

Note: Routine samples are to be placed in 10% neutral buffered formalin. Routine samples must be less than 1 cm thick and include all anatomically distinct portions. Where different, samples from small animals (small) and large animals (large) are indicated.

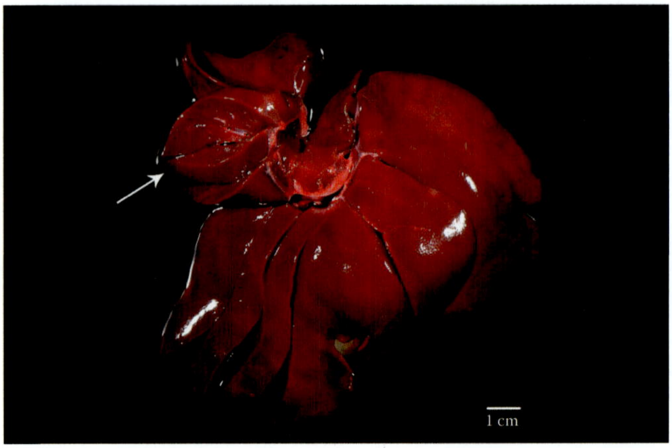

Figure 7.5 Liver, cat. Parallel serial sectioning (bread loafing). Cut surfaces are examined and sections such as those indicated by the arrow are ideal for submittal in formalin.

Heart

Full evaluation of the heart involves examination of the epicardium, myocardium, and endocardium, both major outflow tracts, both atrioventricular valves, as well as the pulmonic and aortic semilunar valves. Routine examination of the heart starts with transection of the heart at the lower one-third (closest to the apex) to assess for abnormalities such as hypertrophy of dilation. Next, the right auricle is incised and the incision continued into the atrium and extended into the right ventricle through the right atrioventricular valve, continued along the interventricular septum and out the pulmonic trunk via the pulmonic semilunar valves. The incision into the pulmonary trunk should be continued into the right and left pulmonary artery branches. Examination of the left side begins with the left auricle which is incised and the incision extended into the atrium and down through the atrioventricular valve into the left ventricle. The endocardium, papillary muscles, chordae tendineae, and left atrioventricular valve are examined. The final cut extends under the left atrioventricular valve into the aorta which should be incised its entire length. The aortic semilunar valves and both coronary ostia are examined.

Bone Marrow Evaluation

The femur is cracked and quality, color, and consistency of the bone marrow is examined by placing a small sample in water. Normal marrow in adult animals is pale-tan to yellow, has a fatty consistency grossly, and will normally float. Marrow in young animals is typically dark red and sinks in formalin, consistent with hematopoiesis. Dark red marrow in an adult animal is abnormal and should always be collected in formalin. Areas of more solid marrow, obvious tumors, and/or areas where there is lysis of the marrow trabeculae and/or bony cortices should be documented and sections collected for histopathology.

Brain and Spinal Cord Evaluation

The head is disarticulated from the body at the atlanto-occipital joint. In some instances, the eyes are removed from their orbits and extraocular tissues removed prior to fixation. The eye should be submerged into water to facilitate evaluation of the retina and tapetum lucidum. Any asymmetry, miosis, or mydriasis should be noted. The oral cavity is closely inspected for evidence of dental disease, oral lesions, or foreign material. The skin is removed from the skull and the subcuticular side evaluated for any evidence of hemorrhage. The skull cap is removed with bone cutters, striker saw, or hand-held (hack) saw. Although the size and shape of the skull varies significantly by species, general landmarks are identified in Figures 7.6 and 7.7. The brain is examined in situ and then removed after severing of the cranial nerves along the ventral aspect of the brain. The pituitary gland is removed from the sella turcica (pituitary fossa). Removal of the spinal cord may be necessary in some cases and is best achieved by completing a dorsal laminectomy with the use of bone cutters or striker saw. For large animals, a standing band saw may be required. In these cases, the lateral aspect of the spinal column is removed. In all animals, once exposed, the dura of the spinal cord is grasped and the spinal nerves transected with scissors or scalpel blade.

Stomach Contents

Starting at the cardia, the stomach is incised along the greater curvature and gastric contents collected, particularly if ingestion of a toxin is suspected. In all cases, gastric contents should be carefully evaluated for the presence or absence of feed material and/or foreign material. In one study of companion animal abuse and neglect, the presence of foreign material was significantly

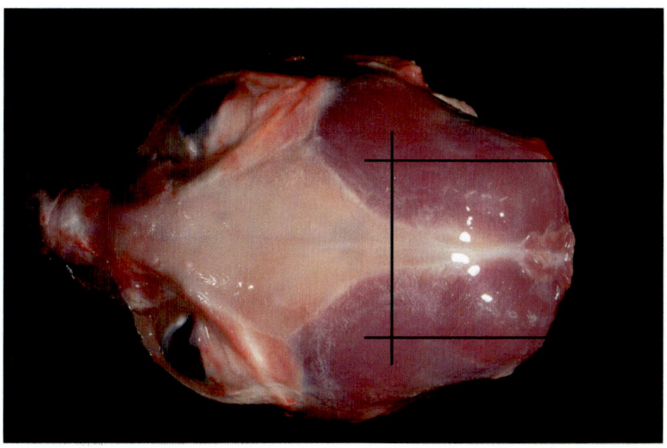

Figure 7.6 Head, cat. Dorsal view. Black lines indicate where cuts should be made.

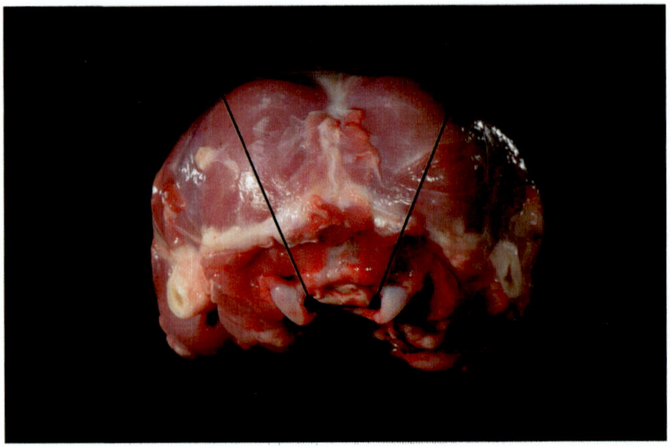

Figure 7.7 Head, cat. Caudal view. Black lines indicate where cuts should be made.

associated with starvation due to exogenous causes (no identifiable preexisting disease) (Gerdin and McDonough 2013). Careful sifting of the contents may be required to find smaller foreign material.

In some cases of malicious poisoning, toxic materials may be embedded within normal feed material which necessitates careful inspection. Accidental poisonings are also common, and while some, such as anticoagulant rodenticide toxicity, may be associated with specific gross lesions, many kill the animal quickly and without suggestive gross changes. Some common toxicants that are easily available include strychnine laced milo seeds (Figure 7.8) and many mole and rodent baits, which may be visualized as irregular fragments of brightly dyed (often green or blue) foreign material. Regardless of the presence or absence of foreign material, gastric contents should be retained frozen for possible toxicology testing.

Fluid Samples

Fluid samples including blood, stomach contents, urine, bile, and ocular (vitreous chamber) fluid may be collected at necropsy. In general, fluid samples should be collected as cleanly as possible; a sterile needle and syringe is recommended where possible. Fluid samples should be collected in a glass tube to prevent any alterations due to interaction with plastics. For biochemical evaluations, ocular vitreous fluid may be particularly valuable as its low cellularity, physiological isolation, and relative resistance to contamination and putrefaction means its composition changes relatively slowly postmortem (Baniak et al. 2014). There is some debate about the reliability of blood for toxicologic testing due to postmortem redistribution which makes predicting antemortem concentrations from postmortem samples fraught with error (Cook et al. 2000). Regardless, the presence of some toxins such as strychnine, cyanide, or zinc phosphide is always supportive of poisoning, and blood should be collected in all forensic necropsy cases. In general, blood should be collected from at least one peripheral vein (femoral is easily accessible).

Figure 7.8 Gastric content, dog: Miloseeds laced with strychnine are admixed with grass and a small cube of steak.

Specialized Forensic Necropsy Procedures

Radiological Studies

Radiological studies should be performed for any case, but are particularly helpful in cases of blunt force trauma, gunshot injuries, and during the examination of charred bodies. Radiographic studies can be used to detect metallic objects such as bullets, jackets, pellets, and knife tips. Computed tomography is also useful during postmortem examination of the body. For more information about forensic radiology, the reader is referred to Chapter 9 (Veterinary Forensic Radiology and Imaging).

Histopathology

Histopathology is the study of the manifestations of disease in tissues under a light microscope. Hematoxylin and eosin (H&E) is the most commonly used stain for routine light microscopic examination. Other histochemical and immunohistochemical stains may be used instead of H&E to highlight specific tissue characteristics, identification of infectious organisms, and identification of various pigments which can accumulate in cells/tissue.

Histopathology is considered to be an important feature regarding the quality of a forensic autopsy and is essential to confirm, refine, or refute findings observed during the gross examination of a body (de la Grandmaison et al. 2010). Histological examination of tissues during forensic autopsies of humans was shown to establish a cause of death alone in 8.4% of cases, traumatic injuries were better documented in 22% of cases, and when the mechanism of death was not shown by gross findings it was discovered by histology in approximately 40% of cases (de la Grandmaison et al. 2010).

In addition to refining or refuting gross examination findings, histology can be used to rule in or out natural disease (such as intestinal adenocarcinoma in an emaciated animal) and it can be used to provide an estimate of the age of an injury such as a laceration or a bruise. In cases of histologic evaluation of wound healing to age a wound, it should be noted that there are significant differences in rates of wound healing between species. Filling time of wounds was faster in dogs compared to cats; as was re-epithelization, wound contraction, and total healing time (Bohling et al. 2004). Similarly, in horses and ponies, second intention healing of wounds was significantly faster in ponies than in horses (Wilmink and van Weeren 2005).

Skeletal Remains

Examination of skeletal remains poses a difficult challenge as most if not all the soft tissue will not be available for examination and skeletons can be incomplete. The forensic examination of skeletons should center on the identification and documentation of boney lesions. Although identification of individuals is a major component of skeletal remains in human forensic cases, in the veterinary forum, identification of the animal can range from species identification to a specific individual. If the skeleton is that of a canid, it is possible to differentiate different species such as the domestic dog and coyote by craniometrics or DNA analysis (Chinnici and Huffman 2014). If a single canid skeleton is identified, the presence of an os penis would confirm the animal is male.

Evaluation of bone for evidence of traumatic injury can be done in order to identify gunshot injuries, predatory bitemarks, fractures, and evidence of natural disease (e.g., osteomyelitis, osteosarcoma). Evidence of boney healing would be consistent with an antemortem injury. Consultation with a forensic anthropologist should be considered in skeletal remains cases.

In some instances, skeletal remains of animals that potentially died of starvation are recovered. Limited data is available regarding analysis of bone marrow fat from recovered intact femurs. It was shown experientially that when femurs with normal bone marrow fat from two different horses were analyzed at 3 or 6 months postmortem, bone marrow fat decreased by 28% after 3 months in one horse and 33% after 6 months in the second horse compared to the contralateral femur (Meyerholtz et al. 2011); however, not enough studies have been performed to validate the use of this test with skeletal remains.

Microbiology, Virology, and Parasitology Studies

In cases where the cause of death is due to a possible infectious etiology, microbiological studies should be performed. Bacterial cultures, fungal cultures, and virus isolation can be performed on numerous tissues and bodily fluids such as material from within an abscess, various body organs, urine, and cerebrospinal fluid. Samples should be collected as aseptically as possible and stored in a petri dish, Whirl-Pak bag, or commercially available bacteriology swab. Samples can be frozen for long-term storage. If the gross appearance is particularly suggestive of a certain type of bacteria or fungus, the laboratory should be notified of your suspicions as some bacteria are more fastidious, slower to grow, or require special culture media. Any potentially zoonotic bacterial or fungal diseases should be discussed with the diagnostic laboratory before samples are sent. In addition to aerobic, anaerobic, mycobacterial, and fungal cultures, molecular diagnostic techniques such as polymerase chain reaction studies can be performed to assess for infectious agents. After the death of an animal, it is common for there to be proliferation of gastrointestinal flora with extension throughout the body with putrefaction. Culture results need to be correlated with gross and microscopic findings.

The presence of internal parasites can be indicative of neglect, and when in significant numbers can contribute to debilitation and/or death. Grossly observable internal parasites are collected in 70% ethyl alcohol. Fresh fecal material is collected into an airtight, nonbreakable container and refrigerated as soon as possible to prevent continued maturation of eggs into larval stages. Fecal material may be stored at 4°C for up to 2 months with minimal maturation of the many stages of parasites (Foreyt 2001). Fecal material should never be frozen as it distorts the eggs beyond recognition. Some organisms, such as Giardia, do not preserve well; therefore, fecal samples should be collected and examined as soon as possible.

If coolants are not readily available or if fecal material needs to be stored for prolonged periods of time, 5–10% neutral buffered formalin in at least a 1:1 and up to 9:1 formalin to feces ratio has been shown to result in the best recovery of nematode eggs in deer (Foreyt 1986) and is recommended for its ease of execution. If DNA studies may be required, 95% ethyl alcohol is recommended. A minimum of 10 g of feces, per test, is ideal.

Toxicology Studies

It is a common misconception that there is a single toxicology test that can identify any toxin within the body. Rather, there are numerous different tests and techniques utilized to identify potential toxicants within the body. During some postmortem investigations or during the scene investigation, suspicious findings may be identified that would suggest possible intoxication of an animal has occurred. An example would be severe hemoabdomen and mediastinal hemorrhage within a deceased dog that does not have a clinical history of an inherited bleeding disorder, recent surgical procedure, or an identifiable mass that ruptured. These findings are suggestive of anticoagulant rodenticide intoxication (Figure 7.9). If a toxin is suspected to have played a role in the death of the animal, consultation with a veterinary toxicologist is recommended. For more information, the reader is referred to Chapter 13 (Veterinary Forensic Toxicology).

Patterns of Injuries

Projectile Injuries

Firearms injuries are often encountered in veterinary forensic cases and are seen in both domestic animal species and wildlife. Gunshot injuries vary in appearance not only because of the type of weapon used but also due to the morphology of animal species involved. A gunshot injury of a bird (due to feathers) or reptile (due to presence of scales) will have different appearances (Cooper and Cooper 2007).

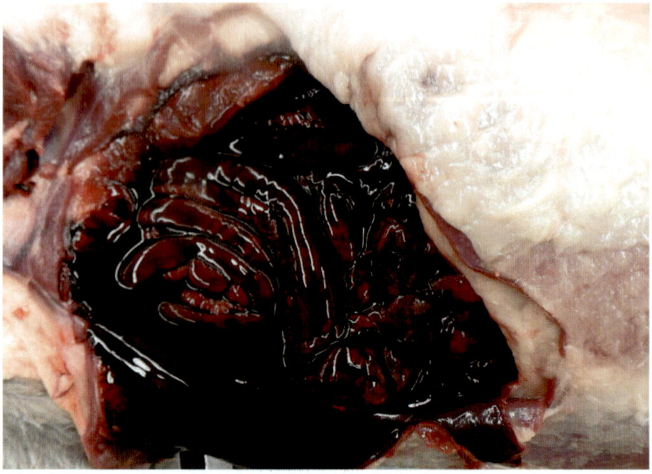

Figure 7.9 Massive intra-abdominal hemorrhage (hemoabdomen).

Handguns, rifles, and shotguns are the main classifications of small arms that are commonly encountered. In the case of handgun and rifle ammunition, the typical construction of ammunition is a metallic cartridge which contains a powder charge that has a bullet set on top of the powder charge and crimped in place. A jacket is often found on small arms projectiles and encases the soft lead core in a shell of harder metal. Upon firing a gun, the bullet is forced out of the cartridge and the cartridge remains within the gun. In the case of shotgun ammunition, there is a plastic cartridge that contains the powder charge which has a wad (felt or plastic disc) or plastic cup that separates the charge from the shot (or slug) which is ultimately ejected from the cartridge upon firing. Air guns which fire projectiles such as ball bearings (BBs) are also encountered.

In cases of firearm injuries, examination of the injuries may allow for determination of the range of fire, trajectory of the projectile, injuries caused by the projectile, and/or type of weapon used to cause the injuries. Radiological studies are important to identify projectiles or fragments that remain within the body. The number of entrance wounds identified during the external examination should equal the number of exit wounds plus the number of retained projectiles. If a discrepancy is noted, possible reasons include a missed wound, projectile fragmentation, or separation of the core from the jacket.

Differentiation between an entrance wound and exit wound is based on characteristics of the wounds. In the case of rifled firearms (handgun or rifle) wounds, entrance wounds are typically round to oval, have an abrasion rim, and are typically the same size or smaller than the projectile (Figure 7.10). In comparison, exit wounds are often irregularly shaped, do not have an abrasion rim and are often the same size or larger than the projectile (Cooper and Cooper 2007; Denton et al. 2006). In wounds resulting from a shotgun, the

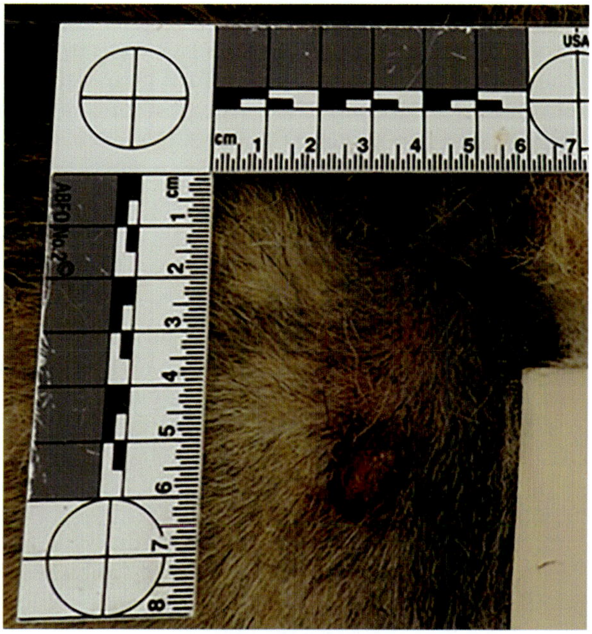

Figure 7.10 Circular wound with an abrasion rim in the skin of a dog consistent with an entrance gunshot wound.

characteristics will vary with distance and angle (Cooper and Cooper 2007). Entrance wounds caused by a shotgun at close range will form a round hole with possible ragged edges; whereas, if the range of fire increases, multiple small round holes instead of a single central hole will be observed. Gunshot injuries should be triangulated using fixed points which will be useful when determining the trajectory of the projectiles. In some instances, only entrance wounds will be identified as all projectiles will remain within the body.

When a projectile is removed from the body, plastic forceps or fingers should be used as contact with metallic objects (such as metal thumb forceps) can damage the projectile. Projectiles should be gently rinsed and dried and wrapped in a soft material and stored in a hard container. The projectile should be photographed with a scale. Evaluation of the projectile by a ballistics expert may allow for further characterization.

Upon determination of the entrance and exit wounds (if any), the trajectory of fire should be determined. The trajectory of fire does not mean that the body was in the actual position nor how the projectile traveled in the air, it simply describes the pathway the projectile took in the body. When determining the trajectory of fire in animals, it should be documented in relation to how the animal is normally positioned.

Limited data is available regarding the determination of range of fire in veterinary species. In human forensics, there are basic characteristics of the gunshot injuries that may prove useful to determine the range of fire and include the presence or absence of soot, presence or absence of stippling (punctate abrasions on the skin), and presence or absence of a muzzle imprint. The range of fire determination from shotguns is determined by measuring the scatter pattern of the shot and is ideally correlated with a test fire scatter pattern from the gun that fired the shot (Cooper and Cooper 2007).

Blunt Force Injuries

Blunt force injuries can be observed during the forensic necropsy. The severity, extent, and appearance of blunt force trauma depends on the amount of force delivered to the body, the region struck, the extent of body surface to which the force is delivered, the nature of the weapon, and the time over which the force is delivered (DiMaio and DiMaio 2001). Blunt force trauma injuries can be observed externally and/or internally. Injuries due to blunt force trauma are divided into four categories: abrasion, contusions, lacerations, and bone fractures.

Abrasions

An abrasion occurs when the superficial layer of the skin (epidermis) is removed by contact with another object. In animals, the severity and size of the abrasion does not always correlate with the severity of an underlying injury (Merck et al. 2013b). Abrasions are initially wet in appearance and do not usually bleed, rather there is leakage of tissue fluid (Munro and Munro 2008). Postmortem lesions can mimic antemortem abrasions as in postmortem dragging of the animal, which is more often seen in large animal species. Insect activity on the body can mimic abrasions (DiMaio and Dana 2007; DiMaio and DiMaio 2001).

There are multiple types of abrasions including grazes, scratches, brush abrasions (scrapes), sliding abrasions, impact abrasions, and patterned abrasions. Brush abrasions are formed when a blunt object scrapes off the superficial layer of the skin with the injury often not extending into the deeper tissue. Sliding abrasions will occur when the animal's body slides across a rough surface. Table 7.4 reviews the various types of abrasions.

Table 7.4 Types of Abrasions Observed during the Forensic Necropsy

Type of Abrasion	Cause
Graze	Projectile such as bullet
Scratch	Fingernails, claws, or sharp edge of an object
Brush abrasion	Blunt object scrapes the body
Sliding abrasion	Body slides across rough surface (such as asphalt)
Impact abrasion	Blunt force impact (perpendicular) to the skin
Patterned abrasion	Imprint of weapon or surface that caused the abrasion

Contusions

A contusion is extravasation of erythrocytes (hemorrhage) into the soft tissue and is due to tearing of blood vessels (veins and/or arteries). Contusions can be confined to the external surface or affect deeper soft tissues, muscle, and internal organs (Panella and Hodge 2013). Tramline bruises occur when an animal or person is struck by a cylindrical object (such as a stick) and appears as a pale linear central area lined on either side by a linear bruise (DiMaio and DiMaio 2001). Tramline bruises have been reported in pigs and cattle (Munro and Munro 2013).

Contusions within the brain can be subdivided into contusion hemorrhage (when vascular injury predominates) or contusion necrosis (with or without hemorrhage); oftentimes contusions occur along a spectrum of these two types (Finnie 2016). Herniation of the brain can result from intracranial hemorrhage such as epidural or subdural hematomas (Figure 7.11).

Bruises are known to change color with time and initially are the product of a combination of natural skin pigment, pigment in extravasated blood, and color added by the inflammatory reaction (Stephenson 1997). As hemoglobin breaks down to bilirubin and biliverden, a bruise will change color through shades of purple, green, orange, and yellow. Assessment of the color of the bruise is considered unreliable to allow for the estimation of aging a bruise in humans except for yellow coloration as this indicates the bruise is probably more than 18 hours old (Stephenson 1997). In veterinary species, it is reported that the changing of color of a bruise between animal species is quite similar; however, the timing at which the changes occur differ and assessment of color may be unsuitable for determining the age of a bruise in veterinary species (Barrington and Jensen 2015). Use of a bruise color chart may be useful when describing and photographing a bruise (Figure 7.12).

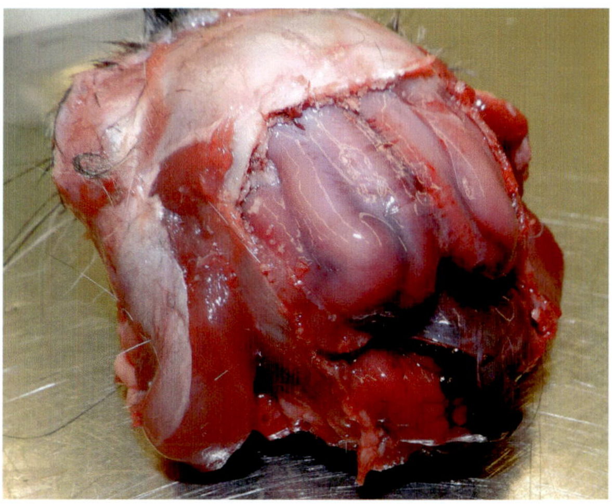

Figure 7.11 Subdural hematoma overlying the cerebellum due to blunt force trauma to the head.

Figure 7.12 Example of a bruise color chart.

Various techniques have been evaluated to allow for estimation of the age of a bruise in multiple animal species (cattle, sheep, chickens, mice, rats, pigs, and rabbits) including histopathology, chemical analysis, and evaluation of mRNA expression at the site of infliction. There are currently no objective scientific reports regarding the aging of bruises in cats, dogs, and horses (Munro and Munro 2013). Based on the limited data in the scientific literature regarding histological evaluation of experimental bruises in animal models, there is consensus that neutrophils are the first leukocyte to infiltrate the site of infliction (Barrington and Jensen 2015). In calves, histologic examination of bruises at 8 hours identified many neutrophils and few macrophages, whereas at 48 hours macrophages were the dominate leukocyte and often contained hemosiderin (McCausland and Dougherty 1978). Extrapolation of data regarding aging of a bruise should be done with caution given that significant interspecies variation can occur.

Lacerations

Lacerations are due to blunt force trauma and result from the tearing of soft tissue due to shearing or crushing force. The edges of a laceration are often irregular and ragged and there is bruising of the margins. In contrast to incised wounds, lacerations have a characteristic known as tissue bridging which is when blood vessels, nerves, and other types of connective tissue remain intact and span the injury (DiMaio and Dana 2007). Tissue bridging is a distinguishing feature that is used to differentiate an incised wound from a laceration (Table 7.5). There may be undermining of the edge of a laceration which would indicate the direction of the impact (Merck et al. 2013b).

Lacerations of internal organs can occur indicating application of a considerable amount of force to the body (Di Maio and Di Maio 2001). Lacerations of internal organs such as the liver and spleen may not have the characteristic feature of tissue bridging as there is little to no interstitial tissue to allow for

Table 7.5 General Characteristics of Lacerations and Incised Wounds

	Laceration	Incised Wound
Cause	Blunt force trauma	Sharp force trauma
Edges	Ragged and irregular	Sharp
Bruising/abrasions?	Yes	No
Tissue bridging?	Yes	No
Presence of foreign material within the wound?	Yes, often present	Usually clean
Type of bone injury	Can see associated fractures	Scoring or chipping of bone is possible

such bridging (Spitz 2006). Massive internal bleeding can result from lacerations of internal organs.

Bone Fractures

In cases of nonaccidental injuries, fractures are often encountered. Causes of fractures include automobile accidents, blunt force trauma, penetration of a projectile, and as a sequela of underlying bone disease. Multiple features of fractures have been reported to raise the suspicion of nonaccidental injury including the presence of multiple fractures, multiple fractures at different stages of healing, and fractures occurring on more than one region of the body (Tong 2014). Fractures should be examined radiographically, grossly, and/or microscopically for evidence of healing ranging from early inflammation to fibrosis to boney callus formation. If multiple fractures are identified, comparison of the age of the fractures should be undertaken as fractures at different stages of healing are suspicious of nonaccidental trauma.

Sharp Force Injuries

Sharp force injures result from the penetration of the skin and/or soft tissue and can be due to scissors, knives, forks, axes, machetes, teeth, or swords, among many others. In contrast to lacerations, sharp force injuries typically have a well-defined edge and do not exhibit tissue bridging (DiMaio and DiMaio 2001). There are three types of sharp force injuries: stab wounds, incised wounds, and chop wounds. Sharp force injuries will often result in loss of massive amounts of blood. In human forensics, air embolisms resulting in death following sharp force injuries have been reported (Campbell and Kerridge 1993; Sarvesvaran 1991). In sharp force injury cases, documentation of the site(s), number, and dimensions of the wounds is imperative. Dissection of the tracts of the injuries and documentation of injuries of internal organs should be undertaken and blood loss percentage should be calculated.

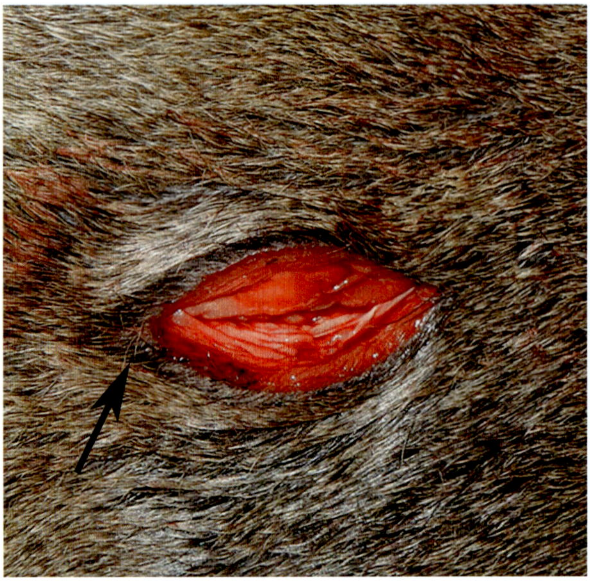

Figure 7.13 Stab wound in the skin of a dog. A stab wound has a greater depth of the wound compared to the length of the wound. Arrow points to blunt end of the wound.

A stab wound is defined as a wound that is deeper than the skin surface length (Figure 7.13). Once the skin is penetrated by the weapon, the weapon can continue to penetrate subcutaneous tissue and internal organs. When measuring the wound, the dimensions of the weapon used are estimated by approximating the edges of the wound and measuring the depth of the wound (Panella and Hodge 2013). Estimation of the dimensions of the wound are problematic as the depth of the wound can be less than, equal to, or greater than the length of the blade and the external length of the stab wound can be less than, equal to, or greater than the width of the blade (DiMaio and DiMaio 2001). A single weapon can result in the creation of wounds of different shapes and sizes.

The wound from a single sharp-edged knife will often have a characteristic V-shaped end and a blunt end. In contrast, a double sharp-edged knife will often have two V-shaped edges. Although these are the characteristic features of single and double sharp-edged knives, rendering an opinion as to the type of weapon at necropsy should be cautioned as single sharp-edged knives can also result in a wound with two V-shaped edges or two blunt ends. The surface of skin surrounding the stab wound should be examined for a patterned abrasion or bruising that was caused by the guard on the knife handle. Other patterns of injury can occur depending on the type of weapon used, a single 2–3 mm hole can be suggestive of an ice pick (Figure 7.14), whereas 2–6 small evenly spaced holes could be suggestive of the tines of a fork.

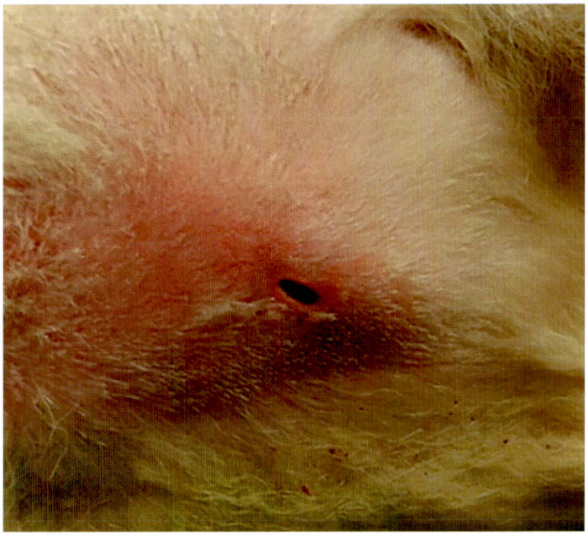

Figure 7.14 Sharp force trauma to the head of a dog. The weapon used in this case was an ice pick.

An incised wound is defined as a wound that has a length on the surface of the skin that is less than the depth of penetration. Incised wounds are often linear. In some cases, the edges of the wound can be jagged if the sharp object used is glass from a broken bottle. Incised wounds can be fatal if there is cutting of a major blood vessel as might be seen in the case of cutting the great vessels and trachea of the neck.

Chop wounds are a combination of sharp edge injury and blunt force trauma (DiMaio and DiMaio 2001). Weapons that cause such injuries include axes, machetes, and swords. The edges are often distinct with or without abrasions and bruising. If the wound penetrates deep to bone, linear boney grooves may be identified which is supportive of a chop type of injury.

Asphyxiation

Asphyxia is a broad term and is used to describe all conditions that are caused by the failure of cells to receive or utilize oxygen (Sauvageau and Boghossian 2010). In forensic situations, asphyxia should be defined as situations where a body does not receive or utilize adequate amounts of oxygen (Sauvageau and Boghossian 2010). There are many subcategories of asphyxia including suffocation (smothering, choking, vitiated airspace/confined spaces), strangulation (ligature strangulation, hanging, manual strangulation), mechanical asphyxia (positional asphyxia, traumatic asphyxia), and drowning (Table 7.6). Postmortem findings in cases of asphyxia may be etiologic specific (such as ligature marked around the neck), whereas other findings are nonspecific and include organ congestion, cyanosis, and fluidity of the blood (McEwen 2016).

Table 7.6 Definition of Terms Used in Classification of Asphyxia

Term	Definition
Suffocation: Smothering	Asphyxia by obstruction of the air passages above the epiglottis (nose, mouth, and pharynx)
Suffocation: Choking	Asphyxia by obstruction of the air passages below the epiglottis
Suffocation: Confined spaces/vitiated atmosphere	Asphyxia in an inadequate atmosphere by reduction of oxygen, displacement of oxygen by other gases or by gases causing chemical interference with the oxygen uptake and utilization
Strangulation: Ligature strangulation	A type of strangulation in which the pressure on the neck is applied by a constricting band tightened by a force (other than gravitational force of the body)
Strangulation: Manual strangulation	A form of strangulation caused by an external pressure on the structures of the neck by hands, forearms, or other limbs
Strangulation: Hanging	A form of strangulation in which the pressure on the neck is applied by a constricting band tightened by the gravitational weight of the body or part of the body
Mechanical asphyxia: Positional asphyxia	A type of asphyxia where the position of an individual compromises the ability to breathe
Mechanical asphyxia: Traumatic asphyxia	A type of asphyxia caused by external chest compression by a heavy object
Drowning	Asphyxia by immersion in a liquid

Source: Sauvageau, A., and E. Boghossian. 2010. Classification of asphyxia: The need for standardization. *J Forensic Sci.* 55:1259–1267.

Mechanical or crushing trauma to the body can result in congestion and petechial hemorrhage cranial to the site of injury (McEwen 2016).

Suffocation

It has been proposed that in the forensic context, smothering is occlusion of the airway above the epiglottis versus choking, which is obstruction of the airway below the level of the epiglottis. If the obstruction extends above and below the epiglottis, then it is recommended to use the lower level airway obstruction to classify the case (Sauvageau and Boghossian 2010). Swelling of the throat from anaphylaxis is a natural cause of choking. Non-natural causes of smothering and choking in veterinary medicine have been caused by small toys, food products, and dental treats (Figure 7.15). In horses, foreign objects

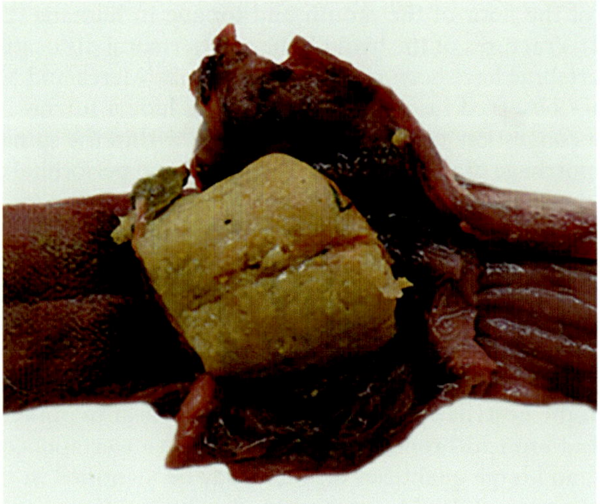

Figure 7.15 Dog treat that is compressing the epiglottis of a dog that resulted in smothering and death of the dog.

in the nasal passages (such as ping-pong balls) can result in suffocation and death. During the forensic necropsy, recovery and documentation of the foreign body is of major importance. If the foreign object is removed prior to postmortem examination, postmortem findings are likely to be nonspecific, and may include congestion, erosion, ulceration, and/or hemorrhage at the site of obstruction.

Asphyxia due to exposure to an atmosphere depleted of oxygen is known by several different terms including vitiated atmosphere, asphyxia in confined spaces, and entrapment. In addition to exclusion of oxygen, asphyxia from gases such as carbon dioxide and carbon monoxide fall within this category (Stern et al. 2014). Toxic gases that are produced in fires include carbon monoxide, carbon dioxide, and hydrogen cyanide. Carbon monoxide is produced by the incomplete combustion of carbon-containing molecules (Prahlow and Barrett 2005). Hydrogen cyanide is formed from the combustion of carbon and nitrogen containing materials (plastics, wool, and silk).

Strangulation

Strangulation is the closure of the blood vessels and/or airways of the neck as a result of external pressure on the neck (Sauvageau and Boghossian 2010). Types of strangulation include hanging, ligature strangulation, and manual strangulation.

In cases of hanging, the structures of the neck are compressed and the tightening of the material around the neck is due to the gravitational weight of the body. Airways may or may not be obstructed in cases of hanging; although, occlusion of blood vessels will occur and result in cerebral anoxia and death. If airway obstruction is to occur it is due to either compression of the trachea or elevation of the floor of the mouth and tongue in humans (DiMaio and DiMaio 2001). Fractures of the hyoid bone and vertebral dislocation/fracture of cervical vertebrae have been reported in animals (Merck and Miller 2013). Other findings observed in cases of hangings include a furrow on the neck with a rim of congestion, abrasions, hemorrhage within the spinal cord, and petechial hemorrhage of the conjunctiva, gingiva, and periorbital areas.

Drowning

Drowning is an extremely difficult diagnosis to make as it is often a diagnosis of exclusion (McEwen and Gerdin 2016). In cases of suspected drowning, it is important to eliminate other possible causes of death as the animal could have been immersed in the water after it was dead. Postmortem findings in cases of drowning are nonspecific and include copious amounts of froth and fluid exuding from the nostrils and copious amounts of clear to pink froth within the trachea and bronchi/bronchioles. Lungs can be atelectatic, congested, or hemorrhagic, and large quantities of water may be identified in the stomach (McEwen and Gerdin 2016; Munro and Munro 2013). Microscopic lesions in cases of animals drowning include intra-alveolar hemorrhage, alveolar overdistention, attenuation of alveolar septa, aspiration of foreign material, and flooding of alveoli with proteinaceous fluid (McEwen and Gerdin 2016).

Diatom testing has been used to diagnose drowning but its reliability is controversial (Munro and Munro 2013). Postmortem diatom contamination in piglets has been reported and diatoms were recovered from the heart, lung, skin, muscles, and bone of piglets that died of causes other than drowning when immersed in water postmortem (Giancamillo et al. 2010).

Thermal Injuries

There are many causes of thermal injury including fire, radiant heat, microwave radiation, electrocution, and exposure to cold (frostbite). The patterns of these types of injuries can be different as are the underlying causes. Thermal and chemical burns are occasionally encountered in dogs and cats. Causes of burns in veterinary medicine include boiling liquids, exposure to caustic chemicals, electric heating pads, and fires. Burns are often asymmetrical lesions and may range from areas of red cutaneous discoloration to erosion and ulceration to overt necrosis. Chemical burns will often have a drip or spatter pattern. There are four degrees of burns which can be fully characterized histologically.

In some instances, the pathologist will be presented with a charred body and it will be necessary to determine if the victim was burnt before or after the animal died. In cases of injuries due to exposure to fire, whether it be exposure to the fire fumes or heat, many pathologic changes can be identified. The two main signs of vital exposure to fire fumes in burned bodies that are reported in the forensic literature (Bohnert et al. 2003; Rogde and Oliving 1996; Stern et al. 2014) include elevation of carboxyhemoglobin in postmortem blood and deposition of soot within the respiratory tract including the larynx, trachea, and bronchi (Figure 7.16). Some cases also have soot deposits in the esophagus

Figure 7.16 Intratracheal carbon material (soot) from a dog that died in a house fire.

and stomach, but soot deposition in the respiratory tract is always present in such cases (Bohnert et al. 2003). Postmortem findings suggestive of vital exposure to heat included burn blisters on the skin, edema and vesicular detachment of the mucosa of the pharynx, larynx, and/or upper esophagus, absence of soot and/or burns in the corner of the eyes (crow's feet), incompletely singed eyelashes, and petechial hemorrhages in the conjunctiva (Bohnert et al. 2003). Microscopic findings supportive of vital exposure to heat include edema and vesicular detachment of the mucosa of the pharynx, larynx, and/or upper esophagus, increased secretion of mucus, and pseudo-goblet cell formation (Bohnert et al. 2003).

In cases of exposure to microwave energy, postmortem findings include fragile skin, pugilistic appearance, and the animal will appear partially cooked. A unique microscopic finding reported with microwave radiation is relative tissue sparing. Relative tissue sparing is confirmed microscopically as the preservation of subcutaneous fat with burning of the epidermis, dermis, and skeletal muscle, due to the high fat and low water content of the panniculus (Surrell et al. 1987).

Electrical burns can be accidental injuries in the case of a puppy chewing on a wire. In this case the burns would be within the oral cavity. Electrocution is also utilized as a form of euthanasia, as in the case of humane euthanasia of swine and has been utilized for euthanasia of dogs used for organized dog fighting. In electrothermal burns there can be singeing of hair, feathers, and skin, elevation of the skin with a sunken center, and burns ranging from first to fourth degree (Schulze et al. 2016). Microscopic examination will be useful to characterize the electrical injuries as metallization of tissue and epidermal cells and nuclei can display fishbone-like elongation (Schulze et al. 2016).

Frostbite is uncommonly encountered in healthy animals, whereas ill animals or those that have not been acclimated to cold temperatures are more susceptible (Miller et al. 2013). Frostbite typically occurs on the tips of the ears, digits, scrotum, and tip of the tail.

Emaciation

Emaciation is defined as the wasted condition of the body. Emaciation can result from two different pathophysiologic mechanisms: cachexia and starvation. Cachexia is a multifactorial, primarily cytokine-mediated wasting that occurs in conjunction with endogenous disease (Gerdin et al. 2016). There are multiple forms of cachexia including cardiac cachexia, cancer cachexia, and renal cachexia. Cachexia is characterized by the voluntary reduction in caloric intake (most, but not all cases), increased protein catabolism, loss of lean body mass, and failure to reverse the catabolic state with proper nutritional support (Freeman 2012; Gerdin et al. 2016; Stricker and Kumar 2013). In cachexia, there is no decrease in basal metabolic rate and cytokines and hormones such as TNF-α, IL-1, and prostaglandins contribute to the development of the cachexic state (Kusewutt and Rush 2007). Loss of lean body mass is a hallmark of cachexia (Freeman 2012), which must be differentiated from sarcopenia, the loss of lean body mass in the absence of disease. Sarcopenia is associated with aging and has been reported in dogs and cats (Freeman 2012). Starvation is characterized by an involuntary reduction in caloric intake, decreased basal metabolic rate, relative sparing of lean body mass until fat stores are depleted, and is correctable by nutritional support (Gerdin et al. 2016). In contrast to weight loss due to cachexia, metabolic adaptations allow fat to be used as the primary fuel source; therefore, preserving lean body mass (Freeman 2012). Starvation typically occurs due to an animal not having access to food, inappropriate diets, and/or inadequate quality/quantity of food (Gerdin et al. 2016; Stern 2013).

Gross and microscopic findings in cases of starvation include loss of muscle mass and absence of subcutaneous adipose tissue, serous atrophy of fat, hepatic and testicular atrophy, follicular (hair follicle) atrophy, and petechial and ecchymotic hemorrhages of the gastric mucosa (Gerdin et al. 2016; Stern 2013). Weighing organs such as the liver is recommended during the postmortem examination to objectively document organ atrophy. It is not uncommon for dogs to have died of starvation to have food identified within the stomach as these animals might have been recently fed by law enforcement, the general public, or the offender. Foreign material such as plastic and Styrofoam (Figure 7.17) has been documented in the gastrointestinal tracts of dogs that have died of starvation (Gerdin et al. 2016; Munro and Munro 2008; Stern 2013).

Serous atrophy of fat is an important finding observed in cases of starvation. Serous atrophy of fat can be observed at the site of any fat depot; however, it is often identified in the epicardium (Figure 7.18), perirenal tissue, and bone marrow (Figure 7.19). Grossly, fat deposits are depleted and clear to yellowish gelatinous material remains (Myers and McGavin 2007). Microscopically,

Figure 7.17 Foreign material in the stomach of a dog that died from starvation due to exogenous circumstances.

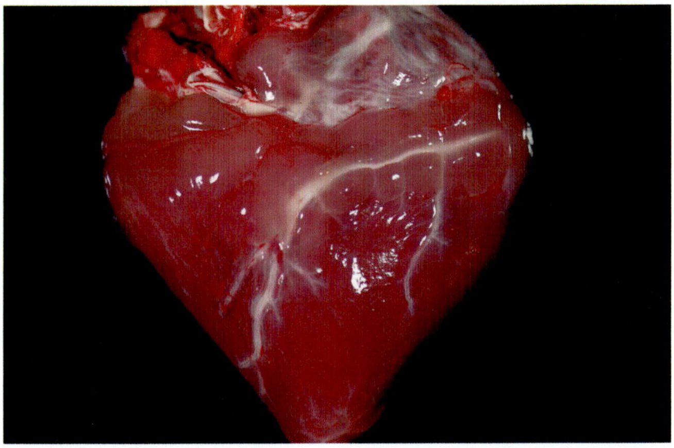

Figure 7.18 Heart, alpaca. Serous atrophy of epicardial fat in an alpaca that died from starvation due to severe dental disease. A coronary artery is visible under the atrophic epicardial fat.

adipocytes are atrophied and interstitial hyaluronic acid mucopolysaccharides are increased. Measurement of the amount of fat in the bone marrow of femurs can be performed to provide a qualitative assessment of bone marrow fat. Testing of bone marrow fat has been validated in dogs, horses, and cattle when femurs were analyzed close to the time of death (Meyerholtz et al. 2011). Animals with serous atrophy of fat had bone marrow fat measured as less than 20% (Table 7.7). In cases where the femur is not available, the humerus has been shown to be a reliable and consistent alternative (Lamoureux et al. 2011).

Figure 7.19 Serous atrophy of bone fat from a goat that died from starvation due to exogenous circumstances.

Table 7.7 Average Bone Marrow Fat Content for Normal Animals

Species	Normal Mean (%)	Normal Range (%)
Canine	82	65–98
Equine	86	63–99
Bovine	91	80–101

Source: Meyerholtz, K. A., Wilson, C. R., Everson, R. J., and S. B. Hooser. 2011. Quantitative assessment of the percent fat in domestic animal bone marrow. *J Forensic Sci.* 56:775–777.

Conclusion

The forensic necropsy is performed to identify, document, and characterize the injuries and/or diseases of an animal in order to determine the cause of death, manner of death, and allow for the collection of trace evidence. The external and internal examinations are the basic parts of the forensic necropsy and are to be performed in all cases. Different patterns of injury are important to recognize as they are caused by vastly different weapons (sharp force injures vs. blunt force trauma) or processes (gunshot injuries, asphyxiation, thermal injuries, etc.). In many forensic necropsies, recognizing these patterns is crucial for determining the cause and manner of death. Complete tissue samples should be collected in all cases and histopathology should be performed when the cause of death cannot be determined after completion of the forensic necropsy. In some cases, more specialized procedures such as radiological studies, toxicological studies, and microbiological testing may be warranted.

References

Baniak, N., Campos-Baniak, G., Mulla, A., and J. Kalra. 2014. Vitreous humor: A short review on post-mortem applications. *J Clin Exp Pathol.* 4:199. doi:10.4172/2161-0681.1000199

Barrington, K., and H. E. Jensen. 2015. Experimental animal models of bruises in forensic medicine—A review. *Scand J Lab Anim Sci.* 41:1–8.

Bohling, M. W., Henderson, R. A., Swaim, S. F., Kinkaid, S. A., and J. C. Wright. 2004. Cutaneous wound healing in the cat: A macroscopic description and comparison with cutaneous wound healing in the dog. *Vet Surg.* 33:579–587.

Bohnert, M., Werner, C. R., and S. Pollak. 2003. Problems associated with the diagnosis of vitality in burned bodies. *Forensic Sci Int.* 135:197–205.

Campbell, P. R., and R. Kerridge. 1993. Fatal traumatic air embolism following a stab wound to the chest. *Aust N Z J Surg.* 63:307–309.

Centers for Disease Control and Prevention (CDC). 2003. *Medical Examiners' and Coroners' Handbook on Death Registration and Fetal Death Reporting.* Hyattsville: CDC.

Chinnici, N., and J. E. Huffman. 2014. Morphological and DNA analysis to determine canid species. *J Penn Acad Sci.* 88:247–253.

Cooper, J. E., and M. E. Cooper. 2007. *Introduction to Veterinary and Comparative Forensic Medicine.* Ames, IA: Wiley-Blackwell.

Cook, D. S., Braithwaite, R. A., and K. A. Hale. 2000. Estimating antemortem drug concentrations from postmortem blood samples: The influence of postmortem redistribution. *J Clin Pathol.* 53:282–285.

de la Grandmaison, G. L., Charlier, P., and M. Durgon. 2010. Usefulness of systematic histological examination in routine forensic autopsy. *J Forensic Sci.* 55:85–88.

Denton, J. S., Segovia, A., and J. A. Filkins. 2006. Practical pathology of gunshot wounds. *Arch Pathol Lab Med.* 130:1283–1289.

DiMaio, V. J. M., and S. E. Dana. 2007. *Handbook of Forensic Pathology*, 2nd ed. Boca Raton, FL: CRC Press/Taylor & Francis.

DiMaio, V. J., and D. DiMaio. 2001. *Forensic Pathology*, 2nd ed. Boca Raton, FL: CRC Press/Taylor & Francis.

Finnie, J. W. 2016. Forensic pathology of traumatic brain injury. *Vet Pathol.* 53:962–978.

Foreyt, W. J. 2001. *Veterinary Parasitology Reference Manual*, 5th ed. Ames, IA: Iowa State University Press.

Foreyt, W. J. 1986. Recovery of nematode eggs and larvae in deer: Evaluation of fecal preservation methods. *J Am Vet Med Assoc.* 189:1065–1067.

Freeman, L. M. 2012. Cachexia and sarcopenia: Emerging syndromes of importance in dogs and cats. *J Vet Intern Med.* 26:3–17.

Gerdin, J. A., and S. P. McDonough. 2013. Forensic pathology of companion animal abuse. *Vet Pathol.* 50:994–1006.

Gerdin, J. A., McDonough, S. P., Reisman, R., and J. Scarlett. 2016. Circumstances, descriptive characteristics, and pathologic findings in dogs suspected of starving. *Vet Pathol.* 53:1087–1094.

Giancamillo, A., Giudici, D., Andreola, S. et al. 2010. Immersion of piglet carcasses in water—The applicability of microscopic analysis and limits of diatom testing on an animal model. *Legal Med.* 12:13–18.

Illinois Coroners and Medical Examiners Association. 2007. Guidelines for the determination of manner of death. http://www.coronersillinois.org/images/laws/guidelines-determination-manner-of-death.pdf (Accessed April 2, 2017).

Kusewitt, D. F., and L. J. Rush. 2007. Neoplasia and tumor biology. In *Pathologic Basis of Disease*, 8th ed., eds. McGavin, M. D., and J. F. Zachary, 279. St. Louis, MO: Mosby.

Lamoureux, J. L., Fitzgeral, S. D., Church, M. K., and D. W. Agnew. 2011. The effect of environmental storage conditions on bone marrow fat determination in three species. *J Vet Diag Invest.* 23:312–315.

McCausland, I. P., and R. Dougherty. 1978. Histological ageing of bruises in lambs and calves. *Aust Vet J.* 54:525–527.

McEwen, B. J. 2016. Nondrowning asphyxia in veterinary forensic pathology: Suffocation, strangulation, and mechanical asphyxia. *Vet Pathol.* 153:1037–1048.

McEwen, B. J., and J. Gerdin. 2016. Veterinary forensic pathology: Drowning and bodies recovered in water. *Vet Pathol.* 53:1049–1056.

Meyerholtz, K. A., Wilson, C. R., Everson, R. J., and S. B. Hooser. 2011. Quantitative assessment of the percent fat in domestic animal bone marrow. *J Forensic Sci.* 56:775–777.

Merck, M. D. 2013. Animal fighting. In *Veterinary Forensics: Animal Cruelty Investigations,* 2nd ed., ed. Merck, M. D., 243–254. Ames, IA: Wiley-Blackwell.

Merck, M. D., and D. M. Miller. 2013. Asphyxia. In *Veterinary Forensics: Animal Cruelty Investigations,* 2nd ed., ed. Merck, M. D., 169–184. Ames, IA: Wiley-Blackwell.

Merck, M. D., Miller, D. M., and P. C. Maiorka. 2013a. CSI: Examination of the animal. In *Veterinary Forensics: Animal Cruelty Investigations,* 2nd ed., ed. Merck, M. D., 37–68. Ames, IA: Wiley-Blackwell.

Merck, M. D., Miller, D. M., Reisman, R. W., and P. C. Maiorka. 2013b. Blunt force trauma. In *Veterinary Forensics: Animal Cruelty Investigations,* 2nd ed., ed. Merck, M. D., 97–122. Ames, IA: Wiley-Blackwell.

Miletich JJ and Lindstrom TL. 2010. Death and the Human Body. In An introduction to the work of a medical examiner. Santa Barbara California: Praeger, pp. 13–20.

Miller, W. H., Griffin, C. E., and K. L. Campbell. 2013. Environmental skin diseases. In *Small Animal Dermatology,* 7th ed., eds. Miller, W. H., Griffen, C. E., and K. L. Campbell, 667–668. Philadelphia, PA: Elsevier.

Munro, R., and H. M. C. Munro. 2008. *Animal Abuse and Unlawful Killing: Veterinary Forensic Pathology.* Edinburgh: Saunders.

Munro, R., and H. M. Munro. 2013. Some challenges in forensic veterinary pathology: A review. *J Comp Path.* 149:57–73.

Myers, R. K., and M. D. McGavin. 2007. Neoplasia and tumor biology. In *Pathologic Basis of Disease,* 8th ed., eds. McGavin, M. D., and J. F. Zachary, 38. St. Louis, MO: Mosby.

Panella, N. J., and S. D. Hodge. 2013. *The Forensic Autopsy for Lawyers.* Chicago: American Bar Association.

Prahlow, J. A., and D. A. Barrett. 2005. A suicide using a homemade carbon monoxide "death machine." *Am J Forensic Med Pathol.* 26:177–180.

Rogde, S., and J. H. Oliving. 1996. Characteristics of fire victims in different sorts of fires. *Forensic Sci Int.* 77:93–99.

Rogers, E., and A. W. Stern. 2013. Veterinary forensics: The veterinarian as the medical examiner. *Today's Vet Pract.* July/August:43–47.

Sarvesvaran, R. 1991. Medico-legal aspects of embolism with a case illustration. *Malays J Pathol.* 13:89–100.

Sauvageau, A., and E. Boghossian. 2010. Classification of asphyxia: The need for standardization. *J Forensic Sci.* 55:1259–1267.

Schulze, C., Peters, M., Baumgrätner, W., and P. Wohlsein. 2016. Electrical injuries in animals: Causes, pathogenesis, and morphological findings. *Vet Pathol.* 53:1018–1029.

Spitz, W. U. 2006. Blunt force trauma. In *Medicolegal Investigation of Death,* 4th ed., eds. Spitz, W. U. and D. J. Spitz. Springfield: Charles C Thomas.

Stephenson, T. 1997. Ageing of bruising in children. *J R Soc Med.* 90:312–314.

Stern, A. W. 2013. Starvation due to neglect: A canine case series. *J Vet Sci Technol.* 4:1–2.

Stern, A. W., Lewis, R. J., and K. S. Thompson. 2014. Toxic smoke inhalation in fire victim dogs. *Vet Pathol.* 51:1165–1167.

Stricker, T. P., and V. Kumar. 2013. Neoplasia. In *Pathologic Basis of Disease,* 8th ed., eds. Kumar, V., Abbas, A. K., Fausto, N., and J. C. Aster, 320–321. Philadelphia, PA: Saunders.

Surrell, J. A., Alexander, R. C., Cohle, S. D., Lovell, F. R., and R. A. Wehrenberg. 1987. Effects of microwave radiation on living tissues. *J Trauma.* 27:935–939.

Thavarajah, R., Mudimbaimannar, V. K., Elizabeth, J., Rao, U. K., and K. Ranganathan. 2012. Chemical and physical basics of routine formaldehyde fixation. *J Oral Maxillofac Pathol.* 16:400–405.

Tong, L. J. 2014. Fracture characteristics to distinguish between accidental injury and non-accidental injury in dogs. *Vet J.* 199:392–398.

Veterinary Genetics Laboratory. Evidence collection. https://www.vgl.ucdavis.edu/forensics/collection.php (Accessed February 6, 2016).

Wilmink, J. M., and P. R. van Weeren. 2005. Second-intention repair in the horse and pony and management of exuberant granulation tissue. *Vet Clin North Am Equine Pract.* 21:15–32.

Wobeser, G. 1996. Forensic (medico-legal) necropsy of wildlife. *J Wildl Dis.* 32:240–249.

Zhou, C., and R. W. Byard. 2011. Factors and processes causing accelerated decomposition in human cadavers—An overview. *J Forensic Legal Med.* 18:6–9.

8

Postmortem Changes and the Estimation of Time Since Death

Jason W. Brooks

Contents

Introduction

Following death, an inevitable and irreversible sequence of physical and chemical changes begins in the body. The order of these changes is largely repeatable, although the rate at which they occur may vary greatly due to a wide range of factors. A thorough understanding of these postmortem processes and the factors that affect them is critical to the estimation of the postmortem interval (PMI).

Estimating the PMI, also known as time since death, is important in many human and animal death investigations, as well as insurance and civil investigations, in order to establish a timeline of events. Formulating an estimate of the PMI may aid the investigator in refining a pool of suspects, corroborating witness statements, and establishing the duration of abuse or neglect (Munro and Munro 2013). Much research on PMI estimation has been conducted on human bodies using both case-based studies and experimental studies; however, relatively little data on PMI estimation in animals are available for use in case applications. As a result, veterinary forensic investigators may attempt to extrapolate from the human data when estimating the time of death in animal cases. Caution must be used, however, as the lack of validation of these methods in animals may present a significant obstacle to the admissibility of this evidence in court. Federal Rules of Evidence (FRE), which are also often adopted by state courts, generally govern the admissibility of evidence. Acceptance and interpretation of FRE rules such as 702 and 703, which govern expert testimony, vary between states. Specifically, in some jurisdictions, *Daubert* standards for admissibility of scientific evidence specify that conclusions must be drawn using the scientific method, based on such foundations as hypothesis testing, peer review and publication, rates of error, and the use of standard controls (Berger 2005). Some of the described techniques may not hold up to this test and, therefore, may not be accepted into evidence unless their reliability and relevance can be demonstrated.

Although time of death estimation has been studied for over a century, the accuracy in estimating PMI has not improved significantly, and no single method can be reliably used (Perper 2006; Swift 2010). Caution should be used when formulating any estimate of time since death, for it is dependent upon multiple factors related to the circumstances of the death and the environment in which the body is located after death. Furthermore, it is well documented that the ability to estimate PMI decreases as the actual time since death increases (Merck and Miller 2013). The investigator must strongly consider that many human death investigations rely heavily on facts revealed through witness testimony or scene investigation to estimate PMI; however, such evidence is often not available in veterinary cases (Brooks 2016). In addition to such investigative techniques, the most commonly used scientific method for the estimation of PMI in casework is the measurement of body temperature to determine the extent of body cooling. The accuracy of temperature-based methods, however, is notoriously low and human models of body cooling may not be appropriate for use in animal cases. This chapter will discuss the typical progression of postmortem changes and a variety of methods, and their limitations, that may be considered by the field investigator to approximate PMI in animal carcasses.

Standard Progression of Postmortem Changes

The investigator must have an understanding of the typical progression of postmortem changes in order to estimate the time since death. These physical and chemical changes depend greatly on environmental conditions such as temperature, oxygen availability, and activity by insects and scavengers (Brooks 2016). The most readily observable physical changes are body cooling, lividity, muscle rigidity, and decomposition.

Body Cooling

The most studied postmortem change is the cooling of the body (algor mortis) after death, which is based on the fact that the body temperature begins to decrease upon death due to the absence of cellular activities that generate heat in the living body. Many research studies have recorded postmortem body temperature changes in humans and animals over time at various sites in the body and under various environmental conditions, however, the ideal model of body cooling for use in the field has not been developed. Numerous variables associated with the body and its environment have been found to significantly affect the rate of body cooling. Despite the difficulties in identifying an optimal model, body cooling may be used to aid in the estimation of the PMI; however, it should be used in conjunction with other methods for the most accurate estimation.

Shortly after death, the body begins to lose heat to the environment and internal temperatures begin to drop. The rate at which this process occurs is dependent on many factors, but there is often a delay between death and the beginning of the internal cooling of the body. This phenomenon, known as the lag phase or temperature plateau effect (TPE), has been shown to vary significantly between studies and has been associated with such factors as animal species, cause of death, body region, body size, surface insulation, and environmental conditions (Al-Alousi 2002; Smart and Kaliszan 2012). Because of this variable lag phase, researchers have had difficulty in formulating models that accurately predict PMI. One of the first attempts to develop a model that accounted for the TPE was to simply add a fixed lag period to the "rule of thumb" that the body cools at a rate of 1°C (1.8°F) per hour after death. By this method, an additional factor of 3 hours was added to account for the TPE (Shapiro 1965). Other authors have since stated that the human body cools at a rate of 0.8–1.1°C (1.5–2.0°F) for the first 12 hours after death, and 0.6°C (1°F) per hour thereafter (DiMaio and DiMaio 2001; Perper 2006). A more complex model was later developed that described the rate of cooling as slowest in the early and late stages and more rapid during the middle stage (Marshall and Hoare 1962). This model is the basis upon which the commonly used nomogram was developed (Henssge 1988). Additional models and refinements continue to be proposed by researchers, but none has been widely accepted for use in casework.

Studies on the cooling of animal carcasses suggest that differences exist between the rate of cooling among various species and that the use of human models may not be ideal for application in animal cases. A major difference cited by some authors is the inconsistency of the TPE in animal carcasses. In a study using pig carcasses, a TPE was observed in only 26% of animals, and in a similar study using dogs, no TPE was detected (Kaliszan et al. 2005; Proctor et al. 2009). The average rate of cooling of dogs in this study was 0.5°C (0.9°F) per hour, which differs from the published estimates of cooling rate for human bodies. Another study using dogs also detected no TPE by rectal temperature measurement, and was able to demonstrate predictable cooling during the first 10 hours after death to permit the estimation of the PMI to a 2-hour interval (Erlandsson and Munro 2007). Studies of wildlife, such as hunter-harvested deer, have also failed to demonstrate a TPE when measuring temperatures in the nasal cavity and thigh muscle (Cox et al. 1994; Hadley et al. 1999). When comparing estimates of PMI using these multiple models, the user quickly determines that the calculated estimates vary across models. Within the first few hours after death, all models will result in a similar PMI; however, as the actual time since death increases, so will the differences between the models. Much of the research conducted on animal carcasses suggests that the rate of cooling of animal carcasses may differ from that of human bodies; however, the variables that affect this process are not yet completely understood. Therefore, the investigator is urged to use caution when applying methods across species.

Lividity

Upon death, blood begins to settle in a gravity-dependent pattern within the body. The resulting purple-red discoloration of the skin and soft tissues is known as lividity or livor mortis. This postmortem pooling of blood may be observed either externally in the skin and mucous membranes, or internally in the organs of the chest and abdomen, typically beginning within 30 minutes to 2 hours after death in humans (DiMaio and DiMaio 2001). It is essential to distinguish livor mortis from hemorrhage or bruising. Livor mortis forms as a direct result of the effects of gravity on blood and, thus, will form as blood settles to the portions of the body that are closest to the ground. Hemorrhage, however, is unlikely to follow such a pattern, and will manifest in areas affected by trauma or other disease. Furthermore, livor mortis is created by the settling of blood within dilated blood vessels, whereas hemorrhage or bruising results from the escape of blood from the vessels and into the surrounding tissues or spaces. Therefore, hemorrhage or bruising of the soft tissues will not blanch or become pale when pressure is applied. Livor mortis, however, depending on its stage of development, may blanch when pressed firmly. In the early stage of livor mortis, applying pressure or moving the body will force blood through the vessels away from the compressed area, leaving the compressed area temporarily blanched until the blood settles again.

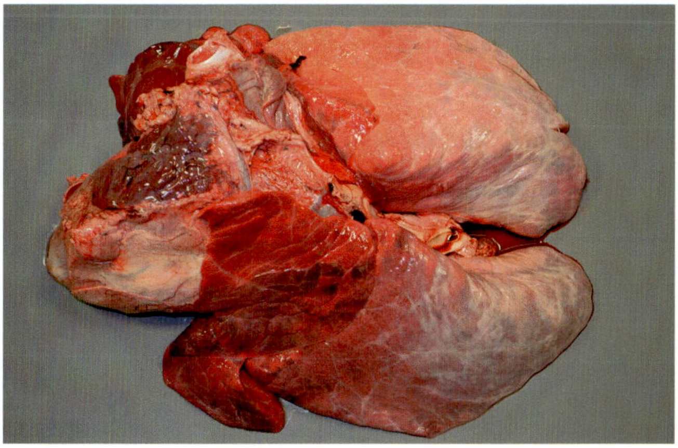

Figure 8.1 Example of lividity.

This phenomenon is known as nonfixed livor mortis. In the later stage of livor mortis, at approximately 8–12 hours, blood begins leaking from the vessels into the surrounding tissues as the vessel walls and the blood cells begin to degrade. When this begins to occur, the blanching in response to pressure is no longer possible and the livor mortis is considered fixed (DiMaio and DiMaio 2001). The investigator may consider this principle if the pattern of lividity on the body is not consistent with the position in which the body was found. This may suggest that the body was moved after livor mortis became fixed (Lew and Matshes 2005). Livor mortis is often not prominent in the skin of many animals, even after removing the hair, though it may be visible on the ears of dogs and is often easily observed within the internal organs (Figure 8.1) (Brooks 2016; Erlandsson and Munro 2007).

Muscle Rigidity

Upon death, the skeletal and cardiac muscle fibers in the body continue to metabolize energy and contract. Eventually, however, because energy is required for the relaxation of muscle fibers, relaxation can no longer occur after the limited supply of energy is depleted. Therefore, the muscle fibers remain in a state of permanent contraction known as rigor mortis, and the musculature of the body becomes increasingly rigid (Saukko and Knight 2004). This state of rigor mortis will persist until it is either physically disrupted by movement of the body or by the early stage of decomposition, resulting in the degradation of the muscle fibers (DiMaio and DiMaio 2001).

There are published intervals for the expected time course for the development of rigor mortis in humans; however, the time required for the onset and resolution of rigor mortis is variable and may differ for other animal species. Typically, in humans, the onset of rigor mortis occurs at approximately 2–6 hours postmortem, and persists for roughly 36 hours, at which time it begins

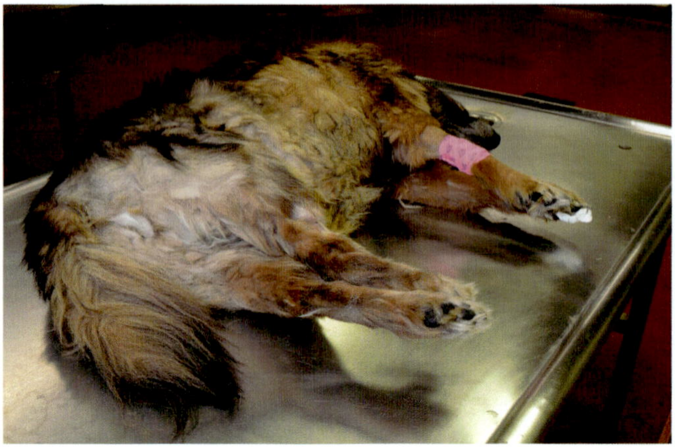

Figure 8.2 Example of a dog in full rigor.

to slowly resolve. This time course, however, is known to vary according to such variables as ambient temperature, antemortem activity, cause of death, and body temperature at the time of death (DiMaio and DiMaio 2001; Saukko and Knight 2004). All muscles in the body are said to be affected uniformly and simultaneously, although the effects of contraction are often reported to be first visible in the small muscle groups of the body, such as the jaw, later developing in the larger muscles of the chest and arms, and finally in the legs (Figure 8.2) (DiMaio and DiMaio 2001). Resolution due to early decomposition typically follows this same pattern. In humans, rigor mortis is more prominent in bodies with greater muscle mass and may be scarcely detectable in bodies with little muscle mass (Martins et al. 2015). In a study using dog carcasses, generalized rigor mortis occurred at less than 1 day postmortem, and rigor mortis of the hind limbs and jaw persisted until 7 days postmortem (Erlandsson and Munro 2007). Little data have been published on the time course of rigor mortis in animals, thus the validity of application of human models is not known. Regardless, the following rule of thumb is commonly used in human cases based on the association between rigor mortis and body cooling (Saukko and Knight 2004). During the first 3 hours after death the body is expected to be warm to the touch and flaccid, with no significant onset of rigor. Between 3 and 8 hours after death, the body is expected to be warm, but notable rigor will be observed. From 8 to 36 hours after death, the body becomes cool to the touch and rigor mortis persists. At any time after 36 hours, the rigor begins to resolve and the body is cool to the touch and flaccid.

Decomposition

To the human observer, the most distinctive postmortem change is the decomposition of the soft tissues. Soon after death, cell membranes begin to degrade and rupture, releasing cellular contents and exposing adjacent cells to degradative enzymes in a type of chain reaction. This form of degradation and digestion of tissues by body enzymes is known as autolysis. A second pathway of decomposition, known as putrefaction, often begins simultaneously because of bacterial proliferation and destruction of tissues. Decomposition has been studied for decades in both animals and humans, and many variables have been found to affect its progress; however, these variables are still not completely understood. There is, however, a largely predictable sequence of stages through which the body progresses after death, but the investigator must consider that many gross changes occur simultaneously in the body and their rates of progression are not entirely linear.

The early literature defines the four phases of decomposition as fresh, bloat, decay, and dry (Reed 1958). These stages, though, were problematic for field application due to the lack of clearly defined starting and ending points. To address this shortcoming, other investigators developed modifications of the four-stage scale, creating both a five-stage scale and a six-stage scale (Galloway et al. 1989; Megyesi et al. 2005; Wilson et al. 2007). Both the five- and six-stage scales are based on multiple descriptive starting points and ending points for each stage. The six-stage scale may be more appropriate for buried bodies or those with a shorter PMI, while the five-stage scale may be better suited to exposed bodies or those with a longer PMI (Brooks 2016). The five-stage scale classifies carcasses as either fresh, early decomposition, advanced decomposition, skeletonization, or extreme decomposition (Galloway et al. 1989).

Despite this relatively uniform progression of gross changes, researchers have long been puzzled by the variation in the rate of decomposition. As a result, one group developed a method for estimating decomposition rate based on accumulated degree days (ADD), a measurement based on the sum of the average daily temperature of each day after death. This was done by assigning decomposition scores to carcasses of known PMI and accounting for time and temperatures to which the remains were exposed (Megyesi et al. 2005). Their results showed that the calculated ADD was responsible for 80% of the variation in decomposition rate of human bodies, suggesting that accumulated temperature exposure was more important than time alone. Although later efforts were made to standardize a "universal" formula for the estimation of PMI using ADD, this approach was found to be unreliable, leaving investigators to consider geographic and climate-associated variables (Cockle and Bell 2015; Vass 2011). Attempts to further refine these methods continue; however, no practical field application has been developed.

Decomposition rate may be affected by a large number of variables. Temperature and moisture are the most well understood, but other variables that may affect decomposition rate include the cause of death, manner of disposition (buried, submerged, bagged, frozen), insulation by clothing or hair coat, oxygen availability, insect activity, scavenger activity, trauma, and other factors (Cockle and Bell 2015). Rapid decomposition of human bodies has been reported under a variety of conditions including high ambient temperatures, high body temperature, obesity, and some forms of natural disease (Zhou and Byard 2011). The presence of clothing on pig carcasses slowed the rate of decomposition and changed the pattern of decomposition by altering insect oviposition sites (Card et al. 2015). Exposure of the body to insects and the heat generated by insect masses is an important factor in the decomposition rate. Rabbits exposed to insects throughout decomposition were found to decompose more rapidly than those initially exposed to insects and then buried (Simmons et al. 2010). Similarly, rabbits exposed to insects for any period of time decomposed more rapidly than rabbits that were never exposed to insects. It has been estimated that exposed surface remains decompose two times faster than submerged remains, and eight times faster than buried remains (Merck and Miller 2013). Scavenger damage to carcasses has also been shown to significantly affect decomposition, resulting in an increased rate of decomposition with possible partial consumption of the carcass (Willey and Snyder 1989). Trauma alone has not been shown to significantly affect the overall rate of decomposition; however, trauma sites provide alternate locations for insect colonization and may affect the pattern of decomposition (Cross and Simmons 2010; Tomberlin and Sanford 2011).

Mummification

It is possible for the body to become desiccated and mummified without completely decomposing if the body is located in dry environmental conditions with low humidity and sufficient ventilation (Lew and Matshes 2005). In this process, the skin becomes tight, yellow-brown to black, and takes on a leathery or parchment paper consistency (Perper 2006). In such an environment, the processes of autolysis and putrefaction are inhibited, and the tissues become dehydrated rather than decomposing. The drying results in changes such as contraction or wrinkling of skin and retraction of the nailbeds (Lew and Matshes 2005). The appearance of the darkened leathery skin may lead untrained observers to presume that these bodies have been burned; however, further examination by a trained investigator will easily distinguish the two.

Methods for Estimating Time Since Death

Despite the number of proposed techniques for estimating PMI, only a small set of these are likely to be of practical use for application in veterinary cases. It is possible for an investigator to be presented with a body in any stage of decomposition from very fresh to very decomposed, therefore one should be familiar with methods applicable to both the early and late postmortem period. These periods may be defined as the periods prior to which and after which the body has equilibrated to ambient temperature, respectively (Al-Alousi et al. 2001a,b; Henssge and Madea 2004). The early postmortem period is the time during which the body core temperature remains higher than the environmental temperature, while the late postmortem period is the time during which the body temperature has become equal to the environmental temperature. Techniques used by the investigator to estimate time since death will differ according to the actual postmortem interval (Figure 8.3). In practice, it is likely that PMI estimation in the early postmortem period will be based largely on gross changes such as muscle rigidity and lividity, rectal

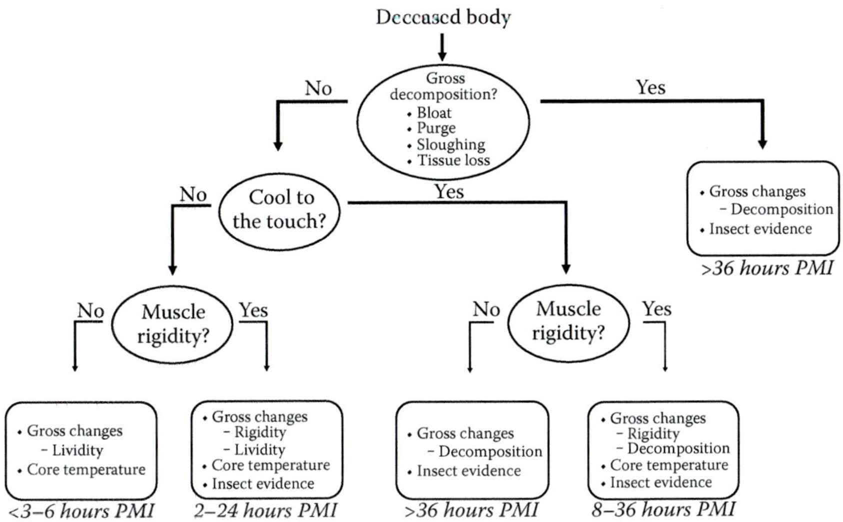

Figure 8.3 Methods used to estimate time since death at various stages.

temperature, and possibly insect activity. In the late postmortem period, however, PMI estimation is often based on insect evidence and gross changes such as muscle rigidity and the stage of decomposition.

Gross Changes

The deceased body undergoes predictable physical alterations including changes of color, muscle rigidity, free gas bloat, production of purge fluid and odorous gases, sloughing of the superficial layer of skin, destruction of soft tissues, and eventual destruction of bone. In the early stages of decomposition, the red to purple gravity-dependent livor mortis may begin within 30 minutes after death and becomes completely developed in humans at approximately 10–12 hours after death, when it becomes fixed and can no longer be blanched with pressure (Lew and Matshes 2005). The amount of time required for fixed livor mortis to occur is variable and may range from 12 hours to 3 days (Saukko and Knight 2004). Rigor mortis often begins at roughly 2–6 hours after death in humans and becomes fully developed by 6–12 hours. Muscle rigidity then begins to resolve as decomposition progresses by approximately 36 hours postmortem (Saukko and Knight 2004).

With the inevitable advance of decomposition, further color changes occur in the skin and soft tissues. Commonly there is green discoloration of the abdominal skin at roughly 24–30 hours after death due to the degradation of hemoglobin (Figure 8.4) (Perper 2006). Body cavities and internal organs often become distended by decomposition gases produced by bacterial putrefaction. This commonly results in bloating of the abdomen followed by bulging of the eyes and tongue. The onset of bloating often develops at approximately

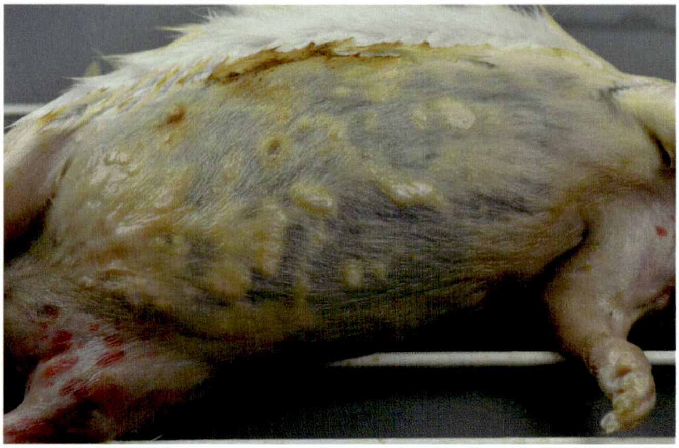

Figure 8.4 Example of green discoloration of the skin due to degradation of hemoglobin.

60–72 hours after death in humans; however, this may occur faster or slower depending on environmental conditions and animal species. Carcasses of herbivores, especially ruminants, are observed by the author to decompose and bloat more rapidly than monogastric omnivores or carnivores, likely due to the residual microbial activity within the gastrointestinal tract (Munro and Munro 2008). As the skin begins to degrade, sloughing of the superficial epidermis may occur, and any body hair in the affected areas may be sloughed along with the underlying skin. As the soft tissues of the body liquefy through autolysis and decomposition, a red-brown liquid is produced, known as purge fluid (Figure 8.5). This purge fluid often leaks from the mouth, nose, and anus or other body openings during the bloating stage (Lew and Matshes 2005).

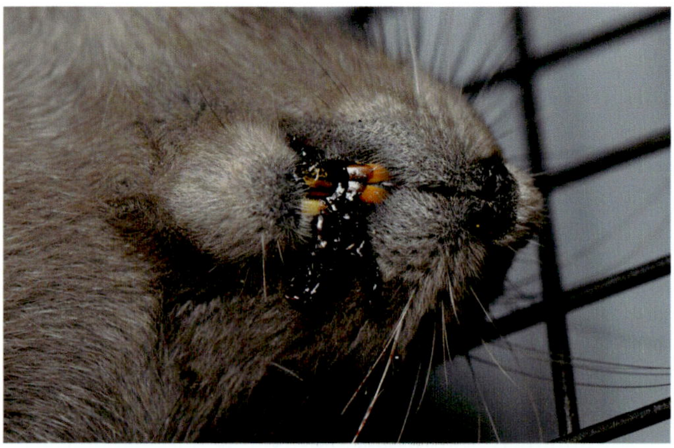

Figure 8.5 Purge fluid leaks from the mouth.

In some cases, pink discoloration of the teeth may occur in dogs at roughly 3 weeks postmortem (Erlandsson and Munro 2007). By several days or weeks after death there is often extensive destruction of the soft tissues by insect activity. Further decomposition or destruction by insects and scavengers is highly variable, but in most cases, will eventually result in skeletonization by several weeks to months after death.

The rate and pattern of decomposition is heavily dependent upon ambient temperature. The overall rate of decomposition increases with higher ambient temperature and decreases with lower ambient temperature. Furthermore, both the rate and pattern of decomposition may be altered by freezing of the carcass (Roberts and Dabbs 2015). A study using frozen pig carcasses demonstrated a slower overall rate of decomposition, less internal putrefaction, and more external drying and insect activity, and a generalized gray discoloration when compared to unfrozen control pigs (Roberts and Dabbs 2015).

Numerous studies in the older literature described a variety of supravital tissue responses for use in estimating PMI including physical, electrical, or chemical stimuli applied to skeletal muscle or the eye (Henssge et al. 2000; Madea 1992). These are not currently considered practical or acceptable methods and will not be further discussed in this chapter. Another noteworthy method, gastric emptying time, was once considered a reliable indicator of PMI. The method was based on the concept that ingested food spent a uniform amount of time being digested in the stomach before being evacuated from the stomach to the small intestine. More recently, however, the time required for gastric digestion and emptying has been shown to be highly variable and subject to many factors. Thus, it is no longer considered to be a valid indicator of PMI (Saukko and Knight 2004).

One group of techniques that has more recently been developed is based on physical changes in the eye. Studies have shown patterns in changes in a wide range of physical characteristics such as corneal opacity, pupillary diameter, retinal vessel changes, retinal color changes, and intraocular pressure (Balci et al. 2010; Jaafar and Nokes 1994). Of these, corneal opacity and intraocular pressure were most strongly associated with PMI. Corneal opacity has been shown to increase significantly at greater than 8 hours after death (Balci et al. 2010). Perhaps of greatest interest to the field investigator is the measurement of intraocular pressure. One study showed that the pressure inside of the eye decreased significantly over the first 12 hours after death when measured by a hand-held tonometer (Balci et al. 2010). With refinement, it is possible that this method may become applicable for use in the field, especially if validated on various species.

Field Application

The interpretation of gross postmortem changes requires careful assessment and documentation of the condition of the body at the scene or in the necropsy room (Figure 8.3). Without moving the body or otherwise disturbing other evidence, the investigator should begin by visually inspecting the body in the position in which it is found. Exposed body areas that are nonhaired or sparsely haired should be examined for purple-red livor mortis within the skin and soft tissues. This settling of blood occurs in gravity-dependent locations; thus, it is expected to develop in portions of the body that are nearest to the ground. If any deviation in this pattern is found, it may suggest that the body has been moved from its original position. The body should also be visually examined for abdominal bloating, gaseous distention of the eyes or other tissues, purge fluid from the body openings, skin discoloration, skin sloughing, and soft tissue destruction or loss. If the body is in an advanced state of decay, there may also be evidence of bone destruction. These criteria should all be assessed visibly without disturbing the body, and should be carefully documented and photographed.

Depending upon the circumstances of the investigation and the role of the individual conducting the examination, permission to move the body for further evaluation should be obtained. When it is possible to do so, the body should be further examined for muscle rigidity by manually attempting to gently flex and extend the joints attached to the muscles of the jaw and the upper and lower extremities. If flaccid, then rigor mortis has either not yet begun or has already passed. If there is moderate resistance, but the joint is capable of manual flexion and extension, then rigor mortis is either beginning to occur or has already reached its maximum and is now beginning to pass. If full rigidity is encountered, then the joint cannot be flexed or extended and the muscle is in full rigor. When rigor mortis begins to pass after a period of muscle degradation begins, the initial rigidity can be overcome by manual force, thus forcing the joint to bend. This is not possible early in full rigor, and only becomes possible after the muscle fibers have begun to decompose sufficiently to allow them to be broken by manual force. The body should also be fully exposed and thoroughly examined on all surfaces for lividity, bloating, purge fluid, skin sloughing, and tissue destruction.

Temperature-Based Methods

The measurement of body temperature to estimate the time of death has been studied for many decades; however, the reliability of temperature-based estimates is questionable in any species and results must be used with caution. When applying this method to animal carcasses, the investigator should account for the species in question rather than simply extrapolating from data generated from studies of human bodies (Munro and Munro 2013). Unfortunately, there is little published data on the postmortem cooling of most animal species, with only a relatively small number of animal studies to provide a basis for species-specific estimates. Therefore, the investigator is left to consider the existing body of knowledge, which is largely based on studies of bodies of humans, pigs, or dogs.

For practical application, there currently exist three methods for interpreting core temperatures in the field. As these were developed by studies on human bodies, caution should be used in their application to animal cases as erroneous results may be encountered given the lack of species specific validation. One method is the "rule of thumb" stating that the body cools at a rate of 1°C per hour after death, plus a factor of 3 hours to account for the TPE (Shapiro 1965). This can be expressed as:

$$\text{PMI (in hours)} = 37°\text{C} - \text{Rectal Temperature °C} + 3$$

Another method is based on an average rate of body cooling of 1.5–2.0°F (0.83–1.11°C) for the first 12 hours after death, followed by 0.55°C (1°F) per hour thereafter (DiMaio and DiMaio 2001; Perper 2006). This can be expressed as:

$$\text{PMI (in hours)} = 98.6°\text{F} - \text{Rectal Temperature °F}/1.5 \text{ or}$$
$$37°\text{C} - \text{Rectal Temperature °C}/0.83$$

For use in animals in which the expected core body temperature differs from that of humans, the formulas of these first two methods may be adjusted by replacing the 37°C (98.6°F) with the expected core temperature for the species of interest (Brooks 2016). The third method is based on a more complex model presented in the form of an easily used chart called a nomogram instead of a manual calculation (Henssge and Madea 2004). Henssge's nomogram is available for use on many websites and is widely published in many textbooks. In addition to rectal temperature, its use requires a measurement of the environmental temperature and estimation of body weight, and it allows for correction due to clothing and environmental conditions.

In addition to these three methods, the investigator should consider critical developments in relevant animal studies. Importantly, many animal studies show that the cooling rate and TPE may differ according to species. Rectal temperature in dogs was found to decrease 0.5°C per hour (Proctor et al. 2009). In this study, the rate of cooling decreased as body weight or body size increased, although body density, sex, and hair coat density had no effect on cooling rate. In another study, rectal temperature in dogs decreased over the first 10 hours after death in a uniform pattern that allowed for the estimation of death to an interval of 2 hours, however, after 10 hours postmortem the reliability decreased significantly (Erlandsson and Munro 2007). The rectal temperature of all dogs in the study reached ambient temperature by 24–48 hours after death.

Before deciding to employ one or more of these methods, the investigator should strongly consider that there is at least a 2-hour margin of error in the first 6 hours after death, at least a 3-hour margin of error in the next 14 hours, and at least a 4.5-hour margin of error in the following 10 hours after death (Kaliszan et al. 2009). In humans, one study found that the nomogram method correctly estimated PMI in only 42.9% of cases, and that the method overestimated PMI for very heavy or large bodies (Hubig et al. 2015; Muggenthaler et al. 2012). The accuracy of the nomogram was eventually improved to within 1.5 hours during the first 6 hours after death by using brain temperature instead of rectal temperature, although the revised method has not been widely adapted due to the difficulty in measuring brain temperature in the field (Henssge et al. 1984).

More recently developed temperature-based techniques, such as measurement of eye or ear temperature, have attempted to improve accuracy of PMI estimation. The application of ear temperature measurements in human bodies by inserting a probe into the ear canal to record the temperature at the eardrum was found to be more accurate than the nomogram method or the other formula methods (Baccino et al. 1996). Investigators concluded that ear temperature was useful in estimating PMI when environmental temperature was above 15°C and showed no TPE. Another series of studies demonstrated the accuracy of eye temperatures for time of death estimation through insertion of a pin probe into the eye (Kaliszan 2013). Eye temperatures showed a faster cooling rate compared to rectal temperatures, showed no TPE, and were not affected by body weight, and the mean error for all cases was 31 minutes within the first 5 hours. These findings suggest that models for PMI estimation using ear or eye temperatures are likely to be improved in the near future and may offer new opportunities for field investigators.

The current understanding of body cooling and the variables affecting it is not sufficiently advanced to provide highly precise time since death estimations. Because of the large inherent error, PMI estimations based on body temperature alone may not be admissible in court and should be used with caution (Hubig et al. 2015; Smart and Kaliszan 2012).

Field Application

The use of temperature-dependent methods requires a basic set of equipment for the measurement of temperatures and other relevant data. Such equipment should include a digital thermometer capable of accurately measuring within a wide range of temperatures from expected body temperature to the environmental temperature, a scale or weight tape for measuring body weight, a calculator, and a nomogram (if this method of interpretation will be used). The investigator should begin by recording the core temperature of the body, preferably by inserting the thermometer probe several centimeters into the rectum, taking caution to avoid disturbing any possible evidence associated with the rectum, especially if sexual assault is suspected. Although other body locations may be used to record core temperature, they will result in artefactual changes to the integrity of the carcass and are not as well documented as rectal temperature. In the future, ear or eye temperature may become more accepted and standardized measurements.

Following the measurement of body temperature, the environmental temperature should be recorded. This is best measured near the location in which the body was found and at the level of the body. Estimation or measurement of the body weight should also be done. This may be accomplished with a scale if the body can be lifted, or with a weight tape for some animal species such as cattle, hogs, and horses. Otherwise, the weight should be estimated by visual examination. Finally, the conditions at the scene must be documented, including the presence or absence of wind, water, and clothing or other insulating covering materials. The collected data can then be applied to the following formulae:

$$\text{PMI (in hours)} = \text{Normal Body Temperature}\,^\circ\text{C} - \text{Measured Rectal Temperature}\,^\circ\text{C} + 3$$

$$\text{PMI (in hours)} = (\text{Normal Body Temperature}\,^\circ\text{C} - \text{Measured Rectal Temperature}\,^\circ\text{C})/0.83$$

$$\text{PMI (in hours)} = (\text{Normal Body Temperature}\,^\circ\text{C} - \text{Measured Rectal Temperature}\,^\circ\text{C})/0.5$$

Additionally, the nomogram method may be used based on temperatures and body weight. It is advised that at least several of these calculations are considered, as each of the formulae will result in a different estimated PMI. The longer the PMI, the greater will be the observed difference in calculations between formulae.

Entomology

Evaluation of the insect life stages found on a deceased body and its immediate environment may provide valuable information for the estimation of PMI and, in some cases, may provide the best estimate of the time of death. To effectively utilize entomology in this manner, it is essential for the investigator to understand the basic principles of insect life cycles and sample collection and storage. When insect evidence is properly collected and delivered to a skilled entomologist, it may be possible to approximate the time at which the insects first colonized the tissue; however, the time of insect colonization does not necessarily correspond to the time of death. Tissue colonization may occur at any interval following death or may, in fact, occur antemortem in the case of an untreated wound. Regardless, the investigator must carefully consider that the life cycles of the insects of interest are sensitive to variations in environmental conditions, so information about recent local weather patterns is often essential for the interpretation of entomological evidence (Tomberlin and Sanford 2011). The identification and evaluation of insects is beyond the scope of practice of most animal forensic, insurance, and civil investigators and is best left in the hands of a forensic entomologist. However, the proper collection and preservation of insects from the body and the environment may easily be learned by the investigator for use in cases in which insect evidence is expected to be of importance.

Field Application

Collection of entomological evidence requires a small amount of advanced preparation including a set of basic equipment and preservatives. The minimum required equipment includes such items as forceps, scoop, fine paintbrush, small shovel, small capture net, paper evidence bags, a variety of vials with screw-top lids and labels, 70–95% ethanol, cooler with ice packs, sawdust or tissue paper, thermometer, and sample collection data sheet. Before collecting any evidence from the scene, it is important to have approval from the authority in charge and to document and photograph any samples in their original location. Begin by collecting any insect stages from the body itself, including from the natural openings of the body, traumatic wounds, any materials covering the body such as clothing or wrapping materials, and at the interface of the body with the underlying material (Amendt et al. 2007). Specimens collected should include larvae and pupae of every shape and size, using different vials for samples of different types and body locations. In general, focus on collecting the most mature insect life stages that are identified. Collect as many of the larvae as possible from each area up to roughly 100 specimens, or when this is not feasible, collect at least 1–10% of the larvae. Recently emerged adults that are not yet able to fly, flying adult flies, and dead adult flies or beetles should also be captured and collected. After collecting insects from the body, search the area surrounding the body over at least a 2-m radius. At an outdoor scene, collect soil samples from up to 10 cm deep at various locations around the body, and collect a control soil sample at a greater distance from the body. Soil samples may be collected into plastic evidence bags and refrigerated until delivery to an entomologist (Maloney and Housman 2014). At an indoor scene, be sure to inspect under carpets, bedding materials, and other items so as to identify all migrating insects (Amendt et al. 2007).

Insect eggs should be collected by moistening a fine paintbrush with water and lightly touching the brush to the egg masses. To maintain live eggs for hatching, the collected eggs should then be placed into a vial lined with moistened tissue paper, and air should be permitted to enter the vial. This may be accomplished by using one or two layers of paper towel or nylon hosiery secured with a rubber band as a lid for the vial. If there will be a delay longer than several hours before eggs can be delivered to an entomologist, a small piece of liver may be provided as nourishment for the newly emerging larvae (Anderson 2013). The time of hatching should also be recorded if any eggs are observed to hatch prior to delivery to an entomologist. To preserve eggs, place eggs into 70–95% ethanol. Similarly, live maggots for rearing should be placed into vials lined with moistened sawdust or tissue paper with liver as needed, permitting air to enter but no insects to escape. Larvae to be preserved must be killed prior to placing in ethanol to prevent putrefaction and distortion. Larvae may be easily killed by immersing in hot water that is near its boiling point for approximately 30 seconds (Amendt et al. 2007). Killed maggots may then be placed into ethanol for preservation. Pupae should be kept alive and stored as for live maggots; there is no need to preserve pupae in ethanol as they lack identifying features (Anderson 2013). Live adults may either be placed directly into ethanol or they may first be killed by placing them in a freezer for approximately 1 hour, or by placing them in a jar containing material soaked in nail polish remover containing ethyl acetate, and then placing the dead insect into ethanol (Maloney and Housman 2014; Tomberlin and Sanford 2011). Recently hatched adult flies that have not yet become capable of flying are of particular interest, and should be placed into vials and kept alive until their wings have fully developed and dried to allow for identification (Anderson 2013). Any other nonliving insect remnants such as empty puparia or beetle feces should be stored in ethanol or in dry vials if thoroughly desiccated (Amendt et al. 2007). Any live specimens for rearing should be stored at a constant and known temperature, generally within a refrigerator (2–6°C), whereas specimens preserved in ethanol may be stored at room temperature. All vials should be carefully labelled, including at least the collection date, specimen ID, and collection location. Transport all specimens to a forensic entomologist ideally within 24 hours of collection while maintaining the chain of custody.

Written and photographic documentation of the scene findings and samples collected is also essential. Many prepared forms are available for use and can be found in a variety of textbooks and websites. Data to be recorded include information about the scene, the body, and the insects observed and collected. In some instances, maggots will be in large masses that generate heat; it is therefore important to obtain the temperature from each mass, as this heat will speed up development of the maggots within the mass (Figure 8.6). The investigator should record temperatures of the body, the maggot masses, the ground or floor surface, soil, and ambient scene temperature (Tomberlin and Sanford 2011). The investigator should obtain weather records from the relevant area, including maximum and minimum temperatures and precipitation for at least the last two weeks prior to the discovery of the body (Maloney and Housman 2014). Photographs of the scene, body, and insect evidence should be routinely taken, and photographs of the surrounding vegetation should also be taken to assist with the interpretation of the insect evidence. This information should be transferred with the specimens to the forensic entomologist.

Although accurate interpretation of insect evidence relies upon insect identification and weather data, some general concepts may be used in the field for more immediate use in roughly estimating the time of colonization. Often, among the first insects to arrive on a dead carcass are the blowflies

Figure 8.6 Maggot mass.

(Anderson 2013). The time delay between death and the first arrival of blowflies is highly variable, but may occur within seconds to minutes or may be delayed by an indefinite interval (Perper 2006). This time lag is a critical feature in the interpretation of insect evidence, as it must be understood that the insect evidence can only be used to calculate an estimated minimum time since death (Saukko and Knight 2004; Tomberlin and Sanford 2011). It is possible, if the time lag between death and colonization was prolonged, that the PMI may in fact be much longer than the time since colonization.

Regardless, once colonization begins, common patterns are frequently observed. Adult female blowflies deposit eggs on the body in predictable locations, including the natural openings of the head such as the eyes, nose, mouth, and ears, and in the anogenital region. This pattern is so predictable that any deviation in this pattern is suggestive of the presence of a wound, as body areas with injured skin or exposed body fluids are often preferentially colonized by insects (Sinclair et al. 2006; Tomberlin and Sanford 2011). While the rate of development of the insect life stages is dependent upon environmental conditions, some general estimates may be used with caution (Saukko and Knight 2004). Blowfly eggs often hatch into the first stage maggots, or first instar, within approximately 8–14 hours after deposition and then to second instar after an additional 8–14 hours. Second instar feed for 2–3 days before molting to third instar and then another 6 days before leaving the host to pupate. At this time, migrating third instar or pupae may be found in the environment surrounding the body. Pupae then emerge as adult flies after roughly 12 days. The entire life cycle of the blowfly requires approximately 18–24 days from egg to adult, depending on environmental conditions. Following the initial colonization of the body by blowflies, additional insect species typically begin to colonize, including other species of flies and beetles.

Botany

Forensic botany is the application of the study of plants to the investigation of a crime. Although not as commonly utilized as other forms of evidence, due to its ubiquitous nature, plant evidence may be very useful in order to establish a geographic association between the victim and suspect and crime scene, refute or confirm testimony, locate and evaluate burial sites, and roughly estimate the PMI (Aquila et al. 2014; Hamilton and Erhart 2012). Botanical evidence may be found in the area surrounding a body, on the suspect, on the victim, or inside of the victim's body and may range from entire plants or leaves to small plant fragments, to microscopic pollen or algae (Merck and LeCouteur 2013). When provided with appropriate samples, it may be possible for a forensic botanist to identify plant species based on taxonomy or DNA sequencing. Based on known geographic distributions of plant species, it may then be possible to determine the area from which the plant fragment originated. It may also be possible, based on plant growth staging, to estimate the time of year that a plant specimen was likely to have been encountered. Botanical evidence may assist in rough approximation of the PMI by estimating the minimum amount of time required for a plant to grow to the observed stage within the body or on the grave of a buried body. Similarly, signs of soil disturbance or anomalous growth of vegetation may indicate to the investigator the possible site of a clandestine grave (Hamilton and Erhart 2012). Exposure to certain poisonous plants may result in death, often following ingestion of the inciting plant (Hardy and Martin 2012). To ascertain this intoxication, the investigator will likely require the expertise of a botanist or toxicologist to identify the plant or toxin to which the decedent was exposed. To fully utilize and interpret botanical evidence, it is essential that appropriate collection techniques are followed and that the samples are evaluated by a capable forensic botanist.

Field Application

Proper collection of plant evidence requires a small amount of basic equipment such as magnifying glass, paper evidence bags and envelopes, newsprint or other large paper for wrapping samples, sheets of corrugated cardboard roughly 12 × 18 inches, similarly sized pieces of plywood for pressing plant materials, strapping material to bind the plywood into a press, a small shovel, scissors, forceps, and glass jars for water collection. After documenting the location and photographing of any relevant plant specimens at the scene, materials may be collected if permission is granted by the authority in charge. A reference sampling of the largest and most common plants in the area of the crime scene should be collected to allow the botanist to develop a complete understanding of the expected plant flora in the microenvironment of the scene. These reference samples may include entire plants with attached roots, leaves, or leaf clusters from trees, and large portions of plants that may be folded and packaged or pressed flat. In general, it is preferable to preserve large plant fragments such as stems and leaves by pressing them flat under light pressure until they completely dry. This may be easily accomplished by creating a plant press using two pieces of plywood and two pieces of corrugated cardboard. Wrap large plant portions flat in a single layer of newsprint paper placed between two layers of cardboard. This may then be placed between two pieces of plywood and pressure applied by tightening several lengths of strapping to compress the plant (Hardy and Martin 2012). The material should remain within the press for several days until dry. After reference samples are collected, trace evidence samples may be collected. These may include large plant portions, which should be stored as described for reference samples, or small plant portions such as seeds, flowers, small leaves, or plant fragments. These materials may be placed directly into paper evidence bags or envelopes and permitted to dry. If DNA analysis is desired, plant materials may be either frozen or desiccated in silica gel (Hardy and Martin 2012; Merck and LeCouteur 2013). The collection of microscopic botanical samples is more complex and should be done in consultation with the botanist. In general, pollen and spores may be collected from the soil into a sterile glass or plastic container using sterile gloves by performing 10–20 pinch collections of the top 1 cm of soil at the scene which are then combined to create a composite sample (Hardy and Martin 2012). Soil samples may be stored at room temperature if thoroughly dry, or otherwise should be frozen. Also, 0.5–1 L of water for pollen, spores, or algae may be collected into a sterile glass or plastic container and frozen. Consult a forensic botanist or forensic botany manual for specific collection protocols.

Laboratory Methods

Although they are beyond the scope of this chapter, the field investigator should be familiar with ancillary analytical methods that may be performed in an accredited forensic laboratory or veterinary diagnostic laboratory. These facilities often employ specialists with expertise in disciplines such as forensic pathology, molecular biology, chemistry, bacteriology, radiology, anthropology, and others. Any referral laboratory should have standard operating procedures in place to maintain a strict and precise chain of custody for all items received for analysis. At such a laboratory, a pathologist may perform histopathology or microscopic review of the tissues or may perform electrolyte assays on body fluids such as blood, ocular fluid, or cerebrospinal fluid. A molecular biologist may conduct analyses to determine the extent of degradation of DNA or RNA. A chemist may measure the degradation of unstable radioisotopes within tissues. A bacteriologist may be able to assay the entire population of bacteria present in the tissues. A radiologist may be able to conduct imaging studies using x-rays or other means to visualize internal body structures. An anthropologist may be called to assist with the identification of bones or the stage of decomposition. While some of these methods, such as histology, biological fluid chemistry, and radiography are best suited for fresh materials, the remaining techniques may be considered for the estimation of PMI when remains are buried or skeletonized or otherwise in an advanced state of decomposition. It is critical to understand the potential contributions of supporting laboratory specialists.

Notably, much attention has been given to chemical analyses of body fluids such as vitreous humor for the estimation of PMI. Vitreous humor has become the preferred fluid sample as it is less subject to contamination and rapid autolysis than blood or cerebrospinal fluid. Decreases in vitreous humor glucose and increases in potassium and hypoxanthine have been well documented in humans by various investigators (Lange et al. 1994; Madea and Rodig 2006; Munoz et al. 2001; Rognum et al. 1991; Rognum et al. 2016; Siddamsetty et al. 2014). Fewer studies have been conducted on animal samples, but a series of studies in dogs demonstrated a similar rise in potassium in vitreous humor as well as other biochemical changes (Schoning and Strafuss 1980a,b,c). Despite the large number of studies on vitreous humor, the chemical analytical methods investigated to date have been imprecise and unreliable and are not currently recommended for use in the field (Madea 2005). With continued refinement, it is possible that these methods may become practical for routine application.

Conclusion

Appropriate interpretation of the data collected from the scene or from the necropsy is critical for producing evidence that is admissible in court. A summary outline of evaluation techniques at various postmortem stages is presented in Table 8.1, and a summarized key for general field interpretation of these data is presented in Figure 8.7. In addition, the investigator should strongly consider the close association between changes in muscle rigidity and

Table 8.1 Methods for Evaluating the Postmortem Interval at Various Postmortem Stages

Postmortem Stage	Time Since Death	Findings	Evaluation Methods
Fresh	0–5 days	No discoloration or insect activity	Core temperature, lividity, rigidity, ocular changes
Bloat	1–21 days	Gray-green discoloration, bloating, skin slippage, hair loss, early insect activity	Soft tissue decomposition, insect evidence, ocular changes
Active decay	3 days–18 months	Moist decomposition of tissues, sagging of flesh, caving of abdomen, extensive insect activity, bone exposure of less than half of the skeleton, mummification may occur	Soft tissue decomposition, insect evidence
Advanced decay	7 days–3 years	Bones with residual body fluids, tissue covering less than half of the skeleton, dry bones	Bone and soft tissue decomposition, insect evidence, botanical evidence
Dry remains	2 months–3 years	Dry bones with weathering such as bleaching, mineral deposition, erosion, or freeze-thaw damage	Bone decomposition, botanical evidence, radiocarbon dating

Early Postmortem Period (Approximately <24–36 hours PMI)

Core Temperature Decrease

A decrease of approximately 0.5–1.5°C per hour may be expected

Gross Changes

Lividity

- Onset (30 minutes–2 hours)
- Fixed and persistent (beginning at 8–72 hours)

Rigidity

- Onset (2–6 hours)
- Fully developed (6–36 hours)

Decomposition

- Bloating (as soon as 1 day)
- Discoloration: gray-green (as soon as 1 day)
- Skin/hair sloughing (as soon as 1 day)

Insect Evidence

Blowfly Life Stages (minimum colonization time)

- Eggs (may be deposited at any time after death)
- 1st instar (8–14 hours)
- 2nd instar (16–28 hours)

Late Postmortem Period (Approximately >24–36 hours PMI)

Core Temperature Decrease

Equilibrates to ambient temperature in 24–48 hours

Gross Changes

Lividity

- Fixed and persistent (beginning at 8–72 hours)

Rigidity

- Full (6–36 hours)
- Resolving (>36 hours)

Decomposition

- Bloating (onset at 48–72 hours, resolution by 7–13 days)
- Discoloration: gray-green (onset at 24–30 hours)
- Skin/hair sloughing (onset 1–5 days)
- Purge fluid (onset at 48–72 hours)
- Soft tissue destruction (3 days–3 years)
- Skeletonization (13 weeks–3 years)

Insect Evidence

Blowfly life stages (minimum colonization time)

- Eggs (may be deposited any time after death)
- 1st instar (8–14 hours)
- 2nd instar (16–28 hours)
- 3rd instar (3–4 days)
- Pupa (9–10 days)
- Adult (18–24 days)

Decomposition is generally slowed by 50% or more during submersion or burial.

Figure 8.7 Changes observed during the postmortem period used for estimating the postmortem interval.

body temperature over time. If the body is flaccid and warm to the touch, it is likely very recently died and rigor mortis has not yet begun. If the body is warm and rigid, it is likely that rigor has recently occurred, but that the core temperature has not yet decreased significantly. If the body is cool and rigid, this suggests that rigor is still active, but that enough time has passed since death to allow for body cooling. Finally, if the body is cool and flaccid, it is likely that the body has been dead long enough to permit both cooling and the complete resolution of rigor mortis.

The investigator is advised to consider that these methods remain imprecise, and that no single method, or even a combination of methods, can be used to estimate PMI with great precision. This does not, however, imply that the estimation of PMI is without value. Data collected from the scene or at necropsy should be considered along with any facts revealed through witness statements or scene investigation. Furthermore, many factors related to the scene will affect the rate at which the described physical and chemical changes in the body will occur. The environmental temperature, humidity, wind, sunlight exposure, insect activity, scavenger activity, method of body disposal, exposure to oxygen, and other variables must all be considered. The experienced investigator should consider the collective body of scientific evidence and investigative evidence when estimating the PMI.

References

Al-Alousi, L.M. 2002. A study of the shape of the post-mortem cooling curve in 117 forensic cases. *Forensic Sci Int.* 125:237–44.

Al-Alousi, L.M., R.A. Anderson, D.M. Worster, and D.V. Land. 2001a. Multiple-probe thermography for estimating the postmortem interval: I. Continuous monitoring and data analysis of brain, liver, rectal and environmental temperatures in 117 forensic cases. *J Forensic Sci.* 46:317–22.

Al-Alousi, L.M., R.A. Anderson, D.M. Worster, and D.V. Land. 2001b. Multiple-probe thermography for estimating the postmortem interval: II. Practical versions of the triple-exponential formulae (TEF) for estimating the time of death in the field. *J Forensic Sci.* 46:323–7.

Amendt, J., C.P. Campobasso, E. Gaudry, C. Reiter, H.N. LeBlanc, and M.J. Hall. 2007. Best practice in forensic entomology—Standards and guidelines. *Int J Legal Med.* 121:90–104.

Anderson, G. 2013. Forensic entomology: The use of insects in animal cruelty cases. In *Veterinary Forensics: Animal Cruelty Investigations*, M. Merck, ed., pp. 273–286. Ames, IA: John Wiley & Sons, Inc.

Aquila, I., F. Ausania, C. Di Nunzio, A. Serra, S. Boca, A. Capelli, P. Magni, and P. Ricci. 2014. The role of forensic botany in crime scene investigation: Case report and review of literature. *J Forensic Sci.* 59:820–4.

Baccino, E., L. DeSaintMartin, Y. Schuliar, P. Guilloteau, M. LeRhun, J.F. Morin, D. Leglise, and J. Amice. 1996. Outer ear temperature and time of death. *Forensic Sci Int.* 83:133–46.

Balci, Y., H. Basmak, B.K. Kocaturk, A. Sahin, and K. Ozdamar. 2010. The importance of measuring intraocular pressure using a tonometer in order to estimate the postmortem interval. *Am J Forensic Med Pathol.* 31:151–5.

Berger, M.A. 2005. What has a decade of Daubert wrought? *Am J Public Health.* 95 Suppl 1:S59–65.
Brooks, J.W. 2016. Postmortem changes in animal carcasses and estimation of the postmortem interval. *Vet Pathol.* 53:929–40.
Card, A., P. Cross, C. Moffatt, and T. Simmons. 2015. The effect of clothing on the rate of decomposition and Diptera colonization on Sus scrofa carcasses. *J Forensic Sci.* 60:979–82.
Cockle, D.L., and L.S. Bell. 2015. Human decomposition and the reliability of a "Universal" model for post mortem interval estimations. *Forensic Sci Int.* 253:136 e1–136 e9.
Cox, R.J., S.L. Mitchell, and E.O. Espinoza. 1994. CompuTOD, a computer program to estimate time of death of deer. *J Forensic Sci.* 39:1287–99.
Cross, P., and T. Simmons. 2010. The influence of penetrative trauma on the rate of decomposition. *J Forensic Sci.* 55:295–301.
DiMaio, V.J., and D. DiMaio. 2001. *Forensic Pathology.* 2nd ed. New York: CRC Press.
Erlandsson, M., and R. Munro. 2007. Estimation of the post-mortem interval in beagle dogs. *Sci Justice.* 47:150–4.
Galloway, A., W.H. Birkby, A.M. Jones, T.E. Henry, and B.O. Parks. 1989. Decay rates of human remains in an arid environment. *J Forensic Sci.* 34:607–16.
Hadley, B.M., L.W. Robins, and D.A. Beffa. 1999. Estimating time of death of deer in Missouri: A comparison of three indicators. *J Forensic Sci.* 44:1124–30.
Hamilton, M.D., and E.M. Erhart. 2012. Forensic evidence collection and cultural motives for animal harvesting. In *Wildlife Forensics: Methods and Applications*, J.E. Huffman and J.R. Wallace, eds., pp. 65–79. Ames, IA: Wiley-Blackwell.
Hardy, C.R., and D.S. Martin. 2012. Plants and wildlife forensics. In *Wildlife Forensics: Methods and Applications*, J.E. Huffman and J.R. Wallace, eds., pp. 145–159. Ames, IA: Wiley-Blackwell.
Henssge, C. 1988. Death time estimation in case work. I. The rectal temperature time of death nomogram. *Forensic Sci Int.* 38:209–36.
Henssge, C., L. Althaus, J. Bolt, A. Freislederer, H.T. Haffner, C.A. Henssge, B. Hoppe, and V. Schneider. 2000. Experiences with a compound method for estimating the time since death. II. Integration of non-temperature-based methods. *Int J Legal Med.* 113:320–31.
Henssge, C., E.R. Beckmann, F. Wischhusen, and B. Brinkmann. 1984. Determination of the time of death by measurement of central brain temperature. *Z Rechtsmed.* 93:1–22.
Henssge, C., and B. Madea. 2004. Estimation of the time since death in the early postmortem period. *Forensic Sci Int.* 144:167–75.
Hubig, M., H. Muggenthaler, I. Sinicina, and G. Mall. 2015. Temperature based forensic death time estimation: The standard model in experimental test. *Leg Med (Tokyo).* 17:381–7.
Jaafar, S., and L.D. Nokes. 1994. Examination of the eye as a means to determine the early postmortem period: A review of the literature. *Forensic Sci Int.* 64:185–9.
Kaliszan, M. 2013. Studies on time of death estimation in the early post mortem period—Application of a method based on eyeball temperature measurement to human bodies. *Legal Med (Tokyo).* 15:278–82.
Kaliszan, M., R. Hauser, R. Kaliszan, P. Wiczling, J. Buczynski, and M. Penkowski. 2005. Verification of the exponential model of body temperature decrease after death in pigs. *Exp Physiol.* 90:727–38.

Kaliszan, M., R. Hauser, and G. Kernbach-Wighton. 2009. Estimation of the time of death based on the assessment of post mortem processes with emphasis on body cooling. *Leg Med (Tokyo).* 11:111–7.

Lange, N., S. Swearer, and W.Q. Sturner. 1994. Human postmortem interval estimation from vitreous potassium: An analysis of original data from six different studies. *Forensic Sci Int.* 66:159–74.

Lew, E.O., and E.W. Matshes. 2005. Postmortem changes. In *Forensic Pathology: Principles and Practice*, D. Dolinak, E.W. Matshes and E.O. Lew, eds., pp. 527–554. New York: Elsevier/Academic Press.

Madea, B. 1992. Estimating time of death from measurement of the electrical excitability of skeletal muscle. *Sci Justice.* 32:117–29.

Madea, B. 2005. Is there recent progress in the estimation of the postmortem interval by means of thanatochemistry? *Forensic Sci Int.* 151:139–49.

Madea, B., and A. Rodig. 2006. Time of death dependent criteria in vitreous humor: Accuracy of estimating the time since death. *Forensic Sci Int.* 164:87–92.

Maloney, M.S., and D. Housman. 2014. *Crime Scene Investigation Procedural Guide.* R.M. Gardner, ed. Boca Raton, FL: CRC Press/Taylor & Francis.

Marshall, T., and F. Hoare. 1962. Estimating the time of death—The rectal cooling after death and its mathematical representation. *J Forensic Sci.* 7:56–81.

Martins, P.A., F. Ferreira, R. Natal Jorge, M. Parente, and A. Santos. 2015. Necromechanics: Death-induced changes in the mechanical properties of human tissues. *Proc Inst Mech Eng H.* 229:343–9.

Megyesi, M.S., S.P. Nawrocki, and N.H. Haskell. 2005. Using accumulated degree-days to estimate the postmortem interval from decomposed human remains. *J Forensic Sci.* 50:618–26.

Merck, M., and R.A. LeCouteur. 2013. Special considerations in animal cruelty cases. In *Veterinary Forensics: Animal Cruelty Investigations*, M. Merck, ed., pp. 69–96. Ames, IA: Wiley-Blackwell.

Merck, M., and D. Miller. 2013. Postmortem changes and the postmortem interval. In *Veterinary Forensics: Animal Cruelty Investigations*, M. Merck, ed., pp. 255–271. Ames, IA: Wiley-Blackwell.

Muggenthaler, H., I. Sinicina, M. Hubig, and G. Mall. 2012. Database of post-mortem rectal cooling cases under strictly controlled conditions: A useful tool in death time estimation. *Int J Legal Med.* 126:79–87.

Munoz, J.I., J.M. Suarez-Penaranda, X.L. Otero, M.S. Rodriguez-Calvo, E. Costas, X. Miguens, and L. Concheiro. 2001. A new perspective in the estimation of postmortem interval (PMI) based on vitreous. *J Forensic Sci.* 46:209–14.

Munro, R., and H.M. Munro. 2013. Some challenges in forensic veterinary pathology: A review. *J Comp Pathol.* 149:57–73.

Munro, R., and H.M.C. Munro. 2008. *Animal Abuse and Unlawful Killing: Forensic Veterinary Pathology.* Philadelphia, PA: Saunders/Elsevier.

Perper, J. 2006. Time of death and changes after death. In *Medicolegal Investigation of Death: Guidelines for the Application of Pathology to Crime Investigation*, W.U. Spitz and D.J. Spitz, eds., pp. 87–183. Springfield, IL: Charles C Thomas.

Proctor, K.W., W.J. Kelch, and J.C. New, Jr. 2009. Estimating the time of death in domestic canines. *J Forensic Sci.* 54:1433–7.

Reed, H.B. 1958. A study of dog carcass communities in Tennessee, with special reference to the insects. *Am Midl Nat.* 59:213–45.

Roberts, L.G., and G.R. Dabbs. 2015. A taphonomic study exploring the differences in decomposition rate and manner between frozen and never frozen domestic pigs (*Sus scrofa*). *J Forensic Sci.* 60:588–94.

Rognum, T.O., S. Hauge, S. Oyasaeter, and O.D. Saugstad. 1991. A new biochemical method for estimation of postmortem time. *Forensic Sci Int.* 51:139–46.

Rognum, T.O., S. Holmen, M.A. Musse, P.S. Dahlberg, A. Stray-Pedersen, O.D. Saugstad, and S.H. Opdal. 2016. Estimation of time since death by vitreous humor hypoxanthine, potassium, and ambient temperature. *Forensic Sci Int.* 262:160–5.

Saukko, P.J., and B. Knight. 2004. The pathophysiology of death. In *Knight's Forensic Pathology*, P.J. Saukko and B. Knight, eds., pp. 52–97. New York: Oxford University Press.

Schoning, P., and A.C. Strafuss. 1980a. Postmortem biochemical changes in canine blood. *J Forensic Sci.* 25:336–43.

Schoning, P., and A.C. Strafuss. 1980b. Postmortem biochemical changes in canine cerebrospinal fluid. *J Forensic Sci.* 25:60–6.

Schoning, P., and A.C. Strafuss. 1980c. Postmortem biochemical changes in canine vitreous humor. *J Forensic Sci.* 25:53–9.

Shapiro, H.A. 1965. The post-mortem temperature plateau. *J Forensic Med.* 12:137–41.

Siddamsetty, A.K., S.K. Verma, A. Kohli, D. Puri, and A. Singh. 2014. Estimation of time since death from electrolyte, glucose and calcium analysis of postmortem vitreous humour in semi-arid climate. *Med Sci Law.* 54:158–66.

Simmons, T., P.A. Cross, R.E. Adlam, and C. Moffatt. 2010. The influence of insects on decomposition rate in buried and surface remains. *J Forensic Sci.* 55:889–92.

Sinclair, L., M. Merck, and R. Lockwood. 2006. *Forensic Investigation of Animal Cruelty: A Guide for Veterinary and Law Enforcement Professionals.* Washington, DC: Humane Society Press.

Smart, J.L., and M. Kaliszan. 2012. The post mortem temperature plateau and its role in the estimation of time of death. A review. *Leg Med (Tokyo).* 14:55–62.

Swift, B. 2010. Methods of time since death estimation within the early post-mortem interval. *Homicide Major Incident Investig.* 6:97–112.

Tomberlin, J.K., and M.R. Sanford. 2011. Forensic entomology and wildlife. In *Wildlife Forensics: Methods and Applications*, J.E. Huffman and J.R. Wallace, eds., pp. 81–107. Hoboken, NJ: Wiley-Blackwell.

Vass, A.A. 2011. The elusive universal post-mortem interval formula. *Forensic Sci Int.* 204:34–40.

Willey, P., and L.M. Snyder. 1989. Canid modification of human remains: Implications for time-since-death estimations. *J Forensic Sci.* 34:894–901.

Wilson, A.S., R.C. Janaway, A.D. Holland, H.I. Dodson, E. Baran, A.M. Pollard, and D.J. Tobin. 2007. Modelling the buried human body environment in upland climes using three contrasting field sites. *Forensic Sci Int.* 169:6–18.

Zhou, C., and R.W. Byard. 2011. Factors and processes causing accelerated decomposition in human cadavers—An overview. *J Forensic Leg Med.* 18:6–9.

9

Veterinary Forensic Radiology and Imaging

Elizabeth Watson

Contents

Introduction

Radiography and other imaging modalities are often important tools in veterinary forensic investigations. An understanding of forensic imaging techniques in live and deceased animals and a cognizance of the advantages and limitations of each imaging modality are valuable goals for the forensic investigator (Table 9.1). Forensic radiography documents evidence of trauma and assists in

Table 9.1 Comparison of Imaging Modalities Used in Forensic Investigations

	Radiography	Ultrasonography	CT	MR
Action and Use				
Action	Ionizing radiation	Sound	Ionizing radiation	Magnetic field
Highly portable	No	Yes	No	No
Temperature dependent	No	Yes	No	Yes
Anesthesia needed	No	No	Yes	Yes
Projectile trauma	+++	+	+++	+
Pregnancy check	+++	+++	X	X
Survey entire animal	+++	X	+++	X
Soft tissue foreign body	+	+	+	+++
Rib fracture	+++	+	+++	X
Thoracic trauma	+++	+	+++	X
Abdominal organ laceration	+	+++	+	X
Bone edema	X	X	X	+++
Fracture healing	+++	+	+	+
Emaciation	X	X	X	+++
Postmortem imaging	+++	+	+++	+

Note: +++ Best use, + Adequate or some use, X Not recommended.

the differentiation of accidental and nonaccidental injury, helps predict chronology of injury, identify and spatially locates foreign objects and projectiles, and discriminates between antemortem skeletal trauma. Radiographic and other imaging studies allow acquisition of objective evidence in a noninvasive manner. Importantly, imaging evidence is perpetual and imaging studies can be re-evaluated at any time during an investigation should additional information become available.

Although the field of veterinary forensic radiology and imaging is broad and encompasses any application of imaging to legal questions, including imaging of archaeological specimens and inanimate objects, this chapter focuses on the utilization of imaging of live and deceased animals in criminal investigations. The terminology "diagnostic imaging" has largely replaced the word "radiology" in clinical medicine due to the expanding variety of imaging modalities; however, the terminology "forensic radiology and imaging" is preferred to "forensic imaging," which commonly refers to creation of an exact copy of a computer hard drive.

Each radiographic or imaging study entered into evidence requires an imaging report. Unlike a document or photograph, a forensic radiographic or imaging study requires an interpretation by an expert and cannot stand alone as evidence. An expert's interpretation of a radiographic study will include a description of the radiographic findings and a conclusion defining the forensic significance of each radiographic abnormality.

In addition to radiography, imaging modalities utilized for medicolegal investigation include ultrasonography, computed tomography (CT), magnetic resonance (MR) imaging, and nuclear scintigraphy and positron emission tomography (PET). Nuclear scintigraphy and PET are functional studies requiring administration of a radiopharmaceutical, only applicable to the live animal, and are not commonly performed in veterinary forensics. Ultrasonography, CT, and MR are useful imaging modalities for medicolegal investigations in both the live and deceased animals.

Radiography in Forensics

Forensic radiography of the live animal is similar to imaging techniques employed in clinical practice. The clinical imaging examination is performed to guide treatment and/or assess disease progression and resolution, and is a regional radiographic study. In contrast, forensic radiography documents evidence of abuse or neglect and can consist of a survey examination of the whole animal. An entire body study represents targeted orthogonal views which cover the whole animal. A single exposure of the entire animal is never acceptable practice in forensic radiography or in veterinary diagnostic imaging, and similarly imaging of an entire baby, or the babygram, is unacceptable in human radiography (American College of Radiology 2006). A single exposure of an entire body or an exposure including multiple body parts results in a poor-quality image due to geometric distortion, inappropriate exposure factors, and reduced resolution. Radiographic images in forensic examinations must possess high detail, adequate contrast, and good spatial resolution, should be precisely positioned and free of artefacts, and must be appropriately identified as to the individual animal, the acquisition date, the imaging facility, and left- or right-side labelling. A minimum of two orthogonal views of each body region is required for adequate localization and complete identification of structure. More than two orthogonal radiographs may be necessary in more complex anatomy or with specific injuries. Although numerous forensic resources recommend radiographic studies of live and deceased animals in medicolegal investigations, specific radiographic imaging guidelines are not widely available to the forensic veterinarian. Orthogonal radiography of the entire body of a large dog could produce upward of 36 images. In an effort to

Table 9.2 Radiographic Views of Live or Deceased Small Animals in Suspected Cases of Abuse

Routine Survey

- Skull: Lateral, ventrodorsal, and rostrocaudal (3 images)
- Cervical spine: Lateral and ventrodorsal (2 images)
- Thorax: Right and left lateral and ventrodorsal (3 images)
- Abdomen: Lateral and ventrodorsal (2 images)
- Pelvis and femurs: Lateral and ventrodorsal (2 images)
- Forelimb: Craniocaudal and lateral of each[a] (4 images)
- Hind limb: Lateral and craniocaudal of each[a] (4 images)
- Pes and manus: Dorsopalmar/plantar views of each (4 images)

Optional Images

- Thorax: Obliques
- Skull: Obliques
- Pelvis: Frog-leg ventrodorsal
- Digits: Oblique laterals

[a] The limb surveys will require more than eight images in large dogs. Rigor or body condition will limit the number of images obtained in deceased animals.

adequately screen the entire animal for trauma and to reduce the number of images and potential x-ray exposure to personnel, a truncated radiographic survey of the entire animal is suggested (Table 9.2). Some adjustments can be made for large dogs and deceased animals in which positioning is not ideal. A review of this first level of imaging and the physical examination findings may dictate further imaging. The transition from film/screen radiographic imaging to digital imaging (CR/DR) has greatly facilitated the time involved in imaging and reduced the expense of obtaining multiple x-ray exposures. It should be recognized that x-ray exposure to personnel is similar in digital and film/screen imaging and the use of protective lead clothing; the use of radiolucent tape, sponges, sandbag-positioning aids and chemical restraints; and the adherence to radiation safety practices of time, distance, and shielding; and the As Low As Reasonably Achievable (ALARA) principle of x-ray exposure are strongly encouraged.

Forensic radiography of deceased animals is performed as a complementary examination with the forensic necropsy. Body condition and rigor mortis may preclude the typical precise positioning performed in the live animal forensic radiographic examination. If the descendant is presented in a container or body bag, an initial image is obtained prior to removing the animal from the container. This ensures that no forensically important material is lost or left in the body bag. If the condition of the body is friable, orthogonal images will be obtained without removal from the container. Since geometric distortion occurs outside the center of the x-ray beam, targeted radiographs are obtained to cover the entire body. Images centered on the more complex anatomy, such as the skull and thorax, are essential in the postmortem radiographic study. The images will be obtained in the manner described for the live animal with limitations given for the condition of the body and rigor mortis. Greater detail will be achieved with collimated images centered on individual body parts. Radiolucent sponges, tape, and sandbags facilitate the positioning. With no need for personnel in the room to position the body, postmortem radiographic exposures are optimized for image quality.

Postmortem radiography can identify abnormal air accumulations within the body, which may not be as easily detected during the postmortem examination, such as pneumothorax, pneumoperitoneum, and in some cases venous air embolism. Additionally, postmortem radiography can be used to identify and localize projectiles, aid in the retrieval of projectiles and foreign material, guide examination in areas not routinely dissected, and alert the forensic pathologist to any potential hazards during postmortem examination. Knowledge of the sequential postmortem changes in the body are necessary for interpretation of postmortem images. Gas accumulation in the hepatic vasculature is one of the earliest postmortem changes and may be seen within the first 12 hours following death (Heng et al. 2008, 2009a). Intravascular gas can be identified in the portal vein, caudal vena cava, femoral artery, the aorta, the cranial mesenteric artery, and the caudal superficial epigastric artery in postmortem radiographic images of the cat and dog (Heng et al. 2008, 2009a). Over time, gas will distribute in the cardiac chambers, great vessels, mediastinum, pleural space, kidneys, and within the spleen (Heng et al. 2008, 2009a,b). The gas within the liver and spleen will first appear as a branching pattern and gradually redistribute into a vesicular pattern owing to collapse of the parenchyma (Heng et al. 2009a). Postmortem gas may also be seen in the shoulder joints or in the colon wall. Gas trapped in the subcutaneous soft tissues (subcutaneous emphysema) and gas in the deeper soft tissues can accumulate over a period of 24–36 hours. An increase in bowel gas may be identified as early as 8 hours following death.

Ultrasonography in Forensics

Ultrasound imaging has a variety of uses in live animal forensic investigation and is widely available, but has some limited utility in postmortem imaging. Because high-quality portable ultrasound equipment is available and does not utilize ionizing radiation, ultrasonography is uniquely suited for the rapid triage of live animals in large-scale animal cruelty investigations (Figure 9.1). Animals can be quickly evaluated in situ for pleural, pericardial, or abdominal effusions, free pleural or peritoneal air, pregnancy, abscessation, and fracture without the need for protective lead clothing or shielding of adjacent personnel. Ultrasound is a useful modality to locate and guide dissection and removal of known projectiles or foreign objects. Guided tissue sampling in live or deceased animals is one of the greatest advantages of ultrasound imaging.

Several factors limit the use of postmortem ultrasonography in forensic investigations. The progressive gas accumulation in the subcutaneous tissues, in the intra-abdominal parenchymal organs, and in the gastrointestinal tract restricts sonographic evaluation. When air is present ultrasound is reflected

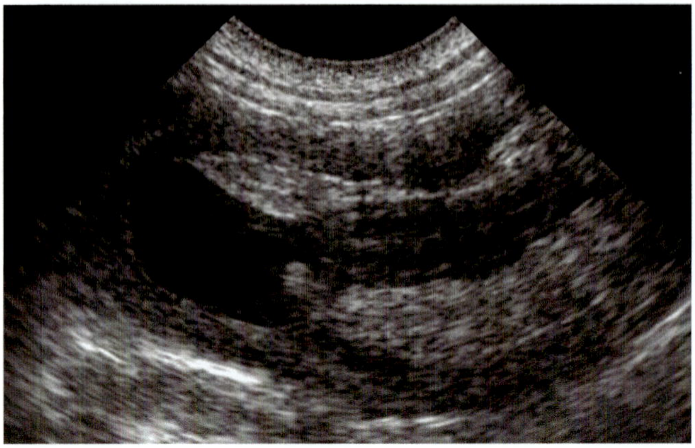

Figure 9.1 Sagittal ultrasound image of an emaciated dog. An intussusception was identified on triage ultrasound. Layers of the bowel wall are visible within the lumen of the intussuscipiens.

at each air-soft tissue interface secondary to differences in acoustic impedance, which describes the resistance of ultrasound travel through tissues. This reflection of sound limits evaluation of the deeper tissues. The reduced flexibility of the deceased body to pressure of the ultrasound probe, increased postmortem echogenicity in the body walls, and difficulties positioning the body for appropriate sonographic windows hamper postmortem sonographic evaluation. Further, low body temperature adversely affects ultrasound contrast resolution. A weak returning signal in adjacent soft tissues is due to diminished differences in acoustic impedance and reflection coefficients, which are a measure of the intensity of the reflected sound.

Computed Tomography in Forensics

Cross-sectional imaging, particularly CT, provides significant advantages over radiography and ultrasound in forensic examination of deceased animals. Although postmortem CT (PMCT) has replaced postmortem radiography in humans, PMCT is currently underutilized in veterinary forensics primarily due to expense and sometimes availability. The superior contrast resolution, the ability to evaluate the body in cross-section, the capability of multiplanar reformatting, and the decreased degradation of the image by poor positioning are advantages of CT imaging over radiography. Similar to postmortem radiographic imaging, PMCT is performed prior to removal of the body from the body bag or container. Because artifacts from metal can somewhat degrade the CT image, any obvious metal on the bag or container, such as a wire identification tag, is removed first. The CT scale can be manipulated to limit the metal streak artifact when the metal is within the body such as a projectile. The animal is placed in dorsal recumbency and imaged completely from the nasal planum through the hind extremities. Precise positioning of the deceased animal with the limbs pulled away from the body wall is often not possible and does not preclude performing the study. With no concerns for radiation exposure, the exposure factors are optimized for imaging the deceased. The skull can be rescanned with a smaller field of view as needed once the initial scan is performed. It is rarely necessary to remove the animal from the body bag for CT imaging. In live animal CT imaging, intravenous contrast material is routinely administered to increase conspicuity of the vasculature. A disadvantage of the native PMCT examination is the evaluation of vasculature. To overcome this disadvantage, advanced techniques for PMCT angiography (PMCTA) are available (Grabherr et al. 2014; Watson and Heng 2017).

Evaluation of the lungs presents an additional challenge in PMCT. Progressing pulmonary atelectasis and internal livor mortis in the thorax are difficult to differentiate from pulmonary disease such as bronchopneumonia and contusion on PMCT. Advanced techniques which mimic the breath hold in live animals are available to supplement the forensic necropsy (Germerott et al. 2010; Watson and Heng 2017). Occasionally, the PMCT and guided tissue sampling may replace the complete forensic necropsy since the body remains intact and this minimally invasive technique may be less objectionable to an owner.

Magnetic Resonance Imaging in Forensics

As with CT, expense and limited availability of equipment constrain the use of the MR in veterinary forensic investigations. Forensic MR imaging in live animals is similar to clinical imaging and requires general anesthesia. A complete MR study is time-consuming compared to CT imaging (Figure 9.2). With no

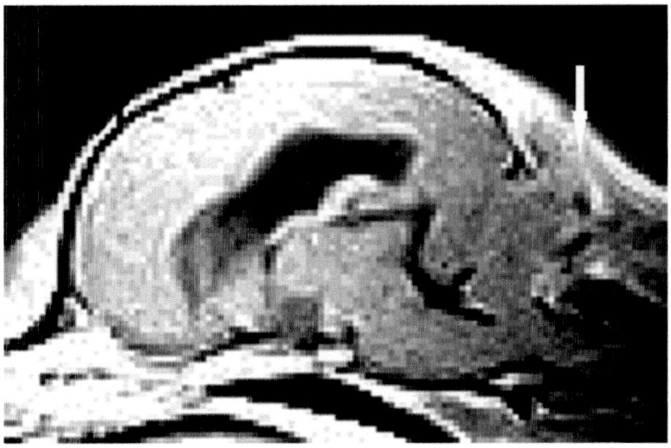

Figure 9.2 Sagittal T2-weighted MR images of a dog following skull trauma. A partial herniation of the cerebellum through a skull fracture is present.

motion artifacts, postmortem magnetic resonance (PMMR) can provide high anatomic detail and excellent contrast resolution, which is greater than that achievable with PMCT. A particular advantage of PMMR is the evaluation of the brain prior to the invasive forensic necropsy. PMMR may be particularly useful in late stages of decomposition when increased liquefaction may be problematic for tissue handing. Additionally, PMMR is a useful supplement to forensic necropsy for differentiation of postmortem and perimortem skeletal trauma through the absence or presence of imaging findings consistent with a vital reaction and to provide additional evidence of emaciation through the identification of serous atrophy of bone marrow fat (Ruder et al. 2011; Sherlock et al. 2010).

In addition to the time-intensive nature of an MR study, the expense, and the limited availability of magnets, temperature dependence represents another potential disadvantage of PMMR. MR contrast resolution will be degraded as the body cools. Below 20°C (68°F), the distinction between fat and soft tissue will be diminished on routine sequences. Diminished contrast between soft tissue and fat does not necessarily preclude the performance of a PMMR study; however, the investigator should be aware of temperature dependence before attempting to image cold or frozen bodies.

The hazards of ferromagnetic implants or foreign objects in MR imaging are widely known in clinical medicine. Survey radiographs are obtained prior to placing the animal in the magnet. The presence of metal in a body is not necessarily a contraindication for PMMR as not all metals are affected by the magnetic field. Only steel containing projectiles are contraindicated in MR imaging owing to their potential to move in the magnetic field and the strong artifact steel projectiles create. MR signal degradation due to the presence of nonferromagnetic metal can be lessened by artifact reduction techniques.

Radiographic Signs of Trauma and Neglect

Radiographic and other imaging studies are useful to identify a wide range of injuries from soft tissue trauma, skeletal trauma, pulmonary contusions and other evidence of intrathoracic trauma, intra-abdominal trauma, intracranial trauma, projectile trauma, secondary signs of drowning and strangulation, and may assist in differentiating nonaccidental trauma from accidental trauma. Imaging studies can also support medicolegal investigations of neglect by providing additional evidence of diminished body fat and condition, identifying serous atrophy of bone marrow fat, and providing evidence of the owner's failure to provide a minimum standard of veterinary care.

Soft Tissue and Skeletal Injury

Soft tissue injuries are commonly evaluated on radiographs in conjunction with skeletal trauma, although other imaging modalities are better at delineating the extent of soft tissue injury. CT and MR imaging provide better soft tissue resolution than radiography for evaluation of soft tissue trauma and CT can rapidly survey large body areas. High frequency ultrasound can detect small accumulations of subcutaneous fluid and bruising; however, ultrasound is not a useful survey modality and is limited to targeted body regions.

Skeletal trauma is typically first evaluated with radiography, since it is a readily available imaging modality appropriate for survey of the whole body. Motor vehicle trauma and falls from heights are common causes of accidental trauma in small animals and are differentiated from nonaccidental trauma by the location and distribution of the fractures and in the context of the reported clinical history and examination findings. Fractures of the skull, teeth, ribs, and vertebrae, injuries to the claws, and evidence of older fractures are more often associated with nonaccidental trauma; whereas fractures of the pelvis, pulmonary contusions, and pneumothorax are more often secondary to a motor vehicle accident (Intarapanich et al. 2016). When rib fractures do occur from a motor vehicle accident, the distribution is primarily on one side of the body; and in a nonaccidental injury, bilateral rib fractures predominate (Intarapanich et al. 2016). Rib fractures are not a frequent injury in high-rise trauma in dogs and cats. Vertebral trauma, spinous process fractures, pulmonary contusions, and pneumothorax are frequent radiographically identifiable high-rise injuries (Gordon et al. 1993; Whitney and Mehlhaff 1987). Facial injuries, tooth fractures, and extremity fractures are additional reported injuries in falls from a height. Additional radiographic features that are reported to suggest nonaccidental trauma rather than accidental trauma include multiple fractures and fractures occurring in more than one body region, presentation with healing fractures, and multiple fractures at varying stages of healing (Tong 2014). Although one study suggested that transverse fractures are more likely to be associated with nonaccidental trauma, transverse fractures in the distal antebrachii of small breed dogs are one of the most common accidental fractures in dogs (Muir 1997; Tong 2014). Transverse, short oblique, or mildly comminuted distal antebrachial fractures occur in small breed dogs after jumping or minor trauma from a fall and are probably more common in the small breed dogs due to morphologic properties of the bone.

It is not uncommon for investigators to attempt application of fracture features of nonaccidental trauma in children to nonaccidental trauma in animals. Within the appropriate context, radiographic features considered highly specific for nonaccidental trauma in children include the classic metaphyseal lesion, posterior rib fractures, spinous process fractures, scapular fractures, and sternal fractures. The classic metaphyseal lesion, a thin fracture at the primary spongiosa of the metaphysis, occurs through a transverse shearing motion in infants and toddlers up to 24 months of age and most commonly in children who are not yet walking. This fracture type is unlikely to occur in dogs and cats since animals are weight-bearing by 3 weeks and physeal closure occurs at a much earlier age in animals than in children. Once the animal or child is walking, physeal fractures are more common.

Thoracic and Abdominal Injury

Thoracic and abdominal injuries are best initially evaluated with radiography. Three radiograph projections, left lateral, right lateral, and ventrodorsal views of the thorax and abdomen are standard. Oblique thoracic views are optional projections for evaluation of the thoracic wall and ribs. Pulmonary contusions are identified as patchy or regional interstitial or alveolar infiltrate with little initial change in lung volume and effacement of the pulmonary vasculature because of hemorrhage in the alveoli. The radiographic pattern of pulmonary contusion cannot be differentiated from other airspace diseases such as bronchopneumonia and edema. The location of the infiltrate and other radiographic signs may help differentiate contusion from edema and pneumonia. Pulmonary contusions are expected to mostly resolve over a period of 72 hours; monitoring by serial images at 24-hour intervals is recommended. Pulmonary contusion can often occur in the absence of rib fracture, particularly in the immature animal due to increased chest compliance. Other signs of thoracic trauma, such as pneumothorax and pneumomediastinum are rapidly detected on thoracic radiographs (Figure 9.3). Pneumothorax may also be rapidly identified by a skilled sonographer on ultrasound. Pneumomediastinum may occur from dissection of gas through cervical soft tissue wounds, secondary to blunt trauma and alveolar rupture, or from esophageal or tracheal perforations. Radiographic signs of abdominal trauma are loss of serosal detail consistent with free peritoneal fluid, rupture of a hollow viscus, and the identification of free peritoneal air, or urinary or ureteral trauma and loss of serosal detail or retroperitoneal contrast. Positive contrast cystography or excretory urography are needed to evaluate the urinary bladder wall integrity. Negative contrast cystography and ultrasound are not appropriate to detect urinary bladder trauma. Ultrasound and CT are the imaging modalities most appropriate to identify liver and splenic lacerations.

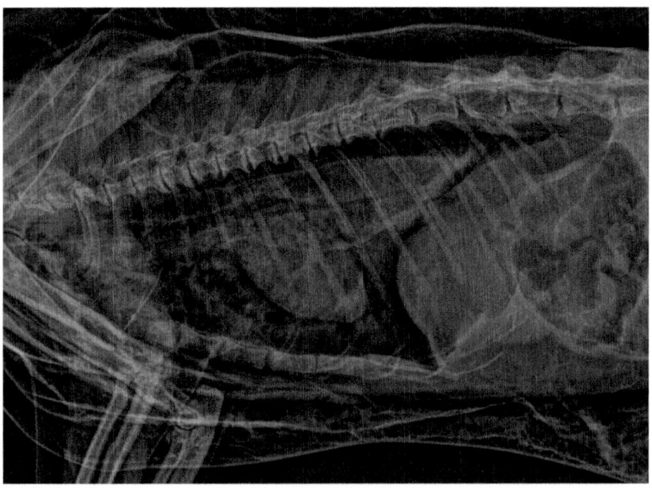

Figure 9.3 Lateral thorax of a cat with large-volume subcutaneous emphysema and pneumothorax.

Intracranial Trauma

Radiography and ultrasonography are of limited value in identification of intracranial trauma. Marked intracranial hemorrhage and contusion may be present without skull fractures. Since ultrasound cannot penetrate bone, ultrasonography is only useful if an open fontanelle is present or skull fractures have provided a sonographic window. Although MR imaging provides the greatest soft tissue resolution, CT is favored for evaluation of intracranial trauma owing to CT's more rapid acquisition time (Figure 9.4). Acute bleeds are hyperattenuating (bright) relative to normal brain parenchyma. With chronicity, hemorrhage becomes isoattenuating and later mildly hypoattenuating. Intracranial hemorrhage on MR also changes over time making identification challenging if a chronology of events is not known.

Projectile Trauma

Projectile trauma refers to firearms, air guns, or occasionally arrows. Orthogonal radiographic images can determine the number of projectiles or projectile fragments and the location of projectiles, assist in trajectory evaluation, and provide some limited information on the type of weapon used. When entrance and exit wounds are inconclusively identified or distinguished on the physical examination, radiographs are contributory to determine whether a projectile is penetrating, meaning the projectile remains within the body, or perforating, meaning the projectile exited the body (Figure 9.5). General knowledge of weapon and ammunition types (shotgun, rifle, handgun, and air rifle) is important to assess the wounding potential of the projectile and to

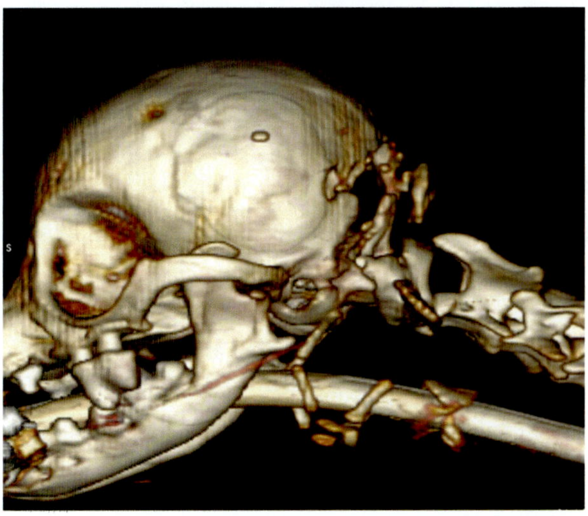

Figure 9.4 CT with 3D reconstruction of a dog with head trauma. Displaced occipital bone fractures are present.

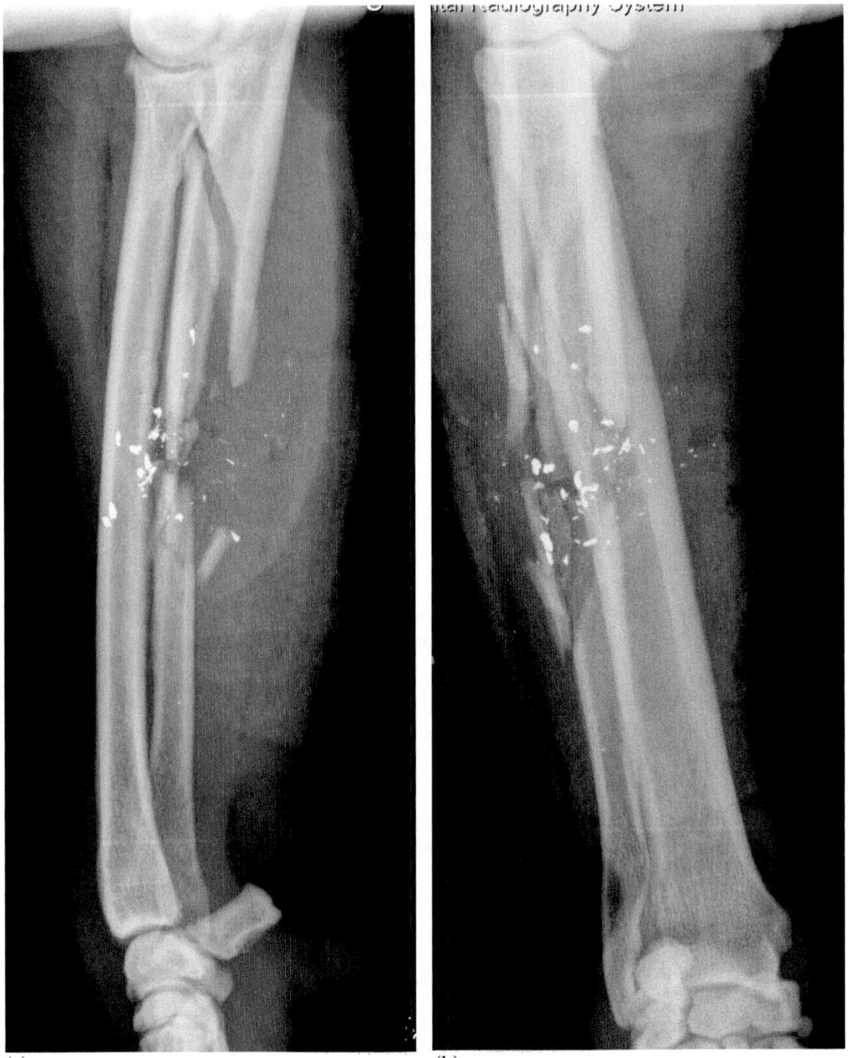

(a) (b)

Figure 9.5 Lateral (a) and craniocaudal (b) views of the antebrachium of a dog. A comminuted gunshot fracture is present. The absence of a large projectile fragment indicates a penetrating wound or that the bullet struck at a tangential angle.

guide retrieval of projectiles during a postmortem examination. The trajectory of a bullet cannot always be determined on orthogonal radiographs. Since the projectile will tumble, the direction a bullet is pointing will not necessarily indicate the direction of travel. A bullet may fragment or deflect from bone and change direction, further complicating trajectory evaluation. Projectile and bone fragments may be propelled along a tract indicating a direction of travel. Gas may be seen within a wound tract but in general gas will distribute along fascial planes and is not useful to delineate a tract. When the projectile penetrates bone, the bone may bevel toward the direction of travel. The greater soft tissue resolution obtained with CT imaging increases the conspicuity of hyperattenuating hemorrhage within a projectile tract. CT may also detect tiny metallic fragments, not seen on routine radiographs, indicating a projectile tract.

Other materials such as pieces of copper jacket or wadding material from shotgun shells may be deposited in a wound and will be of lesser opacity on radiographs than the metal opaque projectiles (Figure 9.6). The location of the jacket fragments should be described to the pathologist since forensically important material will be found on the copper jacket.

The size of a projectile cannot be precisely determined on orthogonal radiographs due to the distance from the image receptor and magnification. An approximation of the projectile size can be determined by a correction factor (CF) if the projectile to focal spot (D) and projectile to image receptor distances (d) are known by using the following equation:

$$\text{CF} = \text{D} - \text{d/D} \times \text{Measured Size} = \text{Actual Dimension}$$

Steel shot, used in waterfowl hunting, and lead shotgun pellets can usually be radiographically differentiated by their shape. The steel shot maintains a round shape on impact, whereas the soft lead shot deforms with impact.

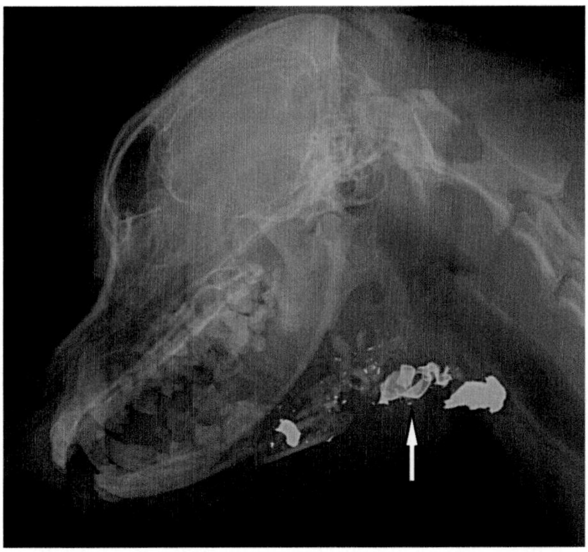

Figure 9.6 Lateral skull of a dog shot in the face with a handgun. Metallic projectile fragments are present. A copper jacket (arrow) is visible as a less opaque material. Numerous mandibular bone fragments, soft tissue swelling, and peritracheal gas are present.

Differentiating steel and lead shot pellets is especially important if MR imaging will be performed since steel shot is ferromagnetic and lead shot is not. Differentiating range of fire (contact, short range, intermediate range, and distant range) for shotgun wounds on radiographs can be challenging. In general, a widespread shot pattern is associated with an intermediate or distant range of fire and a more tightly grouped pattern indicates a contact or short range of fire.

Drowning and Strangulation

Radiographic findings that support drowning are rarely specific and consist of interstitial and alveolar infiltrate primarily in the dorsal aspect of the caudal lung lobes. This caudodorsal distribution of infiltrate can be seen with other causes of noncardiogenic pulmonary edema, such as postictal edema, acute airway obstruction, acute respiratory distress syndrome, toxicities and drug reactions, pulmonary embolism, and with pulmonary hemorrhage. On occasion, aspiration of sand can be identified radiographically as a mineral opaque material in the bronchi. Conspicuity of fluid, sand, and debris in the airways is improved with CT due to the modality's higher soft tissue resolution, cross-sectional imaging, and ability to create multiplanar reconstructions.

Similarly, radiographic findings of strangulation are not specific and noncardiogenic pulmonary edema secondary to strangulation appears radiographically similar to other causes of noncardiogenic pulmonary edema. Soft tissue changes in the larynx are poorly evaluated on radiographs due to the modality's limited soft tissue resolution. Swelling in the larynx is difficult to differentiate from a soft tissue mass or epiglottic retroversion. Since the laryngeal cartilages are not always completely mineralized, fractures of the larynx may be occult on radiographic studies. Fractures of the hyoid bones are reported to be uncommon in small animals; however, fractures may be difficult to evaluate on radiographs due to the summation of the right and left hyoid bones and the cartilaginous junctions, which are indistinguishable from the surrounding soft tissue structure. CT imaging provides greater soft tissue resolution and a cross-sectional view (Figure 9.7) of the hyoid and laryngeal cartilages (Francis et al. 2008).

Body Condition

Measurement of the subcutaneous fat on a thoracic radiograph has demonstrated good correlation with the 9-point body condition score (BCS) in a small number of dogs (Ruder et al. 2011). The subcutaneous fat is measured on the ventrodorsal view at the level of T8 rib head and compared to the length of the T4 body on the lateral view and the width of T8 on the ventrodorsal view. When the animal or body is no longer available or to corroborate the clinically determined BCS, the body condition can be determined by using the described T4 and T8 ratios in regression formulas (Linder et al. 2013). Although CT methods for estimating visceral and subcutaneous fat and the use of dual-energy x-ray absorptiometry (DEXA) for estimating body condition in live animals are described, these methods have not been validated in animals with low body condition scores (Ishioka et al. 2005a,b).

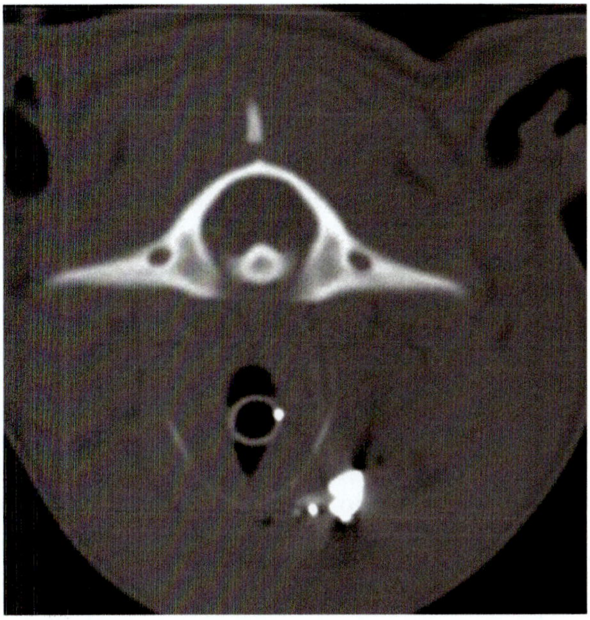

Figure 9.7 CT of a dog with a perforating gunshot wound to the neck. The CT demonstrates the proximity of the large metallic projectile to the cricoid cartilage and airway. Normal streak artifact from metal is present.

Serous atrophy of fat can be histologically identified in emaciated animals and humans (Sherlock et al. 2010; Stern 2013). MR imaging provides a complementary method for detecting serous atrophy of fat in the bone marrow. Although radiography is appropriate to evaluate cortical bone and some changes in medullary opacity or the trabecular pattern, MR imaging is more sensitive in the assessment of the adipose tissue content of bone. Normal medullary bone has a high or intermediate signal on T1-weighted and T2-weighted studies and a low signal on short tau inversion recovery (STIR) images. In contrast, cortical bone has a low signal intensity on T1-weighted, T2-weighted, and STIR sequences. On both high-field and low-field MR imaging systems, serous atrophy is detected as a low trabecular bone signal intensity on T1-weighted images and a high trabecular bone signal intensity on STIR, consistent with an increased fluid content of the bone marrow fat (Sherlock et al. 2010).

Bone Healing and Distinguishing Perimortem and Postmortem Trauma

Osseous changes identified on imaging studies may be localized to the periosteum, cortex, endosteum, medullary cavity, articular surfaces, and nutrient foramen. Recognizing changes within the periosteum is essential to assessing skeletal trauma and healing.

The periosteal membrane, a fibroelastic component covering all bone other than the articular surfaces, is strongly adhered and shares a blood supply with the underlying bone. In immature animals, the periosteum has weaker attachments to the underlying bone and is more active than mature periosteum. A periosteal reaction or periosteal mineralization is the result of numerous types of injury and the appearance of the periosteal reaction may indicate the type of bone injury, when the insult occurred, and the healing process. Periosteal reactions may be continuous or interrupted and described as solid or smooth, lamellated, palisading, spiculated, sunburst, or amorphous. Solid or smooth continuous periosteal reactions will occur at stable healing fracture sites, can indicate subperiosteal hemorrhage, or may be associated with benign processes or inactivity of a previous skeletal injury. A lamellated or onion skin periosteal reaction can occur with repeated trauma and intermittent or cyclical disease processes. The periosteal reaction seen with hypertrophic osteopathy is an example of a palisading reaction, which is most often associated with semi-aggressive processes. This pattern may also be identified with chronic soft tissue inflammation. In an aggressive process, such as a rapidly growing neoplasm, the periosteum will be disrupted from the tight attachment to the underlying bone and will form spicules or an amorphous reaction, sometimes in an interrupted pattern.

Periosteal reaction can be an early indicator of trauma even when no soft tissue wound or fractures are observed. Blunt force trauma or torsional force can disrupt the periosteum from the underlying bone resulting in calcified subperiosteal hemorrhage. The radiographic appearance is smooth continuous periosteum slightly lifted from the underlying bone (Figure 9.8). Periosteal reaction is first seen radiographically 7–10 days following injury; however, it may be seen as early as 5 days in the more active periosteum of the immature animal. Cases of suspected nonaccidental trauma with no underlying osseous lesions should be radiographed 10 days from the initial presentation to screen for an early periosteal reaction.

A periosteal reaction is also the earliest radiographic evidence of fracture healing. The fracture margins will lose sharpness and faint periosteal bone will be observed at the fracture site 5–10 days after injury. Subsequent radiographic signs of healing can be affected by many factors including the age and health of the animal, the blood supply, the fracture gap, the location and type of fracture, and the immobilization or motion at the fracture site. At 10–14 days after the fracture, resorption of bone in the fracture margins may be observed. The earliest sign of callus can be radiographically observed at 14–21 days after fracture (Figure 9.9). Bridging bone and remodeling can be observed 21–30 days after injury and remodeling will continue beyond 30 days.

Radiographic signs of a chronic injury include atrophy of the soft tissues, which can be radiographically observed as early as 2 weeks following injury (Figure 9.10). Comparison of the soft tissues of the contralateral limb will be useful. A marked reduction in soft tissues may occur over several weeks. Two additional signs of chronic skeletal trauma are bone atrophy and post-traumatic osteoporosis, which are a generalized loss of bone opacity distal to and at the

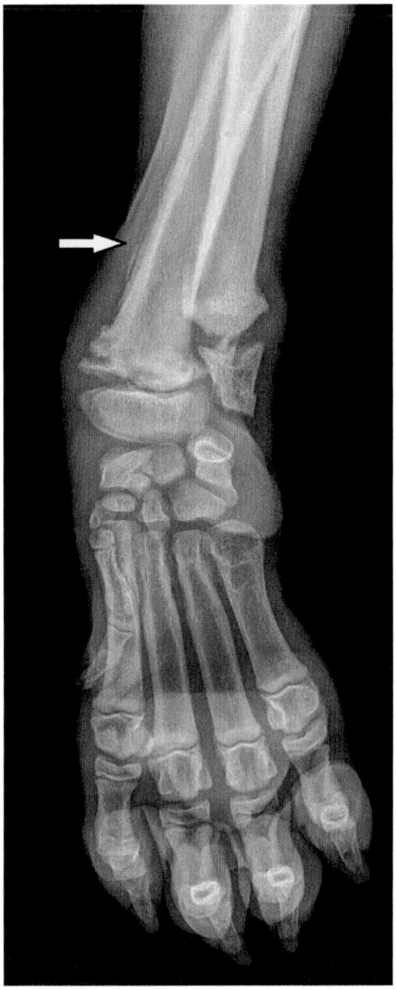

Figure 9.8 Dorsopalmar view of the manus of a 3-month-old dog with a Salter-Harris II fracture of the distal radius. Subperiosteal hemorrhage is present on the medial radial diaphysis (arrow).

injury site and a reduction in the size of the bone, and aseptic necrosis, which is the loss of blood supply to a bone fragment or femoral head epiphysis.

Imaging studies are contributory in the identification of other types of trauma such as luxations, subluxations, physeal fractures, symphyseal fractures, and bone edema or bone bruises. Radiographs are appropriate to identify luxations, subluxations, physeal fractures, and symphyseal fractures. A bone bruise, which represents microfractures, can be caused by blunt force trauma, avulsion trauma, or axial compression. Bone bruises are radiographically occult and are diagnosed with magnetic resonance imaging as T2-weighted

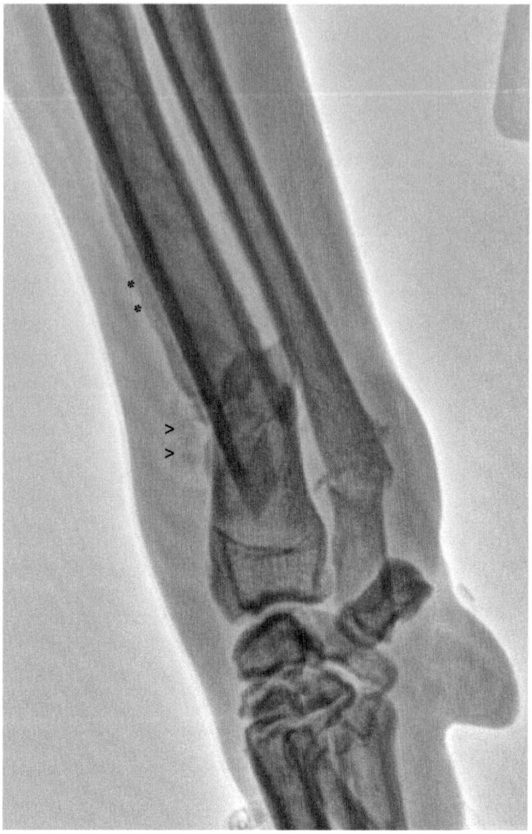

Figure 9.9 Lateral views of a dog with 2-week-old malaligned distal radial and ulnar fractures. A moderate amount of smoothly marginated periosteal bone is present on the cranial aspect of the distal radius (asterisk). Ill-defined new bone without bridging callus is present at the cranial radial fracture site (arrowhead).

hyperintensities and T1-weighted hypointensities as early as 24 hours after an injury.

The use of imaging studies to differentiate antemortem skeletal injury from perimortem trauma centers on the identification of an osseous response. Since a periosteal response will not be radiographically observed for 5–10 days after injury, perimortem fractures will be sharply marginated and show no evidence of a periosteal response. Conversely, an antemortem fracture will show varying degrees of blunting of the fracture margins, periosteal response, or callus, based on the chronicity of the trauma. PMMR can assist in the differentiation of perimortem fractures and postmortem fracture (Ruder et al. 2011). Acute bone fracture results in a high trabecular bone signal intensity on STIR and a low T1-weighted signal. The MRI vitality sign of bone marrow edema is absent when fractures occur postmortem (Ruder et al. 2011).

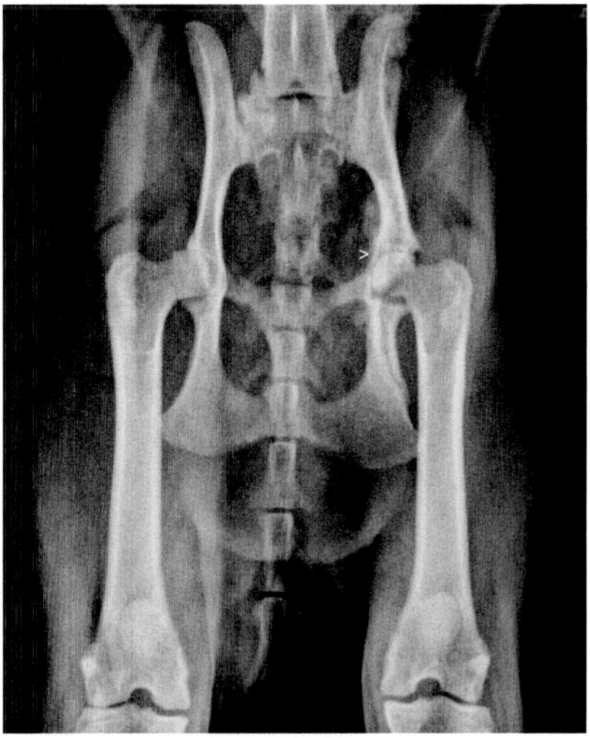

Figure 9.10 Ventrodorsal pelvic view of a cat with a 3-week-old left acetabular fracture and left muscle atrophy (arrowhead).

Poisoning and Foreign Objects

Imaging studies can assist in the identification of ingested or inserted foreign material and poisons. Carbamate and paraquat are known to cause pulmonary edema and paraquat poisoning causes pneumomediastinum in dogs and humans. As the time after death increases, these changes cannot be distinguished from normal postmortem findings. The radiographic identification of gastric foreign material or unexpected gastric ingesta may support intentional or accidental poisoning. Some drugs or toxins are radiopaque and easily identified on radiographs. Others are soft tissue opaque and indistinguishable from the normal gastrointestinal fluid. Phenothiazines, chloral hydrate, tricyclic antidepressants, sucralfate, and iron-containing, iodinated, and potassium-containing drugs are radiopaque in fluid to varying degrees. Metaldehyde pellets and mothballs are radiopaque. On occasion dogs have been used as carriers for drug smuggling through surgical implantation of drug packets. Some drugs such as cocaine and hashish are primarily radiopaque. The material surrounding the drug in round or oval packets, such as latex, plastic wrap, and paraffin, are variably radiopaque. The introduction of foreign objects through the skin or insertion through body orifices may include metal fragments such as from a knife or razor blade, glass, wire, wood, and pencils or pens. Some foreign objects, such as razor blade fragments, are metal radiopaque and teeth or bone are mineral opaque and will be evident on routine radiographs (Figure 9.11). All glass, regardless of lead content, is radiopaque. Other material that is not normally radiopaque may be visualized by the surrounding gas from a stab wound, tract, or body orifice. The practice of radiographing a substance alone will not determine its radiopacity in a body: the substance must be radiographed within a water bath to confirm if it is radiopaque within the body. The superior soft tissue resolution and cross-sectional imaging of CT will increase conspicuity of all foreign materials. Ultrasonography is a useful tool to identify and localize foreign material. Material that is not radiopaque may be visualized as a hyperechoic structure. Wood and plastic objects often demonstrate posterior shadowing. A comet tail artifact may be present deep to metal objects (Figure 9.12).

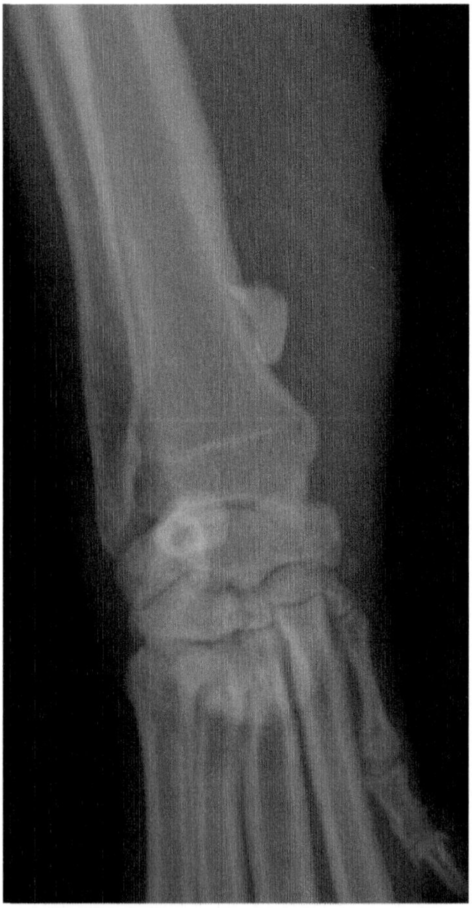

Figure 9.11 Dorsopalmar view of the carpus and distal antebrachium of a mature dog with diffuse soft tissue swelling and bite wounds. A tooth fragment foreign object is visible medial to the distal radius.

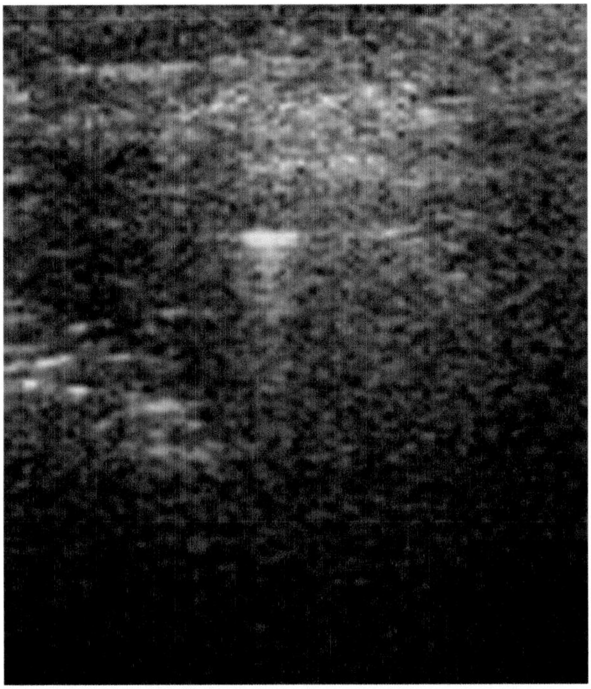

Figure 9.12 A sagittal ultrasound image of a metallic projectile demonstrates a comet tail artifact.

Conclusion

Radiography, ultrasound, CT, and MR have proven to be valuable in several areas of forensic investigations and the noninvasive and perpetual nature of imaging studies is unique compared to other types of evidence. Radiography and the other described imaging modalities can be used to identify skeletal and soft tissue trauma, projectiles, and secondary signs of drowning and strangulation. Other uses may include differentiating nonaccidental trauma from accidental trauma and determining the body condition score of dogs. An understanding of the limitations, advantages, and current use of the available imaging modalities will permit efficient use of imaging in forensic investigations.

References

American College of Radiology. 2006. ACR practice guideline for skeletal surveys in children. In: *American College of Radiology Standards*. Reston, VA.

Francis KA, Goggin JM, Hoskinson JJ. 2008. Imaging diagnosis–laryngeal collapse due to cricoid cartilage fracture. *Vet Radiol Ultrasound*. 49:360–361.

Germerott T, Preiss US, Ebert LC, Ruder TD, Ross S, Flach PM, Ampanozi G, Filograna L, Thali MJ. 2010. A new approach in virtopsy: Postmortem ventilation in multislice computed tomography. *Leg Med (Tokyo).* 12:276–279.

Gordon LE, Thacher C, Kapatkin A. 1993. High-rise syndrome in dogs: 81 cases. *J Am Vet Med Assoc.* 202:118–122.

Grabherr S, Grimm J, Dominguez A, Vanhaebost J, Mangin P. 2014. Advances in postmortem CT-angiography. *Br J Radiol.* 87:20130488.

Heng HG, Teoh WT, Sheikh-Omar AR. 2008. Postmortem abdominal radiographic findings in feline cadavers. *Vet Radiol Ultrasound.* 49:26–29.

Heng HG, Selvarajah GT, Lim HT, Ong JS, Lim J, Ooi JT. 2009a. Serial postmortem abdominal radiographic findings in canine cadavers. *Forensic Sci Int.* 192:43–47.

Heng HG, Selvarajah GT, Lim HT, Ong JS, Lim J, Ooi JT. 2009b. Serial postmortem thoracic radiographic findings in canine cadavers. *Forensic Sci Int.* 188:119–124.

Intarapanich NP, McCobb EC, Reisman RW, Rozanski EA, Intarapanich PP. 2016. Characterization and comparison of injuries caused by accidental and nonaccidental blunt force trauma in dogs and cats. *J Forensic Sci.* 61:993–999.

Ishioka K, Okumura M, Sagawa M, Nakadomo F, Kimura K, Saito M. 2005a. Computed tomographic assessment of body fat in Beagles. *Vet Radiol Ultrasound.* 46:49–53.

Ishioka K, Okumura M, Sagawa M, Nakadomo F, Kimura K, Saito M. 2005b. Computed tomographic assessment of body fat in beagles. *Vet Radiol Ultrasound.* 46:49–53.

Linder DE, Freeman LM, Sutherland-Smith J. 2013. Association between subcutaneous fat thickness measured on thoracic radiographs and body condition score in dogs. *Am J Vet Res.* 74:1400–1403.

Muir P. 1997. Distal antebrachial fractures in toy-breed dogs. *Compend Contin Educ Pract Vet.* 19:137–145.

Ruder TD, Germerott T, Thali MJ, Hatch GM. 2011. Differentiation of ante-mortem and post-mortem fractures with MRI: A case report. *Br J Radiol.* 84:e75–78.

Sherlock E, Mair TS, Murray RC, Blunden TS. 2010. Magnetic resonance imaging features of serous atrophy of bone marrow fat in the distal limb of three horses. *Vet Radiol Ultrasound.* 51:607–613.

Stern AW. 2013. Starvation due to neglect: A canine case series. *J Vet Sci Technol.* 4:1–2.

Tong LJ. 2014. Fracture characteristics to distinguish between accidental injury and non-accidental injury in dogs. *Vet J.* 199:392–398.

Watson E, Heng HG. 2017. Forensic radiology and imaging for veterinary radiologists. *Vet Radiol Ultrasound.* 58:245–258.

Whitney WO, Mehlhaff CJ. 1987. High-rise syndrome in cats. *J Am Vet Med Assoc.* 191:1399–1403.

10

Bitemarks

Examination and Analysis

Katherine E. Kling and Adam W. Stern

Contents

Introduction

Forensic dentistry (forensic odontology) is the application of dental science to legal investigations and is utilized to connect a suspect with a crime by means of bitemark analysis or used in postmortem identification of a person (Giannelli 2007; Pramod et al. 2012). In relation to veterinary forensics, evaluation of dental evidence, specifically bitemarks and oral anatomy, can be used to support or refute the possibility of a specific animal being the perpetrator of the bite. It is important to note that bitemark analysis may involve multiple professionals including a veterinary dentist, veterinary pathologist or general veterinary practitioner, anthropologist, forensic odontologist, and/or law enforcement personnel. Every case will have different circumstances associated with the case, which may include variable number of suspects and/or victims, location, and/or presence or absence of witnesses.

Currently there is intense scientific and legal scrutiny of the field of bitemark identification (Saks et al. 2016). Bitemark analysis is based on the assumption that dentition is individually unique (Kashyap et al. 2015); however, it is not known if this individuality is recorded specifically enough in the bite injury (Sweet and Pretty 2001). Simply put, if there is a high quality bitemark and all probable suspects can be examined (in the case of a closed population of suspects), if appropriate techniques are followed and distortions are reduced, then bitemark analysis can be of value in establishing a link between the bitten person and the potential biter (Senn 2007).

In veterinary forensics, bitemarks may be used to identify an individual or class of individuals (e.g., species of animal). In veterinary species, it is also theorized that no two dental patterns are similar; however, this uniqueness may not be observed in the bitemark. This is due to plasticity and hysteresis of victim skin and orientation variables of the biting suspect. When presented with a potential bite wound, consultation with a veterinary dentist or forensic veterinarian is recommended for examination of the animal as well as to assist with recovery of bitemark evidence and creation of dental impressions and casts. Additionally, consultation with an expert in DNA analysis will allow for performance of DNA testing which can allow for additional supporting evidence to incriminate or exculpate a suspect animal.

It is important to note that an animal can be a bite victim or a perpetrator (biter). Examples of an animal being a victim include a small breed dog that is attacked by a large breed dog, a dog that sustained wounds in an organized dog fight, or a cat that is found deceased in a backyard known to have a dog living on the property. By comparison, the animal as the biter can include the large breed dog that attacked a small breed dog, a dog living on the property where a dead cat with bitemarks is found, or a dog that bit a human. Human-related injuries and fatalities are reported to occur by numerous animal species including canids (dog, wolf, and coyote), felids (domestic cats and large cats including lions and cougars), bears, and alligators to name a few (Clark et al. 1991; Cohrn 2013; Harding and Wolf 2006; Neiburger and Patterson 2002). In the United States, approximately 4.5 million people are bitten by dogs every year with between 10 and 20 fatalities a year (World Health Organization

2013). Some studies suggest there are tens of millions of dog bite–related injuries worldwide (World Health Organization 2013).

Bite injuries made by animals can leave patterns and can result in significant injury or death. Bite injuries can range from abrasions to punctures to massive tearing of soft tissue. In some cases, the animal attacker may be at risk of being euthanized (in judicial or legal consideration of the potential future risk of injury). In addition, the owner of the animal may be held liable; therefore, definitive identification of the biter or at least exoneration of a bite suspect is imperative. It is for this reason that a forensic investigation is performed to substantiate the involvement of the animal suspect(s).

When approaching an animal bite case, the investigation can be divided into five main parts:

1. Witness information (witness statements, animals involved, circumstances)
2. Scene investigation (environmental conditions, bloodstains, foot/paw prints)
3. Animal examination (forensic examination including dental examination, trace evidence collection, photo documentation, production of dental impressions and casts)
4. Bitemark review and comparison to the available physical evidence
5. DNA analysis

This chapter will introduce the veterinary forensic investigator to the basic principles of bitemark analysis and discusses the documentation and appropriate collection of bitemark evidence. We will discuss examination of the animal both as the suspect and victim; however, examination of a human bite victim will not be discussed. Table 10.1 contains a list of commonly used terminology relating to the oral cavity.

Dental Anatomy

Feline and canine dentition, similar to carnivores in general, can be described as having four basic types of teeth, including incisors, canines, premolars, and molars (Figure 10.1). Incisor teeth, which are small and single rooted, serve a purpose of grasping, cutting, and grooming, and the premolar and molar teeth are used for mastication (Bergqvist 2003). The canine teeth in cats and dogs have long crowns anchored by long roots and these teeth are designed for grasping and tearing. The opposing carnassial teeth are the fourth premolar on the maxilla and the first molar on the mandible and these are the largest teeth in the cat and the dog. Each tooth is held in a bony socket within the jaw by a fibrous ligament. The maxillary arch is larger and longer than the mandibular arch and when the mouth is closed the maxillary incisor teeth partially obscure the mandibular incisor teeth.

Table 10.1 Common Dental Terminology

Term	Definition
Apical	Toward the root (apex)
Buccal	Toward the cheek
Coronal	Toward the crown
Distal	Away from the central incisors
Labial	Toward the lips
Lingual	Toward the tongue
Interproximal	Surface between two teeth
Mesial	Toward the central incisors
Occlusal	Facing a tooth in the opposite jaw
Palatal	Toward the palate
Rostral	Region of the nose and mouth

Figure 10.1 Mandible from a dog. The right mandibular canine tooth is denoted by the arrow.

Cats and dogs are diphyodont, meaning that they have both a permanent set of teeth and a deciduous or baby set of teeth. Most deciduous teeth in the dog and the cat have erupted within the first couple of months of life (Table 10.2) and the permanent teeth have erupted by 6–7 months of age (Wiggs and Lobprise 1997; Miller et al. 1993). The modified Triadan system is a system of numbering teeth that assigns different numbers to permanent and deciduous teeth (Figure 10.2). For permanent teeth, 100s are used to describe the teeth

Table 10.2 Approximate Dental Eruption Times for the Dog and Cat				
	Dog	Dog	Cat	Cat
	Deciduous	Permanent	Deciduous	Permanent
Incisors	3–4 weeks	2–5 months	2–3 weeks	3–4 months
Canines	3 weeks	5–6 months	3–4 weeks	4–5 months
Premolars	4–12 weeks	4–6 months	3–6 weeks	4–6 months
Molars	N/A	4–7 months	N/A	4–5 months

Sources: 1. Miller M.E., Christensen G.C., H.E. Evans. 1993. The digestive apparatus and abdomen. In *Anatomy of the Dog.* p. 19. Philadelphia, PA: WB Saunders. 2. Wiggs R.B., H.B. Lobprise. 1997. *Veterinary Dentistry Principles and Practice.* p. 169, Ames, IA: Wiley-Blackwell.

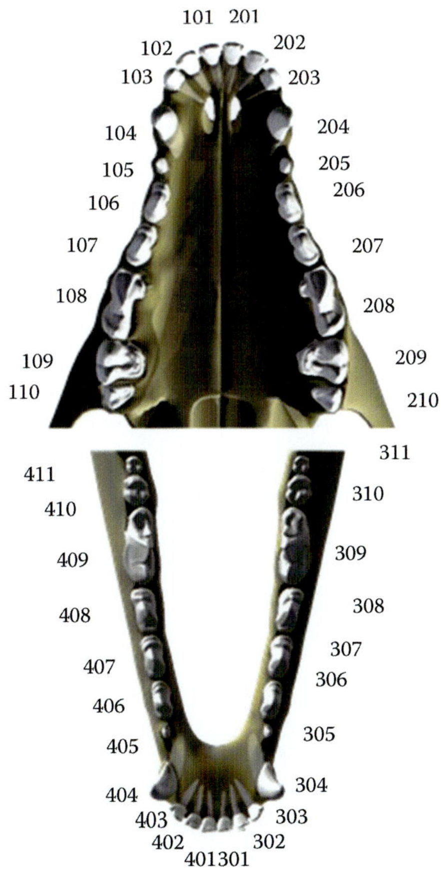

Figure 10.2 Modified Triadan system for the dog.

of the right side of the maxillary arch, 200s for the teeth of the left side of the maxillary arch, 300s for the left mandible, and 400s for the right mandible. Deciduous teeth on the right side of the maxillary arch are 500s; deciduous teeth on the left side of the maxillary arch are 600s; deciduous teeth on the left mandible are 700s and the right mandible 800s (Floyd 1991).

Adult teeth erupt with enamel covering a thin layer of primary dentin surrounding the pulp. As the tooth matures, new dentin is laid down adding density to the tooth and narrowing the pulp canal. If a tooth becomes nonvital, dentin development ceases. For example, a dental radiograph of an 8-year-old dog that sustained irreversible pulpitis will show a tooth with a pulp canal that is wide, in contrast to the rest of the vital teeth in the mouth that will have developed more narrow pulp canals over time (Figure 10.3). In contrast to the continual development of dentin, enamel once lost cannot be regenerated (Nanci 2013).

In both the cat and dog, the mandibles are joined at the midline by a fibrocartilaginous joint, the mandibular symphysis. This symphysis can allow for slight physiologic movement between mandibles especially in cats and brachycephalic dogs. The occlusal relationship that the mandibular canine tooth has with the maxillary third incisor tooth and maxillary canine tooth is called the canine interlock (Figure 10.4). The occlusion of a dog or a cat is determined and described by the relationship between the mandibular and the maxillary arches. In normal occlusion, the maxillary incisors are rostral to the mandibular incisors when the mouth is closed. When the mandibular arch is shorter than the maxillary arch the occlusion is said to be mandibular brachygnathic (mandibular distocclusion). When the mandibles protrude beyond the maxillary arch, the dog or cat is said to be mandibular prognathic (mandibular mesiocclusion).

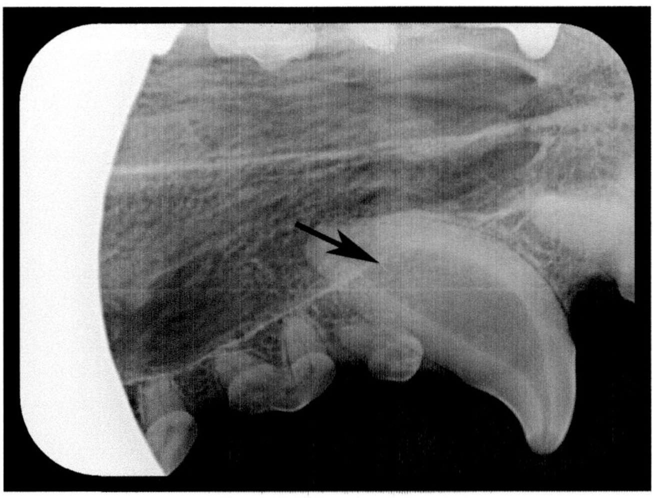

Figure 10.3 Dental radiograph from a dog. Note the pulp canal (arrow).

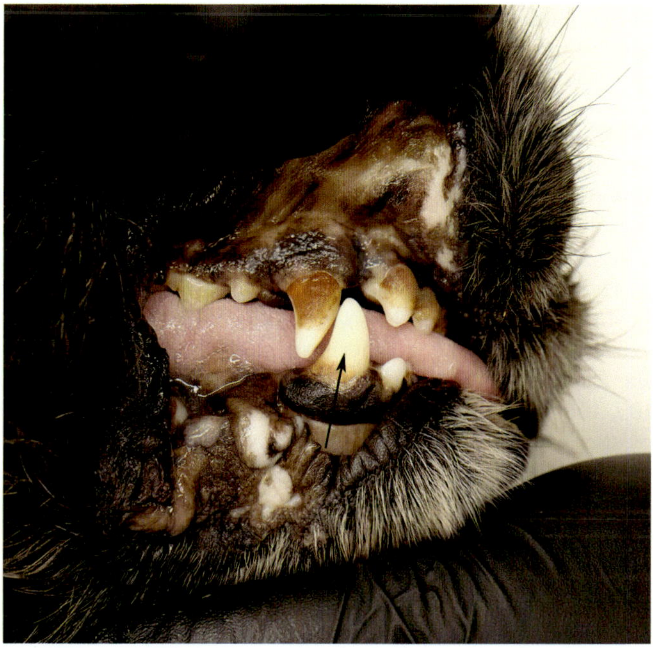

Figure 10.4 Canine interlock. Note the occlusal relationship that the mandibular canine tooth (arrow) has with the maxillary third incisor tooth and maxillary canine tooth.

Canine

Canines have 42 permanent teeth and the dental formula is I3/3, C1/1, P4/4, and M2/3. It is important to note that regardless of species, dental formulas are for one side of the mouth; therefore, the total number of the teeth is the total formula multiplied by 2. This means that the dog has 3 incisor, 1 canine, 4 premolar, and 2 molar teeth on each side of the maxillary arch and each side of the mandibular arch has 3 incisor, 1 canine, 4 premolar, and 3 molar teeth. There are 28 deciduous teeth in the puppy since the first premolar teeth and the molar teeth are nonsuccessional. The dental formula for the puppy is I3/3, C1/1, and P3/3.

The shape of a dog's skull can be described as dolichocephalic, mesaticephalic, or brachycephalic. Some of the more extreme conformations have been breed selected for. A brachycephalic dog can be described as having a shorter skull and this is often accompanied by having a prognathic mandible. Despite the shorter length of the maxillae, the same number of adult teeth often are present and so the teeth are most often rotated and crowded. Breeds of this confirmation include the Pug or English Bulldog. When the skull is elongated, such as is seen in a Greyhound or a Collie, the skull type is dolichocephalic. When the skull is neither short nor elongated but of a more proportionate conformation, the skull is described as mesaticephalic and breeds with this conformation include the Beagle or Golden Retriever. The teeth for dogs with mesaticephalic skull types are often less crowded while dogs with dolicocephalic skull types often have widely spaced premolars.

Feline

Felines have 30 permanent teeth and the dental formula is I3/3, C1/1, P3/P2, M1/M1. This means that the cat has 3 incisors, 1 canine, 3 premolars, and 1 molar on each side of the maxillary arch and on each side of the mandibular arch has 3 incisors, 1 canine, 2 premolars, and 1 molar teeth. It is important to note that several teeth in the cat are normally absent when compared to the dog; when using the modified Triadan system for tooth numbering, the nonexistent teeth are skipped in the numbering system. The adult cat lacks many of the premolars and molars that are present in dogs (105, 110, 205, 210, 305, 306, 310, 311, 405, 406, 410, 411); and of the 30 permanent teeth commonly found in the domestic cat, hypodontia, or the congenital absence of a tooth or teeth is not uncommon (Verstraete and Terpak 1997). Twenty-six teeth make up the deciduous dentition in the kitten and the dental formula is I3/3, C1/1, and P3/2.

Less variation in skull shape is seen in cat when compared to dog breeds; however, the shape of a cat's skull can still be described as dolichocephalic, mesaticephalic, or brachycephalic. In contrast to the canine tooth of the dog, there are lateral grooves in the canine tooth of the cat. Cats, especially pure breeds, are more prone than dogs to tooth resorption that can lead to crown irregularities and crown fractures (Girard et al. 2008).

Examination of the Animal

Regardless if an animal is a perpetrator or victim, a complete forensic examination is warranted in order to characterize the animal's injuries as well as evaluate and collect dental evidence for comparison purposes. With analysis of the bitemarks it may be possible to allow for the identification of the biter. For example, in a closed population, the identification of the suspect may be made by exclusion of all other potential biters. In a general or open population, bitemark analysis can be used to exclude potential bite suspects, although identification of the biter may not be determined.

It is important to note that the suspect or the victim may be presented alive or deceased. Variations in examination techniques may be required. For example, if the suspect animal is an aggressive live dog, the animal may be sedated or anesthetized prior to examination for safety reasons. In certain situations, the suspect animal may not be available for examination as in the case of predation (wild carnivores). If the attack happens outdoors, environmental status, local fauna, and animals' feeding and behavior are important issues to evaluate (Fonseca et al. 2015).

Examination of the Bite Victim

It is important for the examiner to recognize an injury as a potential bitemark. A bitemark is a pattern produced by human or animal dentition and associated structures in any substance capable of being marked by these means (Clark et al. 1991). The type of bite injury will vary by the encounter including species of the offending animal and by the types of teeth used to cause the bite. Bites can cause a variety of injuries including hemorrhage, contusions, abrasions, lacerations, incisions, avulsions, and artifacts (Verma et al. 2013) (Table 10.3). In the case of injuries caused by forceful use of incisors, contusions and small punctures may be observed. Injuries caused by the canine teeth include punctures (Figure 10.5) and tearing of tissue. The shape of the bite wound is dependent on many factors including the size of the biting animal's jaw, occlusion of the jaw, and by the type of bite (partial to complete bite). A partial bite may include only the incisor teeth, whereas a complete bite will involve all the

Table 10.3 Seven Types of Bite Injuries

Type of Bitemark	Definition
Abrasion	A scrape on the skin
Hemorrhage	A profusely bleeding site
Contusion	Ruptured or broken blood vessels (bruise)
Laceration	Punctured or torn skin
Incision	Neat puncture of skin
Avulsion	Removal of the skin
Artifact	A piece of flesh or body part is bitten off

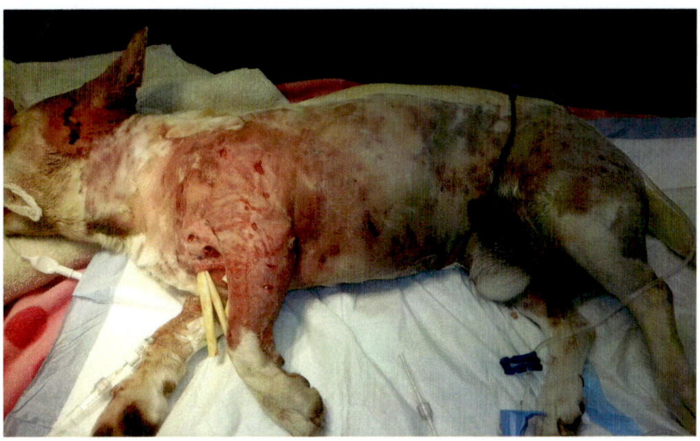

Figure 10.5 Example of a small breed dog that was attacked by a large breed dog. Note the injuries of multiple parts of the body including the forelimb, thorax, and abdomen. Photograph taken after medical intervention was instituted. Photo courtesy of Drs. Meredith Pieper and Christine Davis, Prairie Oak Veterinary Center.

teeth. Victims may also have severe injuries from crushing and can include fractures (skull, neck, ribs) and hemorrhage into body cavities.

The general veterinary practitioner or emergency veterinarian will likely be the first person to evaluate an animal victim with a bite wound. It is important for the person who first identifies the bite wound to accurately describe, preserve, photograph, and collect any evidence. Some animals presented the veterinarian will have severe and life-threatening injuries and the animal will likely need to be stabilized prior to attention being directed toward preservation and collection of evidence from the bite injury.

Examination of the animal victim should include the following:

- *Forensic clinical examination and treatment of the injuries*: A forensic clinical examination should be performed as injuries identified are recorded and stabilization of the animal (if injuries are serious/life threatening) should be performed.
- *Document the injury*: This includes a description of the lesion(s) including the appearance, size, location on the body, and orientation of the lesion.
- *Photographic documentation of the injuries*: Photographs with and without an ABFO (American Board of Forensic Odontology) No. 2 photo scale should be taken. The use of ultraviolet (UV) and infrared (IR) photography may be taken to make some areas of the bitemark more distinct. When appropriate, the bitemark should be photographed over multiple days.
- *Trace evidence collection*: In the case of bite wounds, saliva or blood from the perpetrator will be deposited at the site of the wound. It is therefore imperative that at least two duplicate sets of swabs for DNA testing be collected. When necessary, these must be collected before cleaning the wound.
- *Impressions of the bite wound*: In addition to photographs, it is important that impressions of the wound be obtained.

Examination of the Suspect Biter

As previously mentioned, bites by an animal cause various types of injuries and the type of injuries will vary by the encounter and species of offending animal. The bite suspect will likely be presented first to law enforcement personnel who should immediately have the animal evaluated by a forensic veterinarian. The suspected perpetrator may have injuries that occurred during the attack and/or will likely have evidence of the attack based on the exchange of biological or physical evidence (Locard's Exchange Principle). For example, blood from the victim may be found on the body or in/around the oral cavity of the biter.

Examination of the suspect biter should include the following:

- *Forensic clinical examination and treatment of any injuries*: A forensic clinical examination should be performed as injuries might be identified on the suspect biter. Evaluation of the head including function of the jaw should be performed. A 10-day observation period for signs of rabies may be required (Centers for Disease Control and Prevention 2016). A behavior evaluation is recommended. Claws/nails and appendicular extremities should be examined for the presence of tissue from the bite victim (Bernitz et al. 2012).

- *Evaluation of the teeth*: Examination of the oral cavity including taking of photographs. Observations and measurements of various characteristics should be obtained and can be obtained digitally

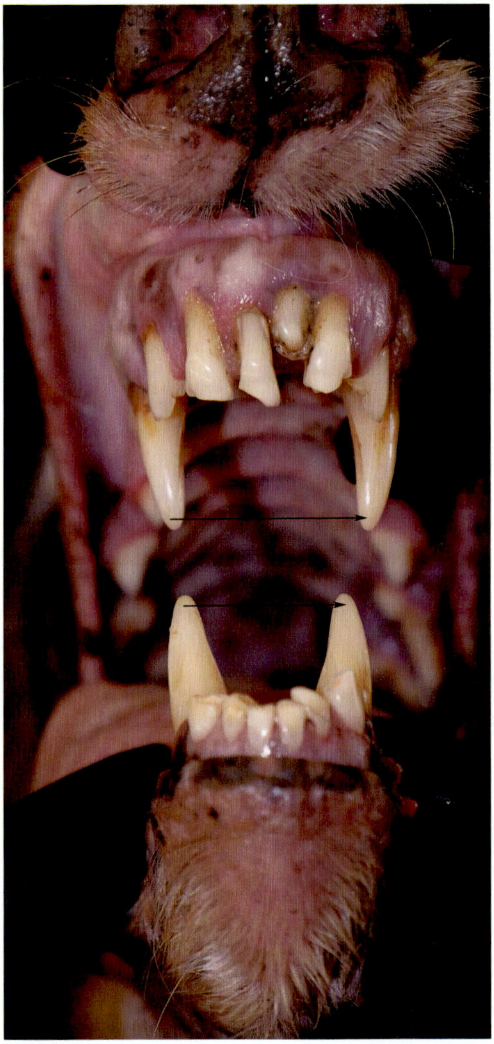

Figure 10.6 Domestic dog showing maxillary (top) and mandibular (bottom) intercanine distance.

including intercanine distance (ICD) (Figure 10.6) at the level of the cusp tips, arch shape, arch width, distance between mesial points of the central incisors, and maximal opening of the mouth. In one study, measurements of the ICD in three different areas on the canine teeth and not just the cusp tips were recommended to accommodate for variance in depth of the bite injuries (Murmann et al. 2006). Photographs of the teeth from multiple angles should be taken including profile and intraoral photographs (Table 10.4). The intraoral photographs should depict the maxillary and mandibular arches. Photographs with and without an ABFO No. 2 photo scale should be taken. Documentation of features of the teeth including missing teeth, fractured crowns, rotated teeth, and teeth out of the aligned dental arch may be useful when evaluating a bitemark. Documentation of the changes from normal occlusion, the malocclusion class, and presence or absence of dental disease (e.g., calculus) should also be recorded.

- *Dental impressions and casts*: Dental impression of both the upper and lower arch should be obtained and it is recommended two sets of casts be produced.
- *Sample bites*: The ABFO recommends obtaining sample bites from suspected human biters (American Board of Forensic Odontology 2016); similarly, sample bites can be collected from a suspect biter animal.
- *Trace evidence collection*: Saliva or blood from the victim may be deposited on the perpetrator, under the nails/claws, or found within the oral cavity. It is imperative that at least two duplicate sets of swabs for DNA analysis be collected. This must be done

Table 10.4 List of Photographic Images to Acquire from a Suspected Human Biter

Extraoral Images	Intraoral Images
Full Face Profile	Anterior view Anterior view with incisal edges slightly opened Anterior view with mandible protruded Anterior view demonstrating maximal open (with scale in place) Lateral view (left) Lateral view (right) Occlusal view (maxillary) Occlusal view (mandibular)

Source: American Board of Forensic Odontology. 2016. ABFO Bitemark Methodology Standards and Guidelines. http://abfo.org/wp-content/uploads/2016/03/ABFO-Bitemark-Standards-03162016.pdf (Accessed April 10, 2017).

Note: Similar photographs can be taken from a suspected biter animal.

without contamination of the site using personal protective equipment (PPE) and sterile swabs. Given the sensitive nature of the collection of DNA, this should be done first during the forensic examination.

In certain instances, the suspect animal may be examined postmortem and a forensic necropsy should be performed in such cases. Regardless if the animal is alive or deceased, examination of the animal for tissue that is from the victim is appropriate. During the forensic necropsy, gastric contents should be examined for ingested tissue from the victim. If the animal is alive, emesis can be induced and vomitus should be collected. Vomitus/stomach contents should be strained to identify any evidence such as tissue or fabric. Fecal material should also be collected as evidence such as recovered fabric from the clothes of a human bite victim. Regardless of the status of the animal, the evidence should be collected and stored appropriately for further analysis. If the animal is deceased, collection of samples and performance of rabies testing is recommended as a positive test result would require postexposure treatment.

Impressions

A dental impression is a way of recording the characteristics of an animal's dentition and surrounding soft tissue structures and it can also be used to make a positive reproduction (Sakaguchi 2012). When choosing an impression material, considerations may include cost, elasticity, working time, accuracy, stability, and ease of use.

Alginate is a commonly used impression material in veterinary dentistry because it is inexpensive and very elastic, meaning it can stretch over long tooth crowns and regain its shape (Nandini et al. 2008). However, impressions made with alginate are susceptible to shrinkage as the water in the material evaporates and therefore alginate is best suited to a scenario when a model can be created almost immediately. Further, in the process of creating the model from an alginate impression, the impression is destroyed.

Polyvinyl siloxane is an impression material in the family of elastomeric materials. The drawback of polyvinyl siloxane has to do with its hydrophobic nature, which in moist environments like the mouth means that this impression material is more likely to develop air bubbles or defects (Perry 2013). However, the clear advantage of using polyvinyl siloxane is the stability it provides. Impressions made with polyvinyl siloxane can be preserved and used for creating multiple models, which is recommended (Bhargava 2012). Prior to collecting full mouth impressions, the mouth of the animal should be prepared in such a way that the teeth should be free of debris by flushing the mouth with saline and drying the teeth. It should be noted that collection of oral swabs for potential DNA analysis be performed prior to flushing the oral cavity. The impressions will be collected from the maxillae and the mandibles separately in two slightly differently shaped trays mainly because the tray to accommodate the mandible must leave room for the lingual frenulum (Figure 10.7). A custom tray might be needed in the case of an animal with unique dentition,

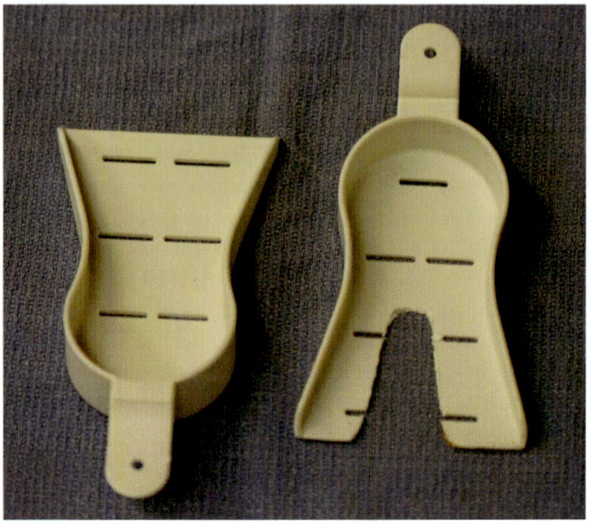

Figure 10.7 Maxillary impression tray (left) and mandibular impression tray (right).

as in a plastic storage bin drawer having been used as an impression tray for an alligator (Cohrn 2013). The lips should be held up and away from the teeth and gingiva when taking an impression. Impression material used should be mixed according to the manufacturer's recommendations. Polyvinyl siloxane is supplied in two containers, a catalyst and a base. When the two are mixed together by hand, polymerization occurs. Latex gloves interfere with this polymerization and should not be worn (Chee and Donovan 1992). A more viscous polyvinyl siloxane should be used in combination with heavy wash polyvinyl siloxane to provide the greatest detail while maintaining stability of the impression (Figure 10.8). The heavy wash should make up the bulk of the impression and the light wash should comprise 1.5–2.5 mm thickness only (Chee and Donovan 1992).

Study Models or Casts

A study model or cast is made from a dental impression and is most commonly created using gypsum products (Figure 10.9). Gypsum products are materials that come from naturally occurring stone and include plaster of Paris, dental stone, and die stone (Sakaguchi 2012). Plaster of Paris is the weakest of the gypsum products and dental stone or die stone are more likely to yield a desirable result. When mixing dental stone, the manufacturer's directions should be followed. Use of too much water may result in a weaker final product. Overmixing will hasten the set time. The water used should be neither cold nor hot as either extreme can slow the setting time (Sakaguchi 2012). The impression can be held firmly on a general purpose dental vibrator while the dental stone is placed in small quantities near the most detailed or important regions of the impression, for example, the canine teeth. Allowing the material to flow into the more detailed areas is the best way to reduce

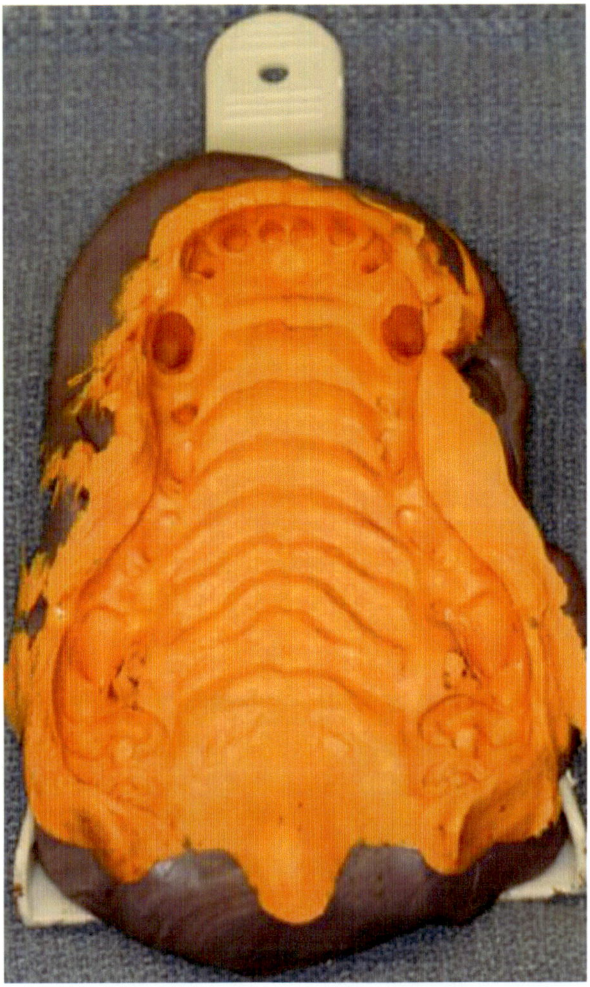

Figure 10.8 Example of an impression from a dog. The orange material is viscous polyvinyl siloxane and the purple material is heavy wash polyvinyl siloxane.

the incidence of air bubbles. The vibrator allows air bubbles to escape resulting in a smoother product. It is recommended that two sets of study casts be produced and all materials including trays, impression, and casts be securely stored (Sweet and Pretty 2001).

Sample Bite

A sample bite/bite impression should be made (Figure 10.10). It is made in a wax medium by impressing the bite wax against the teeth in the mouth by closing the mouth firmly. Make sure to label both the upper arch and lower arch. This bite wax permits the examiner to relate the upper and lower impressions correctly in full occlusion since it can be used to help place the model

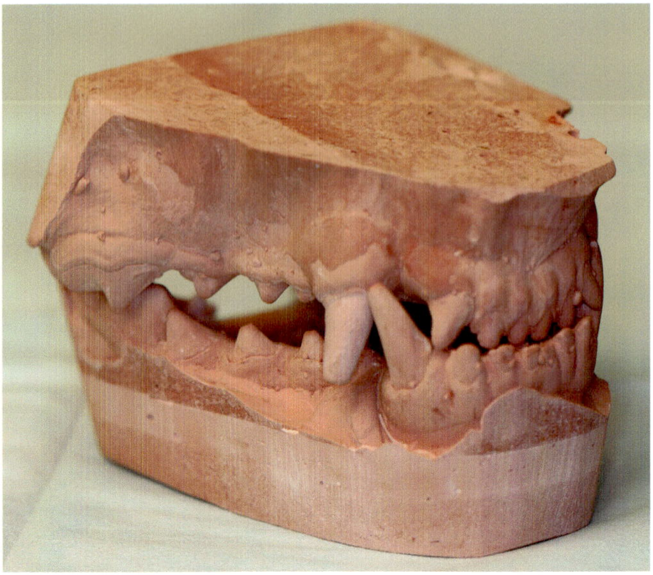

Figure 10.9 Example of a dental cast.

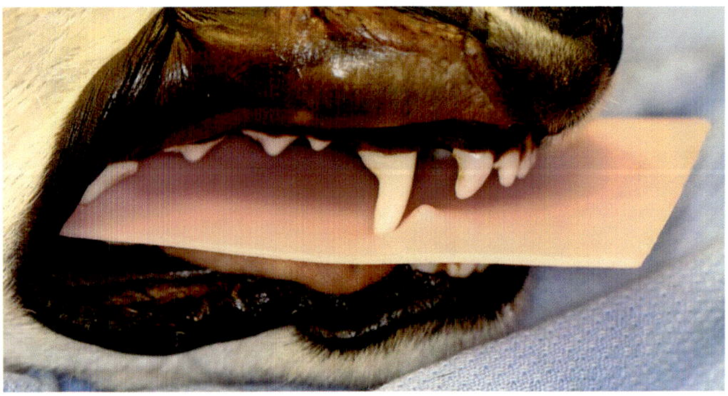

Figure 10.10 Example of a sample bite in wax.

of the maxillary arches and the model of the mandibular arches in occlusion. These test bites should be photographically documented.

Interpretation of Bitemarks

Bitemark interpretation will depend on the quality of the bitemark. A human bitemark severity and significance scale was created to allow for consistent means of describing bite injuries (Pretty 2007). Some bitemarks will be of low forensic significance in relation to bitemark analysis such as complete avulsion

Table 10.5 Description of Bite Injury and Associated Forensic Significance

Description of Bite Injury	Forensic Significance
• Very mild bruising • No individual tooth marks present • Diffuse arches visible • May be caused by something other than teeth • Least severe	Low forensic significance
• Obvious bruising with individual, discrete areas associated with teeth • Skin remains intact	Moderate forensic significance
• Very obvious bruising with small lacerations associated with teeth on the most severe aspects of the injury • Likely to be assessed as definite bitemark	High forensic significance
• Numerous areas of laceration with some bruising • Some areas of the wound may be incised • Unlikely to be confused with any other injury mechanism	High forensic significance
• Partial avulsion of tissue • Some lacerations present indicating teeth as the probable cause of the injury	Moderate forensic significance
• Complete avulsion of tissue • Possibly some scalloping of the injury margins suggestive that teeth may have been responsible for the injury • May not be an obvious bite injury • Most severe	Low forensic significance

Source: Pretty, I.A. 2007. Development and validation of a human bitemark severity and significance scale. *J Forensic Sci.* 52:687–691.

of the tissue; whereas, other types will have high forensic significance such as small lacerations associated with teeth (definite bitemark). Table 10.5 characterizes bitemarks and their associated forensic significance. Dog bitemarks generally have quantity but lack quality; therefore, over-interpretation of bitemarks should be avoided (Bernitz et al. 2012).

Features of Dog and Cat Bitemarks

Bitemark analysis will typically center on the pattern of incisor and canine teeth. It is important to differentiate a bitemark caused by an animal from a bitemark caused by a human. Humans have four incisor teeth per dental arch whereas cats and dogs each have six incisors per dental arch. Animal bites are often distinguished by differences in arch shape and specific tooth morphology.

Generally speaking, dog bites have a narrow arch with deep puncture wounds (Figure 10.11). Dogs have an asymmetrical maxillary and mandibular arch. In one study, the overall arch size ranged from 30–55 mm and was circular to oval in appearance (Kashyap et al. 2015). The incisor morphology is rectangular to oval and canine teeth morphology is oval to round. In a study comparing four breeds of dogs (Pomeranian, German Shepherd, Doberman, and Indian), the shape of the arch, incisor tooth morphology, and canine tooth morphology were similar; however, the arch size was different and there was an increase of ICD between the breeds in the study (Kashyap et al. 2015). In another study comparing the ICD between dogs and humans, medium sized dogs (9.1–23 kg) had similar results to human ICD (Tedeschi-Oliveira et al. 2011). Injuries from dogs may be represented by "V"-shaped holes which are

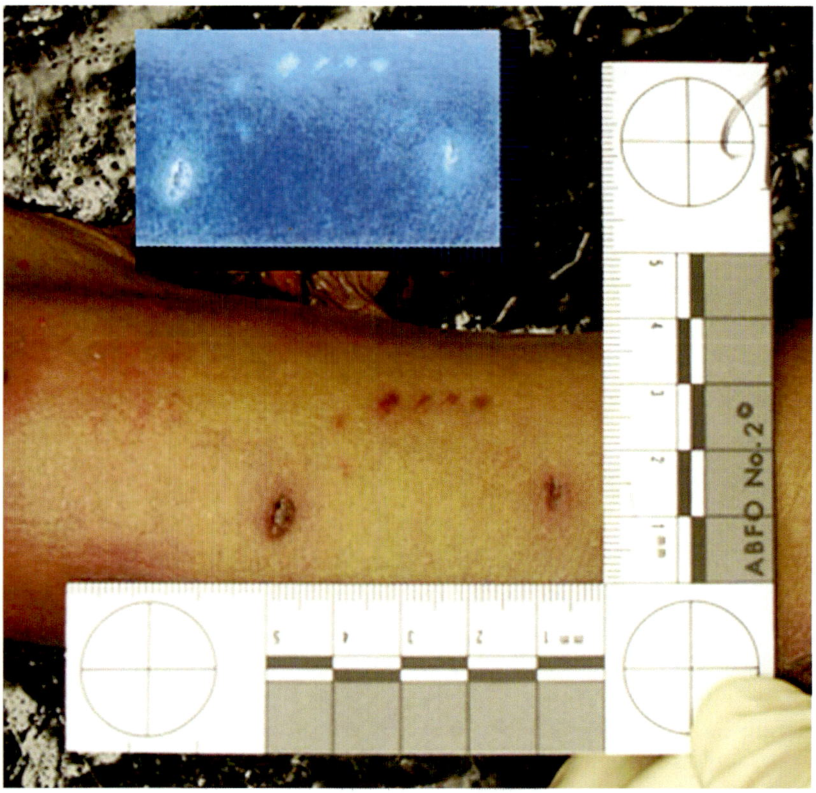

Figure 10.11 Example of a high-quality bitemark on the arm of a human who was bitten by a dog. Note the incisor and canine teeth marks. Insert of bitemark with Photoshop image adjustment. Photo courtesy of Kenneth Cohrn, DDS, DABFO.

produced by anchorage of a canine tooth and subsequent shaking (hole-and-a-tear) (Fonseca et al. 2015).

The cat bite is much shorter and rounder than the dog bite. The anterior portion of the dental arch is very linear (Murmann et al. 2006). Small round puncture wounds are more typical of injuries from a cat bite. In the cat, the mean ICD was 14.7 mm (range 8.3–20.6 mm) (Ratz et al. 1999). It should also be noted that claw marks (parallel scratches) can be found with cat bites.

Excluded versus Not Excluded

A bitemark is a pattern of injury and can be analyzed in order to exclude or not exclude a suspect animal. According to the ABFO (American Board of Forensic Odontology 2016), the following criteria are used for excluded and not excluded. For inconclusive, the criteria specifically mention a human bite; however, the same criteria theoretically can apply to animals.

- *Excluded*: The bitemark demonstrates class and/or individual characteristics that could not have been created by the dentition in question.
- *Not excluded*: The bitemark demonstrates class and/or individual characteristics that could have been created by the dentition in question.
- *Inconclusive*: Although the analyst has concluded the pattern is a human bitemark, there is missing, incomplete, or otherwise insufficient information to form an opinion whether the dentition in question caused the bitemark.

Once it has been established that the injury is a bitemark, the bitemark on the victim can be compared to data obtained from the suspect biter. It is important to note that clusters of bites may make it difficult or impossible to definitively identify individual bites, which was noted in a study looking at predation on penguin and albatross chicks (Ratz et al. 1999). Scientific exclusion of a suspect animal is possible and it is through bitemark analysis that determination if the animal could have bitten the victim can be determined. Intercanine distance can be used to exclude or not exclude a suspect animal. For example, 1 of 3 dogs in a closed population was suspected of biting a 2-year-old child, bitemark is of good quality, and the ICD of the bite wound on the child was 40 mm. The maxillary ICD of dog 1 was 22 mm and the mandibular ICD was 20 mm. The maxillary ICD of dog 2 was 39 mm and the mandibular ICD was 35 mm. The maxillary ICD of dog 3 was 41 mm and the mandibular ICD was 36 mm. Based on the measurements, dog 1 is excluded because it could not have created the bitemark based on the ICD, whereas dogs 2 and 3 are not excluded as possible suspects since it is possible that one of them could have caused the bitemark. One must also consider skin plasticity and hysteresis before excluding a suspect.

The features of the suspected animal's dentition must show a strong and consistent relationship to that of the victim impressions including tooth to tooth and arch to arch with the pattern recorded in the bitten skin. In the case of a poor quality bitemark, an inconclusive opinion might be rendered.

Organized Dog Fighting versus Spontaneous Dog Fighting

In the dog, bitemark analysis should be performed regardless of if the victim was in a spontaneous dog fight or organized dog fight. Dogs in organized dog fights may present with few to hundreds of scars on their bodies as well as fresh bitemarks. Scars will be characterized by areas of alopecia or regrowth of the area with white fur (Miller et al. 2016). Similarly, a dog in a spontaneous dog fight may also present with scars. However, dogs involved in organized dog fighting have a higher prevalence of injuries on the front legs, dorsal and lateral aspects of the head, muzzle, and oral mucosa (Miller et al. 2016). In a study looking at dog bite injuries in groups of dogs by weight, the small dog group had a large number of injuries to the thorax and abdomen, and injuries were more severe and at multiple sites (Shamir et al. 2002). Injuries to the dorsum were more prevalent in small and medium sized dogs and it was theorized this might reflect the fighting strategy of a big dog against a smaller dog opponent (Shamir et al. 2002).

DNA Analysis

Utilization of DNA evidence has been used to both identify human biters and exonerate those who were wrongly imprisoned. Some of the difficulties in comparing a bitemark with impressions/casts from a suspect with the bitemark on a victim supports the use of DNA analysis as an alternative method to bitemark analysis. DNA evidence can be utilized for identification or exoneration of a biter.

Samples used for DNA testing should include sterile swabs from the suspected biter and victim. In animals that are victims, there may be clumping of fur due to saliva from the suspect animal. Clipping of the fur around the wound, while avoiding areas with visible blood, is an appropriate sample that may be used for DNA analysis (Veterinary Genetics Laboratory 2017). Other areas that should be swabbed include regions of nonpenetrating indentations on the skin (from teeth) and any wounds on the victim animal (Merck 2013). It is important to note that swabbing around puncture wounds will be of higher value than swabbing directly within the puncture wound. Swabs from the oral cavity and teeth should be taken from the bite suspect. A sample to be used as control tissue from the bite victim should be taken (e.g., cheek swab [antemortem], skeletal muscle [postmortem]). The use of PPE and sterile technique is essential to avoid collector and environmental contamination of bite wounds and therefore the collection of nontarget DNA.

The double swab technique is recommended as it showed the highest percentage of saliva recovery in one study (American Board of Forensic Odontology 2016; Sweet et al. 1997). This collected material can then be used for extraction of DNA and ultimately compared to DNA from a suspect biter. For more information regarding DNA analysis, the reader is referred to Chapter 11 (DNA Evidence Collection and Analysis).

Conclusion

Animal bites are not uncommon and the outcome of the investigation and collection of evidence relating to bite wound injuries can have significant legal consequences for animals and humans. Veterinarians are in a unique position to be able to collect and identify evidence associated with bite wounds. Consultation with a forensic veterinarian, veterinary dentist, or DNA technician may be of benefit in an investigation. The bite wound evidence may allow for exclusion of suspects and in some instances identification of an attacker. Bitemark analysis is a very valuable tool during the forensic investigation; however, it is important to know the limitations of this field of forensic science.

References

American Board of Forensic Odontology. 2016. ABFO Bitemark methodology standards and guidelines. http://abfo.org/wp-content/uploads/2016/03/ABFO-Bitemark-Standards-03162016.pdf (Accessed April 10, 2017).

Bergqvist, L.P. 2003. The role of teeth in mammal history. *Braz J Oral Sci.* 2:249–257.

Bernitz, H., Bernitz, Z., Steenkamp, G., Blumenthal, R., G. Stols. 2012. The individualisation of a dog bitemark: A case study highlighting the bitemark analysis, with emphasis on differences between dog and human bitemarks. *Int J Legal Med.* 126:441–446.

Bhargava, K., Bhargava, D., Rastogi, P., Paul, M., Paul, R., Jagadeesh H.G., Singla A. 2012. An overview of bite mark analysis. *J Indian Acad Forensic Med.* 34:61–66.

Centers for Disease Control and Prevention. 2016. Rabies. https://www.cdc.gov/rabies/exposure/animals/domestic.html (Accessed April 10, 2017).

Chee, W.W.L., T.E. Donovan. 1992. Polyvinyl siloxane impression materials: A review of properties and techniques. *J Prosthet Dent.* 68:728–732.

Clark, M.A., Sandusky, G.E., Hawley, D.A., Pless, J.E., Fardal, P.M., L.R. Tate. 1991. Fatal and near-fatal animal bite injuries. *J Forensic Sci.* 36:1256–1261.

Cohrn, K.F. 2013. Animal bitemarks. In *Manual of Forensic Odontology,* 5th ed. Senn D.R., R.W. Weems, eds. 325–354. Boca Raton, FL: CRC Press/Taylor & Francis.

Floyd, M.R. 1991. The modified triadan system. *J Vet Dent.* 8:18–19.

Fonseca, G.M., Mora, E., Lucena, J., M. Cantin. 2015. Forensic studies of dog attacks on humans: A focus on bitemark analysis. *Res Rep Forensic Med Sci.* 5:39–51.

Giannelli, P.C. 2007. Bitemark analysis. *Crim Law Bull.* 153:930–954. http://scholarlycommons.law.case.edu/cgi/viewcontent.cgi?article=1152&context=faculty_publications (Accessed April 10, 2017).

Girard, N., Servet, E., Biourge, V., P. Hennet. 2008. Feline tooth resorption in a colony of 109 cats. *J Vet Dent.* 25:166–174.

Harding, B.E., B.C. Wolf. 2006. Alligator attacks in southwest Florida. *J Forensic Sci.* 51:647–677.

Kashyap, B., Anand, S., Reedy, S., Sahukar, S., Supriya, N., S. Pasupuleti. 2015. Comparison of the bitemark pattern and intercanine distance between humans and dogs. *J Forensic Dent Sci.* 7:175–179.

Merck, M. D. 2013. Animal Fighting. In *Veterinary Forensics: Animal Cruelty Investigations,* 2nd ed. Merck M. D., ed. 243–254. Ames: Wiley-Blackwell.

Miller, K.A., Touroo, R., Spain, V., Jones, K., Reid, P., R. Lockwood. 2016. Relationship between scarring and dog aggression in pit bull-type dogs involved in organized dogfighting. *Animals.* 6:72.

Miller, M.E., Christensen, G.C., H.E. Evans. 1993. The digestive apparatus and abdomen. In *Anatomy of the Dog.* 385–462. Philadelphia, PA: WB Saunders.

Murmann, D.C., Brumit, P.C., Schrader, B.A., and D.R. Senn. 2006. A comparison of animal jaws and bite mark patterns. *J Forensic Sci.* 51:846–860.

Nanci, A. 2013. Enamel: Composition, formation, and structure. In *Ten Cate's Oral Histology Development, Structure, and Function,* 8th ed. pp. 122–164. St. Louis, MO: Mosby.

Nandini V.V., Venkatesh K.V., K.C. Nair. 2008. Alginate impressions: A practical perspective. *J Conserv Dent.* 11:37–41.

Neiburger, E.J., and B.D. Patterson. 2002. A forensic dental determination of serial killings by three African Lions. *Gen Dent.* 50:40–42.

Perry, R. 2013. Foundations: Dental impression materials. *J Vet Dent.* 30:116–124.

Pramod, J.B., Marya, A., and V. Sharma. 2012. Role of forensic odontologist in post mortem person identification. *Dent Res J (Isfahan).* 9:522–530.

Pretty, I.A. 2007. Development and validation of a human bitemark severity and significance scale. *J Forensic Sci.* 52:687–691.

Ratz, H., Moller, H., and D. Fletcher. 1999. Predator identification from bitemarks on penguin and albatross chicks. *Mar Ornithol.* 27:149–156.

Sakaguchi, R.L. 2012. Replicating Materials—Impression and Casting. In *Craig's Restorative Dental Materials,* 13th ed., eds Sakaguchi, R.L., Powers, J.M., 277–325. Philadelphia, PA: Mosby.

Saks, M.J., Albright, T., Bohan, T.L., Bierer, B.E., Bowers, C.M., Bush, M.A., Bush, P.J., A. Casadevall et al. 2016. Forensic bitemark identification: Weak foundations, exaggerated claims. *J Law BioSci.* 3:538–575.

Senn, D. 2007. A critical look at the forensic value of bitemark analysis. *Forensic Odontology News.* Winter: 1:6–9.

Shamir, M.H., Leisner, S., Klement, E., Gonen, E., D.E. Johnston. 2002. Dog bite wounds in dogs and cats: A retrospective study of 196 cases. *J Vet Med.* 49:107–112.

Sweet, D., and I.A. Pretty. 2001. A look at forensic dentistry—Part 2: Teeth as weapons of violence—Identification of bitemark perpetrators. *Br Dent J.* 190:415–418.

Sweet, D., Lorente, M., Lorente, J.A., Valenzuela, A., E. Villanueva. 1997. An improved method to recover saliva from human skin: The double swab technique. *J Forensic Sci.* 42:320–322.

Tedeschi-Oliveira, S.V., Trigueiro, M., and R.F. Melani. 2011. Intercanine distance in the analysis of bitemarks: A comparison of human and domestic dog arches. *J Forensic Odontostomatol.* 29:30–36.

Verma, K., Joshi, B., Joshi, H., and P. Reject. 2013. Bitemarks as physical evidence from the crime scene—An overview. 2:605.

Verstraete, F.J.M., C.H. Terpak. 1997. Anatomic variations in the dentition of the domestic cat. *J Vet Dent.* 14:137–140.

Veterinary Genetics Laboratory. Evidence collection. https://www.vgl.ucdavis.edu/forensics/collection.php (Accessed April 12, 2017).

Wiggs, R.B., H.B. Lobprise. 1997. *Veterinary Dentistry Principles and Practice.* 55–86, Ames, IA: Wiley-Blackwell.

World Health organization. 2013. Animal bites. http://www.who.int/mediacentre/factsheets/fs373/en/ (Accessed April 10, 2017).

11

DNA Evidence Collection and Analysis

Kristen M. Webb

Contents

Introduction

Animal deoxyribonucleic acid (DNA) can be collected as evidence directly from an animal itself or from the biological material of an animal recovered at a crime scene. Abuse, theft, predator attacks, dog fighting, traffic accidents, and property damage are all examples of possible criminal and civil matters where an animal can be directly involved as either a perpetrator or a victim. DNA can help to solve such crimes, for example, by being used to identify the remains of a pet that was stolen. DNA may also be recovered when secondary transfer of biological material, most often hair, has occurred. It is highly probable that hairs from a dog or cat will be transferred to a person who has spent time in a home where an animal resides (D'Andrea et al. 1998). Similar transfers may occur in other instances, such as from livestock on farms. As such, when an individual involved in a crime lives or spends time with an animal, they can carry animal hair on their person and deposit it at a location or on an item associated with the crime, a process generally referred to as Locard's Exchange Principle (Thornton 1997). DNA from these hairs can be used to link perpetrators and victims to specific locations and crimes without the animal ever having been present. In one of the most well-known cases involving animal DNA evidence, David Westerfield was convicted and sentence to death for the kidnapping and murder of 7-year-old Danielle van Dam. Here, DNA analysis of dog hair found in the lint trap of David Westerfield's dryer was shown to be a perfect match to DNA collected from the van Dam family dog (Iyengar and Hadi 2013). It is believed that this dog hair was transferred from Danielle to a blanket used to wrap her body and subsequently to the dryer lint trap when the blanket was being laundered. The recovery and use of animal DNA is a relatively new and growing area of veterinary forensic investigation.

Nuclear and Mitochondrial DNA

Two distinct types of DNA are found in nearly every cell of an animal's body—nuclear DNA and mitochondrial DNA. The nuclear genome is contained within the nucleus of a cell while the mitochondrial genome is housed within the cell's mitochondria, organelles that play a role in the production of energy. Mature red blood cells lose their nucleus, mitochondria, and other organelles during phase 3 of erythropoiesis, resulting in the absence of DNA in these cells.

Nuclear DNA is inherited from both parents with the genome being comprised of two copies, one from the maternal side and one from the paternal side. Through genetic recombination during meiosis, an offspring's nuclear genome is unique relative to its parents' and siblings' (monozygotic siblings will have identical nuclear genomes). One drawback of the nuclear genome as it relates to forensic work is its linear shape. Linear DNA molecules are highly susceptible to degradation, which decreases the chances of recovering nuclear DNA from decomposing tissue. Alternatively, a single cell may contain up to 1000 copies of the mitochondrial genome, which has a circular shape. Together these characteristics make mitochondrial DNA more readily available from tissue that has begun to decompose, including the dead cells comprising the shaft of a hair. While more persistent, the mitochondrial genome is passed on solely through the maternal line and never undergoes genetic recombination. These properties result in less genetic variability relative to the nuclear genome and in siblings having identical mitochondrial DNA. Heteropaternal superfecundation occurs when a female releases multiple eggs during ovulation that are then fertilized by different fathers. Superfecundation has been known to occur in humans as well as in animals. The offspring of heteropaternal superfecundation would have the same genetic makeup as half-siblings, with identical mitochondrial genomes inherited from their mother but more distantly related nuclear genomes than full siblings stemming from the unique paternal contributions.

Nuclear DNA Profiles

Pioneered in humans by Sir Alec Jeffreys in 1985, polymorphic regions of nuclear DNA can be used to identify individuals, a technique known as DNA fingerprinting (Jeffreys et al. 1985). The two types of polymorphic loci that are often targeted to develop nuclear DNA profiles are variable number tandem repeats (VNTRs) and short tandem repeats (STRs), also known as microsatellites. The general structure of VNTRs and STRs is the same—short sequences of nucleotides repeated in tandem at a particular location (locus) in the genome. The repeat unit of a VNTR ranges in size from 6 to 100 bases and can be repeated thousands of times at a single locus. While highly discriminatory, obtaining enough starting material to analyze multiple loci of that size can be problematic when considering the often-limited amount of sample available from a crime scene. STR loci consist of repeat units ranging from 1 to 6 bases and are typically repeated 50 to 300 times (Figure 11.1). The smaller size makes STR loci ideal for forensic genetics work (The Forensic Science of Genetics 2017).

Nuclear STR-based DNA profiles have been used in human forensic investigations since the 1990s. The Combined DNA Index System (CODIS) database maintained by the U.S. Federal Bureau of Investigation contains over 4.5 million human STR profiles. A CODIS profile consists of 13 STR loci in the human genome. Once an individual's STR profile is determined, the database is consulted to determine the frequency of the particular combination of

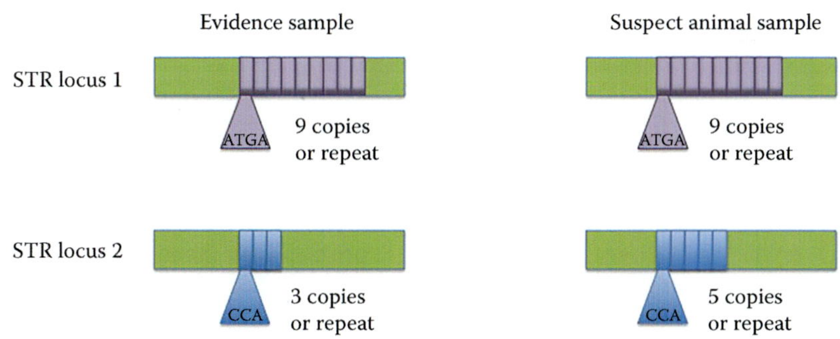

Figure 11.1 Comparison of short tandem repeat (STR) loci from an evidence sample and suspect animal sample. The samples match at the STR locus 1, as they each have nine copies of ATGA repeated in tandem. The samples do not match at the STR locus 2 as the evidence sample contains three copies of the CCA repeat while the suspect animal's DNA contains five copies of CCA. Based on this mismatch alone, the suspect animal can be confidently excluded as being the contributor of the evidence sample.

repeats at each locus and thus the probability that two people could have the exact same profile. Studies have shown that these frequencies, and thus probabilities, can vary between countries and ethnic groups. The recently developed expert system True Allele® (Cybergenetics, Pittsburgh, PA) allows investigators to maximize the utility of forensic mixture samples, or those containing DNA from more than one individual. Interpreting mixture data is challenging in that it is difficult to discern which STR loci belong in a single contributor profile. This system uses advanced statistical analyses to evaluate the likelihood of different combinations of STRs as having been contributed by a single donor and reports the uncertainty through probability (Greenspoon et al. 2015; Perlin et al. 2015). The True Allele system is currently only available for human casework, however, and a comparable system does not exist for veterinary forensic mixture samples.

Work is currently underway to develop standardized forensic STR databases for dogs, cats, and other animals from populations around the world (Berger et al. 2014; Lin et al. 2014; Schury et al. 2014; van Hoppe et al. 2016). Despite the absence of standardized databases, nuclear STR-based DNA profiles have been used for animal identification since the early 1990s. The first case to include a forensic veterinary analysis of animal DNA as evidence was *Beamish v. Her Majesty The Queen*. The victim, Shirley Duguay, disappeared on October 3, 1994 and her body was discovered in a shallow grave eight months later. Within a few days of her disappearance, Duguay's car was found with her blood spatter inside. Recovered nearby was a bag containing a man's jacket and pair of tennis shoes. These items were linked to the case's prime suspect, Duguay's estranged common-law husband, Douglas Beamish, based on size and wear patterns. However, it was white cat hair found in the pocket of the jacket that proved to be the key piece of evidence. While nuclear DNA is rarely recovered from hair due to the absence of nucleated cells in the hair shaft, on occasion epithelial cells will remain on the root from which nuclear DNA can be recovered. In this case, one of 27 hairs possessed such cells. An STR profile of 10 loci was generated and found to be an identical match to the profile of Beamish's parents' pet cat, Snowball (Menotti-Raymond et al. 1997). The probability of a random match at all 10 loci was estimated to be 1 in 7 billion through the sampling of 29 additional unrelated cats (Menotti-Raymond et al. 1997). Douglas Beamish was convicted of murder due, in large part, to the evidence match to Snowball's DNA fingerprint.

Over the past 20 years, additional STR profiles have been developed to reduce the statistical likelihood of a false positive. For example, an initial panel of 11 domestic cat loci and a gender-identifying DNA marker was reduced to 10 STR loci plus the gender identifying marker with a random match probability of 1 in 1.61×10^{13} estimated from over 1000 domestic cats representing 38 breeds (Menotti-Raymond et al. 2012). For domestic dogs, a multiplex genotyping system consisting of 18 STRs along with a gender identifying DNA marker has been developed and tested yielding an average random match probability of 1 in 2×10^{33} using a U.S. regional database (Kanthaswamy et al. 2009). The "Mini-DogFiler" system consists of 16 miniSTRs all less than 205 base pairs in length. This system was created specifically for instances involving degraded DNA (Wictum et al. 2013). The statistical power gained from using a combination of STR loci generates convincing evidence as two animals (excluding monozygotic siblings) having the same repeat number at each locus becomes less and less likely as more regions are analyzed.

Since their inception as evidence, animal STR profiles have been extended beyond companion and farm animals such as cats, dogs, and cows (Putnova et al. 2011). In wildlife forensics, STR profiles have been key pieces of evidence in cases of poaching including of the protected Eurasian badger (Dawnay et al. 2008), the Sardinian mouflon (Lorenzini et al. 2011), and the endangered red- and white-tailed black-cockatoos (White et al. 2009). In each of these cases, an individual was in possession of a protected species. Taking it one step further, it has been shown that human touch DNA, or human DNA left behind on a carcass during the processing of a hunted animal and suitable for STR profiling, can be recovered from culled deer (Tobe et al. 2013). DNA fingerprinting of animals and humans who have committed crimes involving animals has great use in the field of veterinary forensics.

Mitochondrial DNA Profiles

The mitochondrial genome is a small molecule with fewer than 17,000 bases in most mammals. Due to inferior DNA repair mechanisms, the mitochondrial genome has a higher overall average mutation rate relative to the nuclear genome. However, no region of the mitochondrial genome has variation comparable in evidentiary power to that of nuclear repeat loci such as STRs. While repeat regions do exist, they have been shown to vary among an individual's mitochondrial genomes, a phenomenon known as heteroplasmy, making them challenging to analyze. Instead, DNA sequencing of variable regions of the mitochondrial genome is the preferred method for generating mitochondrial DNA profiles. The most variable region of the mitochondrial genome is known as the D-loop (also referred to as the hypervariable region or the control region). This region is between 1000 and 1500 bases and is entirely noncoding, making it more tolerant of mutation. While other regions of the mitochondrial genome have been surveyed for forensic use, including complete mitochondrial genome, the D-loop remains the most popular locus for mitochondrial DNA analysis.

A mitochondrial DNA profile is simply a list of nucleotide differences, or polymorphisms, that occur in an individual's DNA sequence relative to a standard reference sequence. The same reference sequence and comparison approach should be used across the field in the analysis of mitochondrial DNA from a single species such that different profiles can be compared. For example, a 2004 publication provided guidelines for standardizing the way in which domestic dog mitochondrial DNA profiles are generated (Pereira et al. 2004). In dogs, every newly collected sample is compared to the first complete domestic dog mitochondrial genome ever sequenced (Kim et al. 1998 [Genbank Accession Number NC_002008.4]). From this comparison, a list of polymorphisms is generated as well as the location of each polymorphism relative to the reference genome (Pereira et al. 2004). This unambiguous list of single nucleotide polymorphisms is the dog's mitochondrial DNA profile, or haplotype. In cats, the Sylvester Reference Sequence (SRS) is used for the generation of all cat mitotypes (mitochondrial haplotypes). The SRS is a 402 base pairs consensus sequence generated from 1315 cat mitochondrial D-loop sequences (Tarditi et al. 2011). Through comparison to their respective reference sequences, hundreds of dog and cat mitochondrial DNA haplotypes have been identified and can be freely downloaded from the NCBI nucleotide database (https://www.ncbi.nlm.nih.gov/nucleotide).

Mitochondrial DNA is most often used when shed animal hair is found at the crime scene. Naturally shed hair typically lacks the root tag, which contains nuclear DNA, leaving behind only the shaft (nuclear DNA may occasionally be obtained from shed hair if epithelial cells are left behind on the shaft because of self-grooming). Research involving animal mitochondrial DNA isolated from hair shafts has been ongoing since the late 1990s (Angleby and Savolainen 2005; Bekaert et al. 2012; Savolainen et al. 1997; Savolainen and Lundeberg 1999; Schneider et al. 1999; Wetton et al. 2003). These studies have demonstrated the application of utility of mitochondrial DNA isolated from a hair shaft. In one of the earliest cases involving animal DNA, a dog was seen leaving the scene of a traffic accident and was immediately blamed for having caused the crash (Schneider et al. 1999). The car's driver wanted to hold the dog's owner accountable and have them pay for the damages. Three hair fragments were recovered from the front end of the car and the mitochondrial DNA profile of these hairs did not match the profile of the accused dog. Upon learning of the absence of a DNA match, the plaintiff withdrew the suit and the case was dismissed (Schneider et al. 1999).

Similar to nuclear DNA, in order to use mitochondrial DNA as evidence, a DNA profile must be generated from both the biological material recovered from the crime scene as well as an exemplar from the suspect animal. The DNA profiles are compared and if the sequences do not match, the animal can be confidently excluded from having contributed the sample to the scene. If the sequences match, a database must be consulted to determine the frequency of that particular sequence in the general population as D-loop sequences, and even entire mitochondrial genome sequences, can be identical among unrelated individuals. Much research has been done to determine the various D-loop sequences present in the global domestic dog and cat populations. Some sequences can be quite common and not very useful for forensic analysis. For example, a survey of 100 dogs from Sweden revealed that 51% of the dogs carried just one of four common types. The most common sequence, named A11, was found in over 13% of the dogs in the dataset (Angleby et al. 2014). Furthermore, the frequencies of particular sequences can vary quite extensively between geographic populations. In Hawaii, canine haplotype B1 was found in nearly 40% of the dogs while its prevalence in the contiguous U.S. population is just over 13% (Spadaro et al. 2015). In the U.S. cat population, a sequence known as B6 exists at a frequency of just 0.4% compared to a frequency of 28.6% in Ottawa, Ontario, Canada (Arcieri et al. 2016). The frequencies of specific mitochondrial DNA sequences can vary between geographical populations and must be known to estimate the statistical power of the forensic DNA evidence.

While free and publicly available forensic mitochondrial DNA reference databases do not exist for animal populations, private and academic laboratories such as Mitotyping Technologies (State College, Pennsylvania) and the University of California, Davis Veterinary Genetics Laboratory, maintain private databases and will process and analyze samples for a fee. If a suitable database is not available, the evidence may be disregarded by the court. A recent publication titled "Acceptance of Domestic Cat Mitochondrial DNA in a Criminal Proceeding" tells of such an experience in the murder trial of the *State of Missouri v. Henry L. Polk, Jr.* (Lyons et al. 2014). Here, Henry L. Polk, Jr. was charged with the murder of Steven Nolte. Nolte was found severely beaten and nearly decapitated and a single cat hair was lifted from the inside of Nolte's turned-out pants pocket. Mitochondrial DNA analysis was performed on the hair as well as on samples from multiple cats living in the suspect's home. A perfect match was found between the mitochondrial DNA profile of evidence hair and two of the resident cats. Despite the match, the DNA testing and analysis was initially deemed inadmissible because the database used to estimate the frequency of the profile was too small (n = 180 cats). The prosecution had to consult multiple independent, private veterinary genetics laboratories to create a suitably sized database. The mitotype remained unique among the over 400 cats surveyed and the suspect was ultimately found guilty of first degree murder and other charges and was sentenced to life in prison without parole plus 120 years (Lyons et al. 2014).

The minimum number of animals that must be surveyed for a mitochondrial DNA database to be deemed representative of the population varies by species, locus, and geographic region being considered. To determine a sufficient number of animals to sample for a given population, saturation curves are generated. From the curves, saturation threshold sampling points, such as 5% and 1%, can be estimated (Grahn et al. 2015). The points represent the minimum number of animals that must be sampled such that the database represents 95% or 99% of the population diversity, respectively. The creation of a saturation curve, however, requires that many sequences already be available for analysis. For example, a database of just over 1400 D-loop sequences from various cat breeds collected from around the world showed that for most geographic populations, sampling at least 50 cats will satisfy the 5% threshold, meaning that a database of 50 randomly sampled cats should represent the genetic diversity of 95% of the general cat population in a given area (Grahn et al. 2015).

Methods of Collection

When an animal is involved in a crime, many types of biological material that hold the potential to yield viable DNA may be available. All samples collected for processing must be handled according to standard chain of custody protocols. This includes storing samples at a secure location in a labeled, tamper-proof container and at the appropriate storage conditions.

When collecting biological material from which DNA is to be extracted, it is best to contact and follow the procedures of the laboratory performing the analysis. Table 11.1 provides specifics for how to collect crime scene samples,

Table 11.1	Best Practices for Sample Collection[a]
Samples from Live Animals	
Buccal swab	Following a period of at least 30 minutes during which no food or water has been consumed by the animal, cells are collected by inserting a swab and rubbing/swirling between the animal's inner cheek and gum for 15 seconds. The swab should then be air dried for 20 seconds to 1 minute and placed in a paper collection envelope. It is common practice to collect two swabs per animal, one from each cheek. Samples should be processed immediately or may be stored for up to 2 weeks at 4°C. Do not store samples at room temperature, as inherent oral enzymes and bacteria will degrade DNA.
Hair	Up to 30 hairs should be collected from the animal and placed in a paper collection envelope. Do not store samples in a plastic bag as condensation can occur. The entire hair, including the root, should be collected. Store and ship dry and at room temperature.
Feathers	Feathers can yield DNA but the quality and quantity varies based on feather type and age. Feathers with no visible signs of decomposition will yield the best results. Several feathers (2–5) should be collected and placed in a paper bag. Store and ship dry at room temperature.
Blood	Between 0.5 and 1 mL of blood should be collected by a veterinarian using sterile equipment. Blood should be stored in a tube containing an anticoagulant, preferably EDTA (NOT heparin) and kept chilled at 4°C if not being analyzed immediately. Long-term storage at –80°C is appropriate. It is important to minimize repeated thawing and refreezing of samples as this will degrade the DNA. Blood samples should be shipped overnight in a cooler with ice packs.
Samples from Deceased Animals	
Tissue	Only a small amount of fresh tissue is required, usually less than 50 mg (about 1 cm^3), but additional tissue should be collected from degraded remains. If the tissue is fresh and will not be processed immediately, it should be placed in an airtight container and frozen at –20°C. Dehydrated tissue can remain at room temperature until extraction.
Teeth	Intact molars or other large teeth are ideal. Teeth should not be cleaned before being sent to the laboratory. Teeth should be shipped and stored at room temperature.

(Continued)

Table 11.1 (Continued) Best Practices for Sample Collection[a]	
Bone	DNA can be recovered from 3–4 inches of a long bone such as the humerus or femur. Bone should not be cleaned before being sent to the laboratory. Bone should be shipped and stored at room temperature.
Crime Scene Samples	
Blood	Wet blood should be lifted onto dry swabs. Soak 1–2 drops of blood onto each swab. Once dried, the material can be placed in a paper envelope. If dried blood is discovered on an item that is small enough to be moved, the entire object should be taken to the laboratory for processing. If this is not possible, a slightly dampened swab should be used to lift the blood. Moisten the swab head and rub it across the dried blood. The material should be dried before placing in a paper envelope. Blood collected from ice or snow should be placed in a tube and sealed tightly. If possible, the sample should remain frozen and transferred to a –80°C freezer if not processed immediately upon arrival. It is important to minimize repeated thawing and refreezing of samples as this will degrade the DNA.
Saliva	If possible, all or part of the object covered with saliva should be submitted to the laboratory for analysis. If not possible, a swab should be used to collect the saliva, the sample should be allowed to air dry and then be placed in a paper envelope for immediate processing. Placing swabs in airtight containers and freezing at –20°C is appropriate for long-term storage. When collecting saliva from a wound, be careful to avoid the victim's blood, when possible. For animals, fur may be clipped from around the wounded area, again doing your best to avoid blood.
Feces	If the feces are wet, it should be collected in a leak-proof container and frozen at –20°C as soon as possible. Alternatively, the wet feces can be air dried and stored in a paper bag or other breathable container.
Urine/semen	If a large volume of liquid urine or semen is found (minimum 50 mL), it should be collected in a leak proof container and frozen at –20°C immediately. If dried, the object containing the sample should be sent to the laboratory. If not feasible, a moistened swab should be used to collect the dried material, in a manner similar to that of blood and saliva.

(*Continued*)

Table 11.1 (Continued)	Best Practices for Sample Collection[a]
Hair	Loose hairs should be handled to preserve any epithelial cells that may be on the hair shaft. Hairs may be collected and placed in a paper or glass container or collected on a sticky surface such as a fingerprint tape. Do not store samples in a plastic bag as condensation can occur. Store and ship dry and at room temperature.

[a] When collecting biological material from which DNA is to be extracted, it is best to contact and follow the procedures of the laboratory performing the analysis.

such as feces and blood. Collection methods may vary by sample type as well as by whether the sample is fresh or dried. For all collections, appropriate commercially prepared forensic DNA collection kits should be used when available.

The use of a commercial kit can significantly reduce the risk of evidence being challenged due to improper collection and/or handling. Alternatively, collection can be done by modifying other collection materials. For example, a human sexual assault evidence kit can be used for collection, storage, and maintaining a chain of custody. Most importantly, all collection instruments and storage containers should be DNA and DNase free to avoid contamination and preserve the DNA, respectively. DNA is best recovered from materials such as fresh tissue, fresh blood, or cheek cells swabbed from the mouth of a living or very recently deceased animal. The quality and quantity of DNA gradually decreases as samples contain fewer intact cells, with materials such as feces, urine, and vomit being the most challenging. Sample type as well as whether the sample is from a live animal, deceased animal, or crime scene dictate how the sample should be collected (Table 11.1).

Live Animals

Biological material should be collected from all living animals related to and potentially involved in the crime as soon as possible, ideally within the first 24 hours after the crime has occurred. The appropriate experienced professional such as a veterinarian, animal control officer, or law enforcement personnel should perform the collection and maintain chain of custody of each sample.

Generally speaking, the DNA in every cell of the body is the same. This means that minimally invasive sampling procedures are appropriate and preferred for live animals. The most popular minimally invasive sampling procedure is a buccal swab (Figure 11.2). In addition to dogs and cats, DNA has been successfully extracted from buccal swabs taken from many other animals such as horses, cattle, birds, and amphibians. When collecting, it is recommended that no food or water be ingested for 15 minutes prior to sampling. If the sample is coming from a young, nursing animal, the swab should be taken no less than 30 minutes after the last feeding to avoid contamination with the mother's cells. The sampling process involves swabbing the inside of the

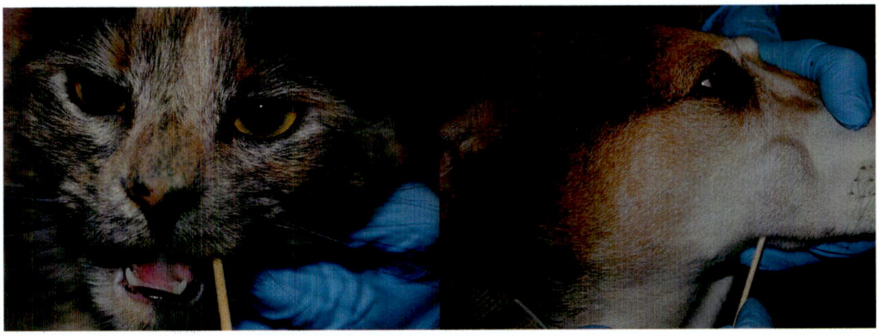

Figure 11.2 Buccal swabs being collected from a cat and a dog.

animal's cheek for 15 seconds, including changing the direction and rotation of the swab. This should result in a visible amount of material being collected. Once dried, the swab should be placed in a paper envelope and transferred to the laboratory for processing (Genomia 2017). For horses, a nostril swab is preferred to a buccal swab. The nostril swab collection process is similar to the cheek swab collection and the swab should be inserted such that the end of the swab remains visible (Halverson 2017).

If a blood sample is needed, it is preferred that the sample be collected by a veterinarian. A fresh, sterile syringe and needle must be used for each animal to avoid cross-contamination. A volume between 0.5 mL and 1.0 mL of unclotted, whole blood is needed and should be transferred to a collection tube containing an anticoagulant. The specific anticoagulant used can vary but must be known as different anticoagulants can potentially inhibit downstream analyses if not first removed from the sample. Heparin, for example, can inhibit the reaction used to amplify target loci and should be avoided. Less problematic anticoagulants include EDTA and sodium citrate. After collection, the tube should be inverted several times to mix (Table 11.1).

Postmortem Specimen Collection

A genetic profile created from animal remains may be used for individual and species identification and to possibly determine the geographic origin of the individual. This type of information can be helpful in cases involving the illegal hunting and trading of endangered species. A 2010 study found that whale meat from Japan's scientific whaling program was being served illegally as sushi at restaurants outside of the country (Baker et al. 2010). Whale meat collected by the scientific whaling program but not used for research may be sold within Japan, but international sales are illegal. Food advertised as containing whale was purchased from restaurants in Seoul, South Korea and Los Angeles, California. DNA sequences were generated from the samples, which allowed for species identification. In some cases, exact matches were discovered between the purchased restaurant meat and whale meat being sold in Japanese markets. As the probability of a random match was extremely low, the researchers considered it to be highly probable that the products originated from the same individuals. The DNA evidence led to the restaurants and sushi chefs being charged with illegally selling an endangered species product (Baker et al. 2010).

If DNA is needed from the remains of a deceased animal, the preferred biological material is tissue. Sufficient amounts of DNA can be extracted from as little as 25 mg of tissue; however, if possible, the entire carcass should be collected. It should be noted that the head and/or distal limbs may be wrapped in white linen sheets or with paper bags over them to prevent loss of evidence of contamination of the sites if evidence is not collected at the scene. Collecting the entire animal would provide adequate material for DNA extraction and allow for the possibility of recovering DNA from other individuals involved in the crime. For example, if the animal scratched or bit an attacker, then DNA from the attacker may be recovered from the animal's nails, teeth, oral cavity, or hair/fur. Once collected, the tissue should be kept chilled. Keeping fresh biological material frozen at –20°C and limiting thawing and refreezing helps to prevent DNA degradation. Once the animal has started to decompose, the tissue is no longer ideal for DNA analysis.

As an alternative to fresh tissue, DNA may be recovered from teeth or bone. In 2009, a necklace made up of 10 wolf teeth was confiscated from the home of a suspected wolf serial killer in Italy. DNA obtained from the teeth was found to match six Italian wolves whose DNA had previously been deposited into a database maintained to monitor the European wolf population. The DNA match was key evidence in proving wolf poaching and identifying the suspected serial killer of the wolves (Caniglia et al. 2010). Teeth are preferred to bone for DNA profiling, with intact molars or other large teeth being ideal. Neither teeth nor bone should be cleaned prior to laboratory analysis (Table 11.1).

Crime Scene Evidence

While an entire carcass or parts of the animal's remains may be recovered during an investigation, more often biological material shed or excreted from the animal is likely to be collected from the scene of a crime. Examples of such biological materials include blood, saliva, hair, urine, and feces. While DNA can be extracted from small amounts of these materials, it is recommended that maximum quantities be collected to increase chances of adequate yield. DNA analysis of these materials can be used to include or exclude an animal from having been present at the scene of the crime. Hair is the most common type of animal evidence collected. Animal hair only contains the more discriminatory nuclear DNA if the follicle is attached or if there is saliva present on the hair from grooming. As such, hairs should be handled carefully to ensure that contamination is kept to a minimum and all DNA present is recovered (Table 11.1).

In addition to direct animal involvement, an individual involved in the crime can carry biological material from an animal on their person to or from the scene, a process known as secondary transfer (Locard's Exchange Principle [Thornton 1997]). A key piece of evidence in a 2000 burglary, robbery, and murder case was dog feces recovered from one of the suspect's tennis shoes. After interrupting a home invasion, three contractors were taken to a barn, bound, and shot execution style. Evidence at the scene included a shoe print found on a piece of wood in the barn. When the suspect's shoes were recovered, it was determined that the shoe print was a match, but alone was not enough to convict the suspect. Dog feces was also found on the shoe. Feces can contain epithelial cells shed from the colon during passage, yielding suitable DNA for analysis. DNA extracted from the feces was a perfect match to DNA extracted from dog feces found in the barn. This match was key in linking the suspect to the crime and he was ultimately convicted of three counts of murder, two counts of robbery, burglary, and attempted robbery (Office of the Clark County Prosecutor 2006).

Laboratory Processing

When a laboratory performs genetic analyses for the purposes of forensic investigation, it is imperative that the laboratory meets the standards of the forensic community to ensure the quality and integrity of the data generated such that evidence is admissible in court. To this end, forensic laboratories are accredited, meaning the laboratory is assessed and formally recognized by a nonprofit professional association as meeting or exceeding a list of standards, including the FBI Director's Quality Assurance Standards. As of 2015, the University of California, Davis Veterinary Genetics Laboratory is the only accredited veterinary laboratory in the United States, having been accredited by the American Society of Crime Laboratory Directors/Laboratory Accreditation Board in 2010 (Kanthaswamy 2015). The lack of accredited labs is due in part to the infancy of the field of animal forensic genetic testing relative to its human counterpart and a lack of standard practices for veterinary forensics. The International Society Animal Genetics (ISAG) Animal Forensic Genetics Standing Committee and the U.S. National Academy of Sciences have made recommendations on the use of animal genetic information in forensic investigations in hopes of generating more accredited laboratories (Linacre et al. 2011; Kanthaswamy 2015).

Consistent with the approaches taken during sample collection, attention must be paid to specimen packaging, labeling, and transport to ensure the reliability of results both in the context of contamination as well as chain of custody compliance. Ideally, all evidence should be individually sealed in a self-sealing envelope, with the investigator's signature across the seal. A barcode system can be employed as a secure means to track a sample along with relevant information including sample type, evidence number, and collection location. Samples should be shipped to the laboratory as soon as possible ensuring that samples are not swapped between time of collection and receipt at the laboratory. All laboratory personnel that handle a sample must complete and sign the appropriate chain of custody documentation. Again, it is recommended that the laboratory performing the DNA analysis be contacted for specific procedures.

When a sample arrives at the laboratory, it is preferred that it be processed immediately. If that is not possible, the sample should be frozen (e.g., –20°C for tissue, −80°C for blood) to limit DNA degradation. The process of DNA extraction involves isolating pure DNA while removing all other cellular components including RNA, proteins, lipids, carbohydrates, and so on. Many commercial extraction kits are available and appropriate for this process. An extraction typically yields between 1 and 500 μg of DNA depending on the amount and type of biological material being used. A successful DNA extraction should yield plenty of DNA for the amplification of the target regions, as a standard amplification requires between just 1 ng and 1 μg of DNA.

The raw data from a nuclear STR profile analysis appears as a series of peaks where each peak represents an amplicon of the target region and the location of the peak along the x-axis indicates the STR size, in nucleotides (Figure 11.3). These data are then converted to a table of locus sizes where each value corresponds to a peak in the raw data. Mitochondrial DNA sequence analysis also results in peaked raw data. However, here each peak represents a

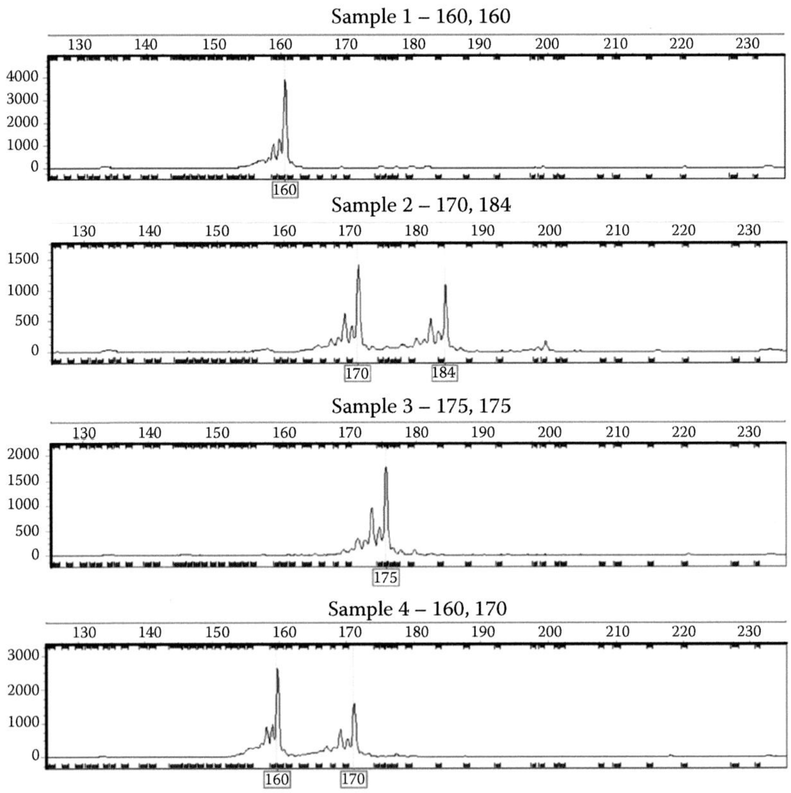

Figure 11.3 Raw data used to create an STR profile. Numbers along the x-axis indicate STR length in nucleotides. Samples 1 and 3 are homozygous meaning they carry identical versions of the STR on their maternal and paternal versions of the DNA while samples 2 and 4 are heterozygous carrying versions of the STR that differ. All four samples differ in their STR profile at this locus.

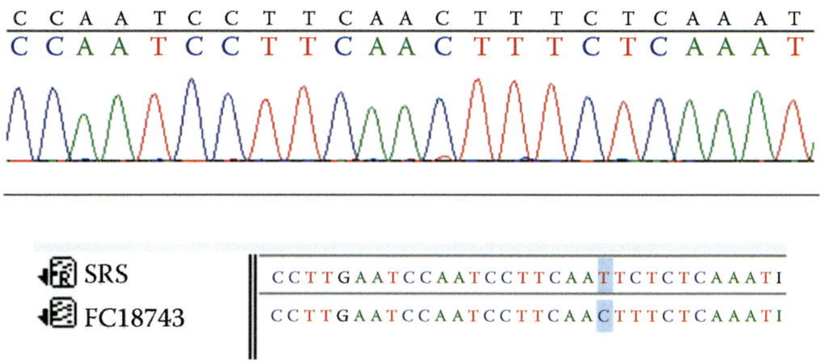

Figure 11.4 DNA chromatogram of a domestic cat D-loop sequence where each peak represents a nucleotide in the DNA sequence (top). Alignment of domestic cat (*Felis catus*) sequence FC18743 to the Sylvester Reference Sequence (SRS) (bottom). A single nucleotide polymorphism in FC18743 relative to the SRS is highlighted.

nucleotide in the DNA sequence. This sequence data is edited and exported as a text file of the nucleotide sequence that is then compared to the reference to determine an individual's mitochondrial DNA haplotype (Figure 11.4).

Contamination

The potential for contamination of a sample with DNA from an outside source exists at every stage of the investigation from evidence collection through laboratory analysis. While human and animal DNA is easily distinguishable, secondary transfer of animal biological material to the scene by an investigator is a very real possibility, from a family pet for example. Limiting incidental activity and ensuring that personnel are aware of their actions at the scene should help to limit inadvertent contamination of evidence. At the scene, the appropriate personal protective equipment (PPE) including gloves should be worn and changed between each sample collected. Each sample should be stored in its own sterile, DNA/DNase-free container. If tools are used during evidence collection, it is preferred that they be sterile and disposable but if not, they should be carefully and thoroughly cleaned between each use to ensure the absence of residual biological material. If the scene is outdoors, dirt and leaf material should be avoided as it can inhibit the subsequent DNA analysis. If evidence is being collected from an injured live animal, every effort should be made to collect the sample prior to treatment (such as cleaning of the wound) to decrease chances of removal of possible trace evidence or contamination of the collection site. Once in the laboratory, gloves should always be worn during the processing of samples and changed in between the handling of material from different animals. Prior to experimental work, all disposables and equipment should be decontaminated through methods such as UV light exposure, which degrades DNA. Ideally, all amplifications of target loci should take place in a dedicated laboratory with negative air pressure. Amplification of target loci, such as STRs or the mitochondrial D-loop, generate millions of copies of DNA from the initial sample. The negative air pressure helps to prevent the escape of DNA into the air of the laboratory and thus prevents contamination. If a dedicated laboratory is not available, bench top work-stations are commercially available that include UV lights for sterilization as well as an air circulation and filtration system. Finally, negative controls (reactions excluding DNA) should be included in all experiments to ensure that DNA carryover has not occurred at any stage of the experimentation.

Conclusion

Animal DNA can be recovered during a crime scene investigation when an animal is the victim, the perpetrator, or when biological material is carried to the scene by an individual involved in the crime. The specific material recovered will determine the type of DNA profile that can be generated. While nuclear profiles are more discriminatory, nuclear DNA is more susceptible to DNA degradation, leaving only mitochondrial DNA for analysis. If a DNA match between an evidence sample and the animal is found, the frequency of that geographically sensitive specific profile in the general population must be determined to estimate the likelihood of a random match. Whether from nuclear or mitochondrial DNA, DNA profiles from animals can be key pieces of evidence in criminal investigations.

References

Angleby, H., and P. Savolainen. 2005. Forensic informativity of domestic dog mtDNA control region sequences. *Forensic Sci Int.* 2–3:99–110.

Angleby, H., Oskarsson, M., Pang, J., Zhang, Y. P., Leitner, T., Braham, C., Arvestad, L., Lundeberg, J., Webb, K. M., and P. Savolainen. 2014. Forensic Informativity of ~3000 bp of coding sequence of domestic dog mtDNA. *J Forensic Sci.* 59:898–908.

Arcieri, M., Agostinelli, G., Gray, Z., Spadaro, A., Lyons, L. A., and K. M. Webb. 2016. Establishing a database of Canadian feline mitotypes for forensic use. *Forensic Sci Int Genet.* 22:169–174.

Baker, C. S., Steel, D., Choi, Y., Lee, H., Kim, K. S., Choi, S. K., Ma, Y. U., Hambleton, C., Psihoyos, L., Brownell, R. L., and N. Funahashi. 2010. Genetic evidence of illegal trade in protected whales links Japan with the US and South Korea. *Biol Lett.* 6:647–650.

Bekaert, B., Larmuseau, M. H. D., Vanhove, M. P. M., Opdekamp, A., and R. Decorte. 2012. Automated DNA extraction of single dog hairs without roots for mitochondrial DNA analysis. *Forensic Sci Int Genet.* 277–281.

Berger, B., Berger, C., Hecht, W., Hellmann, A., Rohleder, U., Schleenbecker, U., and W. Parson. 2014. Validation of two canine STR multiplex-assays following the ISFG recommendations for non-human DNA analysis. *Forensic Sci Int Genet.* 8:90–100.

Caniglia, R., Fabbri, E., Greco, C., Galaverni, M., and E. Randi. 2010. Forensic DNA against wildlife poaching: Identification of a serial wolf killing in Italy. *Forensic Sci Int Genet.* 4:334–338.

D'Andrea, F., Fridez, F., and R. Coquoz. 1998. Preliminary experiments on the transfer of animal hair during simulated criminal behavior. *J Forensic Sci.* 43:1257–1258.

Dawnay, N., Ogden, R., Thorpe, R. S., Pope, L. C., Dawson, D. A., and R. McEwing. 2008. A forensic STR profiling system for the Eurasian badger: A framework for developing profiling systems for wildlife species. *Forensic Sci Int Genet.* 2:47–53.

The Forensic Science of Genetics. http://www.councilforresponsiblegenetics.org/geneticprivacy/DNA_forensics_1.html (Accessed March 29, 2017).

Genomia. 2017. Instructions for animal sampling. http://www.genomia.cz/en/pokyny (Accessed April 1, 2017).

Grahn, R. A., Alhaddad, H., Alves, P. C., Randi, E., Waly, N. E., and L. A. Lyons. 2015. Feline mitochondrial DNA sampling for forensic analysis: When enough is enough! *Forensic Sci Int Genet.* 16:52–57.

Greenspoon, S. A., Schiermeier-Wood, L., and B. C. Jenkins. 2015. Establishing the limits of TrueAllele® casework: A validation study. *J Forensic Sci.* 60:1263–1276.

Halverson, J. 2017. DNA collection from animals. http://joyofdna.com/perpetua-information-guide/dna-collection-from-animals/ (Accessed April 1, 2017).

Iyengar, A., and S. Hadi. 2013. Use of non-human DNA analysis in forensic science: A mini review. *Med Sci Law.* 54(1):41–50.

Jeffreys, A. J., Brookfield, J. F., and R. Semeonoff. 1985. Positive identification of an immigration test-case using human DNA fingerprints. *Nature.* 317:818–819.

Kanthaswamy, S. 2015. Review: Domestic animal forensic genetics—Biological evidence, genetic markers, analytical approaches and challenges. *Anim Genet.* 46:473–484.

Kanthaswamy, S., Tom, B. K., Mattila, A.-M., Johnston, E., Dayton, M., Kinaga, J., Joy-Alise Erickson, B. et al. 2009. Canine population data generated from a multiplex STR kit for use in forensic casework. *J Forensic Sci.* 54:829–840.

Kim, K. S., Lee, S. E., Jeong, H. W., and J. H. Ha. 1998. The complete nucleotide sequence of the domestic dog (*Canis familiaris*) mitochondrial genome. *Mol Phylogenet Evol.* 10:210–220.

Lin, Y. C., Hsieh, H. M., Lee, J. C. I., Hsiao, C. T., Lin, D. Y., Linacre, A., and L. C. Tsai. 2014. Establishing a DNA identification system for pigs (*Sus scrofa*) using a multiplex STR amplification. *Forensic Sci Int Genet.* 9:12–19.

Linacre, A., Gusmao, L., Hecht, W., Hellmann, A. P., Mayr, W. R., Parson, W., Prinz, M., Schneider, P. M., and N. Morling. 2011. ISFG: Recommendations regarding the use of non-human (animal) DNA in forensic genetic investigations. *Forensic Sci Int Genet.* 5:501–505.

Lorenzini, R., Cabras, P., Fanelli, R., and G. L. Carboni. 2011. Wildlife molecular forensics: Identification of the Sardinian mouflon using STR profiling and the Bayesian assignment test. *Forensic Sci Int Genet.* 5:345–349.

Lyons, L. A., Grahn, R. A., Kun, T. J., Netzel, L. R., Wictum, E. E., and J. L. Halverson. 2014. Acceptance of domestic cat mitochondrial DNA in a criminal proceeding. *Forensic Sci Int Genet.* 13:61–67.

Menotti-Raymond, M. A., David, V. A., and S. J. O'Brien. 1997. Pet cat hair implicates murder suspect. *Nature.* 386:774.

Menotti-Raymond, M., David, V. A., Weir, B. S., and S. J. O'Brien. 2012. A population genetic database of cat breeds developed in coordination with a domestic cat STR multiplex. *J Forensic Sci.* 57:596–601.

Office of the Clark County Prosecutor. 2006. http://www.clarkprosecutor.org/html/death/row/stroudp.htm (Accessed April 1, 2017).

Pereira, L., Van Asch, B., and A. Amorim. 2004. Standardization of nomenclature for dog mtDNA D-loop: A prerequisite for launching a *Canis familiaris* database. *Forensic Sci Int*. 141:99–108.

Perlin, M. W., Hornyak, J. M., Sugimoto, G., and K. W. P. Miller. 2015. TrueAllele® genotype identification on DNA mixtures containing up to five unknown contributors. *J Forensic Sci*. 60:857–868.

Putnova, L., Vrtkova, I., Srubarova, P., and L. Stehlik. 2011. Utilization of a 17 microsatellites set for bovine traceability in Czech cattle populations. *Iran J Appl Anim Sci*. 1:31–37.

Savolainen, P., Rosen, I., Holmberg, A., Leitner, T., Uhlen, M., and J. Lundeberg. 1997. Sequence analysis of domestic dog mitochondrial DNA for forensic use. *J Forensic Sci*. 4:593–600.

Savolainen, P., and J. Lundeberg. 1999. Forensic evidence based on mtDNA from dog and wolf hairs. *J Forensic Sci*. 1:77–81.

Schneider, P. M., Seo, Y., and C. Rittner. 1999. Forensic mtDNA hair analysis excludes a dog from having caused a traffic accident. *Int J leg Med*. 112:315–316.

Schury, N., Schleenbecker, U., and A. P. Hellmann. 2014. Forensic animal DNA typing: Allele nomenclature and standardization of 14 feline STR markers. *Forensic Sci Int Genet*. 12:42–59.

Spadaro, A., Ream, K., Braham, C., and K. M. Webb. 2015. Local mitochondrial DNA haplotype databases needed for domestic dog populations that have experienced founder effect. *Forensic Sci Int*. 248:113–118.

Tarditi, C. R., Grahn, R. A., Evans, J. J., Kurushima, J. D., and L. A. Lyons. 2011. Mitochondrial DNA sequencing of cat hair: An informative forensic tool. *J Forensic Sci*. 56(s1).

Thornton, J. I. 1997. The general assumptions and rationale of forensic identification. In *Modern Scientific Evidence: The Law and Science of Expert Testimony*, Volume 2 ed. D. L. Faigman, D. H. Kaye, M. J. Saks, J. Sanders, and E. Cheng. St. Paul, MN: West Publishing Co.

Tobe, S. S., Bailey, S., Govan, J., and L. A. Welch. 2013. Recovery of human DNA profiles from poached deer remains part 2: Improved recovery protocol without the need for LCN analysis. *Sci Justice*. 53:23–27.

van Hoppe, M. J., Dy, M. A., van den Einden, M., and A. Iyengar, 2016. SkydancerPlex: A novel STR multiplex validated for forensic use in the hen harrier (*Circus cyaneus*). *Forensic Sci Int Genet*. 22:100–109.

Wetton, J. H., Higgs, J. E., Spriggs, A. C., Roney, C. A., Tsang, C. S., and A. P. Foster. 2003. Mitochondrial profiling of dog hairs. *Forensic Sci Int*. 3:235–241.

White, N. E., Mawson, P. R., Dawson, R., Bunce, M. A., and P. B. S. Spencer. 2009. Characterization and cross-species utility of 20 microsatellite markers for population and forensic applications in the endangered Carnaby's Black-cockatoo, *Calyptorhynchus latirostris*. *Conser Genet Resour*. 1:341–345.

Wictum, E., Kun, T., Lindquist, C., Malvick, J., Vankan, D., and B. Sacks. 2013. Developmental validation of DogFiler, a novel multiplex for canine DNA profiling in forensic casework. *Forensic Sci Int Genet*. 7:82–91.

12

Animal Behavior for the Forensics Specialist

Elizabeth Stelow and Melissa Bain

Contents

Introduction

When a forensic investigator finds animals as living evidence, or is charged with their care, these animals must be processed in a way appropriate to the investigation. There are special considerations necessary when dealing with live animals as evidence. The chain of custody must be maintained from the confiscation of the individuals through the final disposition. First, someone must be assigned to attend to the care and feeding of the animals. In a court case, this is not likely to be the customary caregivers for these animals, as the suspects may be the ones under investigation. Second, the behavioral evidence may change over time. The animal you see at the crime scene may be in much better, or much worse, condition in as little as a few days; therefore, appropriate documentation must be made quickly. Finally, much of the actual evidence animals have to offer must be obtained through visual observation in addition to physical examination and as needed biomedical samples. In fact, the very next steps in the disposition of the animals may be decided based on a behavioral analysis, in conjunction with other medical and scientific findings.

The goal of this chapter is to address the concept: how does one examine living evidence in the most productive way to provide the best information and the best outcome for the animal? We will cover understanding an animal's body language, the variety of possible behavioral presentations, and how one might assess an animal's temperament. We will also address assessments particular to different crime scenes, including abuse cases, fighting rings, neglect, and hoarding. This chapter ends with notes on different forms of useful documentation of living animal evidence.

Assessing an Animal's Body Language

Most animals are skilled communicators, both within their species and with other species. Communication can include vocalizations. Humans come to learn at an early age, often without being told, what a cat's hiss means and some of the many reasons dogs bark (Pongracz et al. 2011). Subtler communication can take the form of a scent left behind by an animal or the way the animal is holding its ears or tail. This latter form of communication—body posture—is very useful in determining an animal's emotional state or its motivation for a particular action. In addition, body language can suggest medical issues, perhaps arising from the situation under investigation.

Visual cues, as described below, occur in a state of continual shift, depending on the triggers present, the environment, and the animal's resiliency. Changes in body language patterns in an individual should be documented. These changes can help the investigators and caretakers have a more complete picture of the animal's adaptability.

Canine Body Language

A dog can use its posture, ears, mouth, and tail to indicate its intentions and emotions at a given time, in response to the surroundings and specific stimuli.

Figure 12.1 Neutral tail, ears, and posture in a relaxed dog.

Although discussed separately, these elements together provide a complete picture of the dog in that moment (Beaver 1999; Houpt 2011).

- *Posture*—A relaxed upright or reclined posture is the default in a dog that's comfortable with its surroundings (Figure 12.1). This is the state to which all other postures are compared. Alternatively, a very alert dog that is leaning forward toward a stimulus is engaged in a confident way. A dog that is leaning—perhaps even moving—backward or holding its head below its shoulders in response to a stimulus is likely fearful of the situation. If this state persists even without the triggering stimulus, the dog may be generally anxious or fearful. If the hair on the dog's back is erect from the shoulders to as caudal as the hips, the dog is aroused by the situation. The arousal may be due to either fear or excitement.
- *Ears*—Like posture, the ears are held in a neutral position when the dog is comfortable with its surroundings. Forward ears reflect interest in a confident way. Ears held back or tight to the body are indicative of concern or fear. Ears that have been artificially cropped can be difficult to read.
- *Mouth*—The neutral dog mouth has relaxed facial and perioral muscles. If a dog is panting in response to exertion or elevated ambient temperature, the mouth is open but lips are still relaxed. A dog that is displaying aggression will have contracted muscles around the commissures and may even be showing its teeth (Figure 12.2). This can accompany a growl or snarl. If the lips come up in the front in a pucker, the dog is thought to be more confidently aggressive. If the lips are retracted to the sides and toward the ears

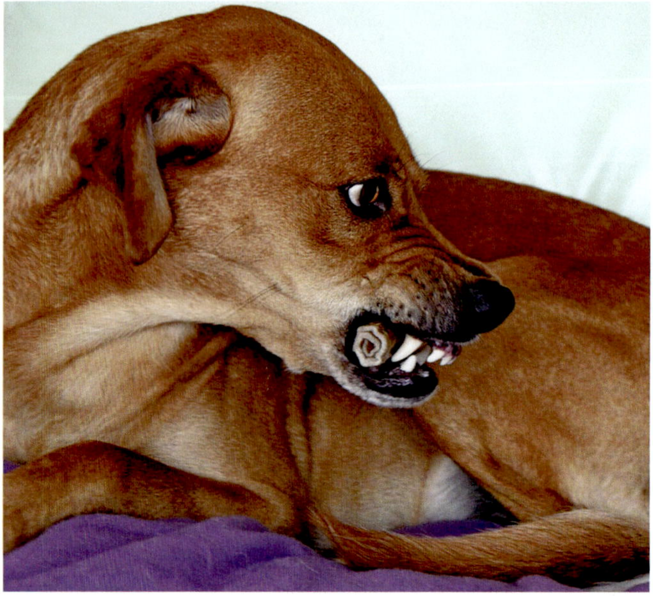

Figure 12.2 Snarling to protect a rawhide treat.

(showing cheek teeth), the dog is thought to be more fearful of the aggression-inducing stimulus.

- *Tail*—A neutral tail is held in the most natural position for the particular breed. This can be curled over the back, as in Akitas and Chow Chows, or held straight and low, like in retrievers. Some dogs have docked tails that make it difficult to know how they are being held. A tail that normally should be held out straight or down that is currently being held over the body is called a "flagged" tail, and indicates confident arousal or aggression. A tail that is tucked under the body indicates concern or fear (Figure 12.3). Rapid wagging of the tail suggests arousal that can be happy, neutral, or aggressive. The neutral tail may be slowly wagging, although this should not be confused with the rigid and rapidly wagging tail of the aroused dog, as wagging is not always a sign of happiness or friendliness.

Taken individually, these visual signals can be of little use; taken together, they present a more complete picture of the dog at that moment. Body language is important when dogs must be housed communally during an investigation, as dogs communicate their intentions and perceived social relationships via posturing. A dog, that puts its head over another's shoulder, or mounts the other dog is asserting a more dominant role. A dog that approaches another with its head lowered and eyes averted, on the other hand, suggests a more submissive stance (Figure 12.4).

Figure 12.3 Tucked tail and lowered head in a frightened dog.

Figure 12.4 Posturing between dogs.

Feline Body Language

Similar to dogs, cats use their vocalizations, postures, tails, and facial features to communicate (Houpt 2011).

- *Posture*—A relaxed cat has soft lines, whether standing, sitting, or recumbent. Whereas, an alert cat has more rigid lines due to tensing muscles, often of the head. Aggressive cats can have two different postures. First, the "Halloween" cat with arched back and puffed/ piloerected tail is the hallmark sign of the fearfully aggressive cat,

Figure 12.5 Piloerection of the tail and lowered head in a frightened cat.

as the cat wants to look as big as possible to deflect the oncoming threat (Figure 12.5). Other fearful cats may remain low to the ground. Conversely, the cat holding its tail head high and front end lower, with a rigid forward approach, is a more confidently aggressive cat.

- *Facial features*—A cat's ears, eyes, and mouth work together to show emotional state. The relaxed cat has equally relaxed facial features, with ears up and eyes and mouth soft. The fearful cat will pull its ears flat back against its head and may widen its eyes and curl its mouth into a hiss (Figure 12.6). A more confident cat may have its ears out to the side and stare straight at its perceived opponent.

Figure 12.6 Hissing with ears back in a frightened cat.

- *Tail*—The neutral cat's tail is held high but relaxed while walking and rests on the ground while sitting or recumbent. The fearful or otherwise aroused cat may piloerect along its tail.

Equine Body Language

Horses also communicate with their tails, body postures, and facial features (Houpt 2011).

- *Posture*—The relaxed horse moves very little compared to the agitated horse. Because horses are prey species, they leave (if possible) when frightened. For the horse forced to stand during something stressful, you may see it hold its rear feet close together or begin to prance. The aggressive horse may try to kick or lift a front or hind leg. A frustrated horse may paw the ground.
- *Facial features*—The relaxed horse will hold its ears in a relaxed upright position and will rotate them in the direction of an interesting sound. That horse's lips will be loose and eyes observant but not darting. The aggressive horse will have its ears pulled back flat against it head, with the extent of the degree to which they are flattened an indication of the intensity of the aggression. Horses may swivel their ears toward objects of interest, including things they find frightening.
- *Tail*—A frightened horse may tuck its tail flat against its rump. A frustrated horse, or one that may become aggressive, may lash its tail forcefully from side to side.

Physiological States

Observing an animal often gives us as much insight into the physiological state of the animal as it does the psychological state. Physically demanding physiological states include pregnancy, lactation, pain, sickness, hunger, thirst, and starvation. We can usually observe whether an animal is well fed or starving, horribly painful or more comfortable, pregnant, or lactating. Sometimes the more nuanced physiologic changes are difficult to identify.

One sign that an animal is well fed and comfortable is that it engages in species-typical body care and maintenance behaviors. The animal might groom casually while we watch (Figure 12.7) or it might sleep or rest with reduced alertness. One must be careful, however, not to confuse grooming as a displacement behavior with relaxed grooming in the comfortable animal or confuse a depressed animal with a resting one.

Animals that are painful, febrile, or suffering from other illnesses may exhibit behaviors indicating illness (Hart 1991). In addition to the more overt signs of illness like vomiting or seizures, subtler signs include curling up and piloerecting to conserve heat, sleeping more than expected, licking or chewing painful body parts, panting out of context, shaking or shivering, reduced

Figure 12.7 Body care in a relaxed cat.

grooming, reduced food intake, and a noticeable increase or decrease in water consumption (Gregory 2004).

Physical illness is not the only acute or chronic problem that should be considered when observing an animal that is having a difficult time coping in its environment or behaving abnormally. While observations about an animal's physical condition are being made, its psychological state will be of interest as well.

Psychological States

Just as an animal can be physically healthy or unhealthy, it can also be psychologically healthy or unhealthy. Stress, fear, and anxiety can manifest as observable behaviors and are often overlooked when assessing the health of an animal; yet one or more can be the underlying cause of problem behaviors like aggression and repetitive behaviors (Gregory 2004). Assessment of these behaviors may require examination of the individual in the environment identified for the investigation (with video recording) and a second neutral location.

To appreciate how they affect the animal, it is important to understand the differences among fear, anxiety, and stress. Fear is defined as "an emotional response due to the presence or proximity of a specific stimulus (e.g., object, noise, individual, social situation) that the pet perceives as a threat or danger" (Landsberg et al. 2013). Fear accompanies an event. Fear/apprehension can arise quickly and, depending on how the situation resolves, can dissipate quickly, too.

Anxiety is defined as "a reaction of apprehension or uneasiness to an anticipated danger or threat" or to an unknown dynamic situation (Landsberg et al. 2013). It is a state rather than an event. Anxious animals are more prone to being fearful in nonthreatening situations. Repeated fear events can cause or exacerbate anxiety and behavioral expression.

Stress is defined as "an altered state of homeostasis which can be caused by physical or emotional factors. This results in psychological, behavioral, endocrine, and immune effects that are designed to handle stress" (Landsberg et al. 2013). In humans, stressors can be external (from the environment or social situations) or internal (illness, or from a medical procedure); in pets, stressors are mainly external, with the animal's personality contributing the internal machinery on which the external stressors act. We tend to think of stress as chronic rather than transient; in pets, it is often the result of frequent and/or intense exposure to fear-inducing stimuli or repeated bouts of anxiety. The animal need not be anxious or fearful to experience stress.

How will the examiner know if these psychological states are being experienced by the animal(s) being examined? There are several behavioral signs to be on the lookout for.

Behavioral Manifestations of Fear, Anxiety, and Stress

Because fears, anxieties, and chronic stress can lead to problem behaviors, it is important to understand this connection. The most common of these behaviors include aggression and abnormal repetitive behaviors.

Aggression is a set of threatening behaviors selected by an animal with the express purpose of increasing the distance from a stimulus (usually a person or other animal). In the dog, these behaviors can include staring, growling, snarling, snapping, posturing, lunging, or biting. Cats may choose to hiss, growl, spit, scratch, or bite. Horses may kick, rear, strike, or bite (Figure 12.8).

Aggression is often due to fear and the need to escape a particular situation. This arises in the frightened animal when it feels trapped, whether caged, cornered, or leashed. Aggression can be limited to growling or snarling, or can

Figure 12.8 Two fighting horses, showing biting and striking.

progress to snapping and biting, depending on the animal's previous experience, the severity of the fear, and the animal's genetic predisposition to display aggression.

Repetitive behaviors can result from a few different diagnoses, such as displacement behavior and compulsive behavior. Displacement behaviors arise when an animal has two very conflicting motivations, such as fight and flight, neither of which is possible; so, the animal engages in something completely unrelated to the situation. These behaviors can also arise when the animal is aroused (or bored) and finds no outlet for his arousal or boredom. A few examples of displacement behaviors in domestic animals include pacing, circling, yawning, lip licking, excessive grooming, and vocalizing (Landsberg et al. 2013).

Compulsive behaviors differ from displacement behaviors in many ways. Most importantly, the start and end of the bouts of these behaviors appear to be outside the control of the animal. Because it lacks control, the animal will often forego normal functions like maintenance behaviors during a bout of compulsive behavior. The animal's lack of control also suggests that the behaviors may lack a specific trigger or context associated with displacement behaviors. The dog may spin in any place at any time. Transitions between active behaviors, sleep/wake states, certain environments, or other situations can increase the chances of these behaviors starting. Examples of common compulsive behaviors in the dog include circling/spinning, "fly-snapping"/air biting, flank sucking, vocalizing, and self-licking. There appears to be certain breed predispositions for some of these behaviors (Landsberg et al. 2013; Moon-Fanelli et al. 2011).

Many resources are available that can address the treatment modalities and strategies of these fearful or compulsive behaviors once they are identified.

Behavioral Assessment/Temperament Tests

The many organizations that take in unwanted or stray pets with the goal of adopting them into new homes would like to know that they are not sending dangerous or highly undesirable pets into innocent households. Additionally, organizations that provide service animals seek ways to test the suitability of an animal for a particular service, like being a guide dog or a police dog. For these reasons, several "temperament tests," more accurately known as behavioral assessments, have been developed. What each test strives to do is uncover different types of aggression or fear that might exist but not be apparent during simple interactions with the animal (Bennet et al. 2015).

While some behavior assessments have proved useful in certain circumstances, they are not without their drawbacks. First, each person administering the assessment must be well versed in the assessment protocol. Then, the assessment should be administered the same way to each animal. Finally, the results must be analyzed properly. Then, even with appropriate knowledge and consistency, studies have shown that these assessments can be relatively nonpredictive for how the animal behaves in other settings at other times

(Bennett et al. 2012). More research is necessary to validate the effectiveness of these tools (Mornement et al. 2010).

Evaluation of Dogs from Specific Situations

One common reason for dogs to be confiscated and left in the care of a protective kennel or shelter is for organized dog fighting confiscations. National Football League quarterback Michael Vick brought the notoriety of dog fighting to the forefront in 2007 when he and three associates were arrested for running a large dog fighting operation on his property. He was convicted of two felony charges and served time in prison.

The 49 dogs that were held at Vick's property were given to a special team for behavior assessment and the recommendation for disposition. These dogs were assessed using, in part, the *American Temperament Test Society* test (American Temperament Test Society, Inc. 2013). Because of testing, one dog was euthanized and the 48 survivors were sent to eight shelters, where the majority remain. Since then, a few of these dogs have been adopted into private homes (Animal Legal Defense Fund 2014; Sieczkowski 2014).

Specific considerations are necessary when examining dogs suspected of coming from an organized fighting group. These dogs are bred with the following characteristics to enhance their capabilities in the pit: increased pain tolerance, very rapid behavioral arousal in response to other dogs, reduced response to canine social signals marking submission, and lack of bite inhibition. The dogs are usually selected for friendliness toward humans, however, so that they are safe to handle before and after fights (Lockwood 2013; McMillan and Reid 2009). Therefore, the primary considerations during physical exam and evaluation have to do with blocking the dog's visual access to other animals and good physical restraint during the examination.

Abused Animals

So often, people assume that the dog who shies from a man's approach or when the broom comes out of the closet was abused by those things in the past. While it is difficult to know for certain what may have happened in the past, fearful dogs that were never socialized to men or to brooms may behave the same way. Similarly, animals that have been neglected and ignored to the point of becoming somewhat feral can be confused with victims of abuse.

Some animals will be included in abuse cases. Abuse can be physical (such as blunt or sharp force trauma, sexual abuse, or extreme forms of neglect) but can also be psychological such as constant punishment leading to learned helplessness (Gregory 2004; McMillan et al. 2015; Seligman and Maier 1967). These types of abuse may present with different physical issues, including healed fractures, wounds, and so on. Behaviorally, the different types of abuse lead to many of the same behavioral characteristics.

Studies have shown that canine victims of abuse have behaviors that differ from the norm in certain identifiable patterns (McMillan et al. 2013, 2015). They are more likely to be aggressive toward people or other dogs. They show increased excitability and hyperactivity. They may be persistent in their attention-seeking behaviors and may show signs of attachment very rapidly. They may engage in more persistent barking and/or increased repetitive behaviors (McMillan et al. 2015). These behaviors should be documented when examining victims of suspected abuse.

Hoarding

Hoarding cases are special cases of animal abuse in that, often, those being investigated had no actual intent to do harm, despite dozens to hundreds of animals being kept in substandard conditions. Furthermore, many cruelty laws do not consider the intense animal suffering that results from hoarding situations; for this reason, careful and thorough documentation is key to a successful prosecution. Also challenging for the forensics team is the sheer number of animals involved, making examination, assessment, documentation, and disposition of the animals a lengthy and resource-intense undertaking (Patronek 2013).

Animals confiscated from hoarding situations, depending on how long they have been there, can be like feral animals (Figure 12.9). They are often deprived of human attention, undersocialized, and neglected (including lack of edible food, clean water, and adequate sanitation); not surprisingly, they often have untreated health issues. Lack of socialization leads to extreme fears, lack of housetraining, cannibalism, over-grooming behavior, and self-mutilation. Other problem behaviors may make these victims difficult to gather and handle during examination or keep confined as evidence (McMillan et al. 2016; Patronek 2013).

Commercial Breeding Enterprises ("Puppy Mills")

Behaviorally, there is a marked difference between puppies that have been transported from commercial breeding enterprises (CBEs) to pet stores and into private homes and those animals retained in CBEs for breeding purposes.

Figure 12.9 A hoarding dog situation.

In addition to having severe health problems stemming from neglect and confinement, breeding dogs confiscated from CBEs are often shy and afraid of people and objects. They are overly sensitive to touch/handling and have reduced emotional range. They are more likely to engage in repetitive behaviors and have increased house soiling. They tend to exhibit less aggression overall than more typical animals (McMillan et al. 2011). By contrast, puppies from CBEs that live in private homes are more likely to be aggressive toward people and other dogs. Like their dams they show increased fears, both social and nonsocial, and increased house soiling (McMillan et al. 2011). While research has been done specifically on CBEs, it also needs to be mentioned that dogs raised in a relatively impoverished environment are more likely to be fearful or aggressive as well (Appleby et al. 2002).

Documentation of Behavioral Evidence

As noted, detailed, objective documentation (including written notes, testing, video and photographic evidence) should be completed early in the investigation and often repeated as needed during a forensics investigation. The key is to document a moment in time—the state of the animal at intake—followed by any additional documentation needed during the animal's confinement. Written documentation should be descriptive and thorough, including any known history, physical examination and laboratory findings, and behavior observations. It should be assumed that any and all documentation will be examined in court. For this reason, written assessments of behavior should be kept objective, however emotionally difficult the situation. It is important to avoid personal written comments not related to the specific examination or testing since all notes are subject to a reciprocal discovery.

Written behavioral documentation should be supplemented with two types of imaging: still photos and video. Photos are useful in documenting body condition, injuries, and markings. They have the benefit of being portable, easily reproducible, and readable without electronic equipment. Videos are useful for documenting gait abnormalities, behaviors, and interactions among members of the group. They have the benefit of including sound as well as moving images to provide a more complete documentation of the living animal. For more information about videography, the reader is referred to Chapter 3 (Videography: A New Tool in Animal Cruelty Investigations).

Consistency in Terminology

It is important that any organization attempting to assess behavioral issues develop terminology that is consistent among all veterinary behaviorists. While there are no national standards for terminology in animal cases, one must take into consideration any terms in use by any governmental or nongovernmental organizations overseeing the case. A clear understanding of the proper spelling, syntax, and definitions of these terms will help to streamline the documentation.

Consistency in "Testing," Documentation, and "Grading"

As alluded to earlier, behavioral assessments are fraught with problems in being able to identify an animal's behaviors. Additionally, there is little proof that they predict future behavior, except in the most severe of cases (Bennett et al. 2012; Diederich and Giffroy 2006). However, they do provide some valuable information. To achieve any potential usefulness, the following guidelines must be met.

Each evaluator should be trained in whichever testing system will be used for the case. The evaluators in an organization must demonstrate good inter-observer reliability. They should also be expected to undergo periodic refresher training to ensure continued consistency within the program.

The assessment content and method should be standardized to establish as much reliability as possible. Such extraneous factors as noise, scents, light, and room structure must be considered as part of the testing paradigm and each may skew the behavioral analysis and the conclusions drawn. The assessment should also be practical to perform. While it may produce more data points, an assessment that is too long or too complicated may not be practical, especially when there are large numbers of animals to be assessed in a single investigation such as in a hoarding investigation.

Conclusion

The behavior of the animals examined and kept as living evidence by a forensics team can provide extensive useful information about the physical and psychological state of each animal on intake, the impact on it of the situation under investigation, its likely adaptability during the investigation, and indications of the best possible outcome for it during or after the investigation. The tools provided in this chapter are tailored to support the forensics team to gather the most useful information about their living animal evidence.

References

American Temperament Test Society, Inc. 2013. Description of the Temperament Test. http://atts.org/2013/01/atts-test-video/ (Accessed March 23, 2016).

Animal Legal Defense Fund. 2014. Animal fighting case study: Michael Vick. Animal Legal Defense Fund. http://aldf.org/resources/laws-cases/animal-fighting-case-study-michael-vick/ (Accessed March 23, 2016).

Appleby, D. L., Bradshaw, J. W. S., and R. A. Casey. 2002. Relationship between aggressive and avoidance behaviour by dogs and their experience in the first six months of life. *Vet Rec.* 150:434–438.

Beaver, B. V. 1999. Canine social behavior. In *Canine Behavior: A Guide for Veterinarians.* Philadelphia, PA: WB Saunders.

Bennett, S. L., Litster, A., Weng, H., Walker, S. L., and A. U. Leuscher. 2012. Investigating behavior assessment instruments to predict aggression in dogs. *Appl Anim Behav Sci.* 141:139–148.

References

Bennett, S. L., Weng, H., Walker, S. L., Placer, M. P., and A. Litster. 2015. Comparison of SAFER behavior assessment results in shelter dogs at intake and after a 3-day acclimation period. *J Appl Anim Welf Sci.* 18:153–168.

Diederich, C., and J. Giffroy. 2006. Behavioural testing in dogs: A review of methodology in search for standardization. *Appl Anim Behav Sci.* 97:51–72.

Gregory, N. G. 2004. *Physiology and Behaviour of Animal Suffering.* Oxford: Blackwell.

Hart, B. L. 1991. The behavior of sick animals. *Vet Clin N Am-Small.* 21:225–237.

Houpt, K. A. 2011. *Domestic Animal Behavior for Veterinarians and Animal Scientists,* 5th ed. Ames, IA: Wiley-Blackwell.

Landsberg, G., Hunthausen, W., and L. Ackerman. 2013. *Behavior Problems of the Dog & Cat.* Philadelphia, PA: Saunders.

Lockwood, R. 2013. Animal fighting. In *Shelter Medicine for Veterinarians and Staff,* 2nd ed. L. Miller and S. Zawistowski, Eds., 441–452. Ames, IA: Wiley-Blackwell.

McMillan, F. D., Duffy, D. L., and J. A. Serpell. 2011. Mental health of dogs formerly used as "breeding stock" in commercial breeding establishments. *Appl Anim Behav Sci.* 135:86–94.

McMillan, F. D., Duffy, D. L., Zawistowski, S. L., and J. A. Serpell. 2015. Behavioral and psychological characteristics of canine victims of abuse. *J Appl Anim Welf Sci.* 18:92–111.

McMillan, F. D. and P. J. Reid. 2009. *Selective Breeding in Fighting Dogs: What Have We Created?* Presented at the Universities Federation for Animal Welfare International Symposium: Darwinian Selection, Selective Breeding and the Welfare of Animals, Bristol.

McMillan, F. D., Serpell, J. A., Duffy, D. L., Masaoud E., and I. R. Dohoo. 2013. Differences in behavioral characteristics between dogs obtained as puppies from pet stores and those obtained from noncommercial breeders. *J Am Vet Med Assoc.* 242:1359–1363.

McMillan, F. D., Vanderstichel, R., Stryhn, H., Yu, J., and J. A. Serpell. 2016. Behavioural characteristics of dogs removed from hoarding situations. *Appl Anim Behav Sci.* 178:69–79.

Moon-Fanelli, A. A., Dodman, N. H., Famul, T. R., and N. Cottam. 2011. Characteristics of compulsive tail chasing and associated risk factors in Bull Terriers. *J Am Vet Med Assoc.* 238:883–889.

Mornement, K. M., Colemen, G. J., Toukhsati, S., and P. C. Bennett. 2010. A review of behavioral assessment protocols used by Australian animal shelters to determine the adoption suitability of dogs. *J Appl Anim Welf Sci.* 13:314–329.

Patronek, G. 2013. Animal Hoarding. In *Shelter Medicine for Veterinarians and Staff,* 2nd ed. L. Miller and S. Zawistowski, Eds., 431–439. Ames, IA: Wiley-Blackwell.

Pongracz, P., Molnar, C., Doka, A., and A. Miklosi. 2011. Do children understand man's best friend? Classification of dog barks by pre-adolescents and adults. *Appl Anim Behav Sci.* 135:95–102.

Seligman, M. E., and S. F. Maier. 1967. Failure to escape traumatic shock. *J Exp Psychol.* 74:1–9.

Sieczkowski, C. 2014. Michael Vick's former dogfighting pups will make you believe in happily ever after. *Huffington Post.* http://www.huffingtonpost.com/2014/04/10/michael-vick-dogs-vicktory_n_5119150.html (Accessed March 24, 2016).

13

Veterinary Forensic Toxicology

Ernest R. Rogers

Contents

Introduction

The practice of veterinary forensic toxicology is defined by the quality of the patient examination, biological sample collection, crime scene sample collection, and selection of the appropriate laboratory and analytical tests performed. Briefly, veterinary forensic toxicology is the assessment of chemicals, toxins, and poisons that may enter the body of an animal. Not all deaths or sicknesses are due to malicious acts. Some are due to accidental exposure and the forensic investigator must be cognizant of the possibility of these accidental intoxications. The investigation of the crime scene and examination of the patient will often give clues as to the nature and cause of the intoxication.

There can be numerous considerations and decisions for the investigator to make before approaching any suspected case involving toxins, poisons, or other chemical agents. Collection of data including photographs of flora, entomological samples, review of the crime scene for indications of the sources of toxins, and collection of biomedical samples from patients must be well planned before entering the environment. Protection and safety of laypersons, first responders, and forensic personnel must be considered before the investigation of any suspected poison or toxic event. The use of personal protective equipment (PPE) by personnel at the scene or treating a patient will depend on the best evaluation of possible chemicals suspected of causing the clinical signs reported at the incident. Finally, the collection of evidence, the sample packaging, chain of custody, and laboratory submission of biological material is critical to the final disposition and assessment of a criminal or civil case.

Scope and Range of Practice

Toxicology and pharmacology are the basis for the understanding of how xenobiotics (poisons, toxins, and drugs) can enter the body, distribute throughout the body, and how they are eliminated. Poisons are those substances derived from chemicals or as may occur by the synthetic manipulation of natural substances. Toxins are those substances biologically derived and may be found in nature. Clinical signs demonstrated by the patient are an essential guide to suggest a rule-out list of possible poisons/toxins/drugs to which the animal was exposed. This understanding will allow for the appropriate collection of evidence (e.g., biological samples for testing) and analysis of that material. As scientists, veterinarians and toxicologists are well qualified to assess the physiological, pathological, clinical laboratory, and histopathological evidence from victims of intoxication. The veterinarian has specific skills in the assessment of live patients in the use of internal medicine techniques such as gastric lavage, endoscopy, ultrasound, and radiographic examination.

The use of toxicology or pharmacology can have implications in criminal, civil, and insurance activity. The use of pharmacological agents has been implicated in diverse circumstances such as competitive animal racing, accidental or intentional illicit drug use in animals, malicious poisonings in companion animals, inadvertent consumption of toxic flora, agroterroist activities for intentional interruption of animal/food sources, animals as unintentional/accidental victims of domestic or international terrorism, and toxic errors in mixing feed or the inappropriate administration of veterinary pharmaceutical in animals (Barigye et al. 2008; Desta et al. 2011; United States Food and Drug Administration 2009).

As with many sciences, the forensic veterinarian may be only one of several forensic professionals in the chain of analysis for a successful case conclusion. Other professionals include toxicologists, pharmacologists, analytical chemists, entomologists, soil scientists, flora experts, and nutritionists. This team of scientists is essential to the chemical analysis and separation of significant critical evidence from confusing or confounding findings in suspicious cases. It must be recognized that the toxicological laboratory, no matter how skilled, cannot appropriately analyze the agent of intoxication without an indication of the class or specific agent suspected. In these cases, the investigation is an essential part of solving the case.

Toxicokinetics and Toxicodynamics

The science of toxicokinetics is the understanding and quantification of how chemical agents are distributed throughout the animal body. Toxicokinetics defines the progress of drugs in the body in a five-step process. The five steps of toxicokinetics are

1. Absorption
2. Distribution
3. Storage/tissue accumulation
4. Biotransformation/metabolism
5. Elimination/excretion

Toxicodynamics is the process by which a chemical agent attacks the target tissue or organ, the nature of the biochemical interaction, and mechanisms that lead to disruption of the normal physiological activity to induce intoxication or poisoning that may result in an insult to the animal. Both areas of toxicology are necessary for an understanding of the facts that are critical to the investigation of criminal, accidental, or civil activity.

Often the nature of a criminal act of poisoning is hidden from direct examination because evidence is removed from the crime scene, perpetrators use commonly available toxins and poisons, and individuals may destroy significant proof of an intoxication. This makes the clinical signs of intoxication essential to the determination of the class or specific agent involved. The collection and documentation of all chemical and biological substances, microbiological insect life and flora at a scene can be important to rule in or rule out toxins related to the investigation.

Absorption is the movement of a chemical from either an external or internal site (e.g., gastrointestinal tract) to the vascular or lymphatic systems of the body. Toxins and poisons can be absorbed in multiple ways including oral/alimentary ingestion, rectal suppositories, parenteral injection, cutaneous absorption, mucous membrane absorption, or inhalation. The physical examination must consider all methods of absorption. In completing the initial examination, the body must be examined for signs of absorption. The method and rate of absorption will determine the level of accumulation of drug, poison, or toxin in the body. Not all toxins will cause sickness or death if absorbed slowly and can be metabolized to an inert or harmless element in the body and subsequently eliminated (Dixit 2007; Gregus 2013). The method of absorption can be influenced by absorption enhancing chemicals such as dimethyl sulfoxide (DMSO) gel that can enhance the transcutaneous absorption (Pathan and Setty 2009). Other factors affecting absorption include molecular size and clinically available format of the product (tablet vs. granular vs. liquid), surface area to which the toxin is applied, the toxicity of the chemical (LD50 for the target species), and the ionized nature of the chemical hydrophilic makeup of the chemical. Physiological factors such as the integrity of the skin or extent of alimentary surface area are other factors that can affect absorption. For parenteral administration, the type of the injection will influence the absorption. In general, absorption will increase with access to the cardiovascular or nervous system (intravascular > intrathecal > intramuscular > subcutaneous). Though these are generally accepted rules of thumb, absorption may vary with the nature of the agent and the target organ (Webster 2001a; Eaton and Gilbert 2013; Gregus 2013).

Once absorbed, the toxin is distributed by either the vascular, lymphatic, or the cerebral spinal fluid. This distribution will facilitate the toxin progression to the target organ. The rate of distribution from the site of absorption will determine the amount of accumulation at the target organ and therefore determine the toxicity at the organ, cellular, or molecular level (Dixit 2007; Webster 2001b). Distribution is affected by many factors including cardiovascular function, perfusion of target tissue/organ, and the ability of the target organ to metabolize the rate of the incoming toxin (Dixit 2007; McClellan 2007; Webster 2001b).

Metabolism of the noxious substance varies by the mechanism of action (MOA) on the target organ (toxicodynamics). The MOA is the biological or chemical action by which the insult affects the body, tissue, or cell. The biochemical systems that metabolize or neutralize toxins are only as effective as the rate of transport to areas of cellular metabolic detoxification, their ability to neutralize toxins, and the speed of the elimination of the xenobiotic. In some cases, the mechanism of detoxification or biotransformation can result in metabolites that are equally as toxic as or even more toxic than the original compound. This is called toxication and may result in bimodal series of signs (Ballie and Rettie 2011). An example is found in cases of ingestion of ethylene glycol, which is then broken down by the body to oxalic acid and glycolic acid, with first stomach upset and then kidney failure.

Elimination of an insulting agent is accomplished by several methods including biochemical processes including hydroxylation, reduction, or oxidation which alters the chemical structure and enhances elimination of toxins. Excretion is the physical removal of the toxin or metabolite from the body where it is returned to the environment. Excretion may occur through the urinary system, lungs (exhaled), through the hepatobiliary system and feces, or through cutaneous excretion. There are physiological compartments that, after excretion, may accumulate chemical residues. Collection of these tissues or biological fluids is essential to the successful identification of a toxic substance. These reservoirs may include hair/fur, skin, liver, kidney, muscle, bile, feces, urine, and alimentary system (Molina 2010). It should be noted that some toxins or their metabolites, after excretion, can be reabsorbed into the body particularly from the feces.

The relationship among the 5 steps with respect to the path of a xenobiotic from absorption to excretion can be described by multiple compartment models. Each step is represented by a compartment model which can be described mathematically for virtual flow among the steps. The mathematical description is complicated by biological, chemical, and molecular factors but is valuable for estimating the absorption, distribution, elimination, and therefore the toxicity of known agents.

The understanding of toxicodynamics allows insight into the molecular and biochemical methods of intoxication. Once in sufficient quantity (concentration) at the target tissue or organ, the insult will cause cellular disruption. Cellular targets of toxicity include cellular lipids, intracellular proteins, and nucleic acids. Methods of cellular disruption include but are not limited to: interference with cellular physical barriers (e.g., calcium/sodium channels), intracellular formation of electrophiles, generation of free radicals, blockage of intracellular metabolic activities, and interference with intracellular and intercellular communications.

For those interested in the specifics and mathematics of toxicokinetics, toxicodynamics, and biochemical or molecular mechanisms affecting cellular physiology, they are referred to review classic texts that are available for review and further general study of the science of toxicology.

Forensic Investigations

The investigation of animal intoxications begins with defining a level of suspicion that either toxins, poisons, drugs (legal or illicit), or chemicals are involved in the activities to be investigated. There are many clues that suggest the involvement of toxins. There should be a heightened suspicion of toxins if there is an acute loss of life in otherwise healthy animal populations. Sudden changes in behavior, increases in aggression, lethargy, and excessive ptylism may be indications of toxin ingestion. The presence of toxic flora in the animal's environment may also be an indication of potential intoxication. Intoxication may be suspected based on the animal's clinical signs (Table 13.1),

Table 13.1 Clinical Signs That Raise the Level of Suspicion of Intoxication
Acute, unexpected sickness in previously healthy animals
Vomiting, diarrhea (with or without blood), inappetence
Oral, facial, or body staining (usually primary colors)
Ulcerations of oral cavity, hypersalivation, dry mouth
Eye, oral or facial irritation, increased rubbing pawing at eyes/face
Chemical/pharmaceutical odor on body
Head pressing, incoordination, ataxia, inability to walk or rise
Seizures, tonic spasms
Delirium, abnormal behavior, increased aggression, acute changes in behavior
Ecchymosis or petechial hemorrhage, epistaxis
Sudden collapse, cardiac arrhythmias
Increased consumption of water
Icterus, skin discoloration, lesions of contact dermatitis
Coughing, dyspnea, cyanosis
Sudden death without precipitating signs

abnormalities identified during the forensic necropsy (Table 13.2), and others may be found at or around the crime scene (Table 13.3).

The ability to ensure the proper identification of an intoxicant is affected by multiple factors including the toxic agent kinetics and dynamics (Table 13.4). In some cases, the toxin may be increased by time since death, accumulation

Table 13.2 Postmortem Abnormities That Raise the Level of Suspicion of Intoxication
Oral, esophageal, stomach or intestinal ulcerations or bloody contents
Organ or tissue ulceration or gangrenous findings
Sloughing of skin at potential contact areas
Enlarged, gas-filled gastrointestinal system
Laryngeal, tracheal, or pulmonary congestion or pulmonary edema
Blood-filled thoracic or abdominal cavity, lack of clotted blood
Brain (vascular congestion)
Oral mucosal or musculature discoloration
Abnormal gastric contents (food not regularly ingested by animal, pills)
Significant increased or decreased rate of onset or dissipation of rigor mortis
Injection site(s), subcutaneous hemorrhage
Organomegaly (splenic, liver, lungs, heart, etc.)

Table 13.3 Findings at a Crime Scene That Raises the Level of Suspicion of Intoxication
Food items placed around crime scene or nearby environs
Nonfood items mixed with or injected into food items (e.g., powders, pellets, liquids)
Toxic flora in or around foraging areas that have been chewed or disturbed
Areas of dead, dying, or chemically burned flora or grass
Chemical or industrial odors
Vomitus containing food or nonfood items
Dead or dying insects, aquaculture, or wildlife
Changes in normal water conditions (odors, colors)
Family history of illicit drug use (drug odors, paraphernalia)
Sponges or material soaked in attractive food products (e.g., bacon grease, broth)
Increased animosity between neighbors and adjacent parties

Table 13.4 Factors That Can Affect Forensic Toxicological Investigations
Time since death
Antemortem body condition (disease status, body condition score)
Species, animal size, weight
Location interned (above, belowground, submerged in water, or covered)
Ambient environmental temperatures, time of year (summer, winter)
Intoxication agent, concentration, dilution (water, feed, attractant food stuffs)
Mode of absorption (oral, parenteral, transcutaneous, inhalation)
Postmortem degradation or predation
Ease of obtaining or availability of poisons (some may be legally restricted)
Confounding environmental chemicals, pesticides, herbicides, or toxic flora

at the target organ/tissue, or by impaired absorption, decreased metabolism, or decreased excretion. In other cases, toxin concentration may be decreased by time as distribution continues to result in the sequestration of natural metabolites, by postmortem redistribution, or environmental factors that may break down toxins and their metabolites.

Intoxication of an animal may be malicious and incited by anger, revenge, or another nefarious motive and initiated by a human suspect. There are multiple alternatives to malicious, criminal inspired poisoning of animals. Alternatives include accidental poisoning, where the toxic or poisonous substance was either improperly handled or stored. In these cases, the victim only has access to the poison by entering restricted areas, opening previously secure containers, or by happenstance in the environment. Signs suggestive of accidental poisonings include that the toxin has been properly secured in a cabinet, but may have leaked from the container or location. Another source of accidental intoxication is the "backyard mechanic" who may fail to completely clean the work area (ethylene glycol) that can lead to a pet intoxication. There have also been cases of toxicological morbidity and mortality due to predation on previously intoxicated carrion (Kelly et al. 2014). In some cases of large animal intoxication, the investigator must consider and investigate the possibilities of accidental feed contamination, the presence of toxic flora (e.g., pokeweed, jimson weed, poison hemlock) in containment areas and pastures (McCartney 2017), and the improper use of veterinary medications by an untrained animal handler. If the toxin hasn't been placed in open areas, there is no sign of the staging or attracting food, then accidental possibilities should be considered.

Not all intoxications are from poisons or toxins. There may also be accidental intoxications from illicit, prescription, or over-the-counter pharmaceuticals. In states where there is legalization of marijuana, there has been increases in canine intoxication. Many of these are accidental ingestion but forced intoxication has been recognized (Poiset 2015; Salvail 2014). There are no specific screening tests for marijuana (tetrahydrocannabinol or THC) in dogs or cats. The use of "at home drug test kits" has been useful in urine screening for this common recreational drug (Figure 13.1) (Teitler 2009). Whether a screening result is positive or negative, an aliquot should be sent to a toxicology laboratory for confirmatory testing. Some authors suggest that the human drug test may result in a false negative, due to possible different urine metabolites in the dog as compared to humans (DeNezzo 2015). Use of urine multidrug test kits are not always effective in identifying marijuana or methadone in urine from dogs with suspected or known exposure to these drugs (Teitler 2009). In the case of marijuana intoxication, the diagnosis should be suspected based

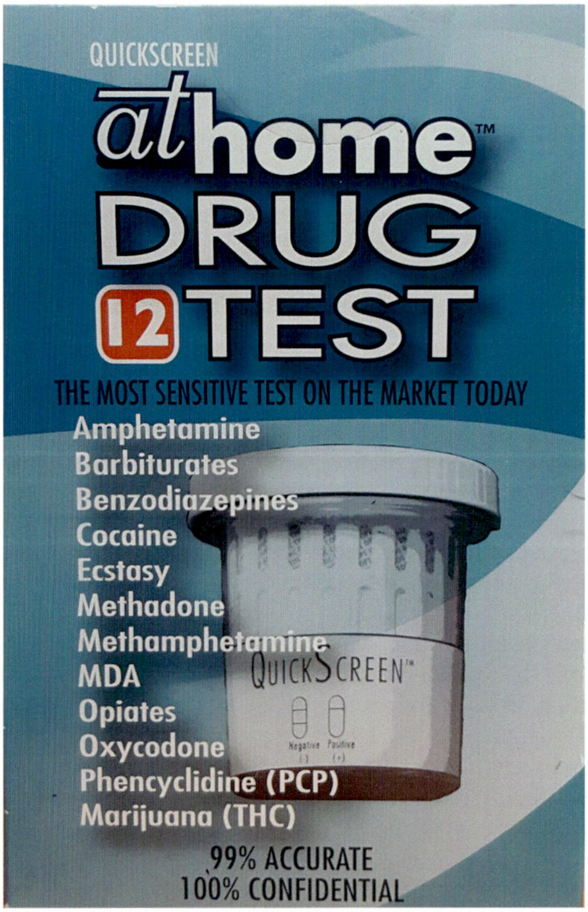

Figure 13.1 Example of a human drug test that may be used as a screening test for illicit drugs in dog urine. These screening tests can yield false negatives (as in the case of marijuana and methadone). Photo courtesy of Dr. Adam W. Stern, University of Illinois.

on clinical signs, patient history, and owner report. Clinical signs include diarrhea, hypothermia, dysphoria (vocalization), ataxia, coma, and death. A dog can start to show clinical signs of marijuana intoxication approximately 60 minutes after ingestion (DeNezzo 2015). The reader is referred to the veterinary literature for clinical signs of alcohol and other illegal or over-the-counter drugs. The exposure of the pet to illicit drugs may be considered animal abuse and should be investigated.

No forensic toxicology examination is complete without a review of the complete medical history of the patient including review of previously prescribed or used veterinary or human pharmaceuticals, homeopathic preparations, food, and antiparasitic agents. This can be used to assess for a possible drug to drug or drug to chemical interaction which could have resulted in illness or death.

Ideally the forensic veterinarian should be included in the crime scene investigation so critical evidence can be identified and collected that may otherwise be lost. A crime scene may be a primary, secondary, or tertiary scene and this must be considered as part of the criminal investigation. A primary crime scene is the location where the suspected criminal act occurred and where the victim is found. This is often the case with a very fast acting poison or one that may disable the victim from moving after ingestion or inhalation (zinc phosphide, carbon monoxide). There have been examples of veterinarians who have initiated necropsies or examined living animals and have been overcome by toxic gases and hospitalized (Centers for Disease Control and Prevention 2012; Drolet et al. 1996). Guidelines for the medical intervention have been written by the American Veterinary Medical Association (2016).

The suspect may, however, to compromise standard forensic techniques, attempt to move, hide, or bury victims. This must be distinguished from a primary crime scene where the toxic element has been removed by the perpetrator. This results in a secondary crime scene, one where the victim is located and a second where the victim was poisoned. Though not conclusive, the presence of vomitus, bloody fluids, evidence of seizure, or disruption of the flora and environment are signs of a primary scene. In rare cases, there may be a third crime scene. This may occur when the victims are transported, by vehicle, to a location from where they were poisoned at one location and died at another location. Signs of a tertiary scene are the presence of pet animals, recently seen in one location being found in another remote location or a group of animals in a single hidden location. An understanding of the variations in crime scenes and locations includes: primary location where victim was poisoned, secondary location when victim is transported (the vehicle), and the tertiary location is where the victim bodies were left and subsequently found (e.g., submerged in water or buried).

Examination of the living animal for toxicological investigation has some additional requirements beyond that for the general forensic examination. The living patient may demonstrate signs unique to the toxic agent (Table 13.5). Video or photographic documentation of the patient can be helpful. The presence of chemical odors (body, breath, and urine) may also be clues to the toxic agent. Noting oral lesions, muscle fasciculation, seizures,

Table 13.5 Select List of Potential Poisons That May Be Used in Malicious Intoxication of an Animal

Chemical	Acute LD50 (Rat)	Characteristics	Route of Absorption	Mechanism of Action	Comments
Arsenic trioxide (laboratory chemical)	LD 50 oral = 10 mg/kg	Solid, white, odorless	Ingestion	Protein thiol inactivation	Skin burns, affects lungs, liver, and kidney
Bromethalin (rodenticide)	LD50 oral = 2 mg/kg Dog LD50 oral = 4.7 mg/kg	Green, solid wax Ingestion Inhalation	Ingestion or inhalation	Uncouples oxidative phosphorylation	Affects brain, increases CSF pressure, incoordination, seizures
Carbon monoxide Car exhaust	LC 50 inhalation = 6600 ppm @ 30 min. exposure	Gas, colorless	Inhalation	Formation of carboxyhemoglobin	Affects cardiovascular system, blood, CVS, lungs, CNS 35% in Hb fatal Flammable gas
Cholecalciferol (rodenticide)	LD50 oral = 42.5 mg/kg Dog LD50 oral = 80 mg/kg	Colorless to white crystals, solid	Inhalation or ingestion	Interferes with receptors affecting calcium and phosphorus cell levels	Activated in body hydroxylation Affects liver and kidneys Uremic breath

(*Continued*)

Table 13.5 (Continued) Select List of Potential Poisons That May Be Used in Malicious Intoxication of an Animal

Chemical	Acute LD50 (Rat)	Characteristics	Route of Absorption	Mechanism of Action	Comments
Sodium cyanide (pesticide)	LD50 oral = 6440 ug/kg Dog LD50 oral = 4.7 mg/kg	Solid, white, bitter almond odor	Ingestion, inhalation, and transcutaneous	Inactivation of cytochrome oxidase (impairs cellular respiration)	Affects central nervous system gastrointestinal system, and cardiovascular system Cyanosis, cardiac arrhythmia, collapse, confusion Toxic gas can be released postmortem
Diphacinone (rodenticide)	LD50 oral = 2.3 mg/kg	Yellow powder	Ingestion	Inhibits formation of prothrombin	Ecchymosis, petechia, epistaxis, internal bleeding
Ethylene glycol (Antifreeze)	LD50 oral = 4700 mg/kg	Liquid, clear, viscous, fluorescent green, and sweet odor	Ingestion	Formation of calcium oxalate crystals and renal failure	Common around cars and is easily obtained
Organophosphate (pesticide)	LD50 oral = 688 (male) -1127 (female) mg/kg gender dependent	White pellet, cabbage smell	Ingestion, inhalation, and transcutaneous	Cholinesterase inhibitor	Diarrhea, vomiting, drooling, and muscle spasms

(*Continued*)

Table 13.5 (Continued) Select List of Potential Poisons That May Be Used in Malicious Intoxication of an Animal

Chemical	Acute LD50 (Rat)	Characteristics	Route of Absorption	Mechanism of Action	Comments
Paraquat (herbicide)	LD50 oral = 150 mg/kg	Dark blue liquid	Ingestion and inhalation	Interferes with electron transfer, forms superoxide radicals	Affects lungs (fibrosis) kidneys, and liver Difficult to obtain in the United States
Sodium fluoride (Compound 1080)	LD50 oral = 31 mg/kg	White, crystalline powder, odorless Ingestion, inhalation, cutaneous contact, eye irritation	Ingestion, inhalation, and transcutaneous	Blocks tricarboxylic acid cycle	Vomiting, seizures, confusion, agitation, cardiac arrhythmias Difficult to obtain in the United States
Strychnine (pesticide)	LD50 oral = 2.6 mg/kg	Fine crystalline powder	Ingestion, inhalation, and transcutaneous	Primary interference with postsynaptic glycine neurotransmitter	Excitation, tremors, and convulsions

(*Continued*)

Table 13.5 (Continued) Select List of Potential Poisons That May Be Used in Malicious Intoxication of an Animal

Chemical	Acute LD50 (Rat)	Characteristics	Route of Absorption	Mechanism of Action	Comments
Thallium (laboratory chemical)	LD50 oral = 44 mg/kg	Dark brown and solid	Ingestion	Interferes with potassium-dependent processes, antagonizes cardiac calcium, inactivates sulfydral groups	Acute intermittent porphyria, peripheral neuropathy, and hair loss Thallium is radiopaque
Zinc Phosphine (rodenticide, insecticide)	LD50 oral = 12 mg/kg	Various forms of powder and pellets	Inhalation and ingestion	Blocks mitochondrial respiration by inhibiting cytochrome oxidase	Weakness, confusion, vomiting, nausea, ataxia, and unconsciousness Postmortem gas generation is toxic

incoordination, ataxia, or skin and mucosal discoloration are indicative signs related to the cause of the intoxication. Collection of biological samples and evidence in a case of potential intoxication may include blood, urine, and fur (Figure 13.2). The animal should be examined for possible injection sites and when appropriate radiographs should be taken. It is recommended that samples are taken in triplicate for security and reciprocal discovery. All elements of the chain of custody must be followed and maintained. Multiple blood and urine samples should be collected for clinical analysis and toxicological analysis; each sample should be stored as appropriate for the procedure anticipated. Lesions and injection sites may be biopsied and submitted for tissue analysis.

When the specific toxic agent is unknown, supportive treatment is indicated. The use of intravenous fluids, activated charcoal, and medications for seizure control, therapeutic enema, and gastric lavage may be helpful. Although discussion regarding clinical support and treatment of intoxication is beyond the scope of this chapter, when a toxic agent is known or suspected, specific antidote administration and supportive medical treatment should be initiated. Much of the pertinent information with respect to antidotes, lethal dose (LD50), first aid, and methods of absorption may be obtained from a Material Safety Data Sheet (MSDS), specific for the suspected toxin. Further, clinical treatment considerations and medical support may be obtained from one of several veterinary poison control centers based in the United States. In all investigations of toxin or poisoning events the forensic veterinarian is encouraged to use the appropriate

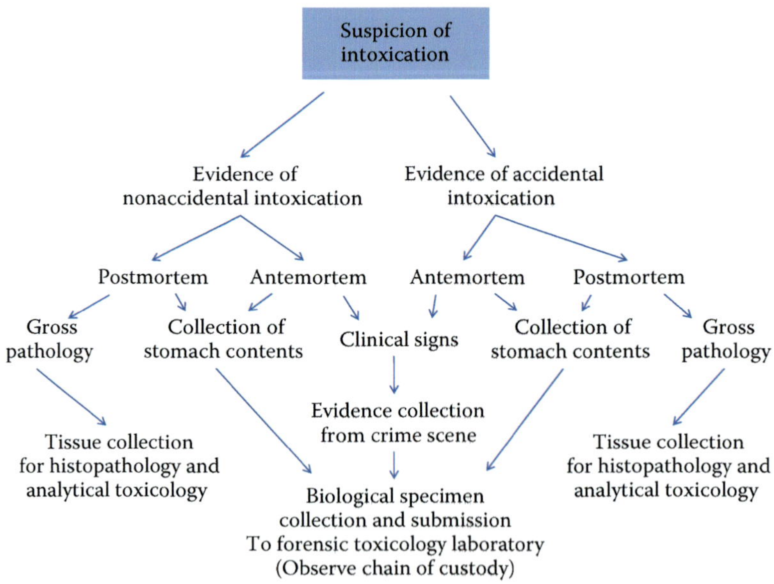

Figure 13.2 Flowchart regarding evidence collection for cases of suspected intoxication.

PPE (American Veterinary Medical Association 2016; Occupational Safety and Health Administration 2006).

The deceased patient presents unique challenges and dangers during the collection of evidence such as tissues and bodily fluids. Once the animal is identified the victim should be isolated and prepared for transportation as any other victim of a crime. In the case of a poisoning event, the postmortem examination should be conducted in a well-ventilated area with the use of appropriate PPE. Without the confirmation of the nature of the toxic agent, all precautions must be observed. Often examination of the suspected crime scene will allow suspicions to be confirmed.

In cases of potential intoxication, tissue collection is more extensive than that of other postmortem examinations. The postmortem examination in an animal poisoning case should include a complete external examination. The extremities should be uncovered and any debris or foreign material between the pads or distal extremities should be collected and stored separately from each paw for future analysis. Combing of the body should be performed on a clean linen sheet or clean butcher paper to be able to collect foreign material that may be relevant to the investigation. Once the external examination is completed and the body photographically documented the body may be shaved or the skin removed to examine for possible injection sites. Tissue samples may be taken at the injection site as evidence. Samples should include all organs, body fluids including vitreous humor, fur, and body surface evidence (Table 13.6).

The internal examination will follow the standard forensic necropsy protocol. Multiple samples should be obtained for several methods of storage including 10% neutral buffered formalin, fresh freezing or refrigerated samples, and maintenance in normal physiological saline (for toxicological analysis).

Entomology has been recognized as a method of establishing time since death (Amendt 2011). The degradation of an animal body may be due to high ambient environmental temperatures, method of disposal of the body, wildlife predation, or time since death. For more information regarding the postmortem interval, the reader is referred to Chapter 8 (Postmortem Changes and the Estimation of Time Since Death). In the case of severe degradation of the body, insect larvae may be collected for entomotoxicology (Iantrona et al. 2001; Pounder 1991). Controversy exists about the quantitative correlation in human toxicology between entomological samples and human muscle concentration (Tracqui et al. 2004). Other concerns surround the toxicokinetics of the drug after being consumed by the insect or larvae and correlation to the human body (Gautam et al. 2013). The distinction between veterinary toxicology and human toxicology is that in many cases in veterinary samples quantitative analysis is trumped by qualitative analysis. This is to say that the presence of any toxin, poison, drug, or chemical in the animal body is cause for suspicion of criminal or accidental activity. Entomological samples (blowfly maggots, dermestid beetles, and other scavenging insects) may be placed in containers for storage (in 0.9% sodium chloride solution, frozen, or in 70% EtOH) and transport depending on laboratory requirements. Analysis of

Table 13.6 Samples to Collect for Toxicological Analysis

Sample	Collection	Comments
Blood	Peripheral blood preferred, postmortem femoral or subclavian vein Minimum 60 mL	(1) Use glass containers; (2) No preservative (serology); (3) Sodium fluoride or potassium oxalate anticoagulants (toxicology); (4) EDTA preservative (DNA); (5) Glass tube with Teflon cap for gaseous toxins
Urine	Ideally, 10–20 mL	Place in red top tube; Screening or confirmatory sample
Bile	Ideally, 10–20 mL	Place in red top tube
Vitreous humor	Ideally, 2–4 mL	Place in red top tube
Skeletal muscle	Preferred tissue sample. 20–50 g per sample; Quadriceps muscle is preferred	Good correlation with drug levels; Collect sterile sample
Liver	Samples from deep right lobe; Avoids contamination of gastrointestinal tract	Good for inhaled toxins/metabolites
Kidney	Standard for collection	Good for heavy metal testing
Brain	Standard for collection	May be more important for histopathology; Limited toxicology data
Lung	Difficult to sample in standard for collection	Lung samples from apex good for inhaled toxins, halogenated hydrocarbons
Spleen	Standard for collection	
Adipose	Standard for collection	Good for pesticide and volatile poisons
Fur/hair	Standard for collection	May give time frame for drug or poison intoxication
Stomach contents	Standard for collection	Good for recent ingestion of toxins/ poison

insects should be accompanied by documentation of local flora. Toxicological analysis should be completed at a certified forensic laboratory.

All sample evidence collection is critical to the successful conclusion of a toxicological investigation. The forensic veterinarian should contact a toxicology analytical laboratory in advance of having to send in samples. There are many laboratories that can and will analyze veterinary forensic samples. Selection of an analytical laboratory must meet several criteria. The laboratory should have experience and protocols for packaging and transportation of toxicological samples, be familiar with the strategy for the chain of custody, be certified as a forensic toxicology laboratory, and have standard procedures and practices. Further, technicians should be certified for the analytical forensic analysis and be prepared and experienced in courtroom testimony.

The certification of a forensic toxicology laboratory is offered by several organizations. Municipal laboratories may be certified by the state or state police in which they reside. The gold standard of certification includes ISO/IEC 17025 accreditation related to testing and calibration accuracy, American Board of Toxicology (ABT) accreditation program, and American Society of Crime Laboratory Directors/Laboratory Accreditation Board (ASCLD/LAB) among others (Adrien 2017; American Board of Forensic Toxicology 2014). Laboratories recognized by these standards support good laboratory practices. The analytical techniques recognized as the gold standard in toxicology include gas chromatography-mass spectrometry (GC/MS) and high-performance liquid chromatography (HPLC). As technology improves, other techniques may surpass these current acceptable methods. The veterinary forensic investigator should have a good working relationship with both the laboratory and the technical personnel to ensure consultations that will result in the appropriate testing and analysis for each situation.

Each laboratory has specific protocols for the collection, packaging, shipping, and submission of toxicological samples. It is recommended that the veterinary forensic investigator contact and initiate a relationship with any laboratory that will be used. The toxicological forensic laboratory will have a manual of appropriate collection and packaging requirements. Analysis of toxicological samples as with histopathological samples will generate invoices and costs for services. If the forensic veterinarian is not prepared to pay for these laboratory services themselves, then consultation and prior approval, by either the lead investigator for law enforcement or the appropriate attorney, is recommended.

Conclusion

The forensic veterinarian is well prepared for the diagnosis and interpretation of toxicological events in animals. The investigation of any crime is necessary to protect our animals. The forensic investigator must be cognizant that toxicological agents may be of danger to both victim and the investigating veterinarian. The astute recognition of clinical signs that raise the suspicion of intoxication is critical. Further, the ability to complete a thorough and detailed crime scene investigation may be the difference between a successful prosecution and failure to demonstrate and/or collect any appropriate evidence. The specifics of toxins, poisons, and chemical agents cannot be reviewed in a single chapter and the interested reader should seek additional education in toxicology from academic sources, MSDS, and fellow forensic scientists and toxicologists. In addition, the investigator must be familiar with and skilled in the appropriate use of PPE.

Forensic toxicology speaks to the story of abuse and death with respect to both our animal patients and humans who may be in contact with the animals. One should be aware that not all intoxications are felonious or malicious. Some are accidental due to errors in feed formulation, inappropriate use of veterinary pharmaceuticals, or the presence of toxic flora.

Veterinary forensic investigators may find themselves involved in criminal, civil, or insurance cases. Each type of case can require a different level of confirmation, evidence presentation, and laboratory analysis. The resolution of any investigation should be directed at the scientific collection, analysis, and presentation of valid scientifically robust testimony encompassing evidentiary facts with the support of the most appropriate toxicological, medical, and biological literature.

References

Adrien, M. 2017. Key advantages of ISO/IEC 17025 accreditation in testing and calibration laboratories. http://www.artipot.com/articles/2075006/key-advantages-of-iso-iec-17025-accreditation-in-testing-and-calibration-laboratories.htm (Accessed May 23, 2017).

Amendt, J., Richards, C.S., Campobasso, C.P., Zehner, R., M.J. Hall. 2011. Forensic entomology: Applications and limitations. *Forensic Sci Med Pathol.* 7:379–392.

American Board of Forensic Toxicology. 2014. Toxicology Laboratory Accreditation Program. http://abft.org/files/ABFT_LAP_Outline_September_2014.pdf (Accessed April 12, 2017).

American Veterinary Medical Association. 2016. Phosphine product precautions. https://www.avma.org/KB/Resources/Reference/Pages/Phosphine-product-precautions.aspx (Accessed March 12, 2017).

Ballie, T.A., A.E. Rettie. 2011. Role of biotransformation in drug-induced toxicity: Influence of intra- and inter-species differences in drug metabolism. *Drug Metab Pharmacokinet.* 26:15–29.

Barigye, R., Mostrom, M., Dyer, N.W., Newell, T.K., G.P. Lardy. 2008. Ethylene glycol toxicosis in adult beef cattle fed contaminated feeds. *Can Vet J.* 49:1018–20.

Centers for Disease Control and Prevention. 2012. Occupational phosphine gas poisoning at veterinary hospitals from dogs that ingested zinc phosphide—Michigan, Iowa, and Washington, 2006–2011. https://www.cdc.gov/mmwr/preview/mmwrhtml/mm6116a3.htm (Accessed May 12, 2017).

DeNezzo, N. 2015. Marijuana toxicity: Don't be afraid to tell your veterinarian if your dog may have been exposed. https://asgvets.com/marijuana-toxicity-in-dogs/ (Accessed February 3, 2016).

Desta, B., Maldonado, G., Reid, H., Puschner, B., Maxwell, J., Agasan, A., Humphreys, L., T. Holt. 2011. Acute selenium toxicosis in polo ponies. *J Vet Diagn Invest.* 23:623–628.

Dixit, R. 2007. Pharmacokinetics and toxicokinetics: Fundamentals and applications in toxicology In. *Veterinary Toxicology: Basic and Clinical Principles*, ed. R.C. Gupta. Atlanta, GA: Academic Press, pp. 25–41.

Drolet, R., Laverty, S., Braselton, W.E., N. Lord. 1996. Zinc phosphide poisoning in a horse. *Equine Vet J.* 28:161–62.

Eaton, D.L., S.G. Gilbert. 2013. Principles of toxicology In. *Casarett & Doull's Toxicology*, 8th ed., ed. C.D. Klaasen. New York: McGraw-Hill, pp. 13–48.

Gautam, L., Pathak, R., Danlami, H.S., M.D. Cole. 2013. Entomotoxicology: Alternative matrices for forensic toxicology. https://www.forensicmag.com/article/2013/08/entomotoxicology-alternative-matrices-forensic-toxicology (Accessed February 14, 2017).

Gregus, Z. 2013. Mechanisms of toxicity In. *Casarett & Doull's Toxicology*, 8th ed., ed. C.D. Klaasen. New York: McGraw-Hill, pp. 49–122.

Iantrona, F., Campobasso, C.P., M.L. Goff. 2001. Entomotoxicology. *Forensic Sci Int.* 120:42–47.

Kelly, T.R., Poppenga, R.H., Woods, L.A., Hernandez, Y.Z., Boyce, W.M., Samaniego, F.J., Torres, S.G., C.K. Johnson. 2014. Causes of mortality and unintentional poisoning in predatory and scavenging birds in California. *Vet Rec Open.* 1:1–13.

McCartney, M. 2017. How to identify poisonous plants. http://www.farmanddairy.com/columns/can-you-identify-poisonous-plants/417636.html (Accessed May 22, 2017).

McClellan, R.O. 2007. Concepts in veterinary toxicology In. *Veterinary Toxicology: Basic and Clinical Principles*, ed. R.C. Gupta. Atlanta, GA: Academic Press, pp. 3–24.

Molina, D.K. 2010. Collection and selection of toxicologic specimen In. *Handbook of Forensic Toxicology for Medical Examiners*, ed. D.K. Molina. Boca Raton, FL: CRC Press/Taylor & Francis, pp. 1–6.

Occupational Safety and Health Administration. 2006. Personal protective equipment. https://www.osha.gov/OshDoc/data_General_Facts/ppe-factsheet.pdf (Accessed February 23, 2017).

Pathan, I.B., C.M. Setty. 2009. Chemical penetration enhancers for transdermal drug delivery systems. *Trop J Pharm Res.* 8:173–179.

Poiset, M. 2015. My dog ate my stash: Pets and accidental marijuana ingestion. http://mjinews.com/dog-ate-stash-pets-ingest/ (Accessed March 31, 2017).

Pounder, D.J. 1991. Forensic entomo-toxicology. *J Forensic Sci Soc.* 31:469–472.

Salvail, A. 2014. Sick dogs in Aspen likely ate marijuana edibles, says vet. http://www.aspentimes.com/news/sick-dogs-in-aspen-likely-ate-marijuana-edibles-says-vet/ (Accessed June 2, 2017).

Teitler, J.B. 2009. Evaluation of a human on-site urine multidrug test for emergency use with dogs. *J Am Anim Hosp Assoc.* 45:59–66.

Tracquil, A., Keyser-Tracqui, C., Kintz, P., B. Ludes. 2004. Entomotoxicology for the forensic toxicologist: Much ado about nothing? *Int J Legal Med.* 118:194–196.

United States Food and Drug Administration. 2009. Melamine pet food recall—Frequently asked questions. https://www.fda.gov/animalveterinary/safetyhealth/recallswithdrawals/ucm129932.htm (Accessed February 12, 2017).

Webster, C.R.L. 2001a. Basic pharmacology: Drug absorption. In *Clinical Pharmacology*, ed. C.R.L. Webster. Jackson Hole, WY: Teton New Media, pp. 2–3.

Webster, C.R.L. 2001b. Chapter 2, Basic pharmacology: Drug distribution. In *Clinical Pharmacology*, ed. C.R.L. Webster. Jackson Hole, WY: Teton New Media, pp. 4–5.

14

Animal Sexual Abuse

Adam W. Stern and Martha Smith-Blackmore

Contents

Introduction

Animal sexual abuse (ASA) is also known by a variety of terms including bestiality, zoophilia, zoosadism, and animal sexual assault. In this chapter, we will use the term ASA preferentially over other terms such as bestiality as these other descriptors explain the motives and behavior of the perpetrator and fail to convey the harm that occurs to the animal. In some cases of ASA, physical harm to the animal may not occur. ASA may include fondling of an animal's genitalia; penetration of the vagina, anus, or oral cavity or oral-genital contact (from person to animal and/or vice versa); masturbation on the animal or masturbation of the animal; use of foreign objects to penetrate an animal; and injuring or killing an animal for sexual gratification as in cases of zoosadism. Involvement of other trauma such as burns, incised wounds, or crushing injuries to the genitalia may also be inflicted. Otherwise unexplained injury to the nipples should raise the index of suspicion that ASA may be implicated. In some cases, a human victim may be compelled to participate in ASA against their will.

ASA may be accompanied by other injuries including blunt force or ligature trauma, tail injuries, ear injuries, and strangulation injuries. These accompanying injuries may be part of the assailant's sexual repertoire, or they may be caused during efforts to restrain the victim. If a victim is not taken by force, other methods may include hormonal manipulation, the use of pharmacologic sedative agents, or behavioral conditioning to encourage sexual behaviors.

Veterinarians should consider ASA as a possible cause for genital trauma and bacterial or protozoal infections and while not always fatal, animals killed in the act of ASA may be presented for necropsy. This chapter provides an overview of ASA and will discuss the clinical and forensic necropsy examinations and techniques for identifying and collecting trace evidence such as semen or lubricants.

Incidence of Animal Sexual Abuse

The true incidence of sexual contact with animals by humans is not known due to a paucity of studies that investigate this in detail, perhaps due to its taboo nature (Munro 2006). ASA is an activity that may be perpetrated by men and women; however, only men can penetrate an animal with a penis, and ejaculate on or in the animal. Because as of yet, data for various crimes are not reported in any consistent manner, the frequency with which it occurs is unknown.

In the Kinsey reports on human sexual behavior, written in 1948 and 1953, 8% of males and 3.6% of postpubescent women claimed to have had sexual contact with animals (Kinsey et al. 1948, 1953). However, their study results were based on nonrandom sampling and an aggressive questioning style (Beirne 2001). More recently, a Brazilian study looking at a population of men for risk factors of penile cancer found that 171 of 492 participants reported to have had sex with animals (Zequi et al. 2012). Individual case reports of ASA can be found in both the veterinary and human medical literature (Blevins 2009; Kirov et al. 2002; Mittal et al. 2000).

Social and Psychological Context

There is not a single demographic group for people who engage in ASA. It is recognized that there is an active counterculture of zoophiles who gather in chat rooms and share animal pornography. This hidden community serves to validate and normalize the practice in a manner similar to pedophiles (Durkin et al. 2006). It may also play a role in the recruitment of neophyte zoophiles. Abel found that a history of bestiality was the single greatest predictor for engaging in future child sexual abuse (Abel 2008). Zoosadists derive pleasure from torturing animals (often but not always sexually); whereas, necrozoophilia is the practice of sex with dead animals. "Opportunistic zoophiles" have normal human sexual encounters but will have sexual encounters with animals if the opportunity presents itself. Aggrawal has suggested these definitions within a 10-tier classification of animal sexual behaviors of people (Aggrawal 2011). More recently, a 5-item classification scheme (affection/intimacy; situational; secondary gain; sexual violence/cruelty; and other) has been suggested (Holoyda 2016; Holoyda and Newman 2014).

Regardless of motivation, the sexual abuse of animals is an imbalance of power because the human has control over the animal, including most aspects of welfare. Therefore, the sexual abuse of a pet can be considered an assault akin to sexual abuse of a dependent child (Beirne 2001). Like children, animals cannot consent to sexual activity in a clear, unambiguous manner. A number of studies have demonstrated ASA as an indicator of past exposure to sexual assault or violence and as a predictor of potential for future violence. A proclivity for sex with animals may be consistent with abusing individuals who cannot voice opposition (Sandnabba et al. 2002). For these reasons, most states require that an offender convicted of bestiality be listed on their state's sex abuser registry (National District Attorney Association 2014).

Animal Sexual Assault Victims

Animal sexual abuse has been reported in both farm animal and companion animal species. ASA has been reported in the horse, donkey, mule, goat, chicken, cattle, sheep, goat, dog, and cat. In a review by Munro and Thursfield of cases of known and suspected sexual abuse, ASA was identified in 21 dogs and 5 cats, and 2 unknown species (Munro and Thursfield 2001). One author (MSB) has documented fatal ASA on a rabbit. Dogs are considered the most frequent victims of ASA (Beetz 2008).

Examination of the Sexually Abused Animal

The clinical examination of the live ASA victim or the forensic necropsy of the deceased ASA victim should be detailed and thorough as there may be evidence to document anywhere on the animal. Examination findings should be recorded in the medical record/necropsy report, with photographs and radiographs when possible. In the living animal, baseline hematology and biochemistry data, urinalysis, and fecal analysis should be performed. This information may be called into service later to rule out other possible causes of lesions raised by the defense. Fecal analysis and rectal examination are important to rule out or contextualize perineal trauma as the defense may suggest self-trauma due to parasitism or impacted anal sacs.

Many of the steps taken during the clinical examination and forensic necropsy in cases of ASA are similar. The examining veterinarian and assisting staff should wear powder free gloves during the examination to avoid introducing contaminating materials. Additionally, use of gloves and other personal protective equipment such as safety glasses is recommended. The animal should be systematically examined with an alternate light source (ALS) to identify trace evidence such as human biological material or lubricants. An ALS examination should cover the entire body (head to toe) in a systematic pattern. Animal victims may remove trace or biological evidence in the course of grooming activities. Biological evidence may be found anywhere on the animal, not only around the perineum. Semen may be found at areas distant from the sexual contact as the assailant may transfer evidence by touching themselves and subsequently contacting the animal. When identified, suspect material should be photographed and then collected by carefully snipping fur with scissors and preserving it in a paper evidence fold. These samples should be labeled and turned over to the law enforcement authority (or sent to an appropriate accredited forensic laboratory) investigating the case while maintaining proper chain of custody protocols. During the initial examination, forensic materials (trace evidence) may be observed requiring specific preservation. Sexual assault evidence collection kits or crime scene collection kits for evidence collection can be ordered from commercial sources, or in an urgent situation may be available from the local human emergency room. Many hospital emergency rooms have a sexual assault nurse examiner (SANE) on duty at all times and this personnel may be a valuable resource to contact and consult before ever being presented with a suspected ASA case.

Swabs taken to examine for trace evidence (semen, DNA, condom lubricants, etc.) should be obtained from multiple sites on the animal including oral, perianal, vaginal or penile and scrotal, and any suspect area identified during the ALS examination. DNA evidence can be helpful to identify the perpetrator and can be utilized to prove that a particular object was used to harm an animal. Dry samples can be collected on a cotton-tipped swab moistened with sterile water. Collected samples must be fully air dried before packaging for preservation in paper and preserved in paper (not plastic) for future analysis. If damp materials are packaged in plastic, mold can develop and denature the DNA evidence. Whenever possible, samples should be collected in duplicate from each site, and unused swabs should be submitted as controls. For more information about DNA collection techniques, the reader is referred to Chapter 11 (DNA Evidence Collection and Analysis).

During the clinical examination of the live patient, it is important to note that body cavity swabs should be collected prior to use of lubricants as lubricants may be identified from samples collected from the animal's vagina or anus, and can provide evidence that sexual contact occurred. The presence of condom lubricants may corroborate witness statements that sexual contact occurred in the absence of semen and in fact will account for the absence of seminal fluid. The presence of condom lubricants in a body cavity is evidence of penetration. Laboratory testing of the lubricant may be able to match brand of condom. The most common lubricant polydimethylsiloxane (PDMS) is not water soluble, so it will not be absorbed although it can be flushed from the vaginal cavity with urination. Some lubricants contain particulate matter such as cornstarch or amorphous silica; hence, the need to wear powder-free gloves during evidence collection. Spermicides such as Nonoxynol-9 may also be detectable from swabs.

After the completion of the ALS examination, the animal should be carefully and thoroughly combed over butcher paper or a clean white cotton sheet to further identify trace evidence such as foreign (human) hairs, dried blood, and so on (if appropriate to the case). Nail clippings and scrapings should be collected for potential analysis as these may contain DNA of the perpetrator. When possible, a witness (e.g., technician, investigator) should be present during evidence collection to corroborate the examination and collection of the evidence and, when appropriate take control of the evidence so that it is properly secured, transported, and stored.

Suspected human genetic material from animal sexual abuse cases will not be processed by veterinary genetic laboratories. Law enforcement officers or prosecutors should submit suspect human origin materials to state or county police laboratory for processing of these samples. Alternative private laboratories may be used for forensic analysis of materials, but they must be ISO/IEC 17025:2005 accredited and licensed in your state. Such laboratories may be used after conferring with the lead investigative law enforcement authority on the case.

Although there are many bench tests available for purchase, it may not be appropriate for veterinarians to perform testing on collected materials. If a commercial kit is used, the serial/lot number, name, and other specific information regarding the test should be recorded. Materials should be collected, logged, and made available to law enforcement officials. DNA testing is very expensive and in some instances, based on discretion of the investigating agency, testing may not be performed. When a lack of financial resources limit submission, samples should be collected and stored appropriately. There is only one opportunity to perform initial evidence gathering and as the case develops funds may be identified to pay for specimen submission.

After collection of swabs for DNA and combing of the animal, full-body radiographs or computerized tomography scan should be performed. Particular attention should be paid to the abdominal cavity for signs consistent with peritonitis, other infections, retained foreign bodies (such as within the reproductive tract or free in the abdominal cavity) or free gas. The diaphragm, body wall, and pelvic floor should be observed for integrity. In the spayed female, objects inserted in the vaginal vault may be forced through the uterine stump into the peritoneal cavity. The limbs and muzzle should be carefully inspected for any indication of periosteal reaction from trauma or binding (such as tape or binding residue and/or bruising).

After imaging procedures, a rectal wash sample should be collected from both male and female animals and a vaginal wash should be collected from female animals (Stern and Smith-Blackmore 2016). Using a disposable plastic pipette or sterile syringe and tubing such as a red-rubber or polyethylene urinary catheter, sterile saline (approximately 10 mL) is infused into the cavity of interest, gently aspirated, then reinfused and reaspirated. The wash fluid (0.9% NaCl) should be stored in a glass tube and submitted for further analysis to a human forensic laboratory for microscopic examination for presence and/or motility of spermatozoa (Merck and Miller 2013; Rao et al. 2005). If the rectum is full of feces, a fecal sample should be collected and can be analyzed for blood, gastrointestinal parasites, and/or analysis of seminal fluid (Merck and Miller 2013). Before submitting materials for analysis, it may be prudent to review items gathered in context with the totality of findings with the investigators/prosecutor to select the most likely salient items for further analysis. Crime labs currently face a tremendous backlog of materials to test and the International Association of Chiefs of Police has called for careful collection and submission of materials to crime labs. Any materials collected should be retained, even if not submitted, until the close of the judicial process to be available in the course of the discovery process.

After performing an ALS examination, radiological studies, and collection of trace evidence, a complete forensic physical examination or forensic necropsy should be performed.

Forensic Physical Examination

The forensic physical examination of the living victim should proceed in the same manner as any regularly performed, systematic physical examination. It also is important to conduct thorough ophthalmic and otic examinations. The ophthalmic examination should include careful inspection of the sclera for injection or petechial hemorrhage consistent with head trauma or possibly increased intraocular pressure from strangulation. The fundic examination should be performed with the same points in mind. Other ophthalmic findings consistent with trauma include hyphema, anterior uveitis, and luxated lens. The ear canals should be palpated for symmetry and hypertrophy, which can occur due to scarring from repeated physical restraint by the ears. The otic examination should include examination of the tympanum if possible. Head trauma can present as contusion or bleeding into the ear canal. The body should be carefully palpated for bumps, swellings, or asymmetry. The animal's behavior should be carefully observed during palpation to take note of any behavioral responses that are suggestive of a pain or panic response. If these are observed, the noted behavior should be recorded in the medical record. Dogs that have been conditioned to perform sexually may assume a position of lordosis during the perineal exam, and some may thrust in response to the penetration inherent in internal examination. Photographs should be taken throughout the examination including both normal and abnormal findings.

If radiographic or forensic physical examination findings are suggestive of peritonitis, a peritoneal fluid sample should be obtained aseptically and submitted for cytology and bacterial culture.

The perineal examination should be careful and detailed, looking for abrasions, lacerations, contusions, broken hairs, and/or foreign material. The rectum should be carefully palpated digitally in both the male and female patient and the vagina should be examined with an otoscopic cone or endoscope if available. If an endoscopic examination is possible, still or video images of any lesions should be captured. With vaginoscopy, lesions should be carefully described in the medical record and diagrammed. In the male patient, the prostate should be carefully palpated for symmetry and behavioral responses consistent with indications of pain. The penis should be extruded from the prepuce and examined for lesions. The urethral opening should be examined for evidence of foreign body insertion. The testes should be carefully palpated for symmetry and signs of pain-related behaviors (Figure 14.1). Attention should be paid to the presence of any discharges and these should be collected for cytologic analysis and bacterial culture.

If anal or vaginal lesions are identified, documentation of the location using a clock-face diagram is helpful. For example, the anal sacs are located at the 4 and 8 o'clock position and the dorsal-most aspect of the anus would be at the 12 o'clock position. The distance of perforations or other lesions from the anus or vulva should be measured. A stretch injury to the anus may cause radial tears.

When pain behaviors or vaginal/rectal guarding are noted in the patient or during the examination, they should be documented. Also, the change in behavior after pain medication is administered should be recorded. This documents that pain was ameliorated through the administration of pain medications, further supporting the diagnosis of a painful condition.

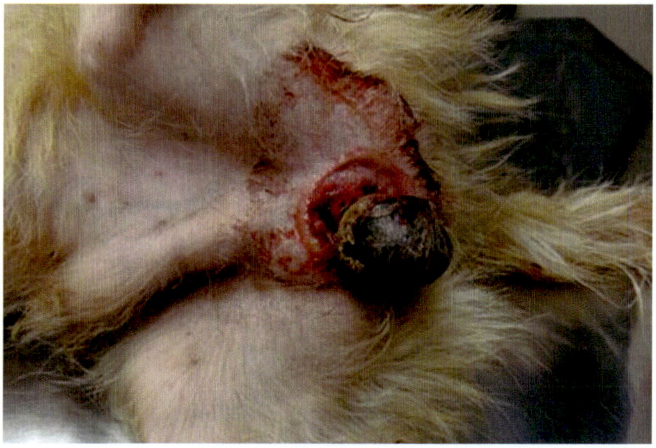

Figure 14.1 Scrotal infarction from a dog that had a rubber band placed around the scrotum.

Forensic Necropsy

As with any forensic necropsy, an external and internal examination should be performed. Findings from the forensic necropsy must be documented to meet the standards required for legal proceedings. Every effort should be made to retain primary evidence so that it may also be tested or reviewed by the defense in the reciprocal discovery process. When a test of vital evidence is anticipated to be a consumptive test, it may be most appropriate to flag this possibility to the legal authorities before proceeding with the testing. Often timing is of importance to ensure expediency of biological specimen analysis.

Similar to other forensic necropsies where nonaccidental injury is suspected, the skin should be reflected and inspected for evidence of blunt force trauma. In cases of suspected ASA, thorough examination of both the gastrointestinal and reproductive tracts is required. Perforation of the rectum, colon, cervix, or uterus can occur and identification of the perforation site would be warranted in cases of foreign body penetration. Similar to the clinical examination, if anal or vaginal lesions are identified, documenting the location of the lesion(s) using a clock-face diagram is helpful.

Pathology of Animal Sexual Abuse

Victims of ASA can have a range of injuries to the genitalia, anus/rectum, and/or nipples, whereas in some instances an animal may lack injuries despite sexual contact. Documented injuries to the anus/rectum and perineum include insertion of foreign objects, sharp force injuries to the perineal region, perianal hemorrhage (Figure 14.2), colonic perforation, anal dilation, and anal tears. Rectal prolapse can occur secondary to rectal and colon injuries and the integrity of the pelvic floor can be disrupted with forceful penetration of oversized objects. Dilation of the anus has been reported in sexually abused animals (Bradley and Rasile 2014; Munro and Thursfield 2001). It should be noted that dilation of the anus commonly occurs postmortem and this should not be confused with anal dilation as an antemortem finding. Histologic analysis of tissue tears can help differentiate antemortem injury from postmortem changes. When size disparity does not allow actual penetration of a body orifice, the entire perineal area may be forcefully invaginated through the pelvic canal. This may result in a large circular "target" lesion of hair loss, contusion or abrasion around the entire perineum, along with disruption of the pelvic floor musculature.

Other types of injuries may be identified in ASA victims, although they are not sexual in origin. These injuries may be related to the force used in restraint or attack prior to sexual assault and include bruising, abrasions (from fingernail scrapings), fractures, thickening of the skin of the pinna or cartilage of the otic canal, and injuries to internal organs such as lacerations of viscera from blunt force trauma, and sharp force injuries (Bradley and Rasile 2014). Ocular changes due to blunt force trauma or asphyxia may include anterior uveitis, hyphema, scleral injection, retinal petechial or ecchymotic hemorrhage or conjunctival petechial hemorrhage may be observed in some cases.

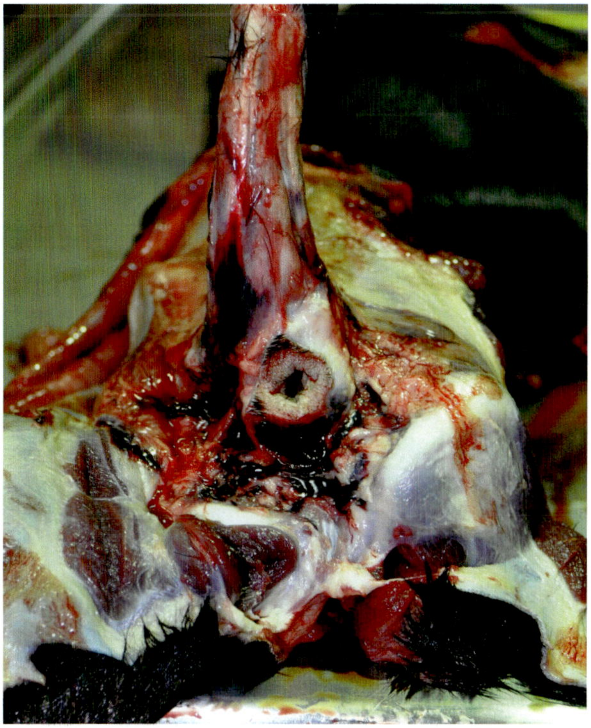

Figure 14.2 Perianal hemorrhage of the dog. Photo courtesy of Dr. Doris Miller, University of Georgia.

Exculpatory Findings

It is important to consider nonsexual causes for the clinical or postmortem findings of an animal examined with a suspicious presentation for sexual assault. Examination findings such as a rectal prolapse can be due to parasitism, vaginal hypertrophy and uterine prolapse due to tissue hypertrophy from estrogen stimulation, genetic predisposition or straining in cases of urinary tract infection or gastrointestinal disease. Transmissible venereal tumor can present with hemorrhagic proliferative lesions that can be mistaken for non-accidental injury on initial inspection. Rectal hemorrhage from hemorrhagic colitis or vaginal hemorrhage/fluid drainage from recent whelping may also mimic findings observed in cases of ASA. Condoms have been found in the rectum of a dog that ingested them incidentally.

Specialized Techniques

Specialized techniques can be utilized during the investigation of ASA cases. These techniques include diagnostic imaging, ALS examination, and tests to identify semen or seminal fluid.

Diagnostic Imaging

Full-body radiographs or computerized tomography should be taken to identify both direct and indirect injuries that might be associated with sexual assault such as musculoskeletal injuries including rib, skull, axial, and appendicular fractures. Injuries to the tail are reported in cases of ASA and include luxation or fracture of the proximal coccygeal vertebrae (Merck and Miller 2013). Repeated forceful manipulation of the tail may result in tail laxity at the proximal coccygeal vertebrae.

Alternate Light Source Examination

ALS has been adapted to medicolegal investigations and these lights can enhance the contrast of biologic evidence against the background or cause the evidence to fluoresce. ALS can be used to identify semen and other bodily fluids. The fluids absorb light at particular wavelengths (excitation spectrum of human semen is 300–480) and then re-emits the absorbed energy at a longer wavelength (emission spectrum is 400–700 nm) (Lee and Khoo 2010; Stoilovic 1991). To clearly observe the photoluminescence effect of semen, use appropriate filters or goggles to filter out strong excitation wavelengths (Stoilovic 1991).

A Wood's lamp is the most common ALS available to the veterinarian; however, the accuracy and sensitivity of the Wood's lamp for identification of biological substances such as urine and semen is questionable. There are recommendations to eliminate the use of the Wood's lamp during sexual assault examinations of humans (Eldredge et al. 2012). It has been shown that other ALS appear to be more useful for detection of human semen including the Bluemaxx BM500, which was 100% sensitive for human semen although not specific (Nelson and Santucci 2002). The use of a Wood's lamp in the absence of any other available ALS is recommended. Practitioners engaging in a forensic practice should add an appropriate semen identifying ALS to their equipment resources. Regardless of the ALS used, in case of identification of a positive stain further laboratory analysis should be performed on samples of interest.

Evaluation for Spermatozoa

Survival times of human sperm in animals is not known. In humans, the survival of human sperm varies and sperm survival is longer in living humans when compared to deceased humans (Platt et al. 2006). Regardless of survivability, the identification of human sperm in the vagina or rectum is supportive of ASA. Evaluation of samples by an accredited human forensic laboratory is advised to ensure the evidence is admissible in a court of law.

If moist materials are collected (such as a moist clump of fur), direct impressions may be made on glass slides for microscopic identification of spermatozoa. Depending on the animal species, sperm can vary in both shape and size and sperm have three distinct regions (head, midpiece, and tail). The most commonly used stain to visualize spermatozoa is the Kernechtrot-picroindigocarmine stain (Christmas tree stain). Nuclear fast red differentially stains the sperm head red and the counterstain picroindigocarmine stains the tail green-blue. When evaluating for human sperm, the acrosomal cap of human sperm stains less intensely red than the nuclear portion of the sperm head compared to canine sperm, which has a light staining of the acrosomal cap, dark red staining of the postacrosomal region, and a colorless region (band) between the acrosome and postacrosomal region (Schudel 2001).

Tests for Seminal Fluid

In many instances spermatozoa may not be recovered in cases of ASA. Reasons for lack of recovery include condom use by the perpetrator, aspermia due to testicular disease or surgical sterilization, lack of ejaculation, the perpetrator was female, or the assault involved the use of a foreign object.

Various screening tests can be utilized to detect the presence of seminal fluid and include screening tests for acid phosphatase (AP) test, prostate specific antigen (PSA), or semenogelin (Sg), or use of mass spectrometry-based proteomics (Hockmeister et al. 1999; Khaldi et al. 2004; Nakanishi et al. 2014; Simich et al. 1999; Stern and Lanka 2015; Van Steendam 2013). Confirmatory tests for human seminal fluid include the microscopic identification of spermatozoa, analysis of short tandem repeat loci from the Y chromosome (Y-STRs), and mass spectrometry-based proteomics (Cotton and Fisher 2015; Martinez et al. 2015; Nakanishi et al. 2014; Santucci et al. 1999; Stern and Lanka 2015). Although some of the tests discussed in this section are practical and easy to use, to date, validation studies are lacking for their use in animals, although some research has been published on species cross-reactivity of several available tests (Miller et al. 2011; Pang and Chang 2007; Sato et al. 2002; Simich et al. 1999; Stern and Lanka 2015).

Acid Phosphatase

AP is primarily localized to the human prostate. AP testing can be performed either by an indirect (blot) testing method or direct testing. In one study looking at direct testing, positive reactions obtained from human oral swabs and a human urine stain have been reported and these results could be misinterpreted as an indication of possible human seminal fluid (Lewis et al. 2013). PSA detection is considered to be more reliable than AP detection after 48 hours for seminal fluid in humans (Khaldi et al. 2004). Limited data regarding AP cross-reactivity to seminal fluid from animals is available. Seminal fluid of several nonhuman primates tested positive for AP, whereas samples from seminal fluid of the dog were negative (Simich et al. 1999). In contrast, AP was detected in seminal plasma from both normal dogs and dogs with prostatic disorders (Bell et al. 1995).

Prostate-Specific Antigen

PSA can be used as a marker of seminal fluid and can be detected in urine of human males aged 12–14 years or greater (Sato et al. 2002). In addition to being found in seminal fluid, PSA is also found in male serum, male urine, apocrine sweat glands, and breast milk of lactating women. Although low levels of PSA can be detected in nonprostatic fluids, this should not be considered to be an issue in sexual assault cases (Graves 1995).

Species cross-reactivity for human PSA have been evaluated from a limited number of animals. PSA cross-reactivity utilizing a PSA membrane test assay was not reported in cat, dog, stallion, pig, and bull (Hockmeister et al. 1999). In a study by Simich et al., semen from dogs tested positive for PSA (mean 44.7 ng/mL) whereas Bell et al. were unable to detect PSA in canine seminal plasma (Bell et al. 1995; Simich et al. 1999). Urine from male cats and dogs showed no reaction using the commercially available "SMITEST" PSA card (Sato et al. 2002).

Semenogelin

Semenogelin I and II (SgI and SgII) are proteins secreted in human semen. Sg assays have been shown to be useful for detection of seminal plasma in forensic samples (Old et al. 2012; Pang and Chang 2007). Semen samples from pig, bull, stallion, cat, dog, and rooster were reported to be negative for Sg utilizing a membrane strip test (Pang and Chang 2007; Stern and Lanka 2015). There was no cross-reactivity for Sg using a commercially available membrane test in various bodily fluids from dogs (seminal fluid, urine, saliva, vaginal secretions, and blood), although in the rectal samples tested a single false positive was detected (Stern and Lanka 2015).

Conclusion

When investigating a case of potential ASA, accurate documentation of lesions or lack of lesions, and behavior of the animal is of crucial importance to the forensic investigation. A complete forensic clinical examination or forensic necropsy must be performed to document any injuries identified in animals that have been sexually abused. Injuries that may be identified and are directly due to ASA include injuries to the anus, rectum, nipples, and penis or vagina. Accompanying injuries identified in ASA victims may include bruises, abrasions, ligature injuries, and/or fractures. The performance of a complete and thorough examination will allow for both the accurate identification of injuries, collection of trace evidence, and superior documentation of the case findings.

References

Abel, G. 2008. What can 44,000 men and 12,000 boys with sexual behavior problems teach us about preventing sexual abuse? Paper presented at the Annual Training Conference of California Coalition on Sexual Offending, San Francisco.

Aggrawal, A. 2011. A new classification of zoophilia. *J Forensic Leg Med*. 18:73–78.

Beetz, A. M. 2008. Bestiality and zoophilia: A discussion of sexual contact with animals. In *The International Handbook of Animal Abuse and Cruelty: Theory, Research, and Application*. F. R. Ascione, ed., pp. 201–220. West Lafayette, IN: Purdue University Press.

Beirne, P. 2001. Peter Singer's "heavy petting" and the politics of animal sexual assault. *Crit Crim*. 10:43–55.

Bell, F. W., Klausner, J. S., Hayden, D. W., Lund, E. M., Libenstein, B. B., Feeney, D. A., Johnson, S. D. et al. 1995. Evaluation of serum and seminal plasma markers in the diagnosis of canine prostatic disorders. *J Vet Intern Med.* 9(3):149–153.

Blevins, R. O. 2009. A case of severe anal injury in an adolescent male due to bestial sexual experimentation. *J Forensic Leg Med.* 16:403–406.

Bradley, N., and K. Rasile. 2014. Recognition & management of animal sexual abuse. *Clin Brief.* Apr:73–75.

Cotton, R. W., and M. B. Fisher. 2015. Review: Properties of sperm and seminal fluid, informed by research on reproduction and contraception. *For Sci Int Genet.* 18:66–77.

Durkin, K., Forsyth, C. J., and J. F. Quinn. 2006. Pathological internet communities: A new direction for sexual deviance research in a postmodern era. *Sociol Spectr.* 26:595–606.

Eldredge, K., Huggins, E., and L. C. Pugh. 2012. Alternate light sources in sexual assault examinations: An evidence-based practice project. *J Forensic Nurs.* 8:39–44.

Graves, H. C. 1995. Nonprostatic sources of prostate-specific antigen: A steroid hormone-dependent phenomenon? *Clin Chem.* 41:7–9.

Hockmeister, M. N., Budowle, B., Rudin, O., Gehrig, C., Borer, U., Thali, M., and R. Dirnhofer. 1999. Evaluation of prostate-specific antigen (PSA) membrane test assays for the forensic evaluation of seminal fluid. *J Forensic Sci.* 44:1057–1060.

Holoyda, B. 2016. *Bestiality in the United States: Legal and Psychiatric Perspectives.* Paper presented at the International Veterinary Forensic Sciences Association conference, St. Petersburg.

Holoyda, B., and W. Newman. 2014. Zoophilia and the law: Legal responses to a rare paraphilia. *J Am Acad Psychiatr Law.* 42:412–420.

Khaldi, N., Miras, A., Botti, K., and S. Gromb. 2004. Evaluation of three rapid detection methods for the forensic identification of seminal fluid in rape cases. *J Forensic Sci.* 49:749–753.

Kinsey, A. C., Pomeroy, W. B., and C. E. Martin. 1948. *Sexual Behavior in the Human Male.* Philadelphia, PA: WB Saunders.

Kinsey, A. C., Pomeroy, W. B., Martin, C. E., and P. H. Gebhard. 1953. *Sexual Behavior in the Human Female.* Philadelphia, PA: WB Saunders.

Kirov, G. K., Losanoff, J. E., and K. Kjossev. 2002. Zoophilia: A rare cause of traumatic injury to the rectum. *Injury.* 33:367–368.

Lee, W., and B. Khoo. 2010. Forensic light sources for detection of biological evidences in crime scene investigation: A review. *Malay J Forensic Sci.* 1:17–27.

Lewis, J., Baird, A., McAlister C., Siemieniuk, A., Blackmore, L., McCabe, B., O'Rourke, P. et al. 2013. Improved detection of semen by use of direct acid phosphatase testing. *Sci Justice.* 53:385–394.

Martinez, P., Santiago, B., Alcala, B., and I. Atienza. 2015. Semen searching when sperm is absent. *Sci Justice.* 55:118–123.

Merck, M., and D. Miller. 2013. Sexual abuse. In *Veterinary Forensics: Animal Cruelty Investigations*, 2nd ed. M. Merck, ed., pp. 233–239. Ames, IA: Wiley-Blackwell.

Miller, K. W. P., Old, J., Fischer, B. R., Schweers, B., Stipinaite, S., and K. Reich. 2011. Developmental validation of the SPERM HY-LIGHTER™ kit for the identification of human spermatozoa in forensic samples. *J Forensic Sci.* 56:853–865.

Mittal, A., Shenoi, S. D., and K. B. Kumar. 2000. Genital lesions following bestiality. *Indian J Dermatol Venereol Leprol.* 66:95–96.

Munro, H. M. C., and M. V. Thursfield. 2001. 'Battered pets': Sexual abuse. *J Small Anim Pract.* 42:333–337.

Munro, H. M. C. 2006. Animal sexual abuse: A veterinary taboo? *Vet J.* 172:195–197.

Nakanishi, H., Hara, M., Takahashi, S., Takada, A., and K. Saito. 2014. Evaluation of forensic examination of extremely aged seminal stains. *Leg Med (Tokyo).* 16:303–307.

National District Attorney Association. 2014. Bestiality as a trigger for sex offender registration. http://www.ndaajustice.org/pdf/Bestiality%20and%20Sex%20 Offender%20Registration.pdf (accessed April 15, 2016).

Nelson, D. G., and K. Santucci. 2002. An alternate light source to detect semen. *Acad Emerg Med.* 9:1045–1048.

Old, J., Schweers, B. A., Boonlayangoor, P. W., Fischer, B., Miller, K. W., and K. Reich. 2012. Developmental validation of RSID-semen: A lateral flow immunochromatographic strip test for the forensic detection of human semen. *J Forensic Sci.* 57:489–499.

Pang, B. C. M., and B. K. K. Chang. 2007. Identification of human Semenogelin in membrane strip test as an alternative method for detection of semen. *Forensic Sci Int.* 169:27–31.

Platt M. S., Spitz, D. J., and W. U. Spitz. 2006. Investigation of deaths in childhood, part 2: The abused child and adolescent. In *Spitz and Fisher's Medicolegal Investigation of Death: Guidelines for the Application of Pathology to Crime Investigation*, 4th ed., W. U. Spitz, and D. J. Spitz, eds., pp. 357–416. Springfield: Charles C Thomas.

Rao, V., Lew, E., and E. Matshes. 2005. Sexual battery investigation. In *Forensic Pathology: Principles and Practice*. D. Dolinak, E. Matshes, and E. O. Lew, eds., pp. 467–485. Oxford: Elsevier.

Sandnabba, N. K., Santtila, P., Nordling, N., Beetz, A. M., and L. Alison. 2002. Characteristics of a sample of sadomasochistically-oriented males with recent experience of sexual contact with animals. *Deviant Behav.* 23:511–529.

Santucci, K. A., Nelson, D. G., McQuillen, K. K., Duffy, S. J., and J. G. Linakis. 1999. Wood's lamp utility in the identification of semen. *Pediatrics.* 104:1342–1344.

Sato, I., Sagi, M., Ishiwari, A., Nishijima, H., Ito, E., and T. Mukai. 2002. Use of the "SMITEST" PSA card to identify the presence of prostate-specific antigen in semen and male urine. *Forensic Sci Int.* 127:71–73.

Schudel, D. 2001. Screening for canine spermatozoa. *Sci Justice.* 41:117–119.

Simich, J. P., Morris, S. L., Klick, R. L., and K. Rittenhouse-Diakun. 1999. Validation of the use of a commercially available kit for the identification of prostate specific antigen (PSA) in semen stains. *J Forensic Sci.* 44:1229–1231.

Stern, A. W., and S. Lanka. 2015. Evaluation of human semenogelin membrane strip test for species cross-reactivity in dogs. *Vet Pathol.* 53:1095–1098.

Stern, A. W., and M. Smith-Blackmore. 2016. Veterinary forensic pathology of animal sexual abuse. *Vet Pathol.* 53:1057–1066.

Stoilovic, M. 1991. Detection of semen and blood stains using polilight as a light source. *Forensic Sci Int.* 51:289–296.

Van Steendam, K., De Ceuleneer, M., Dhaenens, M., Van Hoofstat, D., and D. Deforce. 2013. Mass spectrometry-based proteomics as a tool to identify biological matrices in forensic science. *Int J Legal Med.* 127:287–298.

Zequi, S., Guimaraes, G., da Fonseca, F., Ferreira, U., de Matheus, W. E., Reis, L. O., Aita, G. A. et al. 2012. Sex with animals (SWA): Behavioral characteristics and possible association with penile cancer. A multicenter study. *J Sex Med.* 9:1860–1867.

15

Agroterrorism

Ernest R. Rogers

Contents

Introduction

Since the highly publicized international terrorist attacks of 1993 and 2001 in New York City and the 1995 domestic terrorist attack in Oklahoma City, there has been a heightened concern in recognizing and preventing terrorism. Agroterrorism is a construct under the general category of bioterrorism. For the balance of this chapter, I will be concentrating on crimes against animal life. Agroterrorism, through the introduction of an animal or plant disease, is directed at a country's most vulnerable economic resource, the agricultural industry including animal production (such as beef cattle, dairy cattle, poultry, and swine) and aquaculture industries. The goal of the terrorist is not to destroy our animal or aquaculture resources but to disrupt our economic resources, to hinder domestic and international trade, to disrupt the societal expectation of a safe food source, and create fear of disease in the general population.

The definition of a weapon of mass destruction is "any weapon or device that is intended, or has the capability, to cause death or serious bodily injury to a significant number of people through the release, dissemination, or impact of—(a) toxic or poisonous chemicals or their precursors; (b) a disease organism; or (c) radiation or radioactivity" (Office of the Law Revision Counsel 2017). This definition has only referred to the release of any weapon of mass destruction directed specifically at "persons" and thus is not considered for crimes against animals. The section specifically cited for enforcing terrorism crimes against agriculture is the Animal Enterprise Terrorism Act. It includes force, violence, or threats involving animal enterprises that "intentionally damages or causes the loss of any real or personal property (including animals or records) used by an animal enterprise, or any real or personal property of a person or entity having a connection to, relationship with, or transactions with an animal enterprise" (U.S. Government Publishing Office 2017).

The economics of agriculture and aquaculture are extensive and disruption can lead to severe financial loss and hardships. The beef industry in the United States represents a production value of $6.302 billion (National Cattlemen's Beef Association 2015). The dairy industry in the United States is the sixth largest in the world and represents an annual export volume of $3.71 billion as of August 2011 (United States Department of Agriculture 2017a, 2010). In the United States, the chicken broiler industry, alone, represents $41 billion in trade in the economic marketplace and the poultry and egg industry represents $441 billion including production, jobs, and taxes (Dunham and Associates 2016; United States Department of Agriculture Economic Research Service 2013). Aquaculture, in 2014, had a production value of $386 million divided between freshwater and saltwater produce (National Oceanic and Atmospheric Administration 2015). Although these are not the only economically sensitive industries in the United States, these are likely some of the more vulnerable and high-profile aspects in the agriculture industry.

The threats of agroterrorism have been embraced by the popular media (Norton 2014; Taylor 2014) and studied by multiple government agencies (Office of the Law Revision Counsel 2017; United States Government Publishing Office 2017). The impact of animal involved agroterrorism would include those diseases that both cause high mortality (loss of animal life) and those that have high or even medium morbidity (occurrence of disease in a population). High mortality or morbidity would result in significant loss of production and economics. Additionally, those diseases that are potentially zoonotic may also cause increased health concerns to the public and could result in widespread panic.

The history of agroterrorism is well documented both against animals and humans (Morris 2007; Norton 2014; Taylor 2014). Today, it is recognized that with increases in international travel, the prevalence of foreign animal diseases, and the general lack of vigilance among some in the agriculture and aquaculture food industry, there are weaknesses in security of our food industry including during production and processing. This chapter recognizes that the primary responsibility for the recognition/diagnosis, investigation, and enforcement of the laws related to agroterrorism fall within the jurisdiction of multiple agencies including the United States Department of Agriculture (USDA), Department of Health and Human Services (Norton 2014), and other agencies. However, as a forensic veterinarian, we may have specific skills that, as a first responder, can assist in control and investigation of agricultural-based terrorist attacks.

Weapons of the Agroterrorist

There are multiple chemical and biological agents that may be introduced to the animal production environment. These may include toxins/poisons, viruses, bacteria, parasites, and other disruptive elements. The terrorist may use domestic elements for sabotage or infectious agents grown abroad. Our borders have significant surveillance and protection against weapons such as explosives, toxins/poisons, and other devices of mass destruction. There are comprehensive human resources committed to monitoring subterfuge by individuals. Within the United States, many hard targets receive law enforcement scrutiny to ensure safety. Law enforcement agencies at the municipal, state, and federal levels receive training to monitor and prevent against domestic and foreign terror attacks. In the investigation of a potential bio-agriculture attack, the primary resources are dispatched through the activity and communication of the U.S. Department of Agriculture, Department of Homeland Security, and Health and Human Services (Hurt 2012; Monke 2004; Taylor 2014). The agricultural weapons of mass destruction that meet the criteria of a bioterrorist instrument of economic disruption may be monitored for entry or development within the borders of the United States (Morris 2007; Taylor 2014; United States Department of Agriculture 2017a). Given the covert low-profile nature of bioweapons, surreptitious international and domestic (interstate) smuggling may occur.

We recognize that there are multiple susceptible sites, in animal production and food processing (food chain), that may be vulnerable to attack. The food chain consists of the farm (ranch, breeding facility), livestock holding facilities (stockyards), transportation hubs and vehicles, abattoirs, food processing facilities, and retail outlets.

The list of potential bioagents and nonbiological agents that may be used in an attack include foreign animal diseases of viral, bacterial, or parasitic origin, genetically modified (weaponized) infectious agents, toxins/poisons, chemical weapons, explosives and radiation, or dirty bombs (Hurt 2012; Moats 2007; United States Animal Health Association 2008). The most effective biological weapons would have properties consistent with the following characteristics:

- A bioagent which could be initially introduced by a fomite, aerosolization, or insect vector transmission.
- Animal to animal transmission would occur by direct contact or airborne.
- The bioagent should be stable under a wide range of temperatures and conditions.

- The resulting disease or infectious process would have a long (days to weeks) incubation period.
- The resulting disease would have few initial overt clinical signs.
- The animal would be infectious to other animals before there are clinical signs.

To date, fortunately, there are few natural bioagents that meet all these criteria (Table 15.1). The most likely weaponized biological agent is a foreign animal disease (FAD) (Jayarao 2017; Moats 2007; United States Animal Health Association 2008).

Some vulnerable sites for agroterrorism include the ranch or farm, just before transportation of livestock to a new location, including growing/finishing facilities, stockyards, abattoirs, and holding pens. These sites would allow for the potential distribution of an infectious process to infect large numbers of comingled animals from multiple sources and could cause rapid dissemination of disease in transported and physically stressed animals (Rogers 2003). Comingling of animals (such as at sale barn auctions, stockyards) would increase the chances of disease propagation. Spread of disease in transported animals would result in infected animals being distributed to multiple sites that could be hundreds of miles from the location of the original infection.

There are multiple zoonotic diseases that may have an economic impact on the agricultural industry. Zoonotic diseases may be spread from an infected animal to humans. This may enhance the fear of disease related to human-to-human contact and therefore the spread of the disease within the human population. Although not a terrorist attack, an incident of zoonotic disease that occurred in Hong Kong was an outbreak of avian influenza (H5N1) virus in 1997 (Chan 2002). Initially, the outbreak was found within the poultry industry; human contact resulted in transference of disease to humans. This event created great havoc among the civilian population as fears of infection caused disruption of commerce, restriction of travel, cessation of exports of poultry, and mass euthanasia of avian flocks (Chan 2002).

Possible Signs of Agroterrorism

In considering any possible act of terrorism, the investigator must differentiate an accidental or natural disease infection from a terrorist act. Signs of intentional disease infection or intentional release of a foreign animal disease, or other disease of economic importance, may include changes affecting normal farm or stockyard operations. These may include sudden acute (2–3 days) or subacute illness of multiple previously healthy animals. The discovery of a fomite, open container, or solid/liquid debris at a fence line, adjacent to public access areas where animals are maintained, is cause for suspicion of a potential act of terrorism (Figure 15.1).

There are a multitude of indicators of an agroterrorism attack at the production (farm) level including an increase in numbers of sick or dying animals (Table 15.2). There are also many indicators that are related to the preparation of an agricultural terrorist attack (Table 15.3). These possible indicators

Table 15.1 Select List of Pathogens That Affect Livestock and Poultry

Disease Name	Primary Species Affected	Type of Transmission	Zoonotic	Incubation Period	Animal Mortality	Vaccine Available
Foot and mouth disease	Cloven hoofed animals	Aerosol, direct contact, indirect contact with contaminated fomites	Yes, mild symptoms with very close contact	3–21 days	Low (adults), variable (young animals)	Yes
Anthrax	Herbivores	Spore ingestion, contact, inhalation	Yes	3–7 days	High	Yes
Brucellosis	Cloven hoofed animals	Ingestion of contaminated food products or unpasteurized milk, contact with infected animal abortion products	Yes	3–7 days	Rare in adult animals, induces abortion	Yes
Bovine spongiform encephalopathy (BSE)	Cattle	Ingestion of tissue containing the BSE prion	Yes	2–5 years	Fatal once symptoms appear	No
African swine fever	Swine	Direct contact, feces, urine, tick vector	No	5–15 days	Variable due to virulence, 0–100%	No

(*Continued*)

Table 15.1 (Continued) Select List of Pathogens That Affect Livestock and Poultry

Disease Name	Primary Species Affected	Type of Transmission	Zoonotic	Incubation Period	Animal Mortality	Vaccine Available
Swine vesicular disease	Swine	Body fluids feces, ingestion of contaminated pork products	No	2–6 days	No	Yes
Highly pathogenic avian influenza	Birds, especially chickens and turkeys	Direct contact, fomites human	Yes	1–7 days	Yes, near 100%	Yes
Exotic Newcastle disease	Birds	Direct, body fluids, fomites	Yes	2–12 days	Variable due to virulence	None effective
Rift Valley fever	Cattle, sheep, goats	Insect vector, body fluids, fomites	Yes, very susceptible	12 hours–4 days	Higher in young compared to adults	Yes

(*Continued*)

Table 15.1 (Continued) Select List of Pathogens That Affect Livestock and Poultry

Disease Name	Primary Species Affected	Type of Transmission	Zoonotic	Incubation Period	Animal Mortality	Vaccine Available
Blue tongue	Sheep, cattle, goats, wild ruminants	Insect vector	No	5–10 days	0–50% (sheep), 80–90% (deer)	Yes
Vesicular stomatitis	Equidae, cattle, swine	Insect, direct contact, body fluids, fomites, feed, water	Yes	2–8 days	Rare (cattle and horses)	Yes
Tularemia	Wild and domestic mammals	Contact, ticks, drinking water, contaminated feed	Yes	1–10 days	Yes, 5–15%	Yes

Sources: 1. Moats, J.B. 2007. *Agroterrorism—A Guide for First Responders*. College Station: Texas A&M University Press. 2. Jayarao, B.M. 2017. Agroterrorism: A potential threat to U.S. animal agriculture (Part 1). http://extension.psu.edu/animals/health/biosecurity/fundamentals/agroterrorism-a-potential-threat-to-us-animal-agriculture-i (Accessed April 15, 2017). 3. United States Animal Health Association. 2008. *Foreign Animal Diseases*, 7th Ed. Boca Raton, FL: CRC Press/Taylor & Francis.

Figure 15.1 An example of a fomite placed adjacent to a pasture fence that would allow for direct animal contact and potential disease infection and spread.

Table 15.2 Indicators of an Agricultural Terrorist Attack at the Production Level

- Unusual increase in numbers of sick or dying animals
- Unusual disease of intoxication resulting in illness or death of plants or animals
- Unscheduled or unusual spraying, particularly outdoors and/or during periods of darkness
- Abandoned spraying devices
- Sudden increase in local market pricing on food items that are normally plentiful in supply
- Local reporting of large crop or livestock losses and deaths unrelated to seasonal climatic conditions

Sources: 1. Moats, J.B. 2007. *Agroterrorism—A Guide for First Responders.* College Station: Texas A&M University Press. 2. Federal Bureau of Investigation. 2008. *Criminal Investigation Handbook for Agroterrorism,* pp. 31–42.

of agricultural terrorist attack should be noted by either those veterinarians involved in production medicine or the forensic veterinarian considering the likelihood of a terrorist attack. In addition to these indicators, since 2008 when the FBI's Criminal Investigation Handbook for Agroterrorism was published, the use of autonomous drones (remotely operated flying vehicles) has become a serious threat to any agricultural operation. Drones may be used for the remote distribution of an infective fomite(s), local spraying or distribution of disease producing infectious agents or toxins to otherwise inaccessible

Table 15.3 Indicators That Are Related to the Preparation of an Agricultural Terrorist Attack

- The purchase of agricultural disease cultures or large amount of a highly toxic chemical with cash
- Group or individual inquiring about obtaining samples of agricultural pathogens or asking specific questions about toxicity of a chemical
- The theft or loss of agricultural disease culture or growth media from an academic research institution
- Unusual activity noted in areas where agricultural or livestock disease outbreaks are occurring or have occurred previously
- Shipments of supplies from a laboratory supply company that included growth media, such as blood agar culture dishes
- Unexplained theft of agricultural animals or equipment such as sprayers
- Excessive curiosity about application equipment details, such as spray range
- Unusual interest in the acquisition of vaccines and medications for crop or livestock disease
- Suspicious activities reported at or near livestock feedlots, processing plants, or poultry plants
- Unexplained loitering near pesticide storage areas
- Interest in specific locations of agricultural assets concentrations such as foreign requests for detailed data or travel plans to rural areas
- Noxious or unusual odors not routinely associated with the area

Source: Federal Bureau of Investigation. 2008. *Criminal Investigation Handbook for Agroterrorism*, pp. 31–42.

locations. The presence of a drone, not operated by a known individual, should be reported and investigated. Furthermore, the areas where the drone was seen should be closed and animals from those areas quarantined to those specific areas until an assessment of their disease status can be established. Investigation of unusual fomites, containers, or substances in the pasture or feedlot should be identified, photographed, and marked as evidence.

Another consideration, and possible indicator of introduction of a FAD, would include the travel of foreign nationals, from areas of endemic FAD, who travel to rural agricultural areas without cause or invitation. These individuals present an increasing threat of transboundary animal diseases (TAD) (United States Animal Health Association 2008). This term was developed by the FAO and is defined as "highly contagious epidemic diseases that can spread extremely rapidly, irrespective of national borders" (Levings 2012). These diseases can easily spread and reach epidemic proportions and control/management including exclusion will require cooperation between several countries (United States Animal Health Association 2008). Transboundary animal diseases represent some of the most significant diseases that a terrorist can use in a biological attack against food producing animals.

Security/Investigation Considerations Related to Agroterrorism

In many cases, the small- to medium-sized ranch or farm is a relatively soft security target. Often there is little to no surveillance capability, very few restrictions to public access to pastures, barns/housing, and feeding equipment or water sources at these sites (Figure 15.2). Similarly, many agricultural facilities use pastures and fields for production stock (cattle, small ruminants, and swine) which are also vulnerable to attack through public access (Figure 15.3). Larger facilities, stockyards, large holding facilities, and abattoirs often have improved and higher levels of security. A major vulnerability at these large facilities is the high number of animals in small areas. Second, there is a commingling of animals from multiple geographic areas and increased individual animal stress (due to preconditioning, transportation, and crowding), which results in an increase in endogenous circulating cortisol and subsequently a decrease in disease resistance (Rogers 2003).

Monitoring of animal production facilities for occurrence of disease that could be the result of natural, accidental infections or that may be the result of an agroterrorist attack should be a high priority of any attending clinical or forensic veterinarian. The most vulnerable time at any facility is when there is high vendor or commercial traffic, those times immediately before shipping (dehorning, castration, vaccination), during transportation of animals to a second facility, and post-shipping processing. Currently, the use of a unique USDA identification method (e.g., National Animal Identification System) is one of the best security measures to ensure all animals transported (interstate

Figure 15.2 A medium-sized farm is a low security soft target. Notice the free public access to water, feeding silos, and animal housing. In this case, there is no closed-circuit video surveillance and there are no physical barriers to limit access to animal containment areas. Finally, there are multiple public access county roads surrounding the property.

Figure 15.3 Note the limited security, multiple strand electric fence. A better line of security is to have a 10- to 12-foot buffer zone between the public access area and the pasture fencing.

or internationally) can be tracked from source/birth to slaughter (United States Department of Agriculture 2017b). Additional security measures that may be included are signage warning of limited access, installation of closed circuit television surveillance, and prevention of public access to animal areas and pastures. Pasture security can be enhanced by using a two-fence system creating a space disruption between public access and the barrier fencing for the animals.

If a FAD or an agroterrorist attack is suspected, the veterinarian must inform the appropriate authorities. The primary function of a forensic investigator in the investigation of agroterrorism is to report clinical findings, symptoms, and tentative diagnosis to the appropriate municipal, state, and federal law enforcement authorities (Federal Bureau of Investigation 2008).

Once reported, the forensic veterinarian as well as state and federal veterinarians, law enforcement, and other agricultural investigators will play a role in the following:

- Protect public and individual safety
- Identify possible additional agroterrorism targets
- Attempt to identify any individuals that may have been involved in the distribution of infectious agents
- Advise on the use of the appropriate personal protective equipment for the tentative diagnosis reported
- Restrict or limit travel to and from the affected areas
- Identify any evidence of significance

If an agroterrorism event is suspected, there should be no transportation of animals from the hot zone to any other location. Animals should be confined to the location of the suspected disease event. Further, the individuals involved in the animal care or those that have animal contact should be advised that travel from the infection zone is not in keeping with the expectations of the agricultural authorities (USDA, United States Department of Health and Human Services, United States Department of Homeland Security, and U.S. Food and Drug Administration). Their travel should be restricted without appropriate decontamination and permission from the authorities.

Response to Possible Terrorist Activity

The veterinarian and animal caretakers have responsibilities to care for production animals (and equipment maintenance) including feeding, transporting to other sites, and monitoring the heath status of the herds or flocks. The USDA administers the National Veterinary Accreditation Program (United States Department of Agriculture 2017b). The mission of the National Veterinary Accreditation Program is to "provide accredited veterinarians with the information they need to ensure the health of the nations' livestock and animal population and to protect the public health and well-being" (United States Department of Agriculture 2017b). The skills of the forensic veterinarian may complement those of the federally accredited veterinarian and it is recommended that the forensic veterinarian, who is interested in the area of agroterrorism and foreign animal diseases, seek to obtain certification as a USDA Accredited Veterinarian.

The person or group that attempts to introduce a biological agent, toxin/poison, or other element to incite fear is committing the criminal act of terrorism. This is similar to other criminal activity seen in the general public forum. The initiation of a terrorist attack may start with the introduction of a foreign animal disease (such as a virus or bacteria). This may be accomplished by use of fomites, an insect vector, or aerosolization of an agent.

The first sign of an untoward act may be the discovery of acute illness among previously healthy stock. The initial investigation must include the recognition of signs of illness that may lead to a suspicion of a FAD. Once an unexpected disease is identified or suspected, the point of introduction of this agent should be investigated (Federal Bureau of Investigation 2008).

The suspicion of a FAD does not automatically imply that a terrorist event has occurred. If a FAD is suspected, the attending veterinarian should follow the recommendations of the USDA accreditation program (United States Department of Agriculture 2017b). According to USDA regulations, any foreign animal disease suspicion must be reported to the USDA and State Veterinary Offices as the USDA or state veterinarians will provide instructions on how to proceed including:

- The infected site may be quarantined
- The person(s) in charge of the care of the animals at the site may be quarantined

- Depending on the disease, all transportation of animals may be halted and any recent transportation of animals from the infected area should be traced
- A perimeter may be established outside the infected zone to restrict visitor and commercial traffic
- Samples should not be collected unless specifically instructed to do so by the federal or state veterinary and agricultural authorities

Should there be a suspicion of terrorist involvement, then collection of the on-site biological and medical information is essential and the purview of the forensic veterinarian in concert with the federal agricultural and law enforcement authorities in charge. Any person investigating, working, or entering the infected zone should use the appropriate personal protective equipment.

During the investigation, it will be important to identify a possible source (point source, case definition) for the disease outbreak to help establish a timeline of events. Review with staff any recent unexpected events or visitors that may have had access to the animals directly, the holding facilities, or pastures. An inspection of the animal facilities for foreign objects such as cloths, bottles, spraying equipment, and vials, is essential to identify any potential source of introduction of an infectious/toxic agent. Any unusual objects should be documented, sketched, protected from the elements, as needed, and photographed without attempts to collect evidence, except by an authorized agent of the USDA or other appropriate lead agency (United States Department of Agriculture 2017b). For more information regarding the documentation of evidence, the reader is referred to Chapter 2 (Crime Scene Investigation).

The identification of an agroterroristic action(s) and the assignment of responsibility for such actions are the purview of law enforcement and other governmental agencies. The potential for economic and human health damage is potentially devastating to both the agricultural industry and the public. This type of crime is one where prevention is as important as the investigation. Studies of events involving emergencies and first responders have been found lacking (Gilpen et al. 2009). There are recommendations that additional educational resources and efforts be mustered to improve first responder abilities (Gilpen et al. 2009). The need for education should include other health care professionals and there have been programs that have attempted to recruit additional health care professionals for human health monitoring after a biological or agroterrorist attack. This represents a transdisciplinary partnership and involves the collaboration between academic institutions and health departments at the local and state levels (McKinney et al. 2005).

Recently, several strategies have been presented for detection and monitoring for potential chemical, biological, radiological, nuclear, and/or explosive attacks (CBRNE) or agricultural terrorist attacks. The ranking of possible biological agents by the risk, availability, and opportunity for disease-causing organisms that may be used as a weapon of terror is one such strategy. Although a large amount of work has been put into the risk assessment of potential bioterroristic biological agents, no universally accepted and generic approach applicable to all fields of impact has been developed (Menrath et al. 2013).

In addition to prevention, the use of early detection systems has been studied. Among these are the use of animals as a detector of zoonotic agents that may be used in agroterrorism (Gubernot et al. 2008; Rabinowitz et al. 2006). Current trends in technology represent some of the promising directions for early disease detection. A review of technology of importance in the early diagnosis in the face of a bioterroristic threat/attack includes the development of detection and diagnostic decision strategies for the terrorism response (Bravata et al. 2004). The use of diagnostic laboratory analysis of DNA to help identify infectious agents or use of biochips are other potential detection strategies. A biochip could be useful in the field and offer advantages compared to conventional identification procedures in the laboratory that are tedious, expensive, and time-consuming (Dutse and Yusof 2011).

The establishment of a timeline is essential to any investigation. This will require interviewing all persons involved with the care of animals. Further, all visitors or commercial vendors should be identified and their contact information recorded. Other investigatory steps will be dependent on the animal species involved, the facility's level of security, and the ability to contain the initial contagion.

Government Agencies

All suspected acts of terrorism are reported to hierarchical levels of government and international agencies. Initial reporting is addressed to the USDA APHIS veterinarian and State Veterinary Office. Reportable diseases are defined nationally by the USDA and internationally by World Organization for Animal Health (OIE) (United States Animal Health Association 2008). In a government report, a joint assessment program was developed. This program is the Strategic Partnership Program Agroterrorism Initiative (SPPA) and allows coordination of multiple federal agencies that collaborate in the conduct of assessments in the food and agricultural sector.

In the event of a suspected terrorist attack, law enforcement will be contacted by the federal and/or state veterinarians. The organizations informed include the U.S. Department of Health and Human Services and the Department of Homeland Security, who may investigate any suspected terrorist attacks. Other agencies that may be involved in the investigation include the FBI, state and municipal law enforcement agencies, and veterinary resources including VMS-homeland security and local veterinary emergency resources (Federal Bureau of Investigation 2008; Gilpen et al. 2009; Hurt 2012; Jayarao 2017; Moats 2007; United States Animal Health Association 2008).

There are several international agencies that monitor the geographical distribution and epidemiology of FADs. Most important among these is the OIE, which monitors disease epidemiology and spread worldwide. The OIE maintains a list of infectious diseases for terrestrial and aquatic animals. These diseases, identified by inclusion on OIE maintained and updated active lists, are reported to member countries for worldwide FAD occurrences (Moats 2007; United States Animal Health Association 2008; World Organization for Animal Health 2017). Another active agency includes the Food and Agriculture Organization of the United Nations (FAO). In 1994, the FAO created the Emergency Prevention System for Transboundary Animal and Plant Pests and Diseases (EMPRES). The FAO functions to give early warning, early reaction enabling research, and coordination of EMPRES activities. These and other international agencies are active in warning and predicting the worldwide incidence and spread of animal disease (Moats 2007; United States Animal Health Association 2008).

Conclusion

In general, it is the responsibility of the veterinarian (clinical or forensic) and animal care personnel to first recognize and identify any signs of an unusual animal disease (particularly a FAD) and/or signs of possible criminal/terrorist activity. The federally assigned veterinarian or state veterinarian has the responsibility to confirm the diagnosis, collect biological specimens for testing, and control animal and resource movement when a FAD is suspected or detected. Biotechnology and prevention strategies will be an essential and integral part of the war against agroterrorism.

It must be recognized that the outbreak of a FAD or occurrence of sudden illness, poisonings, or toxin ingestion may also represent a natural or accidental occurrence. The forensic veterinarian should raise the possibility of criminal activity after reviewing all the available evidence surrounding a disease outbreak.

Though all FADs are investigated under the authority of federal and state authorities, the education received by the forensic veterinarian may be useful in controlling the possible crime scene, investigation of the suspicious actions, documentation of events and evidence surrounding any suspected terrorist attack. This may happen before or, when requested, after the state and federal authorities are on scene.

References

Bravata, D.M., Sundaram, V., McDonald, K.M., Smith, W.M., Szeto, H., Schleinitz, M.D., D.K. Owens. 2004. Evaluating detection and diagnostic decision support systems for bioterrorism response. *Emerg Infect Dis*. 10:100–108.

Chan, P.K.S. 2002. Outbreak of avian influenza A (H5N1) virus infection in Hong Kong in 1997. *Clin Infect Dis*. 34 Suppl 2:558–564.

Dunham, J. and Associates. 2016. 2016 Poultry and egg economic impact study. http://poultry.guerrillaeconomics.net/assets/site/res/Poultry%20Impact%20Methodology.pdf (Accessed April 18, 2017).

Dutse, S.W., N.A. Yusof. 2011. Microfluids-based lab-on-chip systems in DNA-based biosensing: An overview. *Sensors* (Basel). 11:5754–5768.

Federal Bureau of Investigation. 2008. *Criminal Investigation Handbook for Agroterrorism*, pp. 31–42.

Gilpen Jr., J.L., Carabin, H., Regens, J.L., R.W. Burden Jr. 2009. Agriculture emergencies: A primer for first responders. *Biosecur Bioterror.* 7:187–198.

Gubernot, D.M., Boyer, B.L., M.S. Moses. 2008. Animals as early detectors of bioevents: Veterinary tools and a framework for animal-human integrated zoonotic disease surveillance. *Public Health Rep.* 123:300–315.

Hurt, B.J. 2012. Agroterrorism as a potential military threat. BiblioScholar.

Jayarao, B.M. 2017. Agroterrorism: A potential threat to US animal agriculture (Part 1). http://extension.psu.edu/animals/health/biosecurity/fundamentals/agroterrorism-a-potential-threat-to-us-animal-agriculture-i (Accessed April 15, 2017).

Levings, R. L. 2012. Emerging and exotic zoonotic disease preparedness and response in the United States—Coordination of the animal health component. *Zoonosis Public Health* 59(s2):84–90.

McKinney, W.P., Wesley, G.C., Sprang, M.V., A. Troutman. 2005. Educating health professionals to respond to bioterrorism. *Public Health Rep.* 120(Suppl 1):42–47.

Menrath, A., Tomuzia, K., Frentzel, H., Braeunig, J., B. Appel. 2013. Survey of Systems for comparative ranking of agents that pose a bioterroristic threat. *Zoonoses Public Health.* 61:157–166.

Moats, J.B. 2007. *Agroterrorism—A Guide for First Responders.* College Station: Texas A&M University Press.

Monke, J. 2004. Agroterrorism: Threats and preparedness. http//www.congressionalresearch.com/RL3252/document.php?study=Agroterrorism+threats+and+Preparedness (Accessed April 15, 2017).

Morris, G.L. 2007. New kind of war: Are we prepared for agroterrorism? www.dtic.mil/get-tr-doc/pdf?AD=ADA470894 (Accessed April 17, 2017).

National Cattlemen's Beef Association. 2015. Beef industry statistics http://www.beefusa.org/beefindustrystatistics.aspx (Accessed March 23, 2017).

National Oceanic and Atmospheric Administration 2015. Aquaculture. https://www.st.nmfs.noaa.gov/Assets/commercial/fus/fus15/documents/03_%20Aquaculture2015.pdf (Accessed February 21, 2017).

Norton, R. 2014. Agroterrorism–Is the threat real? http://www.southeastfarmpress.com/government/agroterrorism-threat-real (Accessed December 11, 2016).

Office of the Law Revision Counsel. 2017. 50 U.S. Code §2302 (1996), Defense Against Weapons of Mass Destructions Act, Chapter 40 Definitions §2302. http://uscode.house.gov/view.xhtml?path=/prelim@title50/chapter40&edition=prelim (Accessed April 15, 2017).

Rabinowitz, P., Gordon, Z., Chudnov, D., Wilcox, M., Odofin, L., Liu, A., J. Dein. 2006. Animals as sentinels of bioterrorism agents. *Emerg Infect Dis.* 12:647–652.

Rogers, ER. 2003 effects of pasteurella haemolytica on pulmonary vascular adrenergic mechanisms. https://vtechworks.lib.vt.edu/handle/10919/5534/browse?type=author&value=Rogers%2C+Ernest+Reginald (Accessed March 12, 2017).

Taylor, D.L. 2014. Agroterrorism: A looming threat to food supply. http://www.thecalifornian.com/story/news/local/2014/09/12/agroterrorism-looming-threat-food-supply/15541125/ (Accessed December 11, 2016).

United States Animal Health Association. 2008. *Foreign Animal Diseases*, 7th ed. Boca Raton, FL: CRC Press/Taylor & Francis.

United States Department of Agriculture. 2010. Overview of the United States dairy industry. http://usda.mannlib.cornell.edu/usda/current/USDairyIndus/USDairyIndus-09-22-2010.pdf (Accessed March 22, 2017).

United States Department of Agriculture. 2017a. NLRAD-NAHRS Reportable disease list. https://www.aphis.usda.gov/aphis/ourfocus/animalhealth/monitoring-and-surveillance/sa_disease_reporting/ct_disease_list (Accessed March 12, 2017).

United States Department of Agriculture. 2017b. National Veterinary Accreditation Program. https://www.aphis.usda.gov/aphis/ourfocus/animalhealth/nvap (Accessed February 1, 2017).

United States Department of Agriculture Economic Research Service. 2013. Statistics & information. https://www.ers.usda.gov/topics/animal-products/poultry-eggs/statistics-information/ (Accessed April 17, 2017).

United States Government Publishing Office. 2017. United States Code §43 (2006)-Public Law 109-374-Nov 27, 2006 Sec. 2, §43 a. 2. (A) https://www.gpo.gov/fdsys/pkg/STATUTE-120/pdf/STATUTE-120-Pg2652.pdf (Accessed April 15, 2017).

World Organization for Animal Health. 2017. OIE-listed diseases, infections and infestations in force in 2017. http://www.oie.int/en/animal-health-in-the-world/oie-listed-diseases-2017/ (Accessed April 15, 2017).

16

The Judicial System

Jon-Henry Barr

Contents

Introduction

When the two sides in a civil dispute—the plaintiff and the defendant—cannot agree to settle their dispute, then the matter must be resolved in a court after the plaintiff sues the defendant. The courtroom itself is usually the last place where attorneys meet to settle their client's differences. In the courtroom, judges will make legal decisions about what laws govern a dispute, and juries will decide what facts of a dispute are truthful or accurate.

Most often, cases are settled between adverse parties because those parties develop reasonable expectations about what is likely to occur at the conclusion of a trial. A settlement also allows each side to participate in the eventual outcome of a dispute, whereas in a trial, the two sides subject themselves to the whims of the judge and the jury.

In criminal cases, the government prosecutes alleged criminals. At the federal court level, the government is generally represented by prosecutors who are referred to as United States Attorneys. United States Attorneys for each federal court district are appointed by the President and approved by the U.S. Senate (Office of The United States Attorneys 2017). Each U.S. Attorney's Office employs numerous other prosecutors who are Assistant U.S. Attorneys (AUSAs), and these prosecutors actually handle the day-to-day activities involved in bringing criminal charges to court.

At the state level, the prosecutors are usually known as the District Attorney (or "DA"), with the prosecuting attorneys employed by the DA known as Assistant District Attorneys (or "ADAs"). In some states such as Florida, the DA is simply known as the "State's Attorney," and in other states such as New Jersey, the DA is known as the County Prosecutor, whose office will employ numerous "Assistant Prosecutors" (or "APs"). Additionally, in most states the DA is an elected official who serves for a specific term of years, while in others the DA is appointed by the governor for a term. District Attorneys are subject to reelection or reappointment, but their employed ADAs continue their work as civil servants regardless of who is responsible for the policies of their local offices. The same holds true for AUSAs (American Bar Association 2017).

Defense attorneys either hail from private law offices or they work as public defenders. As Constitutional law developed in the United States, our courts have determined that the "right to counsel" in criminal cases includes a right to have an attorney represent defendants who are unable to afford their own private counsel (Legal Information Institute 2017a). Public defenders are often reputed to be less effective than private criminal defense attorneys, but most people familiar with the criminal justice system will acknowledge that public defenders generally serve their clients well due to these attorneys' familiarity with criminal laws and local court systems.

The Courtroom

Inside the courtroom, the judge is typically seated on a raised platform facing the attorneys and the litigants (Figure 16.1). Witnesses who are called to testify will step into the witness stand, usually a chair next to the judge, and will be permitted to testify only after swearing (or affirming) to provide truthful testimony. A court reporter will either electronically or stenographically make a record of the statements made by each person in the courtroom. A bailiff is also present to provide security for the court.

Jury Trials

Our federal Constitution, along with each state's constitution, affords those involved in certain civil disputes as well as those charged with felonies a right to a trial by a jury of one's peers (Legal Information Institute 2017c). However, juries are actually not involved with most cases that are brought to state courts. This is because most civil disputes do not involve a large enough sum of money to warrant a jury trial under our laws, and a "small claims"

Figure 16.1 Example of the interior of a courtroom. The basic elements in the courtroom include the judge, attorneys, and defendant (criminal trial) or plaintiff and defendant (civil trial).

judge is assigned to resolve such disputes. On the criminal side, most offenses charged by police are actually misdemeanors or traffic offenses, which are also adjudicated by local magistrates. Additionally, problems regarding family issues (divorce, alimony, child custody, juvenile crime, etc.) only involve judges and not juries. Finally, courts of equity (for cases involving injunctions or demands for specific performance of a contract) also have no juries.

Bench Trials

Trials without juries, which can also be waived sometimes by litigants in civil and criminal cases, are referred to as "bench trials." In bench trials, the judge serves as both the finder of fact and the decider of applicable law, unlike a jury trial in which the jury alone decides what is the truthful version of the facts of a case. Generally, the Rules of Evidence governing the admissibility of evidence and testimony in court are the same regardless of whether a jury is involved in determining the facts of a given case (American Bar Association 2017).

Witnesses

Witnesses provide testimony and can authenticate physical evidence intended to persuade a jury about the facts of a case. In a serious criminal case, felony charges are initially presented to a "grand jury," which simply determines whether enough probable cause exists to indict a person. Grand juries meet in closed and confidential sessions, where defendants and defense attorneys are not permitted to cross-examine prosecution witnesses. However, for the prosecution to actually convict the defendant of an offense, the prosecution is additionally required to prove the defendant's guilt "beyond a reasonable doubt," and to do so before a petit jury (trial jury), where the prosecution witnesses are subject to cross-examination by the defense.

The two distinct types of witnesses are "fact witnesses" and "expert witnesses." Fact witnesses testify in court about their experiences or observations that would tend to prove or disprove something. Expert witnesses are very different. There are three categories of expert witnesses: fact expert, opinion expert, and consulting expert (Frederickson 2016). Expert witnesses are individuals with specialized education, knowledge, or training ("expertise") that enables them to express opinions or draw conclusions based upon their expertise. An expert witness must have his or her qualifications heard by the court prior to being recognized as an expert by the judge, and those qualifications are subject to challenge by the opposing party. Courts will subject veterinary expert witnesses as they would any other expert witness when deciding whether to allow their testimony (Janssen 2007).

Although doctors are often known to serve as expert witnesses, expert witnesses can hail from any recognized profession. An attorney utilizing an expert witness to prove a case will elicit testimony from that expert, which not only establishes the expert's credentials in terms of education, training, and experience, but also to show that the expert is very knowledgeable, thorough, and free from bias or prejudice. Conversely, an opposing attorney will cross-examine the same expert in an effort to minimize the expert's level of education, training, or experience, and possibly demonstrate an inadequate review of relevant facts, taking of "shortcuts," or perhaps a bias or inclination to a predetermined conclusion. A good attorney will also conduct a comprehensive investigation into an expert's background and history to determine if any previous activities or statements could damage the credibility of the expert.

Assisting Counsel as an Expert Witness

An expert witness will typically review a set of facts and then render a written report or opinion about those facts. The expert will usually charge a fee for the report, as well as charge an additional fee for any testimony needed in court. The report is provided to the adverse party or adverse counsel as part of discovery, but the report itself is actually hearsay and inadmissible as evidence unless the expert provides testimony or is subjected to cross-examination, in order to support whatever opinions or conclusions are contained in the report.

Discovery itself is the information and supporting documentation, photographs, audiotapes, videotapes, and related materials that tend to prove or disprove facts presented by one of the parties to a case. In a criminal case, although it is usually the prosecution that must provide discovery to the defense, which substantiates the guilt of a defendant, the prosecution can also demand "reciprocal discovery" from the defense, which might exculpate or alleviate any apparent guilt of that defendant (Legal Information Institute 2017b).

For expert testimony to be admissible in court, the credentials of the expert must be established by the attorney calling that expert. A person can be legally recognized by a judge in the court where the expert's testimony is to be heard. Such recognition is based upon the person demonstrating a level of education, training, and/or experience that gives the person a high degree of knowledge with a subject, which knowledge is "beyond the knowledge of an average juror" (Legal Information Institute 2017b).

Regardless of whether an expert witness is being called by the prosecution (or plaintiff in a civil case) or the defense, it is important to communicate with the attorney who hired the expert. What, exactly, is the attorney looking to accomplish with the expert's testimony? In any medical context, opinion by veterinarians must be provided "within a reasonable degree of medical certainty." If a doctor cannot offer an opinion within a reasonable degree of medical certainty, the doctor's opinion will not be accepted in any court of law. In a veterinary context, can the doctor establish a causation between any signs or symptoms exhibited by an animal and any conduct by humans or other animals? An opinion establishing causation may be countered by another expert who rejects causation, at which point the court's "finder of facts" determines which expert is more credible. In a jury trial, the "finder of facts" is the jury. The judge decides the law that applies to the case, but the judge does not decide who is telling the truth and who is not. In a bench trial, as noted previously, the judge performs both roles.

Evidence

Evidence consists of either testimony or physical evidence; the physical evidence can be films, pictures, audio or videotapes, or any tangible objects. In a criminal case, such tangible objects are often drugs, weapons, or stolen property, and such physical evidence is required to be adequately secured to prevent contamination and ensure that such evidence can be properly tested scientifically, if necessary. To do that, law enforcement officers are trained in procedures to gather evidence, transport and preserve it, including documenting a "chain of custody." A chain of custody is an itemization of exactly who handled the evidence, when it was handled, and where it was stored and/or transported.

If a police officer or government agent cannot account for the whereabouts of, or control over, an item of evidence, then a defendant might exploit that deficiency. A "break" in the chain of custody can imply contamination of the evidence and therefore create a "reasonable doubt" about a defendant's guilt. If physical evidence is damaged or destroyed, a claim of "spoliation" can be made in which "spoiled" evidence can result in a judge instructing a jury to make a negative inference because of that spoliation. At worst, a judge might exclude the evidence altogether, potentially completely disabling a case from going forward.

In criminal matters, evidence is often obtained because of police investigations, which leads to applications for search warrants or the issuance of subpoenas. A Subpoena Duces Tecum is a subpoena for documents or tangible things, whereas a Subpoena Ad Testificandum is a subpoena for live testimony. If, for example, the execution of a search warrant causes the police to need telephone records, they will try to subpoena the telephone records. Those records would presumably reveal which telephone numbers were called, but the nature of such calls would be unknown without testimony from a person who participated in the calls. Once a person is testifying in court, that person is generally prohibited from describing a specific statement made by someone else, which is considered "hearsay," if that statement is being offered to prove the truth of the matter being asserted. There are exceptions to the hearsay prohibition, such as those which permit the admission of "excited utterances" (i.e., "Don't shoot me!") or dying declarations (i.e., saying "Frank stabbed me" just before the declarant dies). Otherwise, hearsay is simply any statement made by someone other than the witness, which statement is used to prove the truth of the matter asserted. While there are numerous exceptions to the hearsay prohibition, as an example it generally means that a witness cannot say, "Mary told me that she saw the defendant robbing the bank." If the prosecutor wants Mary's observations provided to the court, the prosecutor will have to bring in Mary as a witness.

The Rules of Evidence are very complicated and may vary somewhat depending on jurisdiction. However, the legal arguments that attorneys have made over centuries of litigation in American courts have resulted in a body of case law that is far too complex to summarize in a chapter like this one. Suffice it to say that the law is constantly evolving, and that what is or is not hearsay will never be completely answered.

Animal Cruelty Laws

Animal cruelty laws are most frequently found on the books of state statutes, and these laws may differ significantly from state to state. In some places, these laws are only enforced by animal protection law enforcement officers, while in other places any law enforcement officer can bring a charge for such misconduct. Even within a single state, there are different laws applicable to livestock, pets, and wild animals, and a veterinarian should be familiar with these legal regulatory schemes and their differences. Due to the complex nature of animal regulations, specialized training is often preferred for those who actually enforce these laws. Additionally, due to the continual evolution of law, it is important to review official sources for the most current language of any statute (Animal Legal Defense Fund 2017).

Because few attorneys practice law in the area of animal issues, it is not unusual for veterinarians and other animal professionals to teach attorneys about what laws are applicable to a given set of facts. Attorneys unfamiliar with animal statutes and regulations should welcome instruction from non-attorneys who are familiar with such laws, but if the time comes to present a case in court, the lawyer should be relied upon for the proper presentation of the testimony.

Conclusion

Regardless of a person's role in an animal cruelty investigation, knowledge of the judicial system is of major importance. Laws will vary by jurisdiction; the basic principles of jury trials, bench trials, and witness testimony are similar. This knowledge will allow the investigator to be prepared for potential testimony in court, have an understanding of the different types of witnesses, and have an understanding of the different types of evidence.

Note: Much of the information in this chapter is based on the author's experience as a practicing attorney and municipal prosecutor in New Jersey.

References

American Bar Association. 2017. How court works. http://www.americanbar.org/groups/public_education/resources/law_related_education_network/how_courts_work/court_role.html (Accessed April 1, 2017).

Animal Legal Defense Fund. Animal protection laws of the United States and Canada. http://aldf.org/resources/advocating-for-animals/animal-protection-laws-of-the-united-states-of-america-and-canada/ (Accessed April 4, 2017).

Frederickson, R. 2016. Demystifying the courtroom: Everything the veterinary pathologist needs to know about testifying in an animal cruelty case. *Vet Pathol.* 53:888–893.

Janssen, L.A. 2007. The legal system and the veterinarian's role. In *Veterinary Forensics: Animal Cruelty Investigations*, ed. M.D. Merck, pp. 3–1. Ames, IA: Blackwell.

Legal Information Institute. 2017a. *Gideon v. Wainwright*. https://www.law.cornell.edu/supremecourt/text/372/335 (Accessed April 8, 2017).

Legal Information Institute. 2017b. Rule 702. Testimony by expert witnesses. https://www.law.cornell.edu/rules/fre/rule_702 (Accessed April 4, 2017).

Legal Information Institute. 2017c. Sixth Amendment. https://www.law.cornell.edu/constitution/sixth_amendment (Accessed April 8, 2017).

Office of the United States Attorneys. https://www.justice.gov/usao/about-offices-united-states-attorneys (Accessed April 5, 2017).

17

Expert Witness Testimony and Report Writing

Ernest R. Rogers and Adam W. Stern

Contents

Introduction

The veterinarian, whether a general practitioner or forensic investigator, may be requested to become involved with a criminal or civil investigation. The request may include performing a forensic clinical examination, forensic necropsy, collection of crime scene evidence, examination of medical records, or interpretation of other forensic information. The veterinarian may then be asked to give either oral testimony or possibly a written report. In some instances, the testimonial information may be restricted to observation of facts in the performance of one's clinical duties or it may be expanded to include the conclusions and opinions related to a forensic examination. Oral testimony may occur in one of several venues including a deposition at a lawyer's office or in a courtroom setting in a criminal or civil proceeding. Testimony may be as a witness limited to the observed clinical facts and events (testifying witness) or testimony may include clinical events, conclusions, and opinions as to the significance of the clinical facts (expert witness). Additionally, case involvement may include report writing, which may be submitted to the court.

There are benefits and pitfalls to being an expert witness in court. The role of any witness in court is to provide observations, facts, and evidence to the court. The role of an expert witness, such as a forensic veterinarian, is to present evidence and opinions to the court in the context of current acceptable science and medicine. We, as forensic veterinarians, are only interested in facts as presented by the collected evidence. We are not interested in justice or injustice, guilt or innocence, conviction or acquittal. We only gather, examine, analyze, and present the facts or evidence in an unbiased manner for the court or jury to make decisions.

The courtroom is an adversarial forum. In many situations, the prosecutor (criminal case) or the plaintiff's lawyer (civil case) will attempt to discredit the client and any witnesses (testifying or expert) associated with the opposition. Thus, any statements or attempts to undermine a witness's education, credentials, or personal opinions must not be taken personally. The advantage to the expert witness is that, often, the time spent in court allows the individual to better appreciate the nature and process of the justice system.

Veterinarians are educated in both the processes of deductive and inductive reasoning, basic sciences (chemistry, biology, and physics), biomedical sciences, and medical sciences. Many cases involving animal crimes necessitate an understanding of animal behavior, internal medicine, pathology, toxicology, pharmacology, radiology, and surgery. Our background as a veterinarian prepares us well to assist in the clarification of complicated biomedical facts which ultimately will allow for the court to better understand the essential facts of any case. This then will allow laypersons (judiciary, jury, and lawyers) to accurately assign legal significance to the biomedical facts and then assign the appropriate evidentiary and legal weight to the issues in question. We, as scientists, are only interested in the facts as they are pertinent to the legal case in question.

Testifying Witness and the Expert Witness

There are two main types of witnesses, testifying or fact witness (a witness who testifies about directly observed facts related to the case), and the expert witness.

Testifying (Fact) Witness

The fact witness is one who enters court to give testimony of what was observed or gathered directly by the person offering the testimony. This elocution may be either before a judge (bench trial) (Figure 17.1), jurors (jury trial) (Figure 17.2),

Figure 17.1 The judge usually sits behind a raised desk (bench) in the courtroom. The judge mediates and adjudicates all aspects of the trial. In a bench trial, testimony should be directed to the judge. If there is an objection by a lawyer, the witness should stop the testimony until the judge has decided on the issue.

Figure 17.2 The jury is composed of local citizens who are selected by lawyers on both sides of the issue (Voir-Dire). Once accepted as an expert witness, the witness will be judged by the jury based on their professionalism, appearance, diction, and grammar. It is important to maintain visual contact with the jurors as much as possible. In a jury trial, testimony should be directed to the members of the jury.

or in a deposition. In some cases, there is some leniency with the court for conversations overheard by a testifying witness (hearsay evidence). Depositions are usually held at an attorney's office and may be requested by either side. These are often done to allow the attorneys to preview and assess the veracity of the information to be presented, to attempt to intimidate and challenge the expert, or to collect information that may disclose the legal strategy of the opposition. A deposition involves the litigating attorneys, the witness, and a stenographer to record the proceedings. Similar to testimony in a courtroom, the witness is asked questions by the opposition attorney. The discussions can be cordial; however, the witness's consulting attorney is there to guide the witness, ensure that proper questioning guidelines are followed, and assist with the progression of the testimony.

Expert Witness

A witness is only considered an expert when acceptable to the bench (judge) and deemed an expert often limited to their field of testimony, as defined by the judge (Talve 2012). A potential expert witness can be questioned and challenged by the opposing counsel as to their qualifications based on the submitted professional resume or curriculum vitae. These challenges are often an attempt to make the witness appear less credible as to their expert ability to be an interpreter of the scientific and medical facts for the case at hand. The questions asked by the opposing attorney may lead to a harsh, confrontational session that can leave the uninitiated expert shaken. This, of course, is the goal of the opposing counsel. After hearing opposing counsel's questions and follow-up, the judge may declare an individual an expert witness for the trial at hand or simply declare the witness as a testifying witness. The expert witness may be hired by either side in a case, or appointed by the judge to assist in the evaluation of the evidence collected and presented before the court.

Once declared an expert witness by the court, the veterinarian is then, based on education and background, allowed to interpret evidence, render conclusions, and give opinions about the facts of the case (Figure 17.3). Any scientist, veterinarian, or forensic investigator, who is presented as an expert witness, should be prepared for the critical scrutiny of their submitted resume or curriculum vitae. Guidelines suggest a minimum of 10 years of professional activities prior to the date of the testimony (Babinsky and Mangravitti 2004). These should include professional activities including forensic testimony, investigations, teaching, research experience, and education. It is important to recognize that any published or publicly captured opinions (radio, television, scientific articles, social media sites, or electronic blogs) may serve as grounds for a witness challenge. These challenges may be based on personal credibility, reputation, expertise or issues related to bias, conflict of duty, or prejudice. One must be aware that often previously published, unqualified, or dogmatic statements made by a witness may be used to further impeach

Figure 17.3 This is the view from a witness box looking at people (members of the public) seated in the spectator area of the courtroom.

an expert's testimony (Nordsby 2005). The resume or curriculum vitae of the witness is made available to all parties involved in the case and should encompass a complete list of professional activity (Civil Justice Council 2009; Daley 1996). One should be familiar with one's resume review including all public and social media events that are associated with the veterinarian.

The statements made by an expert witness will be used to help to assess the significance and legal weight of the forensic and biomedical evidence within the scope of the trial. Further, the expert witness may give facts that are both known to him personally (observed or obtained by examination of the animal and/or evidence) and those derived through medical or scientific analysis and conclusions. Expert witnesses are expected to discuss both the facts and opinions that are limited strictly to the case without bias, or to coin an old phrase, "the facts ma'am, just the facts." An expert witness can give an opinion based on their examination of the facts, witness statements, medical reports/documentation, and police reports (the totality of the evidence and documentation) for the case. To make statements or give opinions that exceed one's documented expertise can compromise a case. All opinions must be based on appropriate, well grounded, accepted scientific fact (e.g., Frye or Daubert tests and the Federal Rules of Evidence).

The veterinary expert witness must also be aware of the limits associated with evidence collection and presentation, the legal issues of the court (chain of custody, evidence acceptance, the limits of evidence collection, and expert witness conclusions) and the basic legal means for the development of a criminal or civil case. The expertise of a veterinarian in court should be considered with respect to their education, professional activities, and the documented experience that one may have acquired as a result of working in their given field.

The duties of the expert witness include the following (Civil Justice Counsel 2009):

1. Exercise reasonable skill and care with respect to professional codes
2. Maintain perspective with court's objectives
3. Give independent opinions
4. Confine opinions to the judicial matters directly related to the case
5. Consider all material facts and literature
6. Inform the court of any changes of opinion immediately
7. Conform with all procedural and judicial rules and instructions

When consulting with an attorney, all oral communications are privileged and therefore are not available for reciprocal discovery. Reciprocal discovery is the legal requirement for all written evidence, correspondence, investigative reports, notes, and emails to be submitted to the opposing counsel for review. Therefore, when advising on a case, it is prudent to discuss the way in which reports and any other exchange of information will occur. A single email or written letter may compromise a case. In our experience, after reviewing the facts and evidence of the case, defense attorneys prefer oral/telephone reports, whereas, most prosecutors involved in cases prefer to be presented with written reports. The rational for this is that in the indictment or prosecution of a suspect the prosecutor has, based on the evidence and investigation, decided to pursue the case. On the other hand, the defense is notified of the prosecution's intent to indict or press charges and may be seeking to verify the strength of the evidence against his client while seeking information on which to base a defense.

One important issue, with respect to giving testimony, is to recognize the limits of one's expertise and the need to develop working relationships with other forensic experts and lawyers. It is important to review and discuss the testimony one will give under oath with the hiring attorney. The veterinary witness may interact and call for assistance of other forensic experts including forensic veterinarians, toxicologists, pharmacologists, pathologists, ballistic evidence experts, trace evidence experts, and others. When the assessment of the evidence is beyond their expertise, it is appropriate to inform the attorney that another expert might be required. Limiting the answers to those questions that are within our scope of knowledge, experience, and expertise is important as it supports our credibility as an expert witness.

Consulting Expert

Another type of expert is the consulting expert, who while behind the scenes, counsels an attorney on the scientific and medical facts of a case, without committing to testify in court or in a deposition. This expert will assist in preparation for discovery and depositions (including helping the attorney prepare questions for opposing witnesses). A consulting expert will not likely submit a written report or be required for courtroom or deposition testimony. It is important to note that a consulting expert is confidential and not disclosed to opposing counsel. Consulting experts cannot be deposed nor can they be retained by opposing counsel.

Guidelines for Courtroom Testimony

Many animal abuse criminal cases are handled in municipal courts; some may be elevated to state courts though very few will be tried in federal courts. Nonetheless, the expert witness should be aware of three important decisions that govern expert witness testimony. Two guidelines include the Frye Test and the Daubert Test. Both these judicial tests are based on case law and relate to the validity of scientific evidence, opinion, and testimony in the court. The two tests or standards may be cited as guidelines for acceptance of scientific testimony in the state, county, or municipal court. These lower courts may accept either Daubert or Frye tests or a combination of the two. Not all courts submit to either of these guidelines and some have rules and guidelines for the admission of scientific evidence or opinion that are derived from the jurisdiction debate. Although briefly discussed below, there are differences between these two standards but this goes beyond the scope of this chapter. A third standard is one that governs the scientific and expert witness testimony in federal court (and is accepted by some lower courts); this is known as the Federal Rules of Evidence (FRE) (Federal Rules of Evidence 2015).

These standards have been set in an attempt to eliminate unsubstantiated, unfounded, or biased "junk" science from being presented in court as fact. These guidelines serve to test or define the criteria for the veracity, acceptability, and credibility of the witness, the scientific evidence, analysis, and opinions presented. Further, the Daubert test and the FRE also define some of the qualifications necessary to be an expert witness in a court of law. Every witness should be aware of the guidelines that are used in the court (municipal, state, or federal) in which they are to testify. A basic review of the appropriate rules is strongly recommended before trial to be an effective and credible expert witness. Should there be no articulated rules for the court, the expert witness is advised to use FRE as a guidepost for expert testimony. Failing to be aware or follow these guidelines may expose the witness to assertions of bias and perjury, and could result in wholly or partially discredited testimony, and/or ruined professional reputation at a minimum and civil or criminal liability at the worst.

Frye Test

The "Frye Test" is one consideration for the admission of scientific evidence (*Frye v. United States*, 293 F. 1013 [D.C. Cir. 1923]). This set of guidelines was one of the first in the United States and is considered to be "The General Acceptance Test." This is to say that any scientific evidence presented in court must pass legal muster by virtue of its long established general acceptance in the scientific community. This test neither defines the length of time nor gives a definition to the term "general acceptance." The Frye standard, though older in the administration of jurisprudence, is still referred to in some courts as a standalone guidance or in combination with other statutes.

Daubert Test

The "Daubert Test or Standard" for admission of scientific evidence in court is based on case law and is more commonly used in the lower courts. This standard is based on a trilogy of cases that in total form the basis and define the Daubert Standard (*Daubert v. Merrill Dow Pharmaceuticals Inc.*, 509 U.S. 579 [1993], *General Electric Co. v. Joiner*, 522 U.S. 136 [1997], and *Kumho Tire Co. v. Carmichael* 526 U.S. 137 [1999]). Any party involved in the adjudication or trying of a case at trial may raise a "Daubert Motion." This challenge is to exclude the scientific evidence based on lack of basis or may be challenged to the expert's opinion as to the lack of scientific expertise forming the basis of the opinion or testimony (Calhoun 2008).

Federal Rules of Evidence (FRE)

The FRE are a more in-depth set of standards (Federal Rules of Evidence 2015). These guidelines are used primarily by the federal court system. Some lower courts have dispensed with other standards and use the FRE or a permutation of all mentioned standards of scientific acceptance as well. The FRE encompasses multiple scenarios that may arise with an expert witness's testimony. Though all FRE segments pertain to evidence, not all are equally relevant to the veterinary scientific expert witness. Select rules are briefly outlined in Table 17.1.

The most significant FRE are those contained in Article VII. The rules in Article VII pertain to opinions and expert testimony. It is within FRE 701 and 702 that differentiate the types of testimony a lay witness and expert witness can give. Rule 701 states that if the lay witness is not testifying as an expert, then their testimony in the form of an opinion is limited to one that is rational based on the witness's perception, is helpful to clarify facts, understand the given testimony by the witness, and is not based on scientific or other specialized knowledge (Legal Information Institute 2017). In contrast, Rule 702 states that an expert witness is one who is qualified by knowledge, skill, experience, training, or education and this witness may give an opinion if the opinion will help the trier of fact (judge or jury) better understand the evidence, testimony is based on sufficient facts or data, the testimony is based on reliable scientific principles and methods, and the expert has readily applied the principles and methods to the facts of the case (Legal Information Institute 2017).

The most expedient method of establishing the parameters within which the testimony may be given is to discuss the matter openly with the attorney with whom one is working.

Table 17.1 Summary of Select Federal Rules of Evidence

Federal Rule of Evidence	Summary of the Rule
Rule 104	The court must decide on any preliminary questions about whether a witness is qualified, a privilege exists, or the evidence is admissible.
Rule 105	If the court admits evidence that is admissible against a party but not another party, the court must restrict the scope (use) of evidence and must so instruct the jury.
Rule 201	This rule governs judicial notice of adjudicative facts. The court may rule evidence as appropriate without further consideration, if the facts are generally known within the trial court's territorial jurisdiction or the facts can be accurately and readily determined as accurate.
Rule 401	Evidence is relevant if: it has the tendency to make a fact more or less probable than it would be without the evidence and if the fact (evidence) is of consequence in determining an action of the court.
Rule 402	Relevant evidence is admissible unless it violates the U.S. Constitution, a federal statute, the Federal Rules of Evidence, and other rules prescribed by the U.S. Supreme Court.
Rule 403	Evidence may be excluded for unfair prejudice, confusing the issues, misleading the jury (in a jury trial), undue delay, wasting time, or needlessly presenting cumulative evidence.
Rule 603	A witness must give an oath or affirmation to testify truthfully—before testifying.
Rule 607	Any party including the party calling the witness may impeach the witness (attack the credibility of the witness).
Rule 608	A witness's character for truthfulness or untruthfulness—a witness's credibility may be attacked or supported by a witness's character and specific incidences of conduct may on cross-examination be inquired about.
Rule 609	Defines when a party may use evidence of a prior conviction in order to impeach a witness.
Rule 610	A witness's religious beliefs or opinions are not admissible grounds to attack the veracity of the testimony or evidence.

(*Continued*)

Table 17.1 (Continued) Summary of Select Federal Rules of Evidence

Federal Rule of Evidence	Summary of the Rule
Rule 611	The court has control of the scope of the witness's testimony, cross-examination should not go beyond the subject matter, and leading questions are not to be used during direct examination (with some exceptions).
Rule 615	A witness may be excluded from the proceeding of the court (at the request of any party including the court) involved in the case.
Rule 701	The lay witness is not testifying as an expert, then their testimony in the form of an opinion is limited to one that is rational based on the witness's perception, is helpful to understand the given testimony by the witness, and is not based on scientific or other specialized knowledge.
Rule 702	The expert witness is one who is qualified by knowledge, skill, experience, training or education and this witness may give an opinion if the opinion will help the trier of fact (judge or jury) better understand the evidence, testimony is based on sufficient facts or data, the testimony is based on reliable scientific principles and methods, and the expert has readily applied the principles and methods to the facts of the case.
Rule 703	An expert may base their opinion on facts or data of which the expert is personally aware or observed.
Rule 704	Testimony in the form of an opinion is not objectionable because it embraces an ultimate issue.
Rule 706	The court appointed expert witness is an expert who is called by the judiciary to clarify points of a case.
Rule 801	Hearsay means a statement that the person who made the statement does not make it while testifying (at the current proceedings) and a party offers evidence in the truth of the matter asserted in the statement.
Rule 802	Hearsay is not admissible unless acceptable under the Federal Rules of Evidence, federal statute, or based on rules of the U.S. Supreme Court. Hearsay is loosely defined as the repeating of an oral utterance, a written document, or a person's nonverbal conduct.

Source: Legal Information Institute. 2017. Federal Rules of Evidence. https://www.law.cornell.edu/rules/fre (Accessed April 20, 2017).

Risks, Liabilities, and Benefits of Assisting the Legal System

There are many considerations before entering into a relationship with a lawyer in the capacity of a consultant or expert witness. As veterinarians, we must be cognizant that there are both liabilities and benefits to courtroom testimony. A veterinarian may testify on behalf of the prosecution or defense attorney. It is important to remember that courtroom testimony that is well founded in scientific fact and is without prejudice or bias is the best defense to being challenged for accuracy or veracity.

In many states there are laws requiring the reporting of animal abuse or cruelty that, in many cases, based on the professional's experience make it incumbent to report the case to the local authorities. In some of these states there are also legal no-fault protection for those who report suspected abuse; however, this is not true in all states and jurisdictions (Animal Legal Defense Fund 2014).

Where there is legal protection for the reporting of suspected animal abuse, there may be other methods for professional protection (professional liability insurance). Veterinary malpractice insurance covers many situations that the average veterinarian may encounter in the practice of veterinary medicine. This same coverage may include a consulting relationship that includes assisting law enforcement. It is recommended that the practitioner check with their malpractice carrier to understand any limitations or concerns before assisting with an investigation. Reviewing local and state laws as they pertain to reporting animal abuse and liability protection is recommended (Animal Legal Defense Fund 2014, 2016). Courtroom testimony, which is well founded in current, acceptable scientific fact, that is without prejudice or bias is the best defense to being challenged in court.

Though not common, there have been incidents of retaliation against a reporting veterinarian both for reporting a suspected abusive client and for not reporting animal cruelty (Animal Legal Defense Fund 2014). The obvious casualty after reporting abuse could, potentially, be your practice, as rumors are spread to current clients and prospective clients. One must realize that many animal cruelty cases have a "high public emotional quotient" (American Society for the Prevention of Cruelty to Animals 2012; Bennet 2016; Rifkin 2015). These often incite vocal protests, high profile news coverage, and undesired press coverage. The best protection for the veterinarian, in these situations, is to have a working relationship with the local Animal Control Officer, the Humane Law Enforcement Officers ("animal cops"), and other law enforcement officials in the community. Law enforcement, humane law enforcement, animal control, and animal investigation officers are, in most cases, protected under the employing municipalities blanket insurance coverage and by exception from legal liability when performing their legal job without malicious prosecution or intentional false arrest. In general, the civil authorities have more comprehensive liability coverage than forensic veterinarians.

In general, as veterinary professionals, we recognize that conflicts of interest are possible particularly when a local veterinarian, in a limited geographical area, is asked to testify either for the prosecution or the defense. These conflicts may or may not be obvious. The impartial status of an expert witness dictates that there are no conflicts of interest among the prosecution, related involved parties, and the accused. Furthermore, there should not have been a conflicting relationship between the witness and the plaintiff, defendant, the court, prosecutor, or the defense attorney. Other considerations include the sanctity of a Veterinarian-Client-Patient relationship. Relationships among veterinarians are more difficult to assess for conflicts of interest. Suffice it to say that should the collegial relationship between veterinarians extend to a personal relationship, and that veterinarian is a litigant in the proceedings, then likely a conflict exists. Other sources of conflict include possible relationships among litigants either by blood, marriage, or adoption. Always identify if the expert witness is associated with (e.g., director, consultant, agent, or employee) any company or individual either related to the plaintiff or defendant. Before forming an expert witness opinion, recognize that reviewing media or news footage may be a source of prejudice. Social media reports, postings, and blogs are also potential sources of prejudicial reporting. These activities may be questioned in court.

In some cases, expert witnesses are compensated for the time spent preparing a report, discussing a case, and preparation for testimony but never for their conclusions or opinions. It is recommended that a written contract be signed and agreed to by all parties to ensure a meeting of the minds with respect to terms, payment, and accessibility. The consultant should review potential contracts in advance, with an attorney. There are numerous expert witness contracts available on the Internet, and personalizing these documents for the consultant is imperative. In other cases, when working for the prosecution, the prosecutor or judge may offer remuneration to compensate for time in court, writing a report, or completing an investigation. These offers should be confirmed in writing.

The news media often follows and becomes involved in newsworthy animal abuse cases. As a forensic investigator, there may be interactions with the popular media. News media can be deceptive in their approach to a possible information source. Reporters may approach, presenting themselves as an interested citizen, simply asking questions. As an expert witness, the best answer to any question is "no comment" and then offer a referral to the appropriate law enforcement officer, lawyer, or judicial authority. Once one is recognized as being involved in a case, any comment made by an expert witness may jeopardize a legal strategy or compromise a trial verdict.

The Written Report

When requested, an expert may be asked for a written report to be submitted to counsel. The expert report should be as concise as possible. The language used should be descriptive and understandable to the layperson. Avoid the use of medical shorthand without definition or explanation. Once submitted the expert should be aware that there may be a judicial mandate that they appear in court to defend their report. The report is a recitation of the facts, conclusions, and opinions pertinent to the case at hand. It is recommended that the expert ask for a specific list of questions that the hiring attorney wants answered in the written report.

Reports may be completed in several different formats. The report, in general, if more than 3–5 pages should include an executive summary, which is a brief summary of the opinions and conclusions in the report and is limited to several paragraphs. When appropriate there should be an index or table of contents in the report. There should be a section that lists all the testimony, police reports, witness reports, deposition transcripts, photographs, and any other evidence that was reviewed when drawing conclusions, forming opinions, or writing the report. This serves to give notice of the pertinent evidence reviewed.

The expert witness would be wise to give a brief overview of their credentials (such as education and training) and refer the reader to their resume/curriculum vitae in the appendix at the end of the report. This will be reviewed by opposition counsel and the judiciary (Federal Evidence Review 2015; Munroe 2013).

A review of the significant evidence, in narrative form, should be given as concisely as possible. All statements of fact or conclusions based on scientific papers should be cited in the report and listed in an appropriate scientific format (author, year, title, etc.) in the reference section at the end of the document. For credibility, the dates of the references should reflect the most current scientific literature. It is important to include multiple sources for scientific support. Any conclusions should be brief and directed to the point of each statement. Multiple significant issues may be made in point form. Any pertinent documents or pictures of significant evidentiary value can be included in the appendix.

Overall, the conclusions should represent the most objective view of the facts and evidence presented. In no case should the conclusions, drawn from a review of the evidence, exceed the breadth and significance of the observations or evidence available. Over-interpretation of the evidence may result in dismissal of the report and loss of reputation and integrity of the expert.

Any submitted report will be reviewed by the consulting attorney to ensure the language, syntax, and medical/scientific terms in the report can be understood by laypersons. In no case should the opinions or conclusions of the report be changed to meet an attorney's expectation. A good rule of thumb is the inclusion of a statement in the context of the report that explicitly states that the "opinions of this report are given free of coercion," and "conclusions are given in concordance with the accepted, most current medical, forensic, and scientific evidence available to date." Further, it is recommended to include a statement reflecting the author's interpretation of the available evidence. An example is "the author of this report reserves the right to edit, amend, alter, or modify this report in any manner or alter this report based on any additional information or evidence that is provided that may change the opinions and conclusions contained in this report."

The report is a signature of one's credibility, and as such should be free of spelling and grammatical errors. Further, the testifying witness must be aware of the legal elements of chain of custody, search and seizure laws, limits of information from interviews and interrogations to avoid the use of inappropriate evidence collected by others. For example, in New Jersey the forensic investigator or testifying witness is responsible for maintenance of the investigatory notes and evidence collected or examined. This requirement may vary from state to state or country to country so the reader is advised to consult with law enforcement professionals or the prosecutor to ensure complete understanding of their responsibilities under the law as an expert witness or forensic investigator offering an opinion report.

Finally, every expert witness should be aware of some of the potential frailties of forensic evidence presentation and testimony. Subjective bias, conclusion expectation bias, and other issues may lead to prejudiced testimony (Gutheil and Simon 2004). These concerns may be alleviated using well-accepted scientific articles accessed from professional refereed journals and relevant textbooks. The scope of expert testimony allows the witness the latitude to critically evaluate articles, which are available outside the realm of professional journals, and then include these in their opinions with justification.

Conclusion

Veterinarians, as medical professionals, can be instrumental in the assistance in forensic investigations with respect to animal involved criminal activity. When performing our duties during these investigations we are exposed to personal and professional risk. Actions that may be requested by law enforcement officials include the gathering of biomedical or toxicological evidence, assessment of the animal's injuries, assessment of the cause of death, and testimony in court. Though difficult for the neophyte veterinarian, experience in forensics and becoming familiar with the legal processes and procedures may be obtained through additional education and course work. Experience will foster excellence in performance during a forensic investigation, report writing, and courtroom testifying.

Table 17.2 lists several pointers that will allow the veterinarian to prepare to be a testifying witness. The rule of thumb for a veterinarian testifying is as follows: a veterinarian, acting in the capacity as an expert witness, is to use his or her education, scientific and medical knowledge to bring to light pertinent facts of the legal case so that issues that may otherwise be misinterpreted or overlooked by the layperson with respect to the development of the truth are elucidated appropriately without bias.

Table 17.2 General Guidelines for the Expert Witnesses
Has an ethical obligation to assist in the administration of justice
Fee should not be contingent upon the outcome of the case
Compensation should be reasonable and commensurate with time and effort
Must not be an advocate or partisan for either party
Should have recent substantive experience in the area of expertise
Should be adequately prepared for testimony
Should have unbiased opinions
Use opinions based on the medical literature
Opinions based on experience should be clearly defined
Should testify honestly and truthfully without excluding any relevant information
Should avoid conflicts of interest, either actual or potential, with the client or attorneys
Should protect the privacy of records and communications

Source: American College of Legal Medicine. Guidelines on the Ethical Conduct of the Expert Witness. http://c.ymcdn.com/sites/aclm.site-ym.com/resource/resmgr/Docs/ACLM-Expert-Witness-Guidelin.pdf (Accessed March 2, 2017).

References

American Society for the Prevention of Cruelty to Animals. 2012. ASPCA Research shows Americans overwhelmingly support investigations to expose animal abuse on industrial farms. https://www.aspca.org/about-us/press-releases/aspca-research-shows-americans-overwhelmingly-support-investigations-expose (Accessed March 21, 2017).

Animal Legal Defense Fund. 2014. Rankings Stat Sheet 2014: Category 10 - Veterinarian Reporting/Immunity. http://aldf.org/wp-content/uploads/2013/04/Vet-reporting-chart-2014.pdf (Accessed February 15, 2017).

Animal Legal Defense Fund. 2016. Animal Protection Laws of the United States of America and Canada. http://aldf.org/resources/advocating-for-animals/animal-protection-laws-of-the-united-states-of-america-and-canada/ (Accessed February 15, 2017).

Babinsky, S., Mangravitti, J.J. 2004. Introduction. In *Writing and Defending Your Expert Report*, Falmouth, MA: SEAK Inc. Publishers, p. 5.

Bennet, B. 2016. Get tougher on animal cruelty. http://www.publicopiniononline.com/story/opinion/2016/07/29/get-tougher-animal-cruelty/87707942/ (Accessed January 17, 2017).

Calhoun, M.C. 2008. Scientific evidence in court: Daubert or Frye, 15 years later. *Legal Backgrounder.* 23:1–4.

Civil Justice Counsel. 2009. Protocol for the instruction of experts to give evidence in civil claims. http://www.justice.gov.uk/courts/procedure-rules/civil/contents/form_section_images/practice_directions/pd35_pdf_eps/pd35_prot.pdf (Accessed March 2, 2017).

Daley, T.T. 1996. Pretrial preparations can improve a physician's value as an expert witness. *Can Med Assoc J.* 154:573–575.

Federal Rules of Evidence. 2015. http://federalevidence.com/rules-of-evidence (Accessed May 12, 2017).

Gutheil, T.G., Simon, R.I. 2004. Avoiding bias in expert testimony. *Psychiatr Ann.* 34:260–270.

Legal Information Institute. 2017. Federal Rules of Evidence. https://www.law.cornell.edu/rules/fre (Accessed 4/20/17).

Munroe, M.G. 2013. Reciprocal discovery in felony cases (briefly). https://www.merlinusmonroe.com/2013/11/09/reciprocal-discovery-in-felony-cases-briefly/ (Accessed May 18, 2017).

Nordsby, J.J. 2005. Here we stand: What a forensic scientist does In *Forensic Science: An Introduction to Scientific and Investigative Techniques*, 2nd ed., eds James, S.H., Nordby, J.J., S. Bell. Boca Raton, FL: CRC Press/Taylor & Francis, pp. 1–12.

Rifkin, R. 2015. In U.S., more say animals should have the same rights as people http://www.gallup.com/poll/183275/say-animals-rights-people.aspx (Accessed March 17, 2017).

Talve, M. 2012. What is an Expert Witness? In: theexpertinstitute.com/team/michael-talve/ (Accessed September 2016).

Index

Page numbers followed by "f" and "t" indicate figures and tables, respectively.

Index

B

C

D

E

F

G

J

K

L

M

N

O

P

T

U

V

W

X

Z

For Product Safety Concerns and Information please contact our EU representative GPSR@taylorandfrancis.com Taylor & Francis Verlag GmbH, Kaufingerstraße 24, 80331 München, Germany

Batch number: 10722122

Printed by Printforce, the Netherlands